Civil Fraud

Law, Practice & Procedure

First Supplement to the First Edition

Civil Fraud

Law, Practice & Procedure

First Supplement to the First Edition

General Editors

Thomas Grant QC BA (Bristol)
Dip Law, Barrister, Maitland Chambers
Visiting Professor of Politics and Law, Gresham College

David Mumford QC MA (Oxon)
Dip Law, Barrister, Maitland Chambers

SWEET & MAXWELL

THOMSON REUTERS

Published in 2022 by Thomson Reuters, trading as Sweet & Maxwell. Registered in England & Wales, Company No.1679046. Registered Office and address for service: 5 Canada Square, Canary Wharf, London, E14 5AQ.

For further information on our products and services, visit *http://www.sweetandmaxwell.co.uk*

Typeset by YHT 2018 Ltd, Ashford, Middlesex.

Printed and bound by CPI Group (UK) Ltd, Croydon, CR0 4YY.

No natural forests were destroyed to make this product: only farmed timber was used and re-planted.

FSC
www.fsc.org
MIX
Paper | Supporting responsible forestry
FSC® C013604

A CIP catalogue record of this book is available from the British Library.

ISBN (print): 978-0-414-08828-3
ISBN (e-book): 978-0-414-08833-7
ISBN (print and ebook): 978-0-414-08832-0

Authors and Contributors

General Editors

Thomas Grant QC BA (Bristol)
Dip Law, Barrister, Maitland Chambers
Visiting Professor of Politics and Law, Gresham College
David Mumford QC MA (Oxon)
Dip Law, Barrister, Maitland Chambers

Contributors

Rosanna Foskett MA (Cantab); MPhil (Cantab)
Dip Law, Barrister, Maitland Chambers
Benjamin John MChem (Oxon)
Dip Law, Barrister, Maitland Chambers
James Kinman MA (Cantab)
Dip Law, Barrister, Maitland Chambers
Thomas Munby QC MA (Oxon) FCIArb
Dip Law, Barrister, Maitland Chambers
Watson Pringle MA (Oxon)
Barrister, Maitland Chambers
James Sheehan MA (Cantab)
Dip Law, Barrister, Essex Court Chambers
Rebecca Stubbs QC MA (Cantab)
Barrister, Maitland Chambers
Ryan James Turner BA (Hons), LLB (Hons) (ANU); LLM (Cantab)
Barrister, Maitland Chambers
Caley Wright MA (Oxon)
Dip Law, Barrister, Maitland Chambers

The General Editors wish to record their gratitude for her research assistance to:
Danielle Carrington MA (Cantab); LLM (New York University)
Barrister

How to use this supplement

This is the First Supplement to the First Edition of *Civil Fraud Law, Practice & Procedure* and has been compiled according to the structure of the main volume. At the beginning of each chapter of this Supplement, a mini table of contents of the sections in the main volume has been included. Where a heading in this table of contents has been marked with a square pointer, this indicates that there is relevant information in this Supplement to which the reader should refer. Material that is new to the Supplement is indicated by the symbol ■. Within each chapter, updating information is referenced to the relevant paragraph in the main volume.

This Supplement is up-to-date as at 31 December 2021, although some developments have been captured since that date.

TABLE OF CONTENTS

SECTION C
Other Claims

SECTION D
Liability For or Through Others

SECTION E
Relief and Bars To It

SECTION F
Interim Remedies

SECTION G
Trial, Judgments And Enforcement

SECTION H
Cases with an International Element

TABLE OF CASES

TABLE OF CASES

TABLE OF STATUTORY INSTRUMENTS

CHAPTER 1

DECEIT

A. INTRODUCTION

(1) The Foundations of the Tort

1–003 *At the end of footnote 5, add:*

This summary was recently cited by the Supreme Court of Bermuda in *Bidzina Invanishvili et al v Credit Suisse Life (Bermuda) Limited* [2022] SC (Bda) 19 Civ at [634].

(2) The Decision to Allege Fraud

Add new paragraph 1–008A after para.1–008:

1–008A In a claim alleging dishonesty against a corporate defendant, a claimant should, if possible, identify the individuals who are said to have knowledge or an intention or to have engaged in a relevant act or omission on behalf of the corporate defendant as early as possible. However, the failure to plead precise particulars of knowledge or intention that identify those individuals at the outset does not mean that the claim should be struck out.[11a] In many instances, a claimant may not know who, on behalf of a defendant, was the dishonest actor until disclosure is given, even if there is the appearance of a fraud and an evidential foundation sufficient to allow a claim in fraud to be pleaded. It is, therefore, clearly right that the court should not set up an insurmountable bar for a claimant pleading a claim in fraud or lose sight of the difficulties that are commonly faced by a defrauded claimant in pursuing a defendant.

[11a] See *Sofer v Swissindependent Trustees SA* [2020] EWCA Civ 699, per Arnold LJ at [30]–[32] (David Richards and Patten LJJ agreeing), which involved an allegation of a dishonest breach of trust by a professional trustee that was necessary to overcome a trustee exoneration clause in the trust deed.

(3) Advantages of Pleading Fraud

At the end of the paragraph, add: **1–020**

This may be a considerable benefit in some instances, as the grant of a remedy for claims founded on other causes of action may have become statute-barred so that only claims in fraud benefiting from s.32 are likely to be maintainable.

After the first sentence, add: **1–027**

A claimant who obtains a money judgment against an individual based on a fraud or a fraudulent breach of trust may thereby also receive a degree of bankruptcy protection, as the fraudulent wrongdoer will not be released from that debt upon discharge from bankruptcy.[49a]

[49a] Insolvency Act 1986 s.281(3).

B. THE MISREPRESENTATION

(4) Representations of Opinion and States of Mind

In the second sentence of footnote 67, delete the second "at". **1–041**

After the quotation in the first sentence of footnote 68, add:

However, in *obiter,* the Court of Appeal appeared to leave open the door to a claim in deceit being pursued where an implied representation was made that was not known to the mind of the representor: *Property Alliance Group Ltd v Royal Bank of Scotland plc* [2018] EWCA Civ 355; [2018] 1 W.L.R. 3529, per Sir Terence Etherton MR, Longmore and Newey LJJ at [158].

(5) Representations of Intention/as to the Future

(iv) Negotiations and sales talk

After the second sentence, add: **1–049**

To determine whether a representation is simply "sales talk" or a "mere puff" it must be asked whether, objectively judged, a reasonable representee in the position of the representee was entitled to take the representation "seriously".[86a] This requirement that the representation be one that can be taken "seriously" is no more than another way of saying that the reliance by the representee must be reasonable.[86b]

[86a] *MCI Worldcom International Inc v Primus Telecommunications Inc* [2004] 2 All E.R. (Comm) 833, per Mance LJ at [30] (Sir Martin Nourse and Ward LJ agreeing). See e.g. *Carney v NM Rothschild & Sons Limited* [2018] EWHC 958 (Comm), per Judge Waksman QC at [236]–[240].
[86b] See paras 1–126—1–128.

(7) Silence

1–055 *In footnote 104, add the following citation to Property Alliance Group Ltd v Royal Bank of Scotland plc:*

; [2018] 1 W.L.R. 3529

1–060 *In footnote 114, replace the first sentence with:*

Mellor v Partridge [2013] EWCA Civ 477.

Replace footnote 125 with:

Geest plc v Fyffes plc [1999] 1 All E.R. (Comm) 672, per Colman J at 683.

1–062 *Replace footnote 126 with:*

Property Alliance Group, above, at [128]–[132].

(8) Representations and Contractual Warranties

1–065 *After the citation in the final sentence of footnote 131, add:*

per Andrew Baker QC at [16]–[18]

Add new paragraph 1–065A after para.1–065:

1–065A In English commercial practice, a representation or warranty in a contract may be expressed to be subject to information and documents that have been disclosed to the counterparty. Contractual representations or warranties may not, therefore, be entirely true in the sense that the represented or warranted state of affairs exists. The critical feature, though, is that the scope of the representation or warranty is contractually narrowed by disclosing against the representation or warranty in a way that is more efficient (for the disclosing party) than contractually negotiating precise representations and warranties.

(9) Continuing Representations

1–070 *In footnote 140, replace "Cramasco" with "Cramaso".*

C. Knowledge or Recklessness

(1) The Test

Add new paragraph 1–080A after para.1–080:

1–080A The formulation in *Derry v Peek* does not, however, make clear what degree of knowledge constitutes actual knowledge. In particular, Lord Herschell did not spell out whether what is colloquially known as "blind eye" knowledge is sufficient for the purpose of the tort. Blind eye knowledge refers to knowledge that would have been acquired if a person had not consciously shut their eyes to the obvious.[162a] Blind eye knowledge is therefore similar to recklessness—which is described below—but the intention required is different. His Honour Judge Richard Seymour QC held that blind eye knowledge was sufficient to found a claim in deceit in *Renault UK Ltd v Fleetpro Technical Services Ltd.*[162b] It is respectfully suggested that he was right to do so, for in the conscious decision to shut one's eyes to the truth or falsity of a representation there is a level of moral delinquency that ought to be sufficient for the purpose of the tort.

[162a] See generally para.12–038 below in relation to the different types of knowledge.

[162b] [2007] EWHC 2541 (QB), at [130]–[135]. But note the tension in the suggestion by Cockerill J that, while blind eye knowledge is sufficient, a suspicion about "what is going on" does not mean that a representee has a dishonest state of mind: *Roberts v The Royal Bank of Scotland plc* [2020] EWHC 3141 (Comm), at [114].

(2) Awareness of Representation

Move footnote 170 to the end of the quotation. **1–086**

Amend footnote 171 to place the closing parenthesis after the words "Jackson LJ" and delete the closing parenthesis after [77]. **1–087**

(4) Motive Irrelevant

Replace the full stop preceding the quotation with a colon. **1–095**

D. THE DEFENDANT'S INTENTION

(1) Introduction

At the end of footnote 197, add: **1–097**

Compare the rebuttable presumption of inducement in an action for deceit, which is discussed at para.1–134, and the *irrebuttable* presumption of both intention and inducement in an action for bribery, which is discussed at para.7–020.

(2) The Requisite Intention

(ii) What must the representor intend?

At the end of footnote 205, add: **1–103**

See also *Vald Nielsen Holding A/S v Baldorino* [2019] EWHC 1926 (Comm), at [151], per Jacobs J.

In footnote 207, delete the words "per Longmere LJ"

In the final sentence, replace the word "and" with the word "or". **1–108**

E. INDUCEMENT OF THE CLAIMANT

(2) The Test of Inducement

(ii) Nature of the causal contribution required

Replace paragraphs 1–116 to 1–119 with:

1–116 To the above extent the law on inducement is clear. In the first edition of this work, it was said that, in contrast, the precise causal role that a misrepresentation needed to play in the decision of the representee was not entirely clear.[229a] It was nonetheless tentatively suggested that the test of inducement for the purpose of claiming damages for fraudulent misrepresentation is the same as the test for a claim to rescission for fraudulent misrepresentation, namely a lesser standard than "but for" causation. The uncertainty has now been resolved by the judgment of the Court of Appeal in *BV Nederlandse Industrie van Eiprodukten v Rembrandt Enterprises Inc*,[229b] although not in a way that neatly reconciles all authorities.

[229a] Readers should refer to paras 1-116—1-119 of the first edition for a historical survey of the conflicting authorities.

[229b] [2019] EWCA Civ 596; [2020] Q.B. 551. Permission to appeal to the Supreme Court was refused by that court.

1–117 In the case of a fraudulent misrepresentation (as opposed to a negligent or innocent one), a representee is induced by a representation if the representation was "material" in the sense that it was "actively present in the mind of the representee" when he made his decision.[229c] The representee is not, therefore, required to establish that, "but for" the misrepresentation, the representee would not have acted in the way that they did.

[229c] *BV Nederlandse Industrie v Rembrandt*, above, per Longmore LJ at [45] (Peter Jackson and Coulson LJJ agreeing). The Court of Appeal here adopted the language of Bowen LJ in *Edgington v Fitzmaurice* (1885) 29 Ch. D. 459, at 483.

1–118 In recent years, the test for inducement has at times been expressed as requiring only that the representee "might" have acted differently had the misrepresentation not been made, in contradistinction to a test that requires that the representee "would" have acted differently.[229d] To the extent that it is said that the representee "might" have acted differently had the misrepresentation not been made, this is only sufficient if understood in the sense described above. However, the Court of Appeal in *BV Nederlandse Industrie van Eiprodukten v Rembrandt Enterprises Inc* made clear that the court should not undertake a hypothetical inquiry as to what the representee "might" have done if the misrepresentation had not been made.[229e] It has long been the case that the court has considered it inappropriate to engage in counterfactual enquiries as to how the claimant would otherwise have acted, in circumstances where they have been lied to, or of weighing the relative importance of contributing causes.[229f]

[229d] See, e.g., *Marme Inversiones 2007 SL v Natwest Markets plc* [2019] EWHC 366 (Comm), per Picken J at [304], [317].

[229e] [2019] 3 W.L.R. 113, per Longmore J at [34], [45] (Peter Jackson and Coulson LJJ agreeing).

[229f] See e.g. *Reynell v Sprye* 42 E.R. 710, per Lord Cranworth at 728–729; *Smith v Kay* (1859) 7 H.L.C. 750, per Lord Chelmsford at 759 ("Can it be permitted to a party who has practised a deception with a view to a particular end which has been attained by it, to speculate on what might have been the result if

there had been a full communication of the facts?"); *Barton v Armstrong* [1976] A.C. 104, per Lord Cross at 118–119 (a case of rescission for duress, but which was reasoned by analogy to a case of fraudulent misrepresentation: "If it were established that Barton did not allow the representation to affect his judgment then he could not make it a ground for relief ... If on the other hand Barton relied on the misrepresentation Armstrong could not have defeated his claim to relief by showing that there were other more weighty causes which contributed to his decision ... for in this field the court does not allow an examination into the relative importance of contributing causes ..."); *Downs v Chappell* [1997] 1 W.L.R. 426, per Hobhouse LJ at 441 (a deceit case, where it was said that it was "irrelevant to inquire what the representee would have done if some different representation had been made to him ... Such matters are irrelevant speculations").

If understood in this (different) sense, a plea that the representee "might" have acted differently is, therefore, not sufficient to establish the level of inducement required by the tort of deceit. For this reason, it is perhaps best to avoid alleging only that a representee "might" have acted differently if no misrepresentation had been made. **1–119**

In the first sentence, after the text "On any view", but before the comma, add: **1–120**

of the degree of inducement required

Replace footnote 237 with:

'Causation in Misrepresentation' (2015) 131 L.Q.R. 277, at 284.

At the end of the paragraph, add: **1–121**

What the claimant would have done if told the truth is, however, irrelevant in assessing the loss suffered by a claimant. In *Downs v Chappell*,[245a] the Court of Appeal allowed an appeal in part because the first instance judge had asked what the representee would have done if he had been told the truth for the purpose of measuring the loss suffered by the representee:

> "The judge was wrong to ask how [the representees] would have acted if they had been told the truth. They were never told the truth. They were told lies in order to induce them to enter into the contract. The lies were material and successful; they induced the plaintiffs to act to their detriment and contract with [the representor]. The judge should have concluded that the plaintiffs had proved their case on causation and that the only remaining question was what loss the plaintiffs had suffered as a result of entering into the contract with [the representor] to buy his business and shop."[245b]

[245a] [1997] 1 W.L.R. 426.
[245b] *Downs v Chappell*, above, per Hobhouse LJ at 441 (Roch and Butler-Sloss LJJ agreeing).

(iv) Inducement through non-human agency

Replace the sub-heading "Inducement through non-human agency" with "Automatic inducement"

At the end of the paragraph, add: **1–123**

A similar example is where a contract provides that certain obligations accrue or events occur upon a particular representation being made or a document that contains the representation being provided. In that instance, the requirement that a party be induced by the representation is likely to be readily made out.

After paragraph 1–133, add a new heading and the following new paragraph 1–33A:

(ix) Awareness of the Representation

1–133A In order for a claimant to have been induced by a representation, he (or his agent) must generally be aware of the representation on which he is suing.[262a] In most instances, this requirement of awareness follows logically from the need to establish that the representee relied on the representation sued on (for this reason awareness of a representation need not be separately pleaded: it is implicit in a plea of inducement that the representee was aware of the representation). However, awareness may not be required in all instances. For example, if a representation is to be actionable where the representation is made to a computer that produces a standardised response, human awareness of the representation may be unnecessary.

[262a] *Leeds City Council v Barclays Bank plc* [2021] EWHC 363 (Comm); [2021] Q.B. 1027 per Cockerill J at [57]–[67], [113], but see *Crossley v Volkswagen Aktiengesellschaft* [2021] EWHC 3444 (QB), per Waksman J at [92].

(3) Presumption of Inducement

1–134 *In the first sentence, replace the word "law" with "court".*

Replace the second sentence and footnote 264 with:

The presumption is an evidential presumption, rather than a presumption of law, and the onus of proof remains on the representee throughout to prove that they were induced by the misrepresentation.[264]

[264] *BV Nederlandse Industrie van Eiprodukten v Rembrandt Enterprises Inc* [2019] EWCA Civ 596; [2020] Q.B. 551, per Longmore LJ at [43] (Peter Jackson and Coulson LJJ agreeing).

In the final sentence, add quotation marks around the words "very difficult" and at the end of the sentence, add:

so that in some cases a party will need only to rely on the evidential presumption in order to prove their case.

Add new paragraph 1–134A after para.1–134:

1–134A It has been said that in order to rely on the evidential presumption it is necessary for the representee expressly to plead such reliance.[265a] However, it is respectfully suggested that this proposition is wrong for the simple reason that a party does not need to plead matters of evidence. It is necessary only for a claimant to plead that it was induced by the representation in a particular way; the evidence that it relies on to prove that inducement is not a matter that should be pleaded. Indeed, in almost all claims to a remedy for fraudulent misrepresentation, it must be expected that a claimant will rely on the evidential presumption. That being said, until this point of pleading is expressly disavowed, a claimant is likely to be well-advised to expressly plead reliance on the presumption of inducement.

[265a] *Zagora Management Ltd v Zurich Insurance plc* [2019] EWHC 140 (TCC), at [11.32].

(4) Inducement and Causation of Loss

Replace the word "tort" with "induced act". **1–135**

Add new paragraphs 1–135A to 1–135B after para.1–35 as follows:

1–135A However, it is worth mentioning one aspect of causation of loss before departing from this topic. As noted already, it is the loss that is caused by the *induced act* that is remedied by an award of damages; it is not the loss that is caused by the particular way in which the representation was false.[267a] Where a representee is induced to enter into a transaction by a fraudulent misrepresentation, they are entitled to damages for all loss that directly flows from the transaction and not only loss that flows from the misrepresentation, subject, of course, to the "limiting principles" described later in this book.

1–135B An example of the focus of the damages award on the loss suffered as a result of the induced transaction is provided by the Court of Appeal's judgment in *Glossop Cartons and Print Ltd v Contact (Print & Packaging) Ltd.*[267b] The misrepresentations in that case were of a relatively minor nature that were able to be remedied by a moderate degree of expenditure. However, the purchaser had made a bad bargain and substantially overpaid for the assets that it acquired by the induced transaction relative to their market value. It was, therefore, in the purchaser's interests to claim damages for the loss that it had suffered based on an objective market valuation of those assets and the Court of Appeal awarded damages on that basis, despite the extent of the loss suffered being partly attributable to misjudgements made by the purchaser that were unconnected to the falsity of the misrepresentations.

[267a] *OMV Petrom SA v Glencore International AG* [2017] 3 All E.R. 157, per Christopher Clarke LJ at 171 [59] (Black and Kitchin LJJ agreeing).
[267b] [2021] EWCA Civ 639; [2021] 1 W.L.R. 4297.

F. THE LIABILITY OF PRINCIPALS AND AGENTS IN DECEIT

(2) Liability of the Employer/Principal

(i) The test: actual/apparent authority

Replace the sub-heading "(i) The test: actual and apparent authority" with "(i) The test: actual and apparent authority".

Replace the second sentence of footnote 273 with: **1–139**

These principles were recently affirmed and extended by the Supreme Court in *Mohamud v WM Morrison Supermarkets plc* [2016] UKSC 11; [2016] A.C. 677 and *Cox v Ministry of Justice* [2016] UKSC 10; [2016] A.C. 660, as interpreted in *WM Morrison Supermarkets plc v Various Claimants* [2020] UKSC 12; [2020] A.C. 989 and *Barclays Bank plc v Various Claimants* [2020] UKSC 13; [2020] A.C. 973.

At the end of the second sentence of footnote 274, add:

For an example of the application of the principles of vicarious liability in a claim in deceit, see *Hockley Mint Ltd v Ramsden* [2018] EWCA Civ 2480; [2019] 1 W.L.R. 1617, per Sir Terence Etherton MR, Flaux LJ and Carr J at [63].

Add new paragraph 1–142A after para.1–142:

1–142A A claimant who relies on ostensible authority, where an agent had no actual authority, must be able to point to acts on the part of the principal founding their reliance on the apparent authority of the agent and not only to acts of the agent themselves. As the Privy Council has observed:

> "Judges have rightly resisted the notion that an agent can clothe himself with authority."[282a]

There is very good sense in this rule. If a person could, by their act alone, clothe themselves with authority, it would increase the risk of an innocent principal being subject to liabilities to a third party who had dealt with a fraudulent purported agent. In contrast, if an agent is unable to clothe himself with authority, the law creates an incentive for a well-advised third party to seek confirmation of the authority of the agent, or it will run the risk that the principal will not be bound by the putative agent's acts. That is particularly important in cases of fraud, where a director or agent may have entered into transactions with a third party without authority and then absconded with the benefits of those transactions.

[282a] *East Asia Company Ltd v PT Satria Tirtatama Energindo* [2019] UKPC 30; [2020] 2 All ER 294, per Lord Kitchin at [61] (per curiam).

1–145 *At the end of footnote 286, add:*

See further para.1–149.

(3) Agency and the Required Dishonest State of Mind

1–149 *At the end of footnote 292, add:*

, per Birkett LJ at 246.

Chapter 2

CONSPIRACY

A. INTRODUCTION

(2) The Essentials of the Tort

2–007 *At the end of footnote 8, add:*

This summary of the elements of a claim in unlawful means conspiracy was referred to with approval by Sir Ross Cranston, sitting as a Deputy High Court Judge, in *Manek v Wirecard AG* [2020] EWHC 1904 (Comm), at [44].

B. CONSIDERATIONS COMMON TO BOTH TYPES OF CONSPIRACY

(1) The Combination

2–014 *At the end of the paragraph, add:*

It is not necessary for the parties to agree at the outset of the alleged combination to use unlawful means for there to be a conspiracy. It is sufficient if the combination is to use unlawful means at the time they are used.[21a]

[21a] *Raja v McMillan* [2021] EWCA Civ 1103, per Nugee LJ at [64]–[69].

(2) Conspiring with a Company

2–021 *In footnote 39, replace reference to Bowstead and Reynolds on Agency with:*

P.G. Watts (ed), *Bowstead and Reynolds on Agency*, 22nd edn (London: Sweet & Maxwell, 2020), para.9–119.

At the end of footnote 39, add:

In *Raja v McMillan* [2021] EWCA Civ 1103, the Court of Appeal upheld the refusal of the Deputy Judge to strike out a conspiracy claim insofar as it alleged a conspiracy between a company and its sole controller. Whilst accepting at [56] that it was not obvious that there is the requisite combination if all that happens is that a person uses his company to commit an unlawful act, Nugee LJ observed at [57]–[58] that there were arguments the other way, referring to the fact that a sole director could contract with his company and to the decision in *Taylor v Smyth* (see para.2–020(3) above). Nugee LJ also held at [60] that, even if it were right that there is no conspiracy if all that happens is that a director gets his company to do certain things, it does not follow that the same is true if he gets company A to do certain things and company B to do other things.

At the end of footnote 41, add: **2–022**

In *Palmer Birch (a partnership) v Lloyd* [2018] EWHC 2316 (TCC); [2018] 4 W.L.R. 164, a defendant director invoked this argument, in reliance on the principle in *Said v Butt* (see para.3–040 below). HHJ Russen QC rejected the argument (at [212]–[217]) on the basis that, on ordinary principles governing joint torts, if a director were shown to be sufficiently involved in the conspiracy and that his acts (and, where relevant, intention) were sufficiently bound up in the company's acts to make him otherwise liable, then his status as director would not afford him a defence.

At the end of the first sentence of footnote 46, add: **2–024**

Lifestyle Equities CV v Ahmed [2021] EWCA Civ 675; [2021] Bus.L.R. 1020, per Birss LJ at [24]–[49].

(3) Employees and Agents

In footnote 52, amend the first sentence to read: **2–027**

See M. Jones (ed), *Clerk & Lindsell on Torts*, 23rd edn (London: Sweet & Maxwell, 2020), para.23–103.

At the end of the penultimate sentence, add a new footnote 52A: **2–028**

In *Raja v McMillan* (above), Nugee LJ referred at [61] to the dicta of Viscount Simon LC in the *Crofter* case in dismissing an argument that, if one alleged conspirator effectively controlled and/or exerted enormous influence over other alleged conspirators, there could be no conspiracy. There were still two (or more) separate minds, regardless of the level of influence exercised by one over the other.

At the end of footnote 54, add: **2–030**

Various Claimants v Wm Morrison Supermarkets plc [2020] UKSC 12; [2020] A.C. 989, per Lord Reed PJSC at [23]–[26].

(4) Acts Carried Out

At the end of footnote 57, add: **2–031**

For a recent examination and application of this principle see *Lakatamia Shipping Co Limited v Su* [2021] EWHC 1907 (Comm), per Bryan J at [94]–[106] and [816].

C. UNLAWFUL MEANS CONSPIRACY

(2) Intention

At the end of footnote 77, add: **2–040**

Palmer Birch (a partnership) v Lloyd [2018] EWHC 2316 (TCC); [2018] 4 W.L.R. 164, per HHJ Russen QC at [220]; *Pepe's Piri Limited v Junaid* [2019] EWHC 2097 (QB), per Matthew Gullick (sitting as a Deputy High Court Judge) at [73]. Though see the probing analysis of Sarah Worthington QC (Hon) sitting as a Deputy High Court Judge in *Raja v McMillan* [2020] EWHC 951 (Ch), at [53]–[59], discussed further at para.2–043 below, suggesting (without deciding) that unlawful means conspiracy involves a lesser requirement of intention than unlawful interference.

2–042 *Replace footnote 82 with:*

At least where there is uncertainty as to the scope of the class or whether any given member of it will suffer loss: *WH Newsom Holding Ltd v IMI Plc* [2013] EWCA Civ 1377; [2014] 1 All E.R. 1132, at [38]–[41]. The Court of Appeal found that loss to the claimant was not an inevitable consequence of the defendants' actions. *Newsom* was referred to with approval in *Emerald Supplies Ltd v British Airways Plc* [2015] EWCA Civ 1024; [2016] Bus.L.R. 145, at [152]. The Court of Appeal in *Emerald* was willing to accept that, if a defendant intends to cause harm to the members of a particular class, but in fact only some suffer harm, then those who do suffer harm could sue: see at [168]. However, in a cartel case where it is not known whether price-fixing will cause loss to any particular person (e.g. because direct customers may pass on the higher cost to their own customers), the requirement of intention is not made out, and to say that the defendant must have known someone along the supply chain would suffer loss is to expand the class of potential victims to such an extent that it becomes impossible to say that there was an intention to harm a particular claimant. These principles were followed by Barling J in *Media-Saturn Holding GmbH v Toshiba Information Systems (UK) Ltd* [2019] 5 C.M.L.R. 7, in particular at [227]–[239]. In *ED&F Man Capital Markets Limited v Come Harvest Holdings Limited* [2022] EWHC 229 (Comm), at [510]–[512], Calver J rejected the contention (seemingly advanced as a general proposition) that a claimant wishing to rely on the obverse side of the coin argument had to do more than show that the defendant intended to benefit himself at the expense of a class of persons of which the claimant was one. In any event the issue did not arise on the facts of that case: see [529].

At the end of the paragraph, add:

In addition, it seems that the requisite intention may be made out despite the defendants not knowing the claimant's identity, provided that the claimant is in fact the target of the conspiracy.[83a]

[83a] As HHJ Waksman QC held in *CMOC Sales & Marketing Limited v Persons Unknown* [2018] EWHC 2230 (Comm), at [124]–[126], a case argued only by the claimant, but cited with approval in *ED&F Man Capital Markets Limited v Come Harvest Holdings Limited* [2022] EWHC 229 (Comm), per Calver J at [515]–[516].

2–043 *At the end of footnote 85, add:*

The analysis of *Kuwait Oil* in this paragraph was referred to with approval by Calver J in *ED&F Man Capital Markets Limited v Come Harvest Holdings Limited* [2022] EWHC 229 (Comm), at [488].

At the end of the paragraph, add:

However, Sarah Worthington QC (Hon) in *Raja v McMillan*[85a] suggested (on a strike-out application and without finally deciding the point) on the basis of the decisions of the Supreme Court in *Revenue and Customs Commissioners v Total Network SL*[85b] and *JSC BTA Bank v Khrapunov*[85c] that a lesser test of intention may apply in unlawful means conspiracy cases, such that a defendant who carries out a deliberate act with knowledge of its consequences must be taken to intend those consequences. The Court of Appeal[85d] did not find it necessary to address the precise ambit of the requirement of intention.

[85a] [2020] EWHC 951 (Ch), at [53]–[59].
[85b] [2008] UKHL 19; [2008] 1 A.C. 1174.
[85c] [2018] UKSC 19; [2018] 2 W.L.R. 1125.
[85d] [2021] EWCA Civ 1103, at [70]–[75].

2–045 *At the end of footnote 88, add:*

This does not mean that it is a requirement of the tort of unlawful means conspiracy that any of the members of the combination intended to target a specific claimant, a proposition advanced by the defendants in *ED&F Man Capital Markets Limited v Come Harvest Holdings Limited* [2022] EWHC 229 (Comm) and rejected by Calver J at [490]–[528]. The authorities are not thought to support such a requirement, which among other things would be inconsistent with the fact that a given defendant need not know all of the details of a conspiracy to be liable for its consequences; and the fact that blind-eye knowledge may be sufficient to establish intention: see paras 2–124—2–126 below, and *ED&F Man* at [524]–[528]. Perhaps because of the way the argument was put in *ED&F Man*, this paragraph in the main text appears to have been read by Calver J as suggesting that the House of Lords in *Total Network* had intended to revise the test for intention as established in *OBG Ltd v Allan* [2007] UKHL 21; [2008] 1 A.C. 1: see *ED&F Man* at [501]. That is not the case: as set out in para.2–040 above, it is settled that the test for intention to cause loss to the claimant in an unlawful means conspiracy case is as set out in *OBG Ltd v Allan*. Instead, this concept of action "targeted" or "directed" at the claimant—sometimes referred to as "instrumentality"—is best understood as a limiting factor in the scope of what unlawful means can give rise to liability in conspiracy: see para.2–046 below. Whilst Calver J in *ED&F Man* did not accept the suggestion in this paragraph in the main text (and in para.2–086 below) that the House of Lords in *Total Network* had reintroduced this concept (see [501], footnote 80), Arnold LJ adopted a similar analysis to that in the main text in *Racing Partnership Ltd v Done Bros Ltd* [2021] Ch. 277, at [153]. See also paras 2–086A and 2–086B below, where the status and meaning of the concept of instrumentality, and the question of whether intention is relevant to it, are considered further by reference to *ED&F Man* and other cases since the 1st edition of this work.

(3) Unlawful Means or Acts

Amend the final sentence of footnote 93 to read: **2–049**

See to the same effect Jones (ed), *Clerk & Lindsell on Torts*, 23rd edn (London: Sweet & Maxwell, 2020), para.23–108, noting that this is however not the law.

At the end of footnote 112, add: **2–056**

In theory at least, a negligent misrepresentation could qualify as a relevant unlawful act (see *Ivy Technology v Martin* [2019] EWHC 2510 (Comm), per Andrew Henshaw QC (sitting as a Deputy Judge of the High Court) at [13]). In practice however, at least in most cases, it is unlikely that a misrepresentation could be the means by which harm was inflicted on the claimant unless it was deliberately false: see *Taylor v Van Dutch Marine Holding Ltd* [2019] EWHC 1951 (Ch); [2019] Bus. L.R. 2610, per Julia Dias QC (sitting as a Deputy Judge of the High Court) at [300]–[303].

At the end of footnote 116, add: **2–057**

Palmer Birch (a partnership) v Lloyd [2018] EWHC 2316 (TCC); [2018] 4 W.L.R. 164, per HHJ Russen QC at [228]–[234], rejecting the defendant's submission that a breach of contract could not qualify as an unlawful act. In *Ivy Technology v Martin* [2019] EWHC 2510 (Comm), at [66], Andrew Henshaw QC (sitting as a Deputy Judge of the High Court) appears to have considered that it was sufficiently arguable that a breach of contract would not qualify as an unlawful act to require disclosure of the argument on a without notice application, and in *Pepe's Piri Piri Limited v Junaid* [2019] EWHC 2097 (QB) Matthew Gullick (sitting as a Deputy High Court Judge) viewed the point as an open question which it was unnecessary for him to decide (see [72] and [201]). However it does not appear that either judge was taken to *Palmer Birch* or any of the other earlier decisions referred to above.

Replace the final sentence and footnote with: **2–058**

The breach of a directly applicable provision of EU law ought to engage the same principles as the breach of a domestic statute, though this will only now be relevant in relation to conduct pre-dating the UK's exit from the EU.[120]

[120] This is also the view of the authors of M. Jones (ed), *Clerk & Lindsell on Torts*, 23rd edn (London: Sweet & Maxwell, 2020), para.23–89, n.453. To the extent that a provision of EU law has been retained following Brexit, it will form part of English law to which the usual principles will apply.

2–060 *At the end of footnote 122, add:*

In *Magdeev v Tsvetkov* [2020] EWHC 887 (Comm) Cockerill J held, at [381], that, although she rejected the conspiracy claim on other grounds, she would not have done so on the basis that breach of fiduciary duty did not qualify as a relevant unlawful act.

2–061 *Replace footnote 123 with:*

Indata Equipment Supplies Ltd v ACL Ltd [1998] F.S.R. 248, per Otton LJ at 260 (obiter); *Croesus Financial Services Ltd v Bradshaw* [2013] EWHC 3685 (QB), at [114]–[120].

2–073 *At the end of footnote 151, add:*

With effect from the completion of the Brexit transition period on 31 December 2020, the Rome II Regulation forms part of English law as retained EU law, pursuant to s.3 of the European Union (Withdrawal) Act 2018 and subject to the amendments provided for in reg. 11 of the Law Applicable to Contractual Obligations and Non-Contractual Obligations (Amendment etc.) (EU Exit) Regulations 2019/834.

2–074 *Replace footnote 153 with:*

This is also the view of the authors of Collins, Harris (eds), *Dicey, Morris and Collins on the Conflict of Laws*, 15th edn (London: Sweet & Maxwell, 2017), 5th Supplement, para.34–069.

(4) The Defendant Need Not Know that the Acts Carried Out were Unlawful

2–077 *Replace final sentence with:*

Whilst this question had not been given a consistent answer in the decided cases, it has now been settled up to the level of the Court of Appeal, by the decision of that court in *Racing Partnership Ltd v Done Bros (Cash Betting) Ltd*.[159a] This decision is examined below after a summary of the prior case law which is, however, now of mainly academic interest.

[159a] [2020] EWCA Civ 1300; [2021] Ch. 233.

Replace paragraph 2–082 with:

2–082 Many subsequent first instance judges who considered this controversy felt bound to follow *Belmont Finance* over *Meretz*.[169] But others followed the analysis of Morgan J in *Digicel* and the Court of Appeal in *Meretz*.[169a] Subject to further consideration by the Supreme Court, the issue is now settled. In *Racing Partnership Ltd v Done Bros (Cash Betting) Ltd*,[169b] following a detailed analysis by Arnold LJ of the authorities, a majority of the Court of Appeal held that it is not an essential element in the tort of unlawful means conspiracy that the defendant knew that the means employed were unlawful. Ignorance of the law is thus no defence to a claim in unlawful means conspiracy; all that it is necessary to show is knowledge of the facts that gave the relevant unlawful acts their quality of unlawfulness.

[169] *First Subsea Ltd v Balltec Ltd* [2014] EWHC 866 (Ch), per Norris J at [150]–[157] (not affected on appeal [2017] EWCA Civ 186; [2018] Ch. 25); *Capital for Enterprise Fund LP v Bibby Financial Services Ltd* [2015] EWHC 2593 (Ch), per HHJ Pelling QC at [11]–[13] (in *Swain v Swains Plc* [2015] EWHC 660 (Ch), at [135] the same judge had expressed the same conclusion, but without reference to *Meretz*); *Stobart Group Limited v Tinkler* [2019] EWHC 258 (Comm), per HHJ Russen QC at [548]–[573]. In *Lebara Mobile Ltd v Lycamobile UK Ltd* [2015] EWHC 3318 (Ch), at [51], Nicholas Lavender QC (sitting as Deputy High Court Judge) noted the controversy without deciding the point, as

did Freedman J in *Alesco Risk Management Services Ltd v Bishopsgate Insurance Brokers Ltd* [2019] EWHC 2839 (QB), at [379] and [439].

169a In *UPL Europe Ltd v AgChemAccess Ltd* [2017] EWHC 1880 (Ch), at [150], Proudman J expressed the obiter view that she would have followed the decision of Morgan J in *Digicel*; but it appears that neither *Swain v Swains* nor *Capital for Enterprise Fund v Bibby* was cited to her. Similarly, in *FM Capital Partners Ltd v Marino* [2018] EWHC 1768 (Comm), at [95], Cockerill J referred to the analysis in *Meretz* as an accurate statement of the law, but it appears that neither *Belmont Finance* nor the more recent cases referred to in the previous footnote were cited to her. The same is true of the decision of Asplin J in *Lictor Anstalt v Mir Steel UK Limited* [2014] EWHC 3316 (Ch), at [262].

169b [2020] EWCA Civ 1300; [2021] Ch. 233, at [104]–[144] and [171]. Cf. Lewison LJ's powerfully-reasoned dissent at [213]–[265]. Zacaroli J at first instance ([2019] EWHC 1156 (Ch); [2020] Ch. 289) had held that knowledge of unlawfulness was a necessary element of the tort.

At the end of the paragraph, add new footnote 169A: **2–083**

As Zacaroli J observed at first instance in *Racing Partnership Ltd v Done Bros (Cash Betting) Ltd* [2019] EWHC 1156 (Ch); [2020] Ch. 28, at [279], citing the example of an alleged breach of contract, where the question is whether a term prohibits particular conduct.

Add new paragraphs 2–086A and 2–086B after para.2–086:

However, more recent cases have cast doubt on whether this concept—sometimes described as a requirement of "instrumentality"—has any separate aspect of intention to it. In *Racing Partnership Ltd v Done Bros Ltd*,[176a] Zacaroli J dismissed a claim in unlawful means conspiracy based on breaches of the terms and conditions of an online betting exchange, on the basis that those breaches were not directed at the claimants, or the instrumentality of the harm caused to them. In the Court of Appeal, Arnold LJ, giving the majority judgment allowing an appeal on this point, traced the concept of instrumentality through *OBG Ltd v Allan*,[176b] *Revenue & Customs Commissioners v Total Network*[176c] and *JSC BTA Bank v Khrapunov*,[176d] and concluded that: **2–086A**

> "It seems to me that the discussions of instrumentality in the case law tend to conflate two different questions. The first concerns the defendant's intention. As noted above, it is now well established that, in unlawful means conspiracy, the defendant must intend to injure the claimant, although that need not be the defendant's predominant intention and it is sufficient that the defendant intends to advance their economic interests at the expense of the claimant's. To that extent, the defendant's intention must be directed at the claimant. The second question is one of causation. The unlawful means must have caused loss to the claimant, rather than merely being the occasion of such loss being sustained. As I see it, this is the best explanation of the courier service/pizza delivery example: in that example the claimant's loss is caused by customers (who may be presumed not to appreciate that the defendant is systematically breaking the law and some of whom may prefer the defendant's service for other reasons) choosing to place their orders with the defendant, and so the unlawfulness is the occasion for the loss rather than the direct cause of it."[176e]

176a [2019] EWHC 1156 (Ch), [2020] Ch. 289, at [251].

176b [2007] UKHL 21; [2008] 1 A.C. 1.

176c [2008] UKHL 19; [2008] 1 A.C. 1174.

176d [2018] UKSC 19; [2018] 2 W.L.R. 1125.

176e [2020] EWCA Civ 1300; [2021] Ch. 233, at [154].

This would seem to reduce the instrumentality requirement to a simple requirement of factual causation. Calver J reached the same view in *ED&F Man Capital Markets Limited v Come Harvest Holdings Limited*,[176f] citing the judgment of Arnold LJ in *Racing Partnership* and a passage from the judgment of Lord Hamblen in *Secretary of State for Health v Servier Laboratories* **2–086B**

Ltd.[176g] However, *Servier* was an unlawful interference case, and there may be a limit to the extent to which concepts employed in the context of that tort can be carried across into the context of unlawful means conspiracy.[176h] In a dissenting judgment in *Racing Partnership*,[176i] Lewison LJ doubted the basis on which Arnold LJ distinguished the example of the pizza business in the passage cited in para.2–086A above, noting that judges in the Supreme Court decisions referred to in that paragraph appear to have proceeded on the hypothesis that the requirement of "but for" causation was established in that example, but that the concept of instrumentality required something more. In other words, it may be suggested, it is not enough simply that the members of the combination intend to harm the claimant, that one or more of them acts unlawfully, and that those acts in fact cause claimant loss; instead the combiners must intend to harm the claimant by the unlawful means in question (subject to the fact that not every member of the combination needs to know the precise means used: see para.2–124 below). The judgments of Arnold LJ in *Racing Partnership* and Calver J in *ED&F Man* are likely to be followed by a first instance judge but are not altogether easy to reconcile with the judgments in *Total Network* and *Khrapunov* in particular, and may not be the last word on this subject.[176j]

[176f] [2022] EWHC 229 (Comm), in particular at [542]–[546], disapproving para.2–085 of the 1st edition of this work in light of *Racing Partnership*, and to similar effect see [501], as to which see also footnote 88 above. The point appears to have arisen in *ED&F Man* because the defendant argued that it followed from the requirement that the unlawful means be "indeed the means" by which damage was inflicted on the claimant that "any defendant must also have had knowledge of the unlawful means in order to intend them" (see [538]). Calver J rejected this submission, which is inconsistent with the principles and cases referred to in paras 2–124—2–126 below.

[176g] [2021] UKSC 24; [2021] 3 W.L.R. 370, at [92]: "the instrumentality requirement is a causation requirement: the damage to the claimant must be caused in fact through the instrumentality of the third party."

[176h] In contrast to unlawful means conspiracy, unlawful interference requires the unlawful means to be actionable by the third party and—as reaffirmed in *Servier* itself—to have interfered with the third party's freedom to deal with the claimant. These control mechanisms are absent in conspiracy, which is a two-party tort.

[176i] [2020] EWCA Civ 1300; [2021] Ch. 233, at [269].

[176j] The Supreme Court is understood to have granted permission in December 2021 to appeal the decision of the Court of Appeal in *Racing Partnership*, though at the time of this supplement the scope of the appeal is not known to the authors.

(6) Justification in Unlawful Means Conspiracy

Insert new heading (above) and add new paragraph 2–091A:

2–091A In claims for inducing breach of contract, there exists a defence of justification. This is considered in paras 3–066—3–076 below. In two recent cases, an attempt has been made to establish the existence of a justification defence to claims in unlawful means conspiracy. In both cases the attempt failed. This is not surprising: as a matter of principle, it is difficult to see how a defendant held to have been party to a combination to act unlawfully and with an intention to harm the claimant could at the same time be said to have been justified in doing so and thus avoid liability for the resultant damage. The first case is *Palmer Birch (a partnership) v Lloyd*.[183a] HHJ Russen QC held that the defence was not available as a matter of law. He reasoned that, whilst it makes sense for an alleged inducer as an accessory to be able to rely on some independent superior right, liability in conspiracy is of a primary nature and does not arise unless the requisite unlawful means and intention to harm are shown. Any considerations of "justification" are wrapped up in those elements and may in a given case mean that one or both such elements are absent, but there is no room for a freestanding defence of justification. Similarly, in *Global Display Solutions Limited v NCR Financial Solutions Group Limited*,[183b] the defendants sought to raise a defence of justification to a claim in unlawful means conspiracy, on the basis that such a defence would be available to a claim in inducing breach of contract and so should be equally available to a claim in conspiracy to breach a contract. The defence was rejected by Jacobs J on the basis that the conspiracy involved the defendants acting fraudulently and they were not exercising an equal or superior right.[183c]

[183a] [2018] EWHC 2316 (TCC); [2018] 4 W.L.R. 164, at [183]–[193].
[183b] [2021] EWHC 1119 (Comm).
[183c] See [125] onwards. For a discussion of this requirement in the context of inducing breach of contract see paras 3–067—3–075 below.

E. THE DIFFERENT POSITION OF EACH DEFENDANT

(3) Different Conduct

At the end of the paragraph, add new footnote 232a: **2–118**

[232a] As Zacaroli J observed at first instance in *Racing Partnership Ltd v Done Bros (Cash Betting) Ltd* [2019] EWHC 1156 (Ch); [2020] Ch. 289, at [287]: "liability for conspiracy can be established against a person without that person having done more than enter into an agreement with the requisite intention", by contrast (in that case) with liability in breach of confidence, which depends on the defendant having made unauthorised use of the information.

(4) Different Knowledge or Intention

Replace the second sentence of footnote 243 with: **2–121**

Although if a defendant has his own separate aim this may tend to indicate that he did not participate in the conspiracy at all, at least if he did not share the knowledge of the other defendants: see Jones (ed), *Clerk & Lindsell on Torts*, 23rd edn (London: Sweet & Maxwell, 2020), para.23–104. This paragraph in the main text was referred to with approval by David Edwards QC (sitting as a Deputy High Court Judge) in *Salt Ship Design AS v Prysmian Powerlink SRL* [2019] EWHC 2308 (Comm), at [133].

At the end of the paragraph, add new footnote 246a: **2–122**

[246a] This paragraph was cited with approval by Calver J in *ED&F Man Capital Markets Limited v Come Harvest Holdings Limited* [2022] EWHC 229 (Comm), at [523].

At the end of footnote 249, add: **2–124**

This passage from *The Dolphina* was cited with approval in *Standard Chartered Bank India v Registrar of Companies* [2021] EWHC 1566 (Ch), per HHJ Hodge QC at [32], and with apparent approval in *CMOC Sales & Marketing Limited v Persons Unknown* [2018] EWHC 2230 (Comm), per HHJ Waksman QC at [120].

At the end of footnote 252, add: **2–126**

Manek v Wirecard AG [2020] EWHC 1904 (Comm), per Sir Ross Cranston at [45].

(5) Involvement at Different Times

2–127 *At the end of the first sentence of footnote 253, add:*

King v Stiefel [2021] EWHC 1045 (Comm), *The Times*, 4 June 2021, per Cockerill J at [336]–[341], referring to this paragraph in the main text.

F. DAMAGES

2–135 *At the end of the first sentence, add new footnote 277a:*

[277a] *Palmer Birch (a partnership) v Lloyd* [2018] EWHC 2316 (TCC); [2018] 4 W.L.R. 164, per HHJ Russen QC at [245].

Delete final two sentences of footnote 278.

2–137 *In footnote 286, replace the final two sentences with:*

For a criticism of *Lonrho (No.5)* on this point, see J. Edelman (ed), *McGregor on Damages*, 21st edn (London: Sweet & Maxwell, 2020), paras 48–024—48–025. If such losses cannot be claimed, then this is one procedural disadvantage of bringing a conspiracy claim as distinct, for example, from a claim in defamation or malicious falsehood.

At the end of footnote 288, add:

The label "*Wrotham Park*" damages is confusing and may be best avoided, for reasons summarised by Lord Reed JSC in *One Step (Support) Ltd v Morris-Garner* [2018] UKSC 20; [2019] A.C. 649, at [2]–[3].

G. PRACTICAL AND PLEADING POINTS

(1) Burden and Standard of Proof

2–138 *At the end of footnote 290, add:*

For a recent confirmation of the fact that the standard of proof remains the balance of probabilities (in the context of a claim under foreign law making allegations of dishonesty and other serious wrong-doing), see *Bank St Petersburg PJSC v Arkhangelsky* [2020] EWCA Civ 408; [2020] 4 W.L.R. 55, at [39]–[47].

(2) Dishonesty

2–139 *At the end of footnote 291, add:*

Lakatamia Shipping Co Limited v Su [2021] EWHC 1907 (Comm), per Bryan J at [40] and [81].

2–141 *After the first sentence of footnote 296, add:*

This point was recently confirmed by Andrew Henshaw QC (sitting as a Deputy High Court Judge) in *Ivy Technology v Martin* [2019] EWHC 2510 (Comm), at [12].

(4) Other Procedural and Professional Considerations

Add new paragraph 2–148A after para.2–148A:

Whilst it is not necessary to sue all alleged conspirators, or to do so at the same time, careful consideration should be given before deciding to sue alleged conspirators separately. This can be a high-risk strategy. Bringing separate claims concurrently would ordinarily be likely to result in their consolidation by the court, with the claimant having to bear any wasted cost. Doing so consecutively may result in the later claim being struck out as an abuse of process, either (a) on *Henderson v Henderson* grounds—at least if the court and the other parties are not given proper notice of the claimant's intention to bring a second claim in future or (b) if the first claim is unsuccessful, on the grounds that the second claim involves a collateral attack on the decision in the first claim. In *Elite Property Holdings Limited v BDO LLP*,[299a] Nicholas Vineall QC (sitting as a Deputy High Court Judge) refused to strike out a second claim on the first of these bases, but did so on the second. **2–148A**

[299a] [2020] EWHC 1937 (Comm).

At the end of footnote 303, add: **2–149**

This passage, from the 22nd edition, is not reproduced in the 23rd edition.

At the end of footnote 311, add: **2–151**

As explained in footnote 151 above, the Rome II Regulation now forms part of English law as retained EU law, subject to minor amendments.

At the end of footnote 312, add:

The recast Brussels Regulation no longer applies in England with effect from the completion of the Brexit transition period on 31 December 2020, save in respect of proceedings instituted before the end of that period: Civil Jurisdiction and Judgments (Amendment) (EU Exit) Regulations 2019, SI 2019/479, regs 89, 93A; art.67(1)(a) of the EU–UK Withdrawal Agreement.

CHAPTER 3

INDUCING BREACH OF CONTRACT

A. INTRODUCTION

(4) The Tort does not Provide a Remedy for the Party Induced to Breach His Contract

3–006 *At the end of footnote 13, add:*

To the same effect see *Pepe's Piri Piri Limited v Junaid* [2019] EWHC 2097 (QB), per Matthew Gullick (sitting as a Deputy High Court Judge) at [202]–[207].

B. BREACH OF CONTRACT

3–008 *In footnote 20, replace the final sentence with:*

For a contrary view see M. Jones (ed), *Clerk & Lindsell on Torts*, 23rd edn (London: Sweet & Maxwell, 2020), para.23–18.

C. OTHER WRONGS

(3) Equitable Obligations

3–019 *At the end of footnote 44, add:*

Followed in *Davey v Money* [2018] EWHC 766 (Ch); [2018] Bus L.R. 1903, per Snowden J at [712].

(5) Obligations Under a Judgment or Order

Replace paragraph 3–022 with:

3–022 Liability under *Lumley v Gye* has now been recognised as extending to the inducement of breach of obligations under a judgment or order. In *Marex Financial Ltd v Sevilleja Garcia*,[48] the claimant had obtained money judgments against a number of corporate defendants. Subsequently, the individual who controlled the companies (Mr Sevilleja) was alleged to have dishonestly taken steps, after the judgment was handed down, to strip the companies of their assets, rendering them unable to meet their obligations to pay under the judgments. Knowles J dismissed a jurisdiction challenge by Mr Sevilleja founded on the contention that the claim disclosed no cause of action, concluding that the claimant had at least a good arguable case. The judge reasoned that non-payment of a judgment debt was an actionable wrong,[49] and that accordingly the procurement of that wrong could give rise to liability as an accessory.[50] The principle has since been confirmed by Bryan J in *Lakatamia Shipping Co Limited v Su*,[51] holding the analogy with breach of contract to be compelling. Both *Marex* and *Lakatamia* concerned judgments upholding contractual rights. Bryan J considered the analogy particularly strong in that context: since such rights merge in the judgment anything else would lead to the perverse conclusion that the claimant's rights are less well protected once vindicated by the courts. It is however thought to be unnecessary for the judgment to be one upholding contractual rights for the principle to apply.

Add new paragraphs 3–022A and 3–022B:

Ordinary *Lumley v Gye* principles apply in this context. So, for example, the relevant intention is an intention to violate the claimant's rights under the judgment and it is unnecessary to prove an intention to damage the claimant; and the requisite knowledge of the terms of the judgment is the same as in respect of the terms of a contract.[51a] In *Lakatamia*, Bryan J identified one exception to the analogy, concluding (obiter) that there is no room for a defence of justification in the context of inducing non-payment of a judgment debt.[51b] This is considered too broad a proposition. The inducer in the cases discussed in para.3–071 below may well have been entitled to rely on the defence even if the claimant's contractual rights against the contract breaker had been upheld by a judgment. Any other conclusion would entail a judgment elevating the status of the claimant's right vis-à-vis the inducer beyond that given to him by the contract, a conclusion which is difficult to support. **3–022A**

These first instance decisions in *Marex* and *Lakatamia* mark a significant practical development in a claimant's armoury in the fraud context: it will be a common occurrence, particularly in the absence of a freezing order (and sometimes even if there is such an order), that a fraudster will seek to ensure that a company under their control does not comply with a judgment obtained against it by extracting its assets so as to make it judgment proof. *Lumley v Gye* gives a potential right of action against the fraudster in such circumstances. Nevertheless, it is particularly important in this context to distinguish between inducement (which is actionable) and mere prevention (which is not): see para.3–030 below. **3–022B**

[48] *Marex Financial Ltd v Sevilleja Garcia* [2017] EWHC 918 (Comm); [2017] 4 W.L.R. 105. The Court of Appeal refused permission to appeal on this issue (see [2018] EWCA Civ 1468; [2019] Q.B. 173 at [1]) but allowed an appeal on a separate ground, namely that the creditor's loss was reflective of the companies' loss and irrecoverable on that basis. The Supreme Court in turn, by a majority, overturned the Court of Appeal's decision on the grounds that (in summary) the reflective loss principle did not apply to claims brought by creditors in that capacity [2020] UKSC 31; [2021] A.C. 39.

[49] In reliance on earlier authority including *Rubin v Eurofinance SA* [2012] UKSC 46; [2013] 1 A.C. 236, at [9]; some of this earlier authority referred to the juridical basis for the liability being in implied contract.

[50] The judge also held that there was nothing in a further argument that Mr Sevilleja had merely prevented the companies' performance of their obligations. This aspect of his decision is perhaps open to doubt: see para.3–030 below.

[51] *Lakatamia Shipping Co Limited v Su* [2021] EWHC 1907 (Comm), per Bryan J at [120]–[129]. The decision of Knowles J in *Marex* had been referred to with approval in *Palmer Birch (a partnership) v*

Lloyd [2018] EWHC 2316 (TCC); [2018] 4 W.L.R. 164, per HHJ Russen QC at [171]–[172], but the latter case did not concern obligations under a judgment.

[51a] *Lakatamia* at [127]. Intention and knowledge are addressed in paras 3–048 and following below.

[51b] *Lakatamia* at [130]–[131]. The justification defence is considered in paras 3–066 and following below.

D. INDUCEMENT

(3) Mere Prevention of Performance is not Enough

3–030 *Replace footnote 65 with:*

Marex Financial Ltd v Sevilleja Garcia [2017] EWHC 918 (Comm); [2017] 1 W.L.R. 105, at [24]–[26], overturned on appeal [2018] EWCA Civ 1468; [2019] Q.B. 173, itself overturned on appeal [2020] UKSC 31; [2021] A.C. 39 but neither appeal decision addresses this point.

Add new paragraphs 3–030A to 3–030C after para.3–030:

3–030A In *Palmer Birch (a partnership) v Lloyd*,[65a] HHJ Russen QC noted the fine dividing line between prevention and inducement. Following *Stocznia Gdanska SA v Latvian Shipping Co*,[65b] he held that there had been no actionable inducement where a de facto director and funder of the contracting company declined to put the company in funds to comply with some of its payment obligations, in circumstances where he was not obliged to do so and the company was unable to make payment independently.[65c] On the other hand, liability was held to be established in relation to a separate payment obligation where funds had been made available which the judge found should have been allocated to the contracting company. By deciding instead to put the company into liquidation and abusing its separate corporate personality the de facto director was held to have crossed the line from prevention to inducement.

3–030B More recently in *Kawasaki Kisen Kaisha Ltd v James Kemball Ltd*,[65d] a parent company had decided to form a joint venture which took business away from its subsidiary, preventing the subsidiary from performing its contractual obligations to the claimant. Overturning the decision of Teare J that the claimant had an arguable claim against the parent company for inducing breach of contract, the Court of Appeal reaffirmed that prevention of performance is not enough: "There must be some conduct by A amounting to persuasion, encouragement or assistance of B to break the contract with C."[65e] Popplewell LJ also reiterated at [33] the need for the defendant's conduct to operate on the will of the contracting party, which means influencing a choice by the latter whether or not to breach the contract.

[65a] *Palmer Birch (a partnership) v Lloyd* [2018] EWHC 2316 (TCC); [2018] 4 W.L.R. 164.

[65b] *Stocznia Gdanska SA v Latvian Shipping Co* [2001] 1 Lloyd's Rep. 537 per Thomas J, [2002] EWCA Civ 889; [2002] 2 All E.R. (Comm) 768 (CA), discussed in paras 3–041 and 3–044 below.

[65c] [2018] EWHC 2316 (TCC); [2018] 4 W.L.R. 164, at [348]–[356]. In fact in *Stocznia*, the defendant was under a contractual obligation to put its subsidiary in funds; but that obligation was owed not to the subsidiary but to a third party, and Thomas J seems to have considered that obligation to be irrelevant in this context (see [2001] 1 Lloyd's Rep. 537 at [252]).

[65d] *Kawasaki Kisen Kaisha Ltd v James Kemball Ltd* [2021] EWCA Civ 33.

[65e] [2021] EWCA Civ 33, per Popplewell LJ at [32].

In each of *Stocznia*, *Palmer Birch* and *Kawasaki*, some importance was attached to the question of whether the defendant was under any obligation to take steps to enable the contract breaker to comply with its contractual obligations.[65f] Indeed in *Kawasaki*, Popplewell distinguished *Palmer Birch* on the basis that the defendant in *Kawasaki* was under no obligation to direct business to its subsidiary. The presence or absence of an obligation may indeed be important—it may, for example, determine whether the defendant can be shown to have acted unlawfully so as to give rise to potential liability in unlawful interference—but it is less clear why this could make the difference between prevention and inducement for the purposes of the *Lumley v Gye* tort. **3–030C**

[65f] *Stocznia Gdanska SA v Latvian Shipping Co*, per Thomas J at [252]; *Palmer Birch*, per HHJ Russen QC at [167]–[170], [173], [349]–[350] and [361]; *Kawasaki* at [35]–[36], [49] and [51].

(5) Dealings "Inconsistent With" the Contract May Give Rise to Liability

At the end of the paragraph, add new footnote 83a: **3–039**

[83a] Similarly in *Flexidig Limited v A Coupland (Surfacing) Limited* [2019] EWHC 2578 (TCC), the defendant contractor who agreed to carry out work, in circumstances where the claimant asserted that it had a right to carry out that work and that the employer was thus in breach of contract in engaging the defendant, was held at best to have facilitated the employer's alleged breach of contract, falling short of the necessary inducement.

Add new paragraph 3–039A after para.3–039:

The requirement for the inducer to operate on the will of the contracting party, even in a case of inconsistent dealing, was reaffirmed in *Kawasaki Kisen Kaisha Ltd v James Kemball Ltd*.[83a] Popplewell LJ held that inconsistent dealings are not an independent basis for liability but are simply an example of conduct which may amount to inducement because it may constitute a form of persuasion, encouragement or assistance, as was held to have been the case in *Lictor Anstalt*. In the *Kawasaki* case, there were no relevant "dealings" between the defendant (parent) and the contract breaker (subsidiary); all that had happened was that the parent had stopped providing business to the subsidiary. **3–039A**

[83a] *Kawasaki Kisen Kaisha Ltd v James Kemball Ltd* [2021] EWCA Civ 33, at [40]–[51].

E. COMPANIES AND AGENTS

(1) The Rule in Said v Butt

Replace footnote 87 with: **3–040**

The statement now found in Jones (ed), *Clerk & Lindsell on Torts*, 23rd edn (London: Sweet & Maxwell, 2020), para.23–39 that, if a director has ordered or procured the breach by the company, then he may be liable in tort given that he possesses the requisite knowledge and intention, was held by Gloster J in *Crystalens Ltd v White*, unreported, 7 July 2006, at [10]–[15] not to provide any support for deviation from the principle in *Said v Butt*.

(2) Shareholders May Claim the Protection of the Principle

Insert new paragraphs 3–044A and 3–044B after para.3–044:

3–044A The application of the rule in *Said v Butt* to shareholders raises potentially intricate issues where parent and subsidiary companies have common directors or employees, through whom it is alleged that the parent induced a breach of contract by the subsidiary. In *Bumi Armada Offshore Holdings Limited v Tozzi Srl*,[96a] the Singapore Court of Appeal held that, in such a case, it is necessary to examine two issues: (i) whether those individuals were acting for the subsidiary and/or the parent, and, if they were acting for the parent, (ii) whether the circumstances are such that the parent can properly be held liable for inducing its subsidiary's breach of contract.[96b] As to the second of these issues, the court held that the parent would not be liable if it was merely pursuing in good faith its own interest in its capacity as shareholder. Something more than an actual act of inducement is required, such as a finding that the parent was pursuing an interest unrelated to (or possibly in addition to) its capacity as shareholder, or possibly a lack of good faith. Otherwise, the principle of separate corporate personality would be undermined.[96c] The court also pointed[96d] to the conceptual difficulty in identifying an inducement in a case where the same individual does the same thing on behalf of both the subsidiary and the parent.

[96a] [2018] SGCA(I) 05 (Sundaresh Menon CJ, Beverley McLachlin IJ and David Neuberger IJ).
[96b] *Bumi Armada Offshore Holdings Ltd v Tozzi Srl*, above, at [41].
[96c] *Bumi Armada Offshore Holdings Ltd v Tozzi Srl*, above, at [42], [45] and [47].
[96d] *Bumi Armada Offshore Holdings Ltd*, above, at [56].

3–044B *Bumi* was followed by Julia Dias QC (sitting as a Deputy High Court Judge) in *Uavend Properties Inc v Adsaax Ltd*,[96e] a case in which the subsidiary and parent had common directors. The fact that they had been appointed as directors of the subsidiary by the parent company did not mean they carried out their duties as such on behalf of the parent, and nor did anything else in the setup justify such a conclusion.[96f] Although the directors necessarily wore two hats, on the facts their relevant acts had been carried out in their capacity as directors of the subsidiary.[96g] This decision also illustrates the difficult questions of attribution of knowledge and intention which may arise in this context.[96h]

[96e] *Uavend Properties Inc v Adsaax Ltd* [2020] EWHC 2073 (Comm). At [126], the Deputy Judge held (obiter) that the defendant/parent bears the burden of proof on the issue of whether it was acting in good faith in pursuing its interests as shareholder. However, this is perhaps questionable in light of the authorities cited in n.92 above.
[96f] *Uavend Properties Inc v Adsaax Ltd*, above, at [49]–[70].
[96g] *Uavend Properties Inc v Adsaax Ltd*, above, at [79], [89]–[95]. An argument based on vicarious liability of the parent for the acts of the directors also failed for several reasons, including that the directors themselves were able to rely squarely on *Said v Butt* and that they were not acting in the course of employment by the parent: see [128]–[136].
[96h] *Uavend Properties Inc v Adsaax Ltd*, above, at [102]–[106].

F. Intention and Knowledge

(2) Intention Defined

At the end of footnote 104, add: **3–050**

Though it has been suggested that the intention requirement is less stringent in the context of unlawful means conspiracy: see para.2–040 above (n.77).

At the end of footnote 109, add: **3–052**

Similarly, in *Kawasaki Kisen Kaisha Ltd v James Kemball Ltd*, considered in para.3–030A above, the necessary intention was not even arguably shown where the breach of the subsidiary's contract with the claimant could not be said to be the end sought by the parent company or a means to an end, "as distinct from merely being the foreseen or intended consequence" (per Popplewell LJ at [34] and [52]). It is thought that "intended consequence" should here be understood in the sense of a known or foreseen consequence of the parent's intentional acts. If the parent had actually intended to bring about a breach of contract by the subsidiary, then (subject to the separate question of whether the parent induced a breach or merely prevented performance) it is not easy to see why it would not have been liable on the basis that a breach of contract was either the end sought by the parent or a means to that end.

(3) Knowledge of the Contract (and that it will be Breached) is Necessary

At the end of the paragraph, add new footnote 114a: **3–055**

[114a] In *The Beans Group Limited v Myunidays Limited* [2019] EWHC 320 (Comm) at [97]–[101], Martin Griffiths QC (sitting as a Deputy High Court Judge) followed a dictum of Jenkins LJ in *DC Thomson & Co Ltd v Deakin* [1952] Ch 646, at 694, to the effect that a defendant who entered into an inconsistent contract with the contract breaker without knowledge of the claimant's prior contract would be liable if, having become aware of the claimant's contract, he continued with his inconsistent contract knowingly and actively and damage to the claimant is proved. This principle has been little explored. Query whether, in such circumstances, by the time the defendant acquired knowledge of the claimant's contract, he would have an available defence of justification on the basis of an equal right to the right enjoyed by the claimant.

At the end of footnote 122, add: **3–059**

This is consistent with the view expressed in *John v Lucasfilm Ltd. LLC* [2018] EWHC 624 (QB), per Veronique Buehrlen QC (sitting as a Deputy High Court Judge) at [79].

At the end of footnote 127, add: **3–061**

See also *Uavend Properties Inc v Adsaax Ltd* [2020] EWHC 2073 (Comm), per Julia Dias QC at [100], rejecting a submission that "reckless indifference" could be established if blind-eye knowledge could not: "it makes no difference whether the requisite mental element is described as blind-eye knowledge, Nelsonian blindness or reckless indifference. They are all labels for the same thing, which is a conscious decision not to enquire for fear of discovering an inconvenient truth. An element of deliberation is therefore required which distinguishes the situation from one of negligence or even gross negligence."

(6) No Liability Where the Defendant Honestly but Mistakenly Believes that there will be No Breach of Contract

Insert new paragraph 3–065A after para.3–065:

3–065A In *Allen v Pollock*,[138a] the claimant's employee left to join the defendant employer in circumstances which the trial judge found to give rise to a breach of the employee's restrictive covenants. The defendant had received advice to the effect that the relevant covenant was probably unenforceable. The Court of Appeal considered this sufficient to avoid liability and rejected a submission that an absolute belief that there would be no breach of contract was required. Lewison LJ held on the contrary that, if the defendant has an "honest doubt" about whether a contract as a whole is binding or enforceable, or believes it to be "probable" that the relevant term is unenforceable, then that would be sufficient to avoid liability.[138b] He considered it important as a matter of policy that people should be able to act on legal advice, also observing realistically that such advice is rarely unequivocal.[138c] Lewison LJ expressly left open the possibility that advice to the effect that it was merely "arguable" that no breach would be committed would be insufficient to avoid liability.

[138a] *Allen v Pollock* (*Allen (t/a David Allen Chartered Accountants) v Dodd & Co Ltd*) [2020] EWCA Civ 258; [2020] Q.B. 781.
[138b] *Allen v Pollock*, above, at [28]–[33]. Both David Richards and Rose LJJ agreed.
[138c] *Allen v Pollock*, above, at [34].

G. JUSTIFICATION

(3) What Counts as an "Equal or Superior Right"?

3–074 *At the beginning of footnote 157, insert:*

Pepe's Piri Piri Limited v Junaid [2019] EWHC 2097 (QB), per Matthew Gullick (sitting as a Deputy High Court Judge) at [218].

H. DAMAGES

(2) Particular Principles Governing the Assessment of Damages

3–078 *At the end of the first sentence, add new footnote 168a:*

[168a] Though in *Antuzis v DJ Houghton Catching Services Limited* [2021] EWHC 971 (QB), Griffiths J awarded aggravated damages assessed at 20% of the damages represented by the claimants' basic money claims, saying at [155] that "Recovery of the money due now, even with interest, will not compensate the Claimants for the whole effect upon them of their exploitation, manipulation and abuse by the Defendants at the time in question, and in the manner that I have outlined above. The means of inflicting this abuse was the First to Third Defendants' systematic denial of the Claimants' statutory rights. I am not compensating them for personal injury, because this is not a personal injury claim. In awarding aggravated damages, I am recognising that the effect of non-payment and under-payment was extreme, because of its total and cumulative impact on them."

3–080 *Replace footnote 173 with:*

J. Edelman (ed), *McGregor on Damages*, 21st edn (London: Sweet & Maxwell, 2020), para.48–004 and following in particular; and Jones (ed), *Clerk & Lindsell on Torts*, 23rd edn (London: Sweet & Maxwell, 2020), Ch.27.

CHAPTER 4

UNLAWFUL INTERFERENCE

C. UNLAWFUL ACTS

(2) The Unlawful Act Must be Actionable by the Third Party

At the end of footnote 25, add: **4–013**

In *Pepe's Piri Piri Limited v Junaid* [2019] EWHC 2097 (QB), a claim in unlawful interference failed because the alleged wrongful acts of the defendants involved (essentially) causing, encouraging, permitting or facilitating the breach by the third party of its contract with the claimant, whereas this was not unlawful as against the third party: see [202]–[207], and the discussion in para.3–006 above.

(3) What Wrongs Qualify as Unlawful Acts?

4–021 *At the end of footnote 39, add:*

The 23rd edition of *Clerk & Lindsell* retains reference to the concerns expressed in the 22nd edition, but the authors conclude on balance that breach of contract ought to be held to constitute unlawful means for the purposes of the tort referred to here as unlawful interference: see para.23–87.

4–024 *At the end of footnote 50, add:*

In *Marex Financial Ltd v Sevilleja* [2017] EWHC 918 (Comm); [2017] 4 W.L.R. 105, it does not appear to have been in dispute that it was arguable that a breach of fiduciary duty qualified as an unlawful act in principle, subject to the interference requirement (as to which see para.4–35 below).

4–025 *At the end of footnote 51, add:*

Alesco Risk Management Services Limited v Bishopsgate Insurance Brokers Limited [2019] EWHC 2839 (QB), at [376].

(5) Must the Defendant Know that what He is Doing is Unlawful?

Replace paragraph with:

4–032 There was previously a conflict of authority in the context of unlawful means conspiracy as to whether liability depended on the defendant knowing that what was done pursuant to the conspiracy was unlawful (as opposed to knowing the facts that made the conduct unlawful), such that ignorance of the law would amount to a defence. Subject to further consideration by the Supreme Court, the issue is now settled: in *Racing Partnership Ltd v Done Bros (Cash Betting) Ltd*[70] following a detailed analysis by Arnold LJ of the authorities, a majority of the Court of Appeal held that it is not an essential element in the tort of conspiracy to injure by unlawful means that the defendant knew that the means employed were unlawful. The recent cases do not specifically consider the defence in the context of unlawful interference, save for a brief conclusion in one of them that there was a serious issue to be tried on the question for the purposes of an interim injunction.[71]

[70] *Racing Partnership Ltd v Done Bros (Cash Betting) Ltd* [2020] EWCA Civ 1300; [2021] Ch. 233, at [104]–[144] and [171]. This decision, and previous authorities on the issue, are considered at paras 2–077—2–082 above.
[71] *Lebara Mobile Ltd v Lycamobile UK Ltd* [2015] EWHC 3318 (Ch), at [51].

D. INTERFERENCE

4–034 *At the end of the paragraph, insert new footnote 75a:*

[75a] It nevertheless remains necessary to establish damage to the claimant's economic interests. In *Chalfont St Peter Parish Council v Holy Cross Sisters Trustees Incorporated* [2019] EWHC 1128 (QB), Swift J rejected a claim in unlawful interference where the only interest said to have been damaged by the defendants was the claimant council's exercise of its public functions, holding at [95]–[101] that an extension beyond damage to economic interests was not justified either by principle or authority.

Delete the final sentence of footnote 76. **4–035**

Replace the second sentence of footnote 78 with:

This decision was overturned on appeal on the separate basis that the claim was barred by the rule against recovery of reflective loss [2018] EWCA Civ 1468; [2019] Q.B. 173, a decision in turn overturned by the Supreme Court [2020] UKSC 31; [2021] A.C. 39.

At the end of footnote 86, add: **4–038**

This passage from *Emerald Supplies* was referred to by Barling J in *Media-Saturn Holding GmbH v Toshiba Information Systems (UK) Ltd* [2019] EWHC 1095; [2019] 5 C.M.L.R. 7, at [244] and following. In the *Media-Saturn* case the defendants were alleged to have formed a price-fixing cartel. Barling J held that it was arguable that, even though the defendants entered into the price-fixing arrangements voluntarily and knowingly, they nevertheless thereby affected each other's freedom to deal with the claimant, sufficient to give rise to a potential claim in unlawful interference.

Insert new paragraph 4–038A after para.4–038:

The requirement that the defendant's conduct should affect the third party's freedom to deal with the claimant was reaffirmed by the Supreme Court in the face of a challenge by the claimants in *Secretary of State for Health v Servier Laboratories*.[87a] The defendants had obtained a patent of a prescription-only drug, which was later revoked by the European Patent Office (EPO). The claimant health authorities, which funded the cost of drugs dispensed by the NHS, brought a claim in unlawful interference on the grounds that the defendants had obtained, defended and enforced the patent by practising deceit on the EPO and the English court, which caused the claimants loss by delaying the entry of generic versions of the drug into the market, something the defendants were alleged to have intended. It was common ground that the EPO and the English court had had no dealings with the claimants, and so unless it could be shown that the "freedom to deal" requirement was not a necessary element of the tort, the claim was unsustainable. The Supreme Court held that Roth J had been right to strike out the claim (and the Court of Appeal right to uphold that decision) on the basis that the "freedom to deal" requirement was indeed a necessary element of the tort. This was part of the ratio in *OBG Ltd v Allan*, in which the House of Lords had specifically taken the opportunity to clarify the elements of this tort and the inducement tort.[87b] - Moreover, there was no sufficient basis for departing from *OBG*. No real-life examples of the decision causing difficulty had been identified. On the contrary, Lord Hamblen set out a number of strong reasons for following the House of Lords' decision in *OBG*, chief among them that, in summary, "The dealing requirement performs the valuable function of delineating the degree of connection which is required between the unlawful means used and the damage suffered",[87c] and "minimises the danger of there being indeterminate liability to a wide range of claimants".[87d] **4–038A**

[87a] [2021] UKSC 24; [2021] 3 W.L.R. 370.

[87b] *Secretary of State for Health v Servier Laboratories*, above, per Lord Hamblen JSC at [26], [57] and [63]–[74].

[87c] *Secretary of State for Health v Servier Laboratories*, above, at [94].

[87d] *Secretary of State for Health v Servier Laboratories*, above, at [95].

F. JUSTIFICATION

4–045 *At the end of footnote 102, add:*

In *Palmer Birch (a partnership) v Lloyd* [2018] EWHC 2316 (TCC); [2018] 4 W.L.R. 164, the defendants submitted that the justification defence recognised in claims for inducing breach of contract (considered in paras 3–066—3–076 above) extended beyond that tort and was also available in claims for unlawful means conspiracy. HHJ Russen QC rejected this argument (see the discussion in para.2–091A above), in terms which apply equally to unlawful interference, though the decision may be obiter in relation to the latter tort: see [183]–[193] and [201].

G. DAMAGE

4–047 *At the end of footnote 106, add:*

And in *Palmer Birch* (above), per HHJ Russen QC at [244]–[245], where the judge held that the "damages at large" approach justified the court attempting its best assessment of the heads of financial loss suffered (and proved to have been suffered) by the claimant; and that (in the case of unlawful interference, as with unlawful means conspiracy) the conduct of the defendant and the nature of the wrongdoing is likely to form a significant part of that assessment.

CHAPTER 5

INTIMIDATION

A. INTRODUCTION

(1) Nature of the Tort

At the end of footnote 1, add: **5–001**

See more recently *Morley (t/a Morley Estates) v The Royal Bank of Scotland Plc* [2020] EWHC 88 (Ch) (Kerr J) and [2021] EWCA Civ 338; and *Global Display Solutions Ltd v NCR Financial Solutions Group Ltd* [2021] EWHC 1119 (Comm).

At the end of footnote 13, add: **5–006**

A further example is *Morley (t/a Morley Estates) v The Royal Bank of Scotland Plc* [2020] EWHC 88 (Ch), per Kerr J at [196] and following.

B. THE THREAT

(1) Introduction

5–010 *At the end of paragraph, add:*

The existence of a coercive threat is the essence of the tort. An attempt in a recent case to argue that the tort of intimidation could be made out by reference not to threatened unlawful conduct, but to actual unlawful conduct, was rejected, the judge holding that "a threat express or implied is indeed an essential ingredient of the tort of intimidation."[18a]

[18a] See *Global Display Solutions Ltd v NCR Financial Solutions Group Ltd* [2021] EWHC 1119 (Comm), per Jacobs J at [477], a conclusion founded on the judge's careful analysis of *Rookes v Barnard* [1964] AC 1129.

(2) Threat to be Distinguished from Warning

5–011 *At the end of the paragraph, add footnote 19a:*

[19a] The distinction between a threat and a warning was discussed in *Morley (t/a Morley Estates) v The Royal Bank of Scotland Plc* [2020] EWHC 88 (Ch), per Kerr J at [241]–[247]. Having concluded that the words spoken were a threat, the judge continued: "The question is whether it was a threat to do an unlawful act. [The defendant's employee's] disdainful and aggressive tone and demeanour at the meeting, unpleasant though they were, are not sufficient. What matters is whether what he threatened the bank would do was something unlawful."

5–013 *At the end of the second sentence, add footnote 23a:*

[23a] The analysis of the law in these two sentences was approved by Jacobs J in *Global Display Solutions Ltd v NCR Financial Solutions Group Ltd* [2021] EWHC 1119 (Comm), at [484]. He also approved, subject to the precise meaning of the phrase "bad thing", the following submission made by counsel for the defendant: "... the threat in order to be a threat has to be coupled with a demand. The defendant has got to say to the claimant: 'You've got to do something or else I'm going to do something bad to you', and the bad thing has to be unlawful. And if the defendant merely says that he will do something without coupling it with a demand, it's not a threat. And when the defendant has already done something in the past, it's not a threat either, unless he's impliedly threatening that he might do it again, in which case it could be a threat."

5–014 *At the end of footnote 26, add:*

Hence in *Godwin v Uzoigwe* [1993] Fam. Law 65, Stuart-Smith LJ explained, in a modern slavery case, that "assaults and the implied threats of further assaults if [the claimant] did not behave in the manner required of her [by the defendants] are sufficient in themselves to justify the conclusion that the tort was made out."

(3) Unlawful Acts

(i) Acts which would be actionable by the claimant

5–017 *At the end of footnote 33, add:*

There is an interesting discussion of the meaning of an unlawful act in *Morley (t/a Morley Estates) v The Royal Bank of Scotland Plc* [2020] EWHC 88 (Ch) per Kerr J at [248]–[267]. The judge concluded, at [267], that the defendant was threatening to do an act which was not unequivocally unlawful and hence the tort was not made out. It "was threatening to do an act which might or might not turn out to be unlawful....To be unlawful, the act would have to be unlawful vis-à-vis the claimant and not just in the abstract."

In footnote 49, replace the reference with the following reference: **5–026**

A. Tettenborn, *Clerk and Lindsell on Torts, 23rd ed (London: Sweet and Maxwell, 2020)*, para.23–73.

(v) Blackmail

At the end of the paragraph, insert footnote 56a: **5–029**

[56a] The decision in *Al Nehayan* was considered further by the Court of Appeal in *Times Travel (UK) Ltd v Pakistan International Airlines Corporation* [2019] EWCA Civ 828; [2020] Ch 98; and on appeal by the Supreme Court in the same case at [2021] UKSC 40. These decisions are discussed in Ch.15.

D. ACTUAL COERCION

At end of first sentence, insert footnote 65a: **5–033**

[65a] An example of a case where it was held that coercion was not made out is *Morley (t/a Morley Estates) v The Royal Bank of Scotland Plc* [2020] EWHC 88 (Ch) (Kerr J) and [2021] EWCA Civ 338.

CHAPTER 6

MALICIOUS FALSEHOOD

B. ELEMENTS OF THE TORT

At the end of footnote 13, add: **6–006**

For a further restatement of the elements of the cause of action, see *Peck v Williams Trade Supplies Ltd* [2020] EWHC 966 (QB), at [12] and following.

(2) Relating to the Claimant

At the end of footnote 17, add: **6–010**

There is a strict pleading requirement, similar to what pertains in the law of defamation, requiring the claimant to set out the precise words published and alleged to be false, and their meaning: *BHX v GRX* [2021] EWHC 770 (QB), at [55(10)]–[55(11)].

(3) Falsity

At the end of footnote 20, add: **6–012**

In *Peck v Williams Trade Supplies Ltd* [2020] EWHC 966 (QB), Nicklin J explained, at [13]: "In most malicious falsehood cases, the issue of falsity requires a determination of the meaning of the published statement. Although the Court's task when assessing meaning for the purposes of malicious falsehood claims has many similarities to the exercise that has to be performed in defamation claims, there are material differences. Most importantly, the single-meaning rule—a cardinal principle in defamation—does not apply to malicious falsehood: *Ajinomoto Sweeteners SAS v Asda Stores Limited* [2011] QB 497 [35]. Once the single-meaning rule has been despatched, with it goes the objective assessment of the meaning that the notional ordinary reasonable reader would understand the words to bear. In consequence, whereas in defamation, inquiry into what individual publishees understood the words to mean is (with limited exception in some cases on the issues of harm and damage) irrelevant, in a malicious falsehood claim, the subjective understanding of the individual publishees (if they can be identified) is likely to be an essential element of establishing causation of damage." However where there has been publication to a large, but unquantifiable, number of publishees, it is usually impossible to ascertain what meaning(s) they understood the words complained of to bear. In those circumstances, a malicious falsehood claim can be maintained in respect of any meaning that a substantial number of people who read the words would reasonably have understood the words complained of to bear: at [16]. On the other hand where the publication is to a single individual, the only relevant question is what meaning did the publishee understand the publication to bear and, if there is a dispute about it, whether *this* meaning is an available meaning for the purposes of malicious falsehood—see observations of Tugendhat J in *Ajinomoto Sweeteners Europe SAS v Asda Stores Ltd* [2010] Q.B. 204, at [31].

6–014 *At the end of footnote 22, add:*

See further *Qatar Airways Group QCSC v Middle East News FZ LLC* [2020] EWHC 2975 (QB), per Saini J at [145] and following.

(5) Damage

(ii) Need for proof of special damage?

6–022 *At the end of footnote 40, add:*

See further *Tinkler v Ferguson* [2020] EWHC 1467 (QB); [2020] 4 W.L.R. 89, at [44] and [93]; and, on appeal, [2021] EWCA Civ 18; [2021] 4 W.L.R. 27, at [76] and following.

CHAPTER 7

BRIBERY

A. INTRODUCTION

(1) Introduction

7–002 *Replace the third sentence with:*

The starting point is that the principal is entitled to be confident that his agent will act impartially, and that the agent's duty and interest will not be placed in actual or potential conflict.[4]

[4] *Daraydan Holdings Ltd v Solland International Ltd* [2005] EWHC 622 (Ch); [2005] Ch. 119, per Lawrence Collins J at [52]: "An agent should not put himself in a position where his duty and interest may conflict, and if bribes are taken by an agent, the principal is deprived of the disinterested advice of the agent, to which the principal is entitled. Any surreptitious dealing between one principal to a transaction and the agent of the other is a fraud on the other principal." See also *Wood v Commercial First Business Ltd.* [2021] EWCA Civ 471; [2021] 3 W.L.R. 395, considered at para.7–007 below.

At the end of the paragraph, add new footnote 4a:

[4a] But note that "agent" and "fiduciary" are for the purposes of the law of bribery used in a loose sense; and the Court of Appeal in *Wood v Commercial First Business Ltd* [2021] EWCA Civ 471; [2021] 3 WLR 395 held that it was an unnecessary and potentially misleading complication to enquire whether the relationship between the bribed agent and principal was truly a fiduciary one. The real question is whether the "agent" owes a duty to give information, advice or recommendation on a disinterested or impartial basis (see at [48]). See further paras 7–006—7–008A below. In this chapter, the terms "agent" and "fiduciary" are used as convenient shorthands for a person owing duties of the sort identified by the Court of Appeal in *Wood*.

(2) Fiduciary Basis of the Law of Bribery

Replace sub-heading and paragraphs 7–006 to 7–008 with the following:

(2) Basis of the Law of Bribery

7–006 Bribery is a wrong which "is sui generis and defies classification".[12] In the first edition of this book it was suggested that "the law of bribery is, in its fundamentals, a manifestation of the law of agency and fiduciary duties", albeit the terms "agent" and "fiduciary" were said to be used in a wide sense for these purposes, extending beyond those who have the authority to alter their principal's legal relations, and those such as trustees and directors who are classically regarded as subject to fiduciary obligations. Thus in one leading case it was said that in this context "fiduciary relationship" is used "in a very loose, or at all events a comprehensive sense":

> "…for the present purpose a 'fiduciary relation' exists (a) whenever the plaintiff entrusts to the defendant property, including intangible property as, for instance, confidential information, and relies on the defendant to deal with such property for the benefit of the plaintiff or for purposes authorised by him, and not otherwise…and (b) whenever the plaintiff entrusts to the defendant a job to be performed, for instance, the negotiation of a contract on his behalf or for his benefit, and relies on the defendant to procure for the plaintiff the best terms available."[13]

To similar effect, in *Novoship (UK) Limited v Mikhayluk,* Christopher Clarke J said:

> "The recipient of the bribe (or the person at whose order the bribe is paid) must be someone with a role in the decision-making process in relation to the transaction in question e.g. as agent, or *otherwise someone who is in a position to influence or affect the decision* taken by the principal."[14]

[12] *Mahesan v Malaysia Government Officers' Co-Operative Housing Society Ltd*, above, at 383. For one thing, bribery gives rise to remedies at common law as well as in equity: see below, at paras 7–051, 7–058, 7–061 and following.
[13] *Reading v The King* [1949] 2 KB 232 (CA), per Asquith LJ at 236; confirmed in *Reading v The King* [1951] AC 507, per Lord Porter at 516.
[14] [2012] EWHC 3586 (Comm), at [108] (emphasis added).

In *Wood v Commercial First Business Ltd*[15] the Court of Appeal conducted a thorough survey of the caselaw and took this one step further, deciding that it was "unnecessarily elaborate, and perhaps inaccurate" to ask whether there was a fiduciary relationship between the person bribed and the claimant principal. Instead: **7–007**

> "The question...is the altogether simpler one of whether the payee was under a duty to provide information, advice or recommendation on an impartial or disinterested basis. If the payee was under such a duty, the payment of bribes or secret commissions exposes the payer and the payee to the applicable civil remedies. No further enquiry as to the legal nature of the relationship is required."[16]

[15] [2021] EWCA Civ 471; [2021] 3 W.L.R. 395.
[16] Per David Richards LJ at [48].

Thus the foundation for the application of the civil law of bribery is the existence of a duty to provide disinterested advice, recommendations or information. That may or may not arise out of a fiduciary relationship; but it adds nothing to the analysis (and may confuse it) to ask that further question. It is the duty to be honest and impartial that matters.[17] In this chapter we therefore use the terms "agent" and "fiduciary" (which are used in many of the older cases) in a sense that now must be understood as reflecting this modern conception of the relevant duty. According to the Court of Appeal in *Wood*, the one situation in which it remains necessary to enquire as to whether fiduciary duties are owed is in the unusual case (considered below) of the "half-secret" commission, where it appears that relief (such as rescission) will only lie if receipt of the payment involves a breach of fiduciary duty, properly so-called.[17a] **7–008**

[17] *Wood*, above, at [92].
[17a] *Wood*, above, at [80]–[84], [100].

Nevertheless, the unyoking of the law of bribery from that of fiduciary obligations should not be understood as relaxing the requirements for a claim in bribery. In fact, what it does is shift the focus on to what matters: the existence of a duty of honesty and impartiality, however arising and however characterised, with which receipt of an undisclosed payment or other form of benefit (or promise thereof) creates a real risk of conflict. But this remains a strict requirement, and can fail to be satisfied even in cases in which one might readily have characterised the relationship as involving a sort of agency. Thus in *Conway v Eze* it was held that a "property acquisition agent", who introduced a property deal to a purchaser (after the purchase price had been agreed in principle) and then facilitated the parties in reaching an exchange of contracts and had a limited authority to instruct solicitors to that end was not an agent in the sense required to engage the law of bribery.[17b] **7–008A**

[17b] [2018] EWHC 29 (Ch), at [96]–[115]; upheld on appeal at [2019] EWCA Civ 88. See also *CH Offshore Ltd v Internaves Consorcio Naviero SA* [2020] EWHC 1710 (Comm) (intermediaries who brokered a charterparty not agents for either party such as to engage law of bribery).

B. THE INCIDENTS OF THE CLAIM IN BRIBERY

(12) Informed Consent and Disclosure

7–043 *At the end of footnote 86, add:*

In *Medsted Associates Ltd v Canaccord Genuity Wealth (International) Ltd* [2019] EWCA Civ 83; [2019] 1 W.L.R. 4481, it was held that sophisticated investors who were taken to know that some commission was being paid to a broker did not need to be told the actual amount of the commission for the broker to comply with its obligations. A similar conclusion was reached in *CH Offshore Ltd v Internaves Consorcio Naviero SA* [2020] EWHC 1710 (Comm), where the fact of payment but not the amount was known to the complaining party, which was a commercial entity that was aware of the relevant market rates and chose not to enquire as to the precise amount being paid.

(13) Bribery and Ex Turpi Causa

Add new paragraph 7–044A after para.7–044:

7–044A In contrast, in the (post *Patel v Mirza*) case of *Medsted Associates Ltd v Canaccord Genuity Wealth (International) Ltd*, it was suggested (without deciding the point) that a claim for damages representing commissions of which a broker had been deprived when the third party contracted directly with the clients might not be barred on public policy grounds by reason of the commissions having been (it was assumed, contrary to the decision in the case) kept secret from the clients. The Court of Appeal would, had it been necessary to decide the point, have given more weight to the considerations that the third party was aware of the non-disclosure and that to deprive the broker of damages entirely would be disproportionate, since it had reasonably earned at least some commission.[91a] Similarly, in *Bank St Petersburg PJSC v Arkhangelsky* the Court of Appeal upheld a decision that there was an insufficient connection between alleged bribery and a counterclaim for dishonest conspiracy to deny the latter on public policy grounds, and noted that denial of the counterclaim would not be a proportionate response to the illegality "bearing specifically in mind that punishment for bribery is generally a matter for the criminal courts."[91b]

[91a] [2019] EWCA Civ 83; [2019] 1 W.L.R. 4481, per Longmore LJ at [48]–[51].
[91b] [2020] EWCA Civ 408; [2020] 4 W.L.R. 55, per Sir Geoffrey Vos C, at [89]–[92].

7–045 *Replace the first sentence with:*

Where the third party agrees to pay the principal's agent a sum of money which is characterised as a bribe in its more conventional sense of a payment for a corrupt purpose, then it is likely that the agent will be unable to enforce the contract *to* bribe on public policy grounds.[92]

[92] As accepted in *Honeywell International Middle East Ltd v Meydan Group LLC* [2014] EWHC 1344 (TCC); [2014] Lloyd's Rep. 133, at [185].

C. REMEDIES

(3) Rescission

(ii) Rescission as of right

In footnote 112, replace the reference to Bowstead and Reynolds with: **7–051**

Watts (ed), *Bowstead and Reynolds on Agency* (2021), para.8–223.

At the end of the first sentence in footnote 112, add:

; *Wood v Commercial First Business Ltd.* [2021] EWCA Civ 471; [2021] 3 W.L.R. 395, at [99]–[101].

(iii) A "half-way house

At the end of the paragraph, add: **7–053**

It was similarly cited without disapproval by the Court of Appeal in *Wood v Commercial First Business Ltd*,[117a] the Court of Appeal explaining that in the case of a half-secret commission the relevant liability was not for bribery, in the sense considered in this chapter, but rather for breach of fiduciary duty. Thus in such case, in contrast to a case of a fully-secret bribe, it was necessary to determine whether the party receiving the commission owed fiduciary duties (and not just the duty of disinterested advice that suffices to engage the law of bribery).

[117a] [2021] EWCA Civ 471; [2021] 3 W.L.R. 395, at [80]–[84], [100].

Add new paragraph:

Another case in which the fact that commission would be received was known to the clients, but not the amount in fact received, was *Medsted Associates Ltd v Canaccord Genuity Wealth (International) Ltd*.[117b] There, however, the Court of Appeal held that, whilst in some limited respects the relationship between clients and broker was fiduciary, because the clients were sophisticated investors, there was no fiduciary obligation on the broker to disclose more—and thus the question of relief did not arise. In contrast, in *Wood v Commercial First Business Ltd*[117c] disclosure by brokers that they "may receive fees from lenders" was held not to be sufficient to make the commissions half-secret, since the brokers had also agreed to tell the borrowers the amount of the fees and their failure to do so carried with it the implication that no fees were being paid in the particular cases; they were thus fully secret commissions. **7–053A**

[117b] [2019] EWCA Civ 83; [2019] 1 W.L.R. 4481.
[117c] [2021] EWCA Civ 471; [2021] 3 W.L.R. 395.

(4) Proprietary Liability in Respect of the Bribe

At the end of footnote 121, add: **7–056**

This statement now needs to be qualified by the analysis of the nature of the relationship that gives rise to liability for a bribe in *Wood v Commercial First Business Ltd.* [2021] EWCA Civ 471; [2021] 3 W.L.R. 395. See para.7–007 above.

Add new paragraph 7–056A after para.7–05:

7–056A One unresolved question is whether the above analysis applies where the recipient of the bribe is not a fiduciary in the strict sense, but owes on some other basis a duty to give disinterested information, advice or recommendation, it now being clear that the latter suffices to engage the law of bribery, at least for the purposes of the remedies of rescission, restitution and damages.[127a]

[127a] *Wood v Commercial First Business Ltd.* [2021] EWCA Civ 471; [2021] 3 W.L.R. 395.

(5) Restitutionary Liability

7–060 *At the end of footnote 135, add:*

Because a claim for restitution of bribe moneys is not concerned with compensating a loss, the claimant's recoveries from third parties do not affect the relevant defendant's restitutionary liability: *Marino v FM Capital Partners Ltd* [2020] EWCA Civ 245; [2021] Q.B. 1, at [46]–[55].

(7) Account of Profits

7–070 *At the end of the paragraph, add footnote 152a:*

[152a] Because dishonest assistance requires dishonesty on the part of the assister; it also requires that the agent is a fiduciary, whereas it is now established that this is not necessary to establish liability for a bribe: see para.7–007 above.

CHAPTER 8

CONVERSION

A. INTRODUCTION

Replace footnote 6 with: **8–002**

M. Bridge (ed), *Benjamin's Sale of Goods*, 11th edn (London: Sweet & Maxwell, 2020). In cases concerning actual or purported agents, reference should also be made to P.G. Watts (ed), *Bowstead and Reynolds on Agency*, 22nd edn (London: Sweet & Maxwell, 2020), articles 83 to 89. Cases involving corporate agents or transfers of goods across jurisdictional boundaries will require reference to specialist works on such subjects.

B. THE ELEMENTS OF THE TORT

8–003 *At the end of the paragraph, add footnote 7a:*

[7a] This passage was cited with approval in *Tuke v Hood* [2020] EWHC 2843 (Comm), per Jacobs J at [184].

(1) The Current or Prior Existence of Corporeal Personal Property

(ii) The position in relation to intangible property and electronic data

8–007 *At the end of the paragraph, add:*

It is overwhelmingly likely that the same considerations apply to digital currencies, such as Bitcoin.[13a]

[13a] See for example the analysis in *AA v Persons Unknown* [2019] EWHC 3556 (Comm); [2020] 4 W.L.R. 35 per Bryan J.

(2) Possession or an immediate right to possess the goods superior to any enjoyed by the defendant

(i) Possession

8–012 *Replace footnote 20 with:*

See, in particular, F. Pollock, *Pollock and Wright on Possession in the Common Law* (Oxford: Clarendon Press, 1888) (still the leading textbook on the subject) and the useful summaries in A.P. Bell, *Modern Law of Personal Property in England and Ireland* (London: Butterworths, 1989), pp.33–61 and Bridge et al, *The Law of Personal Property*, 2nd Edition, (London: Sweet & Maxwell, 2019), paras 2–001—2–060.

8–014 *Replace footnote 22 with:*

See M.A. Jones, A.M. Dugdale and M. Simpson (eds), *Clerk & Lindsell on Torts*, 23rd edn (London: Sweet & Maxwell, 2020), paras 16–24, 16–54.

(iii) Possession, and rights to possess, are what is important, not ownership as such

8–019 *Replace footnote 29 with:*

See M.A. Jones, A.M. Dugdale and M. Simpson (eds), *Clerk & Lindsell on Torts*, 23rd edn (London: Sweet & Maxwell, 2020), para.16-62.

8–021 *Replace footnote 32 with:*

See M.A. Jones, A.M. Dugdale and M. Simpson (eds), *Clerk & Lindsell on Torts*, 23rd edn (London: Sweet & Maxwell, 2020), paras 16–150—16–151.

(3) Conduct which is (A) Deliberate; (B) Inconsistent with the Claimant's Rights and (C) so Extensive as to Exclude the Claimant from the Possession and use of the Goods in Question

(iii) So extensive as to exclude the claimant from the possession and use of the goods in question

Replace footnote 36 with: **8–029**

See M.A. Jones, A.M. Dugdale and M. Simpson (eds), *Clerk & Lindsell on Torts*, 23rd edn (London: Sweet & Maxwell, 2020), para.16–02.

Replace footnote 37 with: **8–031**

See M.A. Jones, A.M. Dugdale and M. Simpson (eds), *Clerk & Lindsell on Torts*, 23rd edn (London: Sweet & Maxwell, 2020), paras 16–07—16–34.

C. REMEDIES

Replace footnotes 43 and 44 with: **8–037**

[43] See M.A. Jones, A.M. Dugdale and M. Simpson (eds), *Clerk & Lindsell on Torts*, 23rd edn (London: Sweet & Maxwell, 2020), para.16-100.
[44] See M.A. Jones, A.M. Dugdale and M. Simpson (eds), Clerk & Lindsell on Torts, 23rd edn (London: Sweet & Maxwell, 2020), paras 16-110–16-115.

Chapter 9

ESTABLISHING A TRUST

B. SOME FUNDAMENTALS OF TRUST LAW

(3) Conventional Categorisation of Trusts by Method of Creation

9–008 *Replace footnote 2 with:*

[2] See L. Tucker, N. Le Poidevin and J. Brightwell, *Lewin on Trusts*, 20th edn (London: Sweet & Maxwell, 2020), para.8-002; J.McGhee and S. Elliott, *Snell's Equity*, 34th edn (London: Sweet & Maxwell, 2019), para.21-020.

At the end of footnote 3, add:

Thus, the position remains clear at first instance: see *Re CC Automotive Car Group Limited* [2019] EWHC 2771 (Ch), at [83] and following.

C. EXPRESS TRUSTS

(2) Overview of Requirements for the Creation of an Express Trust

9–010 *At the end of footnote 5, add:*

See the recent analysis in the Court of Appeal of the purchaser's interest under a specifically enforceable contract of sale in *Ezair v Conn* [2020] EWCA Civ 687; [2020] BCC 865, at [47] and following.

(3) Requirements 1: The Declaration of Trust–Certainty of Words/Intention, Necessary Formalities, Bona Fides and Sham Trusts, Illegality of Trust etc

9–013 *At the end of footnote 10, add:*

Likewise *Ong v Ping* [2017] EWHC Civ 2069; [2017] W.T.L.R. 1365, at [58] and *Pleshakov v Sky Stream Corp* [2021] UKPC 15, at [48].

At the end of footnote 13, add:

But contrast *Marley v Rawlings* [2015] A.C. 129, at [19], [23], *Armstrong v Armstrong* [2019] EWHC 2259 (Ch) and *Bowack v Saxton* [2020] EWHC 1049 (Ch).

At the end of footnote 14, add:

But evidence of subsequent conduct inconsistent with the existence of a trust was relied upon as an aid to construction of the relevant words in *Hilton v Cosnier* [2018] EWHC 2728 (Ch), at [24]. Of course, subsequent inconsistent conduct by the beneficiaries may also demonstrate that the relevant trust has been brought to an end with their consent under the so-called principle in *Sauders v Vautier* (an analysis which appears to underlie the alternative reasoning of Falk J in *Re Pekalp Properties Limited* [2019] EWHC 90 (Ch), at [111] and following).

At the end of footnote 16, add:

Another recent example is *Re Pekalp Properties Limited* [2019] EWHC 90 (Ch), per Falk J at [103]–[111], where the relevant document was construed as evidencing an intention (never carried into effect) to create a trust in the future, rather than creating a trust immediately.

At the end of the paragraph, add:

While the rule is traditionally expressed (and analysis traditionally focused) upon the intention of the alleged settlor, it is important to appreciate that the intentions of others may be relevant in certain circumstances: for example, a contractual counterparty in circumstances where the trust is made for consideration, or the intended trustee in circumstances where the trust is established by transfer of property.[17a]

[17a] Thus an intention to create an express trust may come to naught if the property is transferred to a recipient who takes it on a different basis: see *Goyal v Florence Care Ltd* [2020] EWHC 659 (Ch) where an intended trust restriction was never communicated to the solicitors in question who accordingly received funds on trust for their own clients in the usual way. Conversely, where the recipient intends to take as trustee (or acts as if he were doing so) a resulting trust or constructive trusteeship *de son tort* may arise even absent the requisite intention on the part of the settlor, as explored later in this chapter.

At the end of footnote 28, add: **9–014**

In *Cameron v Cameron* [2021] EWHC 229 (Ch), at [98]–[103] analogies were drawn between the requirement for signed writing in s.53(1)(c) and the qualifications which apply in relation to signature by mark or by another at the direction of the signatory in the context of the Law of Property (Miscellaneous Provisions) Act 1989 and in the case of wills; but *quaere*.

At the end of footnote 30, add: **9–015**

See also *Dalkilic v Pekin* [2021] EWHC 219 (Ch), at [304]–[308].

At the end of footnote 35, add: **9–016**

In *Knight v Knight* [2019] EWHC 915 (Ch); [2019] 2 P&CR DG14, at [89]–[90], HH Judge Matthews QC (sitting as a Judge of the High Court) adopted the express trust analysis with a resulting trust in the alternative, albeit without reference to the academic literature.

At the end of footnote 49, add: **9–020**

Obviously this does not arise where the trust is entirely unilateral and it is therefore the interest of the settlor alone which is decisive: *Painter v Hutchison* [2007] EWHC 738 (Ch), at [115] and *Re Munir (a bankrupt)* [2021] EWHC 278 (Ch), at [47].

At the end of footnote 50, add:

See also *Re Munir (a bankrupt)* [2021] EWHC 278 (Ch), at [48], adopting what was said in *Minwalla* on this topic.

Replace footnote 61 with: **9–025**

[61] See the helpful review in Ch.6 of L. Tucker, N. Le Poidevin and J. Brightwell, *Lewin on Trusts*, 20th edn (London: Sweet & Maxwell, 2020).

9–027 *At the end of the paragraph, add footnote 63a:*

63a See now the decisions in *Crown Prosecution Service v Aquila Advisory Limited* [2019] EWCA Civ 588; *Knight v Knight* [2019] EWHC 915 (Ch); [2019] 2 P.&C.R. DG14, at [98] and following; and *Ball v De Marzo* [2019] EWHC 1587 (Ch), at [36]–[53].

(4) Requirements 2: The Beneficial Property–Certainty of Subject Matter, the Need to Constitute the Trust, Trusts of Future Property etc

9–028 *At the end of the first sentence, add new footnote 63b:*

63b Note, however, that the boundaries of what constitutes "property" in English law remain potentially debatable: see *AA v Persons Unknown* [2019] EWHC 3556 (Comm); [2020] 4 W.L.R. 35 in relation to the status of crypto-currency.

At the end of the paragraph, add:

However, the surrounding factual context may in some cases make clear what is obscure on the face of the document.[68a]

68a See *Armstrong v Armstrong* [2019] EWHC 2259 (Ch) and *Bowack v Saxton* [2020] EWHC 1049 (Ch), at [31]–[32].

(5) Requirements 3: The Beneficial Interests–Certainty of Objects, the Need for Human or Charitable Objects, Perpetuities and Accumulations etc

9–033 *Replace footnote 80 with:*

80 See the references collected in L. Tucker, N. Le Poidevin and J. Brightwell, *Lewin on Trusts*, 20th edn (London: Sweet & Maxwell, 2020), para.5-051.

9–036 *Replace footnote 84 with:*

84 See, for instance, the treatment in Ch.6 of L. Tucker, N. Le Poidevin and J. Brightwell, *Lewin on Trusts*, 20th edn (London: Sweet & Maxwell, 2020).

D. RESULTING TRUSTS

(1) The Two Types of Resulting Trust

9–037 *At the end of the paragraph, add new footnote 84a:*

84a It has been held that these two types of resulting trusts are exhaustive: see *Re Bhusate* [2018] EWHC 2362 (Ch), per Chief Master Marsh at [64].

(2) Type 1: Unexplained Transfers and Purchases in the Name of Another

9–040 *After the words "gratuitous payment" in the first sentence, add new footnote 85a:*

85a In *Wood v Watkin* [2019] EWHC 1311 (Ch); [2019] BPIR 1265, it was accepted by ICC Judge Barber (in reliance on *Carlton v Goodman* [2002] EWCA Civ 545, at [22(v)]) that undertaking a liability under a mortgage used to fund the purchase price may qualify as a contribution to the purchase price so as to give rise to a resulting trust in some circumstances. Relatedly, a recent review of authorities bearing upon the significance of agreements to discharge mortgage payments may be found in *Tahir v Faizi* [2019] EWHC 1627 (QB).

Replace footnote 87 with:

[87] See J. McGhee and S. Elliott, *Snell's Equity*, 34th edn (London: Sweet & Maxwell, 2019), para.25–011, and *National Crime Agency v Gui Hui Dong* [2017] EWHC 3116 (Ch), at [38].

Replace footnote 88 with:

[88] See the references gathered in L. Tucker, N. Le Poidevin and J. Brightwell, *Lewin on Trusts*, 20th edn (London: Sweet & Maxwell, 2020), paras 10-025 and following.

At the end of footnote 89, add:

In *Wood v Watkin* [2019] EWHC 1311 (Ch); [2019] BPIR 1265, at [82] and following, ICC Judge Barber held that the presumption applied to adult children; and that was followed in *Farrell v Burden* [2019] EWHC 3671 (QC) per Freedman J.

At the end of footnote 90, add: **9–041**

But see *Wood v Watkin*, above, at [94] and following for an example of analysis to the opposite effect.

At the end of footnote 94, add:

See to similar effect *Cobussen Principal Investment Holdings Limited v Akbar* [2020] EWHC 2805 (QB).

At the end of the paragraph, add:

(6) Perhaps most straightforwardly, there continues to be a steady flow of cases in which the presumption of resulting trust is successfully invoked.[96a]

[96a] Among other cases cited in this section, see *Ali v Dinc* [2020] EWHC 3055 (Ch), at [267] and following.

At the end of footnote 100, add: **9–043**

In *Ali v Dinc* [2020] EWHC 3055 (Ch), in a passage which is probably *obiter* at [272]–[278], Sarah Worthington QC (sitting as a Deputy High Court Judge) preferred the analysis of the Chief Master in *Dong* to that of Mr Strauss QC in *Lohia*.

(3) Type 2: Transfers which Fail to Dispose of the Whole Beneficial Interest

Replace footnote 107 with: **9–045**

[107] For example, as a gift with further obligations grafted onto it so as to engage the so-called rule in *Lassence v Tierney* or rule in *Hancock v Watson*. See (for a convenient explanation of that rule) L. Tucker, N. Le Poidevin and J. Brightwell, *Lewin on Trusts*, 20th edn (London: Sweet & Maxwell, 2020), at para.9–022.

(4) A special Case of Type 2: "Quistclose" Trusts

9–047 *At the end of footnote 112, add:*

See also the further recent summary by the Court of Appeal in *First City Monument Bank Plc v Zumax Nigeria Limited* [2019] EWCA Civ 294; [2019] W.T.L.R. 511.

At the end of footnote 116, add:

The intended limitations must be certain, but will be deemed sufficiently certain so long as the court can say that a given application of the money does or does not fall within its terms: *Twinsectra*, above, at [15] and *Ali v Dinc* [2020] EWHC 3055 (Ch), at [238].

At the end of the paragraph, add:

Nevertheless, the Court of Appeal has endorsed *Bieber* and the correctness of the passage cited above in *First City v Zumax.*[119a]

[119a] Above, at [23] and [36]. That has since applied in *Ali v Dinc* [2020] EWHC 3055 (Ch), at [240]–[246], where Sarah Worthington QC (sitting as a Deputy High Court Judge) expressed the perhaps unorthodox view that it was the understanding of the transferee alone, rather than the transferor, which was important.

9–049 *At the end of footnote 120, add:*

But see the reliance on such evidence in *Ali v Dinc* [2020] EWHC 3055 (Ch), at [244].

At the end of the paragraph, add:

Although the authorities speak most often of the intentions and understanding of the transferor, they must of course be shared objectively by the transferee (the state of whose conscience ultimately justifies the existence of the trust).[121a]

[121a] See *Ali v Dinc* [2020] EWHC 3055 (Ch), at [245], although the statement that the transferor need not understand that there should be any proprietary consequence must be debatable in light of *Bieber.*

9–050 *At the end of the paragraph, add:*

Where the purpose remains theoretically possible but the transferor demands the return of the property, difficult questions may arise which have not yet been addressed in great detail in the authorities. It has been suggested that the default assumption is for the arrangement to be revocable at will unless otherwise provided, but also that risk of commercial uncertainty in some contexts may lead to a ready inference that it has been "otherwise provided"; and also held that the arrangement may be terminable under general law without regard to any agreed terms in circumstances where the arrangement was not proceeding according to plan, the transferee was in breach and the transferor needed to protect his proprietary interest.[123a] Potentially more difficult still is the question of when a beneficial interest may be acquired by a party whose receipt of the property is the ultimate purpose of the *Quistclose* trust.[123b]

[123a] See *Ali v Dinc* [2020] EWHC 3055 (Ch), at [249]–[253].
[123b] See *Deluxe Property Holdings Ltd v SCL Construction Ltd* [2020] EWHC 3354 (TCC), at [32] and following, and the authorities there cited.

D. CONSTRUCTIVE TRUSTS

(1) The Nature of Constructive Trusts

Replace footnote 129 with: 9–055

[129] See *Selangor United Rubber Estates Ltd v Cradock (No.3)* [1981] 1 W.L.R. 1555, at 1582, per Ungoed-Thomas J; *Paragon Finance v DB Thakerar* above, per Millett J at 409; *Central Bank of Nigeria v Williams* [2014] UKSC 10; [2014] AC 1189, per Lord Sumption JSC at [7]–[11] and per Lord Neuberger PSC at [57]–[67]. But see C. Mitchell, P. Mitchell and S. Watterson, *Goff & Jones: The Law of Unjust Enrichment*, 9th edn (London: Sweet & Maxwell, 2016), paras 38–19—38–23 for a robust defence of traditional terminology.

(2) Constructive Trusts Arising from Impugnable Transfers/ payments (without Prior Fiduciary Relationship)

At the end of footnote 136, add: 9–058

Where the rescinded contract had provided for the contracting party (A) to procure that property was transferred by a third party (B), it has been described as a novel question unsuitable for summary judgment whether the constructive trust arises in favour of A or B: *Vale SA v Steinmetz* [2020] EWHC 3501 (Comm), at [32] and following (undisturbed by the appeal on a separate point at [2021] EWCA Civ 1087).

At the end of footnote 145, add: 9–061

That distinction is now further supported by the judgment of Lewison LJ (with whom the rest of the Court of Appeal agreed) in *Nasrullah v Rashid* [2018] EWCA Civ 2685; [2020] Ch. 37, at [53], approving the analysis in *Snell's Equity*. See to like effect the judgment of Falk J in *Taylor v Khodabakhsh* [2021] EWHC 655 (Ch), at [89]–[92] (although doubting the applicability of any of the law concerning void or voidable transactions to the case of a court order impugned for fraud under the principles in *Takhar v Gracefield*).

At the end of footnote 147, add:

In *Global Currency Exchange Network Ltd v Osage 1 Ltd* [2019] EWHC 1375 (Comm) [2019] 1 WLR 5865, at [40]–[48], Andrew Henshaw QC (sitting as a Deputy High Court Judge) accepted that *Halley* was binding, but distinguished it on the facts where investors had received "even as a result of fraudulent misrepresentation, real shares in a real company".

Replace footnote 148 with: 9–062

[148] And hence an action in conversion will lie: see M.A. Jones, A.M Dugdale and M. Simpson (eds), *Clerk & Lindsell on Torts*, 23rd edn (London: Sweet & Maxwell, 2020), para.16–37.

At the end of footnote 149, add:

In *Scott v Bridge* [2020] EWHC 3116 (Ch), at [146] and [148]–[151] that reasoning was extended to the case of a gratuitous recipient of a mistaken transfer.

At the end of footnote 151, add:

See to similar effect the judgment of Lewison LJ (with whom the rest of the Court of Appeal agreed) in *Nasrullah v Rashid* [2018] EWCA Civ 2685; [2020] Ch, 37, at [53].

9–064 *At the end of footnote 161, add:*

For reference to academic criticism of the wider decision in *Westdeutsche* to limit the scope of proprietary remedies, see *Ali v Dinc* [2020] EWHC 3055 (Ch), at [220]–[222].

At the end of footnote 162, add:

Ali v Dinc [2020] EWHC 3055 (Ch), at [222]–[227]. But contrast the straightforward reliance on the main *ratio* of *Westdeutsche* in *Scott v Bridge* [2020] EWHC 3116 (Ch), at [141]–[147].

At the end of the paragraph, add new footnote 167a:

[167a] The relevant passage of *Ali v Dinc* (above) post-dated *Re D & D Wines* but appears to have been argued without reference to it.

(3) Constructive Trusts Arising from Fiduciary Relationships

9–071 *At the end of the paragraph, add:*

Indeed, it appears that the rule can extend to profits made by the fiduciary taking advantage of a corporate opportunity which is itself unlawful.[173a] It seems (although the authority on the point may still be in a state of development) that such a trust may also arise where the relevant payment or benefit is received into the hands of a company owned and controlled by the defaulting fiduciary.[173b]

[173a] *Crown Prosecution Service v Aquila Advisory Limited* [2019] EWCA Civ 588.
[173b] See *FM Capital Partners v Marino* [2018] EWHC 2905 (Comm), at [58]–[69]; and more generally Ch.11, at paras 11–117—11–121.

(4) Constructive Trusts Arising from a Prior Agreement or Understanding

9–077 *At the end of sub-paragraph (3), add:*

The trend of the authorities is clearly that all three do, but particularly in the case of "common intention constructive trusts" it is unclear to what extent all of the authorities and principles established in the domestic context remain applicable outside it.

At the end of the paragraph, add:

In addition, while these categories are generally treated as distinct, there is considerable uncertainty as to whether they truly are (as addressed further below in this section).[186a]

[186a] Indeed, some authorities proceed on the basis of an overarching principle which applies whenever property is received by a transaction by which the parties intend that it should be held for the benefit of others (even absent an express trust): see for example *Dalkilic v Pekin* [2021] EWHC 219 (Ch), at [295] and following; and *Potier v Treasury Solicitor* [2021] EWHC 1524 (Ch), at [40] and following.

9–079 *At the end of footnote 187, add:*

See *Iranian Offshore Engineering and Construction Company v Zavarei* [2020] EWHC 2497 (Comm), at [47] and following for the continued importance of financial contribution in some cases.

Replace paragraph 9–080 with:

The principles governing "common intention constructive trusts" of the sort described above have been developed overwhelmingly in cases relating to ownership of a family home. There are some eminent judicial statements providing support for the view that they reflect policy considerations which are only applicable in such cases and should accordingly be confined to them.[190] But the current trend of authority appears to be towards the view, recently endorsed by the Court of Appeal in *Kahrmann v Harrison-Morgan*, that common intention constructive trusts can arise in investment or commercial contexts, albeit not necessarily on the same principles which apply in the context of a co-habiting couple.[191] Precisely what the relevant principles may be in the commercial context is still uncertain.[191a] Conceptually, there is room for debate as to whether these are better regarded as extensions of the common intention constructive trust properly so called, or of the related categories of constructive trust addressed in the following sections, namely: the so-called "*Pallant v Morgan*" constructive trust considered in the following section (which the Court of Appeal has now held is to be considered as a species of common intention constructive trust, while casting doubt on the correctness of that analysis)[192]; and with the constructive trust to prevent the use of a statute as an instrument of fraud / enforce an undertaking to respect an unprotected interest in land.[192a] **9–080**

[190] See *CrossCo v Jolan* (above), per Etherton LJ at [85]–[87] (dissenting) and the citations gathered there. For a recent practical example see *Re Bhusate* [2018] EWHC 2362 (Ch), per Chief Master Marsh at [66].

[191] See *Geary v Rankine* [2012] EWCA Civ 555; *Agarwala v Agarwala* [2013] EWCA Civ 1763; *Bhushan v Chand* [2015] EWHC 1298 (Ch); *Sandhu v Sandhu* [2016] EWCA Civ 1050; *Matchmove Ltd v Dowding* [2016] EWCA Civ 1233 (a case of former friends); *Price v Saundry* [2019] EWHC 496 (Ch), at [20] (a case of business partners); *First National TrustCo (UK) Ltd v Page* [2019] EWHC 1187 (Ch), at [246] and following (upheld, without any appeal on the instant point, at [2020] EWCA Civ 107); *Kahrmann v Harrison-Morgan* [2019] EWCA Civ 2094, at [98]–[99]; and *Oberman v Collins* [2020] EWHC 3533 (Ch); [2021] W.T.L.R. 267, at [130]. In *Pickering v Hughes* [2021] EWHC 1672 (Ch) the point does not seem to have been raised.

[191a] See *Kahrmann* (above). In *First National Trust 4Co (UK) Ltd v Page*, above, at [246], Joanna Smith QC (sitting as a Deputy High Court Judge) accepted the earlier Court of Appeal decision in *De Bruyne v De Bruyne* [2010] EWCA Civ 519 as establishing that common intention constructive trusts would arise outside cases of co-habiting adults; and that in that wider context, there was no need to establish detrimental reliance, but rather a close focus on the circumstances in which the transferee came to acquire the property and upon the existence of unconscionable or inequitable conduct. But this is hard to square with the approach of the Court of Appeal in *Kahrmann* (above), and may be better regarded as an application of the different species of constructive trust considered at para.9–087 below.

[192] See *CrossCo* (again), per Arden LJ at [129], with whom MacFarlane LJ agreed. But that must now be read in the light of *Generator Developments Ltd v Lidl UK GmbH* (below).

[192a] See the reasoning of Fancourt J in *Archibald v Alexander* [2020] EWHC 1621 (Ch); [2020] 2 F.L.R. 1123.

At the end of footnote 196, add: **9–083**

Bulled v Petrie [2020] EWHC 2485 (Ch); *Brent London Borough Council v Johnson* [2020] EWHC 2526 (Ch).

Replace paragraph 9–087 with:

Constructive trust to prevent use of a statute as an instrument of fraud/ Undertaking to respect an unprotected interest in property. There is a third category of constructive trust which may arise to give effect to a prior agreement **9–087**

or understanding. It is founded on the principle that a person may not unconscionably rely upon the absolute character of a transfer of property to defeat a beneficial interest which, according to the true bargain between the parties, was to belong to another; in such circumstances the person who takes the transfer (usually the purchaser of land), although his title takes priority under the rules of conveyancing and land registration, may be found to hold that title on constructive trust in whole or part for the benefit of the party whose inadequately formalised or registered rights he agreed to respect. The bulk of the authorities[210] suggest that the principle is limited to cases where a transfer of land might allow the transferee to take free of another party's interests, and in which the transferee has undertaken a new obligation not otherwise existing to give effect to the relevant interests. But it is not clear that this is the case, in circumstances where the Court of Appeal has characterised the principle in broader terms on the basis that a constructive trust can arise to prevent a statute being used as an instrument of fraud (in the broader equitable sense of that word);[210] or more broadly still on the principle that a constructive trust may arise to prevent unconscionable or inequitable conduct in the form of a denial or refusal to carry out the agreement to hold the property for the benefit of the third party which was the only basis upon which the property was transferred.[210a] It is fair to say that the relationship between this category of constructive trust, the "common intention constructive trust" and the *Pallant v Morgan* equity remains less than clear.

[209] *Lyus v Prowsa Developments Ltd* [1982] 1 W.L.R. 1044; *Ashburn Anstalt v Arnold* [1989] Ch. 1; *Lloyd v Dugdale* [2001] EWCA Civ 1754; [2002] W.T.L.R. 863, at [50]–[52]; *Chaudhary v Yavuz* [2011] EWCA Civ 1314; [2013] Ch. 249; *Groveholt v Hughes* [2012] EWHC 3351 (Ch); [2013] 1 P. & CR 20.

[210] *Rochefoucauld v Boustead* [1897] 1 Ch. 196; *Bannister v Bannister* [1948] 2 All E.R. 133.

[210a] *De Bruyne v De Bruyne* [2010] EWCA Civ 519; [2010] 2 F.L.R. 519, applied in *Archibald v Alexander* [2020] EWHC 1621 (Ch); [2020] 2 F.L.R. 1123. See also *Deluxe Property Holdings Ltd v SCL Construction Ltd* [2020] EWHC 3354 (TCC), at [39]–[47], where a constructive trust was held to arise on this basis in respect of a VAT repayment received by a company from HMRC which was intended to be for the benefit of the customer who had borne the burden of paying the tax.

(5) Other Categories of Constructive Trust Less Directly Relevant in the Fraud Context

9–088 *At the end of sub-paragraph (1), add new footnote 209a:*

[209a] See *Ezair v Conn* [2020] EWCA Civ 687; [2020] BCC 865, at [47] and following.

At the end of the paragraph, add:

(6) Also, trusteeship "de son tort", which may arise when a recipient of property undertakes the role of a trustee, regardless of the intentions of the transferor.[210a]

[210a] See the prominent recent example in *High Commissioner for Pakistan v Prince Muffakham Jah* [2019] EWHC 2551 (Ch); [2020] Ch 421, at [249] and following, where an allegation of express trust failed due to lack of authority on the part of the settlor's officer who created the trust.

CHAPTER 10

BREACH OF TRUST

B. ESTABLISHING A BREACH OF TRUST

(1) Suitable Trust to Found Liability in Breach of Trust

At the end of the paragraph, add: **10–006**

On the other hand, a trustee of a *Quistclose* trust (for example) is likely to be in a similar position to an express trustee.[4a]

[4a] See *Patel v Barlows Solicitors* [2020] EWHC 2753 (Ch); [2021] 4 W.L.R. 6, at [248]; *Ali v Dinc* [2020] EWHC 3055 (Ch), at [247].

(2) Locus Standi to Sue for Breach of Trust

10–008 *Replace footnote 6 with:*

[6] See L. Tucker, N. Le Poidevin and J. Brightwell, *Lewin on Trusts*, 20th edn (London: Sweet & Maxwell, 2020), para.41–071 and following for a more detailed consideration of the position of those with various sorts of (more or less remote) interests under a trust.

At the end of the paragraph, add:

An alleged breach of trust by the trustee may also amount to an exceptional circumstance to justify the beneficiaries bringing claims against third parties which could otherwise only be brought by the trustees.[9a]

[9a] See *Roberts v Gill & Co* [2010] UKHL 22; [2011] 1 A.C. 240; *Hamblin v World First Ltd* [2020] EWHC 2383 (Comm).

(3) The Breach of Trust

10–010 *Replace footnote 12 with:*

[12] See L. Tucker, N. Le Poidevin and J. Brightwell, *Lewin on Trusts*, 20th edn (London: Sweet & Maxwell, 2020), paras 41-010 and following; and *Televantos* [2015] Conv 348, Turner [2015] CLJ 188.

Replace footnote 13 with:

[13] See, for example, C Mitchell, D.J. Hayton and P. Matthews, *Underhill & Hayton Law of Trusts and Trustees*, 19th edn (London: LNUK, 2016), paras 87.01-87.30.

10–013 *At the end of footnote 18, add:*

In other cases, the position may turn on close construction of the communications between the parties or the surrounding facts. Contrast *Levack v Philip Ross & Co* [2019] EWHC 762 (Comm); [2019] PNLR 20; *Goyal v Florence Care Limited* [2020] EWHC 659 (Ch); and *Patel v Barlows Solicitors* [2020] EWHC 2253 (Ch), at [225] and following.

(4) Fraudulent Breach of Trust

10–014 *At the end of footnote 20, add:*

That analysis (including the element at (ii)(c) importing the possibility of a finding of fraud based on objective unreasonableness) appears to have been accepted as correct by the Court of Appeal in *Sofer v Swiss Independent Trustees SA* [2020] EWCA Civ 699; [2020] W.T.L.R. 1075.

10–015 *At the end of the paragraph, add new footnote 21a:*

[21a] See the detailed treatment by the Court of Appeal of what is and is not required of such a pleading in this context in *Sofer v SwissIndependent Trustees SA* [2020] EWCA Civ 699; [2020] WTLR 1075.

C. DEFENCES

(2) Relief from Liability under Section 61 Trustee Act 1925

At the end of footnote 26, add: **10–019**

See also *Patel v Barlows Solicitors* [2020] EWHC 2753 (Ch); [2021] 4 W.L.R. 6, at [256] and following.

D. LIABILITY FOR OTHERS

(1) Liability for the Acts of Co-Trustees

Replace footnote 45 with: **10–028**

[45] *Townley v Sherborne* (1633) Bridg. 35; and see the learned consideration of the old authorities in L. Tucker, N. Le Poidevin and J. Brightwell, *Lewin on Trusts*, 20th edn (London: Sweet & Maxwell, 2020), paras 41-094 and following; and C. Mitchell, D.J. Hayton and P. Matthews, *Underhill & Hayton Law of Trusts and Trustees*, 19th edn (London: LNUK, 2016), paras 96.1-96.9, now more relevant again following the repeal of s.30(1) Trustee Act 1925. For the potential liability of a solicitors' firm for the breaches of trust by a partner within that firm acting qua trustee of a trust under s.10 of the Partnership Act see *Walker v Stones* [2001] Q.B. 902.

E. POSITION BETWEEN THOSE RESPONSIBLE

(1) Contribution

Replace footnote 52 with: **10–031**

[52] The impact of the receipt of a direct or indirect benefit by some trustees from the breach may be a subtle matter: see L. Tucker, N. Le Poidevin and J. Brightwell, *Lewin on Trusts*, 20th edn (London: Sweet & Maxwell, 2020), para.41-089; and C Mitchell, D.J. Hayton and P. Matthews, *Underhill & Hayton Law of Trusts and Trustees*, 19th edn (London: LNUK, 2016), para.97.13.

F. REMEDIES

At the end of the first sentence, add new footnote 55a: **10–034**

[55a] Note that where an account is necessitated by a breach of trust, the trustee may be required to pay the costs of that account regardless of whether sums are ultimately found payable: *Sheffield v Sheffield* [2018] EWHC 2360 (Ch); [2019] W.T.L.R. 295. Compare *Price v Saundry* [2019] EWCA Civ 2261; [2020] W.T.L.R. 233.

C. Defences

(2) Relief from Liability under Section 61 Trustee Act 1925

[illegible] 10-319

See also [illegible] v Sutton [2020] EWHC [illegible] (Ch); [2020] 4 W.L.R. [illegible] at [2[illegible]] and following.

D. Liability [illegible]

(1) Liability for the Acts of Co-Trustees

[illegible] 10-328

[illegible]

E. Position [illegible] Responsible

(1) Contribution

[illegible] 10-341

[illegible]

F. [illegible]

[illegible] 10-3[illegible]

[illegible]

CHAPTER 11

FIDUCIARY DUTIES

B. WHEN FIDUCIARY DUTIES ARE OWED

(2) What Gives Rise to Fiduciary Duties?

11–011 *At the end of footnote 17, and before the full-stop, add:*

; *Lehtimäki v Cooper* [2020] UKSC 33; [2018] 3 W.L.R. 1470, at [44]

11–012 *In the first sentence, after the first parenthesis, add new footnote 19a:*

[19a] *Al-Nehayan v Kent* [2018] EWHC 333 (Comm); [2018] 1 CLC 216, per Leggatt LJ at [163].

11–013 *At the end of footnote 21, add:*

A broker who owes a duty to give his client impartial information, advice or recommendations has also been said not to be (without more) a fiduciary, at least in the strict sense of owing the full panoply of obligations of loyalty; but this more limited duty is sufficient to engage the law of bribery and secret commissions: see *Wood v Commercial First Business Ltd* [2021] EWCA Civ 471; [2021] 3 W.L.R. 395; and see Ch.7.

11–014 *At the end of footnote 22, add:*

This was cited by Lady Arden in *Lehtimäki v Cooper* [2020] UKSC 33; [2018] 3 W.L.R. 1470, at [48], with the qualification that the concept of "reasonable expectation" may not be appropriate in every case.

11–016 *At the end of footnote 25, add:*

This was adopted by HHJ Hodge QC as the "key test" in *Al-Dowaisan v Al-Salam* [2019] EWHC 301 (Ch), at [108].

At the end of the paragraph, add: **11–017**

The enquiry is objective, involving the normative question of whether the nature of the relationship is such that one party is entitled to repose trust and confidence in the other, and specifically trust and confidence in them to put aside their own interests and act solely in the interests of the principal.[26a]

[26a] *Al-Nehayan v Kent* [2018] EWHC 333 (Comm); [2018] 1 CLC 216, per Leggatt LJ at [163]–[165].

(3) Fiduciary Duties in the Commercial and Contractual Context

At the end of footnote 27, add: **11–020**

The final sentence of this passage was cited with approval by Lady Arden in *Lehtimäki v Cooper* [2020] UKSC 33; [2018] 3 W.L.R. 1470, at [51].

At the end of footnote 31, add: **11–022**

But for an example of a case where fiduciary duties were held not to be inconsistent with the existence of a contract that stipulated only for a duty of care, see *Courtwood Holdings SA v Woodley Properties Ltd* [2018] EWHC 2163 (Ch), per Nugee J at [135]–[137].

At the end of the cited passage, add new footnote 48a: **11–031**

[48a:] See also *Medsted Associates Ltd v Canaccord Genuity Wealth (International) Ltd* [2019] EWCA Civ 83; [2019] 1 W.L.R. 4481, per Longmore LJ at [45]: "It is the scope of the agent's obligation that is important, not the fact that he may correctly be called a fiduciary."

(4) Fiduciary Duties Arising Outside the Settled Categories of Relationship

(i) Directors to Shareholders/Other Third Parties

At the end of footnote 56, add: **11–034**

For an English case where a fiduciary duty was held to be owed to shareholders on a similar basis, see *Platt v Platt* [1999] B.C.L.C. 745—apparently the only such case.

At the end of footnote 58, add:

Likewise, the mere fact that the director is purchasing shares from the shareholder does not suffice to give rise to fiduciary duties (absent any other circumstances amounting to a special relationship): *Vald. Nielsen Holding A/S v Baldorino* [2019] EWHC 1926 (Comm), at [745] and (for the analysis of the salient facts of the case) [747]–[758].

(ii) Shareholders to each other

In footnote 64, replace the text after the semi-colon with: **11–039**

but contrast the position of members of a charitable company, who were held in *Lehtimäki v Cooper* [2020] UKSC 33; [2018] 3 W.L.R. 1470 to owe a fiduciary duty of single-minded loyalty in relation to the passing of a special resolution sanctioning a disposition of the company's assets. Note, however, that this duty was owed to the purposes/objects of the charity, rather than to the company or other members; and that it would not necessarily arise in all circumstances in which the member might be called on to vote.

(iii) Other relationships involving companies (de facto directors, shadow directors and third party advisers)

11–040 *At the end of footnote 70, add:*

In *Instant Access Properties Ltd (in liquidation) v Rosser* [2018] EWHC 756 (Ch), Morgan J suggested (at [259]) that the correct approach is not to ask, separately, whether a person is a shadow director and then what duties he owed as such, but rather to ask the composite question of whether, looking at all the facts in the round, the person conducted himself in such a way as to subject himself to fiduciary and other director's duties, and if so in what respects.

At the end of the paragraph, add:

It has been held that the significance of the words "to the extent that" is that there must be some relationship or causal connection between the instruction which founds the shadow directorship and the act or event in respect of which a fiduciary duty is said to be owed—unless it can be said that the shadow director's instructions are pervasive and extend over the full range of directors' decision making.[70a]

[70a] *Standish v The Royal Bank of Scotland Plc* [2019] EWHC 3116 (Ch).

(iv) Joint venturers

11–047 *At the end of footnote 84, add:*

; and *Al-Nehayan v Kent* [2018] EWHC 333; [2018] 1 CLC 216, at [153]–[166], where a close personal relationship of trust and confidence was insufficient to give rise to fiduciary obligations in what was essentially a commercial venture, in which the supposed fiduciary was not acting in any managerial capacity.

(v) LLPs (limited liability partnerships)

11–049 *At end of the paragraph, add:*

Members also owe the LLP (subject to agreement to different effect) obligations under regulations 7(9) and 7(10) of the Limited Liability Partnership Regulations 2001, to account for profits from any competing business, and any benefits from transactions concerning the LLP or from use of its property, name or business connection. These have been said to be "closely analogous" to equitable duties.[87a]

[87a] *Recovery Partners GB Ltd v Rukhadze* [2018] EWHC 2918 (Comm), per Cockerill J at [94].

11–050 *At the end of footnote 88, add:*

; *McTear v Eade* [2019] EWHC 1673 (Ch), at [139]–[140].

(vii) Brokers/introducing agents and their clients

Replace paragraphs 11–055—11–056 with and add new paragraph 11–056A:

11–055 It may seem that what distinguished *Hurstanger* and *McWilliam* on the one hand from cases such as *Pickup* on the other is therefore the level of sophistication of the borrower client. But some doubt is cast on that by the decision in *Medsted Associates Ltd v Canaccord Genuity Wealth (International) Ltd*,[99] where it was held that a broker who introduced wealthy and experienced investor clients (interested in trading contracts for difference) to a financial services institution, in return for a share of the commission charged by the institution to the clients, *did* owe obligations which could legitimately be categorised as "fiduciary" (because the broker impliedly represented that the terms offered by the institution were competitive and to that extent the clients reposed trust and confidence in it); but it was further held that the scope of those obligations was limited and did not extend to requiring disclosure of the amount of commissions that the broker received from the institution, because the clients, being financially sophisticated, must have assumed that the broker was receiving some payment.[100]

[99] [2017] EWHC 1815 (Comm); and on appeal at [2019] EWCA Civ 83; [2019] 1 W.L.R. 4481, at [32].
[100] [2019] EWCA Civ 83; [2019] 1 W.L.R.. 4481, per Longmore LJ at [34]–[47].

The cases in this area received a careful review by the Court of Appeal in *Wood v Commercial First Business Ltd.*[100a] It was there held, consistently with *Hurstanger*, *McWilliam* and *Medsted*, that a broker which was bound to make a disinterested selection of a mortgage product to put to its client "owed duties which engaged the law applicable to bribes and secret commissions" and that "to the extent that it is necessary" these could be characterised as "fiduciary",[100b] *but* that it was not necessary to go that far for relief with respect to the commissions (rescission) to be available. In so doing the Court of Appeal shifted the focus of enquiry towards the content of the duty owed (was it to give impartial information, advice or recommendations?) and away from its characterisation as "fiduciary" or not. The Court further held that *Pickup* was wrongly decided, in that in that case too there was meant to be an exercise of judgment on the part of the broker as to what best fitted the borrower's requirements, which required an "impartial and disinterested view" and was sufficient to impose a fiduciary duty on the broker "in the limited sense in which that term is used in this context".[100c] **11–056**

[100a] [2021] EWCA Civ 471; [2021] 3 W.L.R. 395.
[100b] *Wood v Commercial First Business Ltd*, above, at [110].
[100c] *Wood v Commercial First Business Ltd*, above at [125]–[126].

A broker whose role is purely "ministerial" will likely not owe fiduciary duties. Thus, where a broker merely effected an introduction and conveyed communications between two principals, he was held not to owe fiduciary obligations that precluded the taking of undisclosed remuneration;[101a] and likewise a property agent, who had introduced a deal to a potential purchaser, and then performed a ministerial role in facilitating the progress of the deal and carrying out certain specific instructions for the purchaser, was held not to owe fiduciary obligations such as to engage the law of bribery (in respect of a payment by the seller).[101b] Conversely, where an introducing agent negotiated the terms of the sale of a hotel on behalf of the purchasing joint venture, and advised the venture in connection therewith, there was said to be "no doubt" that it owed fiduciary duties, even though the purchase agreement was concluded between vendor and purchaser directly.[101c] **11–056A**

[101a] *CH Offshore Ltd v Internaves Consorcio Naviero SA* [2020] EWHC 1710 (Comm) (although the intermediary was said to owe an obligation to pass on communications honestly).
[101b] *Conway v Eze* [2018] EWHC 29 (Ch), upheld on appeal at [2019] EWCA Civ 88.
[101c] *FHR European Ventures LLP v Mankarious* [2011] EWHC 2308 (Ch); [2012] 2 B.C.L.C. 39, at [99] (the first instance decision, which was not doubted on this point on appeal).

C. SOME OTHER GENERAL POINTS ON FIDUCIARY DUTIES

(2) Dishonest Breaches of Fiduciary Duty

11–062 *At the end of footnote 110, add:*

See also *First Subsea v Balltec* [2017] EWCA Civ 186; [2018] Ch 25, per Patten LJ at [64]: "For a breach of trust to be fraudulent it is not enough to show that it was deliberate. There must be an absence of honesty or good faith. This can include being reckless as to the consequences of the actions complained of."

(3) The Duration of Fiduciary Duties

11–067 *At the end of footnote 116, add:*

See also s.170(2) of the Companies Act 2006 and para.11–136 below.

11–069 *At the end of footnote 118, add:*

In *Recovery Partners GB Ltd v Rukhadze* [2018] EWHC 2918 (Comm), at [91], Cockerill J noted three points of importance about *In Plus Group Ltd*: (a) it was an exceptional case; (b) what was key was the absence at the relevant time of any dual role on the part of the defendant; and (c) this was because there was a full exclusion of the defendant from decision making and participation as director.

Add new paragraph 11–069A after para.11–069:

11–069A When a company is restored to the register, having been dissolved or struck off, the deeming provision in s.1032(1) of the Companies Act 2006 (that "the company is deemed to have continued in existence") does not mean that directors who ceased to be such upon dissolution or striking off were deemed to have continued in office so as to owe fiduciary duties throughout.[118a]

[118a] *Davies v Ford* [2020] EWHC 686 (Ch), at [371]–[395].

D. THE CORE DUTIES

(2) The "Core" Proscriptive Duties: Introduction

11–074 *After the second sentence, add:*

As it was put by Lady Arden in *Lehtimäki v Cooper*, "'the distinguishing obligation' of a fiduciary is that he must act only for the benefit of another in matters covered by his fiduciary duty. That means that he cannot at the same time act for himself."[121a]

[121a] [2020] UKSC 33; [2018] 3 W.L.R. 1470, at [45].

(3) The Obligation to Avoid a Conflict Between Duty and Interest

11–087 *Replace footnote 144 with:*

[144] See J. McGhee, S. Elliott, *Snell's Equity*, 34th edn (London: Sweet & Maxwell, 2020), para.7-022 and the cases cited there.

(5) The Obligation Not to Profit from the Fiduciary Position

At the end of footnote 166, add: **11–095**

Keystone Healthcare Ltd v Parr [2019] EWCA Civ 1246; [2019] 4 W.L.R. 99, at [15].

(6) The Core Duties Applied: The Diversion of Commercial Opportunities

Insert "(b)" after "and" in line 11. **11–111**

After the comma in the first sentence, add footnote 200a: **11–113**

[200a] *Foster Bryant Surveying Ltd v Bryant* [2007] Bus L.R. 1565, per Rix LJ at [76]–[77].

At the end of sub-paragraph (1), add footnote 200b:

[200b] For consideration of what it means to say that an opportunity is being "actively pursued" (or is "maturing") see *Recovery Partners GB Ltd v Rukhadze* [2018] EWHC 2918 (Comm), at [54]–[68].

At the end of footnote 209, add: **11–115**

The latter proposition was confirmed in *Burnell v Trans-Tag Ltd* [2021] EWHC 1457 (Ch), at [409]–[413].

At the end of footnote 211, add:

See also *Recovery Partners GB Ltd v Rukhadze* [2018] EWHC 2918 (Comm), per Cockerill J at [73]: "The underlying basis of the liability of a fiduciary who exploits after his resignation a maturing business opportunity of the company is that the opportunity is to be treated as if it were property of the company in relation to which the fiduciary owed fiduciary duties."

After the mark for footnote 211, insert:

Alternatively (and perhaps more coherently), it could be said that steps taken prior to the resignation to plan the future exploitation of the opportunity themselves amounted to breaches of the fiduciary duty of good faith, which occurred while the duty was owed but only manifested themselves after resignation.[211a]

[211a] See the explanation of *CMS Dolphin* (above) by Rix LJ in *Foster Bryant Surveying Ltd v Bryant* [2007] EWCA Civ 200, at [69]. Laying the groundwork for diverting an opportunity in the future can of course amount to a present breach of the fiduciary duty of good faith: *Kingsley IT Consulting v McIntosh* [2006] EWHC 1288 (Ch), at [53]. The touchstone of liability is whether in taking the relevant steps the director is acting in good faith in the best interests of the company: see *Shepherd Investments Ltd v Walters* [2006] EWHC 836 (Ch), at [108], and *Recovery Partners GB Ltd v Rukhadze* [2018] EWHC 2918 (Comm), at [83].

In the final sentence, replace "the following section" with "sub-section (8)".

(7) Profit Made by/Opportunity Diverted to a Company or Partnership

At the end of the paragraph, add: **11–117**

Similarly, the fiduciary may have arranged for the profit, which he could have taken personally, to be received by a company.[212a]

[212a] As in *FM Capital Partners v Marino* [2018] EWHC 2905 (Comm), at [58]–[69].

11–121 *At the end of the paragraph, add:*

Finally, since profit made by a fiduciary in breach of his duty is impressed with a constructive trust, a company into whose hands the profit has been diverted would be exposed to a proprietary claim, subject to the usual defences to such claims.[225a]

[225a] See *FM Capital Partners v Marino* [2018] EWHC 2905 (Comm), at [67]; and see generally Ch.23.

(8) The No Conflict and No Profit Duties as they Appear in the Companies Act 2006

(i) Self-dealing

11–127 *At the end of the second sentence, insert new footnote 226a:*

[226a] The carve-out in s.175(3) is not limited to transactions or arrangements directly between the director and the company, but is to be read as having the same scope as the disclosure obligation in s.177(1): *Somerville v 1051 GWR Ltd* [2019] CSOH 61, at [22].

(iv) Duration of the duties

11–136 *At the end of the paragraph, insert footnote 230a:*

[230a] See *Burnell v Trans-Tag Ltd* [2021] EWHC 1457 (Ch), at [409]–[413].

(9) Defences: Fully Informed Consent of the Principal

11–139 *In footnote 235, replace the reference to Medsted at first instance with:*

but contrast *Medsted Associates Ltd v Canaccord Genuity Wealth (International) Ltd* [2019] EWCA Civ 83; [2019] 1 W.L.R. 4481, where it was held (reversing the first instance Judge) that sophisticated investors who must have assumed that some commission was being paid to a broker did not need to be told the amount of the commission.

Add new paragraph 11–142A after para.11–142:

11–142A Company law also allows for the ratification of acts of a director that would otherwise be a breach of fiduciary duty through the approval of the relevant acts by the shareholders, either by formal resolution or informally. In the first case (formal resolution), this is now governed by s.239 of the Companies Act 2006. The second (informal approval), is under the common law "*Duomatic*" principle.[242a] The latter cannot avail the director unless the approval is unanimous and with knowledge of the relevant facts; nor can it avail him where: (a) the company is insolvent or approaching it, such that the duty to consider the interests of creditors is engaged;[242b] or (b) the acts in question are *ultra vires*, unlawful or involve dishonesty.[242c]

[242a] Named after *Re Duomatic Ltd* [1969] 2 Ch 365. This is preserved by s.239(6) of the Companies Act 2006.

[242b] *BTI 2014 LLC v Sequana S.A.* [2019] EWCA 112, at [143] and [220]. See paras 11-160-11-165 below.

[242c] Thus an unlawful return of capital could not be approved in this way: *Satyam Enterprises Ltd v Burton* [2021] EWCA Civ 287. For dishonesty, see *Auden McKenzie (Pharma Division) Ltd v Patel*

[2019] EWHC 1257 (Comm), per Robin Knowles J at [16]; *Tonstate Group Ltd v Wojakovski* [2019] EWHC 3363 (Ch), per Zacaroli J at [14]–[16]; *Ciban Management Corpn v Citco (BVI) Ltd* [2020] UKPC 21; [2021] A.C. 122, at [43].

E. OTHER DUTIES AND CONSTRAINTS ASSOCIATED WITH FIDUCIARIES

(4) The Director's Best Interests Duty in the Context of Potential Insolvency

Replace paragraphs 11–162 and 11–163 with:

In *BTI 2014 LLC v Sequana S.A.* the Court of Appeal (David Richards LJ) examined these and numerous other authorities on the question of whether, and if so at what point, the creditors' interests duty is engaged before actual insolvency, and came to the following conclusions (which, unlike previous English *dicta* on the point, formed part of the *ratio* of the case):[277] **11–162**

(1) That the duty to consider the interests of creditors may be triggered before (as well as at) the onset of actual, established insolvency; and
(2) That this would be so where the directors know or should know that the company is or is likely to become insolvent, "likely" in this context meaning "probable" (and thus a "real risk" of insolvency was insufficient).

Where the company is in a state of insolvency (or probable insolvency) such as to engage the creditors' interests duty, then it is not possible for the shareholders to ratify acts on the part of the directors taken in disregard of those interests.[278] **11–163**

[277] [2019] EWCA 112; [2019] 1 B.C.L.C. 347, at [213]–[221].
[278] *West Mercia Safetywear Ltd (In Liquidation) v Dodd* [1988] B.C.L.C. 250. The case only goes as far as considering actual insolvency; but the point it establishes is that the condition which engages the creditors' interest duty is coextensive with that which bars ratification—one is a necessary corollary of the other. See *BTI 2014 LLC v Sequana S.A.* [2019] EWCA 112; [2019] 1 B.C.L.C. 347, at [143] and [220].

At the end of footnote 283, add: **11–164**

This point was left undecided by the Court of Appeal in *BTI 2014 LLC v Sequana S.A.* [2019] EWCA 112; [2019] 1 B.C.L.C. 347, at [222], save for the observation that if the directors knew or ought to know that the company was presently and actually insolvent, it was hard to see that the creditors' interests could be anything but paramount.

(5) A Fiduciary Duty of Disclosure?

In the first sentence, after "other matters" and before the parenthesis, insert: **11–169**

which he (if acting in good faith) would consider it to be in the company's interests to know[287a]

In the first sentence, replace the semi-colon (in the penultimate line) and the text following it with:

. The duty of disclosure has been said (obiter), on the same basis, to extend to breaches by the director which are themselves "innocent",[289a] a proposition which has the counterintuitive consequence that a non-fiduciary breach of duty by a director could in in some circumstances effectively be converted to a fiduciary breach (with the remedial and other consequences that follow) by dint of the director consciously not disclosing it.[289b] Further, and again because the touchstone is what is considered to be in the best interests of the company, the duty can, in an appropriate case, require that the disclosure be made not to the board, but to the shareholders.[290]

[287a] *GHLM Trading Ltd v Maroo* [2012] 2 B.C.L.C. 369, at [195].

[289a] *Keymed (Medical & Industrial Equipment) Ltd v Hillman* [2019] EWHC 485 (Ch), per Marcus Smith J at [116].

[289b] The failure to disclose something that one considered to be in the best interests of the company to disclose would also amount to deliberate concealment for the purposes of deferring the limitation period under s.32(1)(b) of the Limitation Act 1980: see *IT Human Resources plc v Land* [2014] EWHC 3812 (Ch), per Morgan J at [136].

[290] *GHLM Trading Ltd v Maroo* [2012] 2 B.C.L.C. 369, at [196]–[200].

Add new paragraph 11–169A after para.11–169:

11–169A The duty to disclose wrongdoing identified in *Item Software* has been held to apply to fiduciaries who are not directors;[290a] but it is suggested that, on the reasoning of *Item Software*, that should only be true of fiduciaries who, by analogy with directors, owe the good faith duty in the sense considered above.

[290a] *Hanco ATM Systems Ltd v Cashbox ATM Systems Ltd* [2007] EWHC 1599 (Ch), per Peter Smith J at [65], cited with apparent approval by Vos J in *Bank of Ireland v Jaffery* [2012] EWHC 1377 (Ch), at [301].

11–170 *After the citation in the first sentence of footnote 292, insert:*

(finding that the analogy applies at least where the director has received company property).

(6) Other Equitable Limitations upon the Exercise of Powers

11–174 *At the end of footnote 296, add:*

But the exercise of a statutory power which creates property rights recognised at law will be voidable rather than void, if in breach of these constraints which operate in equity: *ibid*; see also *Stobart Group Ltd v Tinkler* [2019] EWHC 258 (Comm) [453]–[488] (exercise of the board's power to allot shares in a company for an improper purpose voidable rather than void).

11–175 *Replace footnote 299 with the following:*

[299] Such as a Mental Health Act receiver (*Pitt v Holt* [2013] UKSC 26; [2013] 2 A.C. 108, at [57], [97]), a director (*Hunter v Senate Support Services Ltd* [2005] 1 B.C.L.C. 175, at [165]–[180]) and an administrator (*Brewer v Iqbal* [2019] EWHC 182 (Ch), at [46]–[51]).

(7) A Director's Trustee-Like Duty not to Misapply Company Property?

11–183 *Add the following citations to footnote 314:*

Selangor United Rubber Estates Ltd v Cradock (No.3) [1968] 1 W.L.R. 1555, per Ungoed-Thomas J at 1575C-D; *Burnden Holdings (UK) Ltd v Fielding* [2018] UKSC 14; [2018] A.C. 857, at [11]; *Auden McKenzie (Pharma Division) Ltd v Patel* [2019] EWCA Civ 2291; [2020] B.C.C. 316, at [57].

Replace the final sentence with: **11–188**

In the particular context of a director's personal liability for the payment of an unlawful dividend, there are two conflicting lines of old authority on the question. More recent obiter observations in the Court of Appeal and Supreme Court are to the effect that the strict view is to be preferred;[321] but in *Burnden Holdings (UK) Ltd v Fielding*, Zacaroli J disagreed, concluding (after a thorough review of the authorities) that the position can be summarised as follows:

> "First, directors, although not trustees, were to be treated as if they were trustees in relation to the company's funds. Second, if they knew the facts which constituted an unlawful dividend, then they would be liable as if for breach of trust irrespective of whether they knew that the dividend was unlawful. Third, however, if they were unaware of the facts which rendered the dividend unlawful then provided they had taken reasonable care to secure the preparation of accounts so as to establish the availability of sufficient profits to render the dividend lawful, they would not be personally liable if it turned out that there were in fact insufficient profits for that purpose. Fourth, they were entitled to rely in this respect upon the opinion of others, in particular auditors, as to the accuracy of statements appearing in the company's accounts."[321a]

[321] *Revenue and Customs Commissioners v Holland, In Re Paycheck Services 3 Ltd* [2010] 1 W.L.R. 2793, per Lord Hope at [45]–[47] (Supreme Court); and ([2010] Bus L.R. 259), per Rimer LJ at [81]–[84] (Court of Appeal).

[321a] [2019] EWHC 1566 (Ch), at [139] (stating the law as at the end of the 19th Century) and [157]–[159] (concluding that the law remained materially the same now).

At the end of footnote 323, add: **11–189**

; *Byers v Chen* [2021] UKPC 4, at [91]–[93] (putting it in terms of there being a duty on the director to take reasonable steps to intervene).

CHAPTER 12

KNOWING RECEIPT

A. INTRODUCTION

(1) The Nature of the Claim and its Elements

At the end of the paragraph, add new footnote 2a: **12–003**

[2a] See, for recent applications of this three-step formulation, *Brent London Borough Council v Alan Davies* [2018] EWHC 2214, per Zacaroli J at [557]; *Iranian Offshore Engineering and Construction Co v Dean Investment Holdings SA* [2019] EWHC 472 (Comm), per Butcher J at [175]; *Tuke v Hood* [2020] EWHC 2843 (Comm), per Jacobs J at [177]; and *Dhir v Flutter Entertainment Plc* [2021] EWHC 1510 (QB), per Griffiths J at [205]–[208]. In a number of cases, the Courts have adopted a six-step approach, based on the analysis in L. Tucker, N. Le Poidevin and J. Brightwell, *Lewin on Trusts*, 20th edn (London: Sweet and Maxwell, 2020) at para.42–023 and following: see, for example, *First National Trustco (UK) Ltd v Page* [2019] EWHC 1187 (Ch), per Joanna Smith QC at [280] and following.

12–007 *In footnote 7, replace the references starting after the semi-colon in the third line, in the fourth line and in the first half of the fifth line with:*

J. McGhee, *Snell's Equity*, 34th edn (London: Sweet & Maxwell, 2020), para.30–071; L. Tucker, N. Le Poidevin and J. Brightwell, *Lewin on Trusts*, 20th edn (London: Sweet & Maxwell, 2020) para.42–032.

In footnote 8, replace the reference starting after the semi-colon towards the end of the second line with:

McGhee, *Snell's Equity* (2020), paras 30–073 and 30–074.

B. RECEIPT OF THE CLAIMANT'S ASSETS

(1) The Claimant's Assets or their Traceable Proceeds

12–013 *In footnote 16, replace the second sentence with:*

Note, however, Tucker, Le Poidevin and Brightwell, *Lewin on Trusts* (2020), para.42–041.

12–015 *Replace the second sentence with:*

They do not include contractual rights under executory contracts,[20] a mere "corporate opportunity"[20a] or (probably) most forms of information.[21]

[20a] *Davies v Ford* [2021] EWHC 2550 (Ch), per David Holland QC at [246]: "A mere 'corporate opportunity', that is the uncontracted prospect of business, cannot constitute the property of a company for the purposes of knowing receipt." The Scottish case of *Commonwealth Oil and Gas Co Ltd v Baxter* [2009] CSIH 75 at [94]–[95] was cited with approval as representing the law of England and Wales.

At the end of footnote 22, add:

In *Tuke v Hood* [2020] EWHC 2843 (Comm), it was argued (based on [383] of the judgment in *Madoff* and *Lewin on Trusts*, 20th edn, para.42–054) that the principle applied only where there was a contract for full value without notice by a bona fide purchaser. In that case, Wright had sold cars to JD Classics Limited ("JDC"), from whom Hood had subsequently acquired them. Wright alleged that neither JDC nor Hood was a bona fide purchaser for value without notice of his claims to the cars. Jacob J held that the principle was applicable because, even though it was alleged in the proceedings that the contracts in question had been procured by fraud, no claim had been made to set those contracts aside: see [181]. In those circumstances, the judge did not consider "that there is the starting point for a claim for knowing receipt. Since there is no starting point, the issue [of] whether Mr Hood, as onward recipient from JDC, could successfully argue that he was a bona fide purchaser from JDC for value without notice—does not arise." An appeal in this case is outstanding.

Add new paragraph 12–015A after para.12–015:

12–015A Similarly, there can be no liability for knowing receipt where, at the moment of receipt, the beneficiary's equitable interest in the property received is destroyed or overridden under the law governing the transfer of the underlying asset.[22a] The issue does not arise under the general property law of England and Wales since a recipient of trust property with sufficient knowledge of the breach cannot be a bona fide purchaser for value of the legal estate without notice. However, where foreign law is applicable, the recipient may obtain good title despite knowledge of the breach of trust. In addition, it has been suggested that the issue may arise in the context of statutory schemes for registration of title, including the Land Registration Act 2002, under which the proprietor's title is unaffected by impropriety in the transfer or any unregistered interest.[22b] Whilst there can be no claim for knowing receipt where the equitable interest is destroyed, it is evident that this does not preclude a claim for dishonest assistance which is fault-based rather than receipt-based.[22c]

[22a] *Byers v Samba Financial Group* [2021] EWHC 60 (Ch): the trustee of a Cayman Islands trust of which a Cayman Islands-registered company, SICL, was a beneficiary transferred shares in securities in breach of trust to a bank. Under Saudi Arabian law, the effect of the bank's registration as owner of the shares was to end SICL's proprietary interest in the shares. As the claimant did not have any continuing proprietary interest in the shares which were transferred, no claim in knowing receipt was possible. Had the claimants alleged and proved dishonesty on the transferee's part, it would not have been necessary to establish a continuing proprietary interest in the securities at the moment of receipt by the bank; but no dishonesty was alleged. An appeal in this case is outstanding.
[22b] *Byers*, above, per Fancourt J at [106] (*obiter*): "But, absent dishonesty or a pre-existing equity, a registered transferee of land, whose title has priority under the 2002 Act over the equitable interest of the beneficiary, is not liable in knowing receipt, even if he has knowledge that the transfer was made in breach of trust."
[22c] See para.13–005 below.

Replace footnote 24 with: **12–016**

See, e.g., L. Tucker, N. Le Poidevin and J. Brightwell, *Lewin on Trusts* (2020), para.42–036, cited in *Crypton Digital Assets Ltd v Blockchain Luxembourg SA* [2021] EWHC 1172, at [51].

(2) "Receipt"

In footnote 34, replace the first sentence with: **12–018**

See McGhee, *Snell's Equity* (2020), paras 30–069 and 30–075—30–076.

In footnote 38, replace the second sentence with: **12–021**

See also McGhee, *Snell's Equity* (2020), para.30–069.

C. ARISING FROM A BREACH OF FIDUCIARY DUTY OWED TO THE CLAIMANT

(1) The Requirement

At the end of sub-paragraph (b), add new footnote 50a: **12–027**

The point was reiterated by the decision of Nugee J in *Courtwood Holdings SA v Woodley Properties Ltd* [2018] EWHC 2163 (Ch). In that case, the judge referred back to the judgment of Morritt LJ in *Brown v Bennett* [1999] 1 B.C.L.C. 649, who invoked that of Hoffmann LJ in *El Ajou v Dollar Land Holdings plc* [1994] BCC 143, to the effect that "the plaintiff must show, first, a disposal of his assets in breach of fiduciary duty" (at 154). Morritt LJ went on to say that a successful claimant must then show that the receipt is "the direct consequence of the alleged breach of trust or fiduciary duty of which the recipient is said to have notice" (at 655). Nugee J considered what Morritt LJ meant by the term "the direct consequence". He held, at [188], that he was in "no real doubt" that what was meant by the receipt being the "direct consequence" of the breach of trust or fiduciary duty was that "the disposition itself is in breach of trust or breach of fiduciary duty". He repeated the point again at [190]: "It is not enough that the disposition follows, and is caused by, other breaches of trust or fiduciary duty". See also [201], where the judge explained that the reason for the requirement that the disposition itself be in breach of trust or fiduciary duty is that that is the basis on which the beneficial interest in the property disposed of does not pass to the recipient.

12–030 *At the end of footnote 53, add:*

See also the decision of Nugee J in *Courtwood Holdings SA v Woodley Properties Ltd* [2018] EWHC 2163 (Ch), at [13] and [177] and following.

12–035 *At the end of the first sentence, add new footnote 55a:*

For the circumstances in which knowledge can be attributed to a principal or a company, see Ch.19. For a recent example, see *Recovery Partners GB Limited v Rukhadze* [2018] EWHC 2918 (Comm), at [452]: the knowledge of the individual defendants could be attributed to the corporate defendants who were the "corporate alter egos" of the individual defendants and who were "created essentially for the purpose of the transactions in issue in these proceedings".

D. KNOWLEDGE/UNCONSCIONABILITY

(1) The Knowledge Requirement

12–039 *At the end of footnote 60, add:*

See also *Courtwood Holdings SA v Woodley Properties Ltd* [2018] EWHC 2163 (Ch); *Brent LBC v Davies* [2018] EWHC 2214 (Ch), at [558]; *Iranian Offshore Engineering and Construction Company v Dean Investment Holdings SA* [2019] EWHC 472 (Comm), at [175]; and *Payroller Ltd (In Liquidation) v Little Panda Consultants Ltd* [2020] EWHC 391 (QB), at [81]. In *Brent LBC v Davies* [2018] EWHC 2214 (Ch), Zacaroli J referred to the approach taken by Stephen Morris QC (sitting as a Deputy High Court Judge) in *Armstrong v Winnington Networks Ltd* [2013] Ch 156 and explained, at [563], that "While the *Baden* classification remains useful as guidance, rigid adherence to it is no longer appropriate following *Akindele*".

12–044 *After the reference to HHJ Pelling in brackets in the eighth line of footnote 64, add:*

At [107], HHJ Pelling QC held that Mr Tilly knew or wilfully shut his eyes to the fact that the transfer "was made in breach of the trust obligations" imposed by an agreement, the "relevant facts" for the purpose of this case including, therefore, the existence of a transfer in breach of trust.

At the end of the first sentence, add new footnote 64a:

[64a] In *First National Trustco (UK) Ltd v Page* [2019] EWHC 1187 (Ch), one area of dispute between the parties was whether it was necessary for the recipient of the trust property to know that it had been transferred in breach of trust, or whether it was sufficient to know "relevant facts". Joanna Smith QC, (sitting as a Deputy High Court Judge), expressed herself "a little reluctant to delve into this question in circumstances where the Court of Appeal made it clear in *Akindele* that the touchstone in relation to knowledge was "unconscionability" and that this was a general test to be applied." Nevertheless, at [282], she rejected (obiter) the suggestion that it was necessary to show that the defendant realised that the transaction was obviously or probably in breach of trust (adopting the conclusions of Stephen Morris QC in *Armstrong GmbH v Winnington Networks Ltd*, quoted at para.12–042 above). See also *Payroller Ltd (In Liquidation) v Little Panda Consultants Ltd* [2020] EWHC 391 (QB), per Freedman J at [81]:"It is not necessary for the defendant to know all the facts associated with the wrong and it is sufficient that he knew enough of the facts surrounding the misapplication of the property to make it unconscionable for him to retain the benefit of the receipt."

12–045 *Replace footnote 69 with:*

L. Tucker, N. Le Poidevin and J. Brightwell, *Lewin on Trusts* (2020), para.42–064; and McGhee, *Snell's Equity* (2020), para.30–072.

(2) The Relevant Time

Replace footnote 70 with: **12–047**

See L. Tucker, N. Le Poidevin and J. Brightwell, *Lewin on Trusts* (2020), para.42–083.

Replace footnote 72 with: **12–049**

See L. Tucker, N. Le Poidevin and J. Brightwell, *Lewin on Trusts* (2020), para.42–083.

CHAPTER 13

DISHONEST ASSISTANCE

B. BREACH OF TRUST OR FIDUCIARY DUTY

(1) The Underlying Relationship

At the end of footnote 27, add: **13–013**

See also *FM Capital Partners Ltd v Marino* [2018] EWHC 1768 (Comm), per Cockerill J at [82].

C. ASSISTANCE/PROCUREMENT

(1) What Amounts to Actionable Assistance

13–020 *At the end of footnote 39, add:*

This gloss (albeit as expressed in a different text) was endorsed by the Court of Appeal in *Group Seven Ltd* v *Nasir* [2019] EWCA Civ 614; [2020] Ch 129, at [110].

(4) Causation

13–025 *At the end of footnote 50, add:*

See also *Group Seven Ltd* v *Nasir* [2019] EWCA Civ 614; [2020] Ch 129, at [110], confirming (post *Novoship*) that the relevant causal connection is between breach (rather than assistance in that breach) and loss.

At the end of footnote 51, and before the full-stop, add:

; *Otkritie International Investment Management Ltd v Urumov* [2014] EWHC 191 (Comm), per Eder J at [456] and [458]; *Iranian Offshore Engineering and Construction Company v Dean Investment Holdings SA* [2019] EWHC 472 (Comm), per Butcher J at [170]

13–028 *At the end of the paragraph, add:*

In *Group Seven Ltd* v *Nasir* the Court of Appeal confirmed that the latter case was concerned only with a claim for account of profits, and that the approach in *AIB Group* was indeed to be applied to a claim for compensation against a dishonest assister.[57a]

[57a] [2019] EWCA Civ 614; [2020] Ch 129, at [110].

D. DISHONESTY

(1) The Legal Test

13–036 *Replace the final sentence of footnote 69 with:*

See further footnote 72a below.

Replace the final sentence with:

The Supreme Court in *Ivey v Genting Casinos (UK) ltd (t/a) Crockfords)*[72] expressed the view (albeit in a different context) that the test established in *Barlow Clowes* represents English law, and the Court of Appeal has now applied that test to dishonest assistance claims on a number of occasions.[72a] The position can therefore now be regarded as settled. The Court must ascertain: (i) the defendant's actual state of knowledge or belief[72b] as to the facts; and (ii) whether, in light of that state of mind, the defendant's conduct was honest or dishonest applying the objective standards of ordinary decent people. This standard of appraisal (at the second stage of the analysis) is a purely objective one: there is no further subjective element to the test.

[72] [2017] UKSC 67; [2018] A.C. 391, at [62].

[72a] *Group Seven Ltd* v *Nasir* [2019] EWCA Civ 614; [2020] Ch 129, at [58]; *Stanford International Bank Ltd v HSBC Bank plc* [2021] EWCA Civ 535; [2021] 1 W.L.R. 3507, at [41]; *Natwest Markets Plc v Bilta (UK) Ltd* [2021] EWCA Civ 680, at [130]. Permission to appeal to the Supreme Court was apparently refused in *Group Seven* on the basis that it did not raise an arguable point of law. For earlier authorities see the original n.69 of the first edition of this work.

[72b] In *Group Seven*, above, the Court of Appeal observed (at [61]) that beliefs falling short of knowledge (even in the blind-eye sense) could still be relevant as forming "part of the overall picture to which the objective standard of dishonesty is to be applied" (albeit in that case there was held, reversing the Judge at first instance, to be blind-eye knowledge of the facts which constituted the breach of trust).

Add new paragraph 13–036A after para.13–036:

The test for dishonesty in a dishonest assistance claim is no different when applied to a large corporation: dishonesty, in the sense considered above, still has to be established on the part of one or more individuals representing the corporation. It is not possible to aggregate two separately innocent minds to make a dishonest whole.[72c] **13–036A**

[72c] *Stanford International Bank Ltd v HSBC Bank plc* [2021] EWCA Civ 535; [2021] 1 W.L.R. 3507, at [42]–[48].

(2) Knowledge of the Underlying Trust or Fiduciary Relationship

At the end of footnote 77, add: **13–038**

In *Group Seven Ltd* v *Nasir* [2019] EWCA Civ 614; [2020] Ch 129, at [103]–[104], the Court of Appeal, while declining to decide the issue, expressed the view that the test for dishonesty as now clarified should not be complicated by the specification of a minimum required *content* of the knowledge or belief that the defendant had to have.

For criticism of this approach and a defence of the more restrictive mental element of actual knowledge or blind-eye knowledge, see Davies, "The mental element of accessory liability in equity", LQR 2022 138 (Jan) 32–57.

(3) Doubts, Suspicions and Recklessness

Replace the text in footnote 84 after the citation of Manifest Shipping with: **13–043**

, which was endorsed by the Court of Appeal in the context of a dishonest assistance claim in *Group Seven Ltd v Nasir* [2019] EWCA Civ 614; [2020] Ch 129, at [60].

At the end of the first sentence of footnote 85, before the full-stop, add:

, endorsed in the dishonest assistance context by the Court of Appeal in *Group Seven Ltd v Nasir* [2019] EWCA Civ 614; [2020] Ch 129, at [59]. See also *Twinsectra*, above, at [22].

At the end of footnote 87, add:

See also *Natwest Markets Plc v Bilta (UK) Ltd* [2021] EWCA Civ 680, where the Court of Appeal rejected the submission that it was sufficient to prove dishonesty to show that a trader had a degree of doubt about the legitimacy of trading that would lead him to go to the compliance officer but refrained from doing so: that was an unwarranted dilution of the legal test.

E. VICARIOUS LIABILITY

(1) Dubai Aluminium

13–048 *At the end of footnote 100, add:*

Other senior appellate authority on the principles of vicarious liability includes *Various Claimants v Catholic Child Welfare Society* [2013] A.C. 1; *Cox v Ministry of Justice* [2016] A.C. 660; and *Barclays Bank plc v Various Claimants* [2020] A.C. 973. For a review of these authorities in the context of a dishonest assistance claim, see *Natwest Markets Plc v Bilta (UK) Ltd* [2021] EWCA Civ 680, at [143] and following.

F. NEGLIGENCE LIABILITY

13–051 *In footnote 103, delete the second and third sentences, and add at the end of the first sentence:*

and (by the Supreme Court) at [2019] UKSC 50; [2020] A.C. 1189.

CHAPTER 14

UNJUST ENRICHMENT

A. INTRODUCTION

(1) What is Unjust Enrichment?

14–002 *At the end of the second sentence, add footnote 2a:*

[2a] For a recent reiteration of this principle, see *Dargamo Holdings Ltd v Avonwick Holdings Ltd* [2021] EWCA Civ 1149, per Carr LJ at [106].

(4) Pleading a Claim in Unjust Enrichment

Add new paragraph 14–012A after para.14–012:

14–012A For instance in *Barton v Gwyn-Jones*[13a] the claimant brought a claim for the reasonable value of his services (a quantum meruit) on the basis that the defendant had been unjustly enriched at his expense. The court was not content to have the language of quantum meruit used without identifying the underlying nature of the claim. The Court observed that the term "quantum meruit" covers two different claims: a claim in unjust enrichment where the enrichment is services, and a contractual claim arising from breach of an implied agreement for reasonable renumeration for services. The claimant's counsel submitted that the claims were "two sides of the same coin". The Court of Appeal rejected that submission[13b]: the claims are different causes of action requiring proof of different elements to establish liability.

[13a] *Barton v Gwyn-Jones* [2019] EWCA Civ 1999; [2020] 2 All E.R. (Comm) 652.
[13b] *Barton v Gwyn-Jones*, above, per Asplin LJ at [42] and Davis LJ at [76].

14–013 *At the end of footnote 14, add:*

See also *Samsoondar v Capital Insurance Company Ltd* [2020] UKPC 33, where Lord Burrows said, at [18]: "The ideal pleading of a statement of case by the claimant should indicate that the claim is for restitution of unjust enrichment and should identify facts that satisfy each of those three elements. While it may be desirable, it is not essential, that the words "unjust enrichment" are used but the claimant must identify sufficient facts to show how those three elements are satisfied: see *Goff and Jones, The Law of Unjust Enrichment* (eds Mitchell, Mitchell and Watterson, 9th ed (2016), para.1–38). The important purpose of a statement of case is to ensure, as a matter of fairness, that the defendant knows the case it has to meet."

C. ENRICHMENT AT THE EXPENSE OF THE CLAIMANT

(1) A Direct Transmission of a Benefit from Claimant to Defendant

Add new paragraph 14–052A after para.14–052:

The requirement that a claimant show that he has directly provided a benefit to the defendant was extended by the Supreme Court in *Prudential Assurance Co Ltd v HMRC,*[54a] where the court held that in cases based on a money payment, the claimant cannot recover the value of the opportunity to use the money, quantified as interest, because the defendant only acquires this benefit "indirectly": the opportunity is not directly derived from the claimant's payment, but from the defendant's failure to repay the face value of the money immediately upon receipt see also para.14–028 above. However, this principle does not apply in cases "where the benefit conferred is not the transfer of property outright, but the transfer of the right of possession (and the concomitant right of use) of property which the transferor is entitled to terminate at will".[54b] In such cases "it is appropriate to treat each period during which the right of possession and use subsists as an independent transfer of value. That would be consistent with the fact that the objective valuation of the benefit is itself time-dependent (viz a market rate for use for a particular period). That is very different from the position where there is an outright transfer of money or property, which the transferee subsequently uses (in which case the subsequent use of the money or property will not involve a further and independent transfer of value)." **14–052A**

[54a] *Prudential Assurance Co Ltd v HMRC* [2018] UKSC 39; [2019] A.C. 929: see, in particular at [71]–[74].

[54b] *School Facility Management Ltd v Governing Body of Christ the King College* [2020] EWHC 1118 (Comm); [2020] PTSR 1913 per Foxton J, at [437]. The Court of Appeal upheld the decision of Foxton J but the judgments do not in terms address his analysis on this point: [2021] EWCA Civ 1053.

At the end of footnote 60, add: **14–057**

This case concerned parents who sold their home ("the first property") and bought, from the proceeds, a house for their daughter ("the second property"). The claimant bank had a charge over the first property. They agreed to the release of this charge on the basis that they would acquire a charge over the second property. Solicitors sent the bank a charge over the second property, whereupon the bank agreed to the release of its charge over the first property. However, the charge over the second property was defective; the daughter had never agreed to its creation, and her signature on the relevant document had been forged. The bank's claim was successful. The most orthodox, and convincing, explanation of the reason for the success of the claim is that given by Lord Reed in *Investment Trust Companies* at [65]: the bank "had mistakenly authorised the use of its proceeds of sale of the first property (which it could otherwise have required to be applied to discharge the debt owed to itself) to purchase the second property, thereby providing the defendant with a benefit at its expense."

D. UNJUST FACTORS

(1) The Importance of Justifying Grounds, or the "Presence of Basis Bar"

Add new paragraph 14–066A after para.14–066:

14–066A Compare, however, the Court of Appeal's decision in *Barton v Gwyn-Jones*.[72a] By an oral agreement, a company agreed to pay B £1.2 million "if" he introduced a purchaser for its property who bought it for £6.5m. B introduced a purchaser who initially offered £6.5m but, due to the possible impact of HS2, in due course paid £6 million for the property. The company refused to pay B any money at all on the grounds that the property sold for less than the identified target purchase price. As B had no claim on the express terms of the contract, he brought a claim for the reasonable value of his services (a quantum meruit) on the ground that the company had been unjustly enriched at his expense by the introduction of the purchaser. At first instance, the judge rejected this claim on the basis that it would undermine the parties' contractual arrangements, relying on *Costello v MacDonald, Dickens & Macklin*.[72b] The Court of Appeal allowed the appeal. Asplin LJ, who gave the leading judgment, considered that the case fell to be determined by construing the terms of the contact. She considered that the contract "was entirely silent as to what was to happen if the sale completed for a purchase price of less than £6.5 million"[72c] with the result that the contract did not exclude a claim in unjust enrichment.[72d]

[72a] *Barton v Gwyn-Jones* [2019] EWCA Civ 1999; [2020] 2 All E.R. (Comm) 652.
[72b] *Costello v MacDonald, Dickens & Macklin* [2011] EWCA Civ 930; [2012] Q.B. 244.
[72c] *Costello v MacDonald*, above, at [32]. See also Males LJ at [62].
[72d] See, for stringent criticism of this decision, *Day and Virgo, "Risks on the contact/unjust enrichment borderline"*, LQR 2020, 136 (July) 349–354.

(3) Mistake

14–071 *At the end of footnote 74, add:*

In that case the House of Lords established that restitution may be granted for payments made under mistakes of law, as well as mistakes of fact. The mistake of law in this case was that local authorities had the power to enter into interest rate swap agreements. Such agreements were commonplace, until the House of Lords decision in *Hazell v Hammersmith and Fulham LBC* [1992] 1 A.C. 1 (albeit that there was no legal precedent upon which the councils can be said to have relied to establish that such transactions were inter vires: see [1999] 2 A.C. 349, at 362). In the wake of that decision, several councils recovered, by claims for restitution, sums which they had paid in connection with interest rate swaps agreements on the grounds that they had been paid pursuant to a mistake.

14–072 *At the end of footnote 77, add:*

The line between mistake and misprediction is vexed and difficult to draw. For a recent demonstration of this problem, see *Elston v King* [2020] EWHC 55 (Ch); [2020] BPIR 501. Elston was adjudged bankrupt whilst holding five pension policies. His trustee in bankruptcy informed him that, because Elston could have elected to take his pension payments (even though he had not), those payments could be made the subject of an income payments order pursuant to s.310(7) of the Insolvency Act 1986, in reliance on the judgment of a deputy judge in *Raithatha v Williamson* [2012] EWHC 909 (Ch); [2012] 1 W.L.R. 3559. In the face of the trustee's threat to make an application for such an order, Elston entered into an income payments agreement. Less than a month later, in *Re Henry* [2014] EWHC 4209 (Ch); [2015] 1 W.L.R. 2488 another deputy judge declined to follow *Raithatha*, and the Court of

Appeal later upheld his decision [2016] EWCA Civ 989; [2017] 1 W.L.R. 391. Thereafter Elston attempted to recover the money he had paid to the trustee in unjust enrichment as paid under a mistake of law. The primary basis on which relief was refused was that Elston had not been mistaken about the law; he had simply failed to predict that it would change. The judgment proceeds on that basis that *Kleinwort Benson* is not authority for the proposition that reliance on a law which is later declared to be wrong necessarily gives rise to a mistake. The judgment introduces a distinction between the dramatic over-turning of a well-established and unquestioned rule of law on the one hand, and the overturning of a single decision on a "new and difficult" point on the other ([28], footnote 41), bearing in mind factors such as the level of the court in the appellate structure, whether the point was novel, and whether permission to appeal had been granted. For spirited criticism of the decision, see *Trotter, Mistakes and mispredictions,* LQR 2021, 137 (Apr), 212–216. A similar factual matrix existed in the Privy Council decision of *Samsoondar v Capital Insurance Co Ltd* [2020] UKPC 33; [2021] 2 All E.R. 1105. For commentary, see *Hedley, Restitution and Car Crashes: a simple case of mistake*, CLJ 2021, 80(1), 36–39. The conceptual difficulty underlying both of these decisions is the very notion that the party seeking restitution was operating under a mistake at all. Elston and Capital were both relying on legal decisions which, at the time of the transactions in question, cannot be said to have been wrong; neither can realistically be said, as a matter of subjective belief, to have been mistaken about the status of those decisions. Rather, each simply failed to appreciate the direction that the law, or precedent, would, in the future, take. It is only because of the declaratory view of the common law—viz that judges do not create law but reveal what has always been—that the language of even deemed mistake can be invoked.

(5) Individual Incapacity

In footnote 99, replace the reference to the 32nd edition of Chitty on Contracts with a reference to the 33rd edn (the paragraph numbers remain unchanged). **14–084**

(6) Total Failure of Consideration/Basis/Condition

At the end of footnote 100, add: **14–085**

See also *Dargamo Holdings Ltd v Avonwick Holdings Ltd* [2021] EWCA Civ 1149, per Carr LJ at [80].

At the end of the first sentence, add footnote 103a: **14–089**

[103a] There are rare instances where it is possible to bring a claim for unjust enrichment even though there is a subsisting contract. However, it has been stressed that the "courts should continue to keep a tight rein" on this: *London Trocaedro (2015) LLP v Picturehouse Cinemas Ltd* [2021] EWHC 2591 (Ch), per Robin Vos sitting as a Deputy High Court Judge at [173]. One of the reasons for such restraint arises from the interplay between the law of contract and the law of restitution. It was considered, obiter, in that case that despite the "inelegance" resulting from the analysis, failure of basis could not provide a defence to a contract claim for payment of a benefit, even though the law of unjust enrichment would subsequently allow for recovery of that same benefit: see at [171]. Therefore, as a matter of practicality, if failure of basis is put forward as a defence to a contractual claim, it has been suggested that it should be pleaded by way of counterclaim in unjust enrichment and set-off, see *Universal Advance Technology Limited v Lloyds Bank Plc* [2016] EWCA Civ 933.

At the beginning of footnote 106, add: **14–090**

For recent confirmation of the position, see *Dargamo Holdings Ltd v Avonwick Holdings Ltd* [2021] EWCA Civ 1149, per Carr LJ at [102].

In the second sentence, after the semi-colon, add footnote 106a:

[106a] With regard to this assessment, the Court of Appeal in *Dargamo Holdings Ltd v Avonwick Holdings Ltd* [2021] EWCA Civ 1149 recognised that, in an appropriate case, the court may need to "look beyond the terms of the contract for a wider understanding of the context of an unjust enrichment claim", per Carr LJ at [132]. However, the court also emphasised that where "the basis of the consideration is expressly and unconditionally set out on the face of a valid and subsisting

contract. . .there is no proper scope for inquiring into an alternative basis that is plainly contrary to the express basis freely agreed by the parties", at [133]. The court reiterated that "the parties are simply being held to the express terms of the contract into which they chose to enter and with which terms they have fully complied on all sides. The law of unjust enrichment does not provide a means of subverting that agreement", at [137]. For a recent application of this principle, see *Football Association Premier League Ltd v PPLive Sports International Ltd* [2022] EWHC 38 (Comm), per Fraser J at [102].

F. REMEDIES

(1) Personal Restitutionary Awards

Add new paragraph 14–123A after para.14–123:

14–123A In *Vodafone Ltd v Office of Communications,*[153a] mobile network operators brought an action to recover licence fees which they had paid to Ofcom pursuant to regulations which were later quashed. Regulations dating back to 2011 had fixed rates, which Ofcom then sought, by way of regulations made in 2015, to increase. Mobile network operators paid the 2015 rates for 2 years when it later transpired that they were only liable at the lower 2011 rates. They sought restitution of the excess of the 2015 rates over the 2011 rates. The action was brought in reliance on the "*Woolwich*" principle (based on *Woolwich Equitable Building Society v Inland Revenue Commissioners*[153b]), which entitles anyone who has paid to a public body taxes or levies that are not lawfully due to recover that money. In its defence, Ofcom argued that the appropriate measure was the excess paid over the hypothetical lawful regulations that it could have (but had not) introduced. The Court of Appeal rejected the application of the counterfactual principle and held that it was impermissible to take into account the hypothetical performance of even administrative steps. It was for the Court to determine what sums the defendant was entitled to receive. The claimants were entitled to recover in unjust enrichment the sums in excess of this which they had paid. This is, perhaps, unsurprising in the context of public law principles governing the conduct of public law bodies.

153a *Vodafone Ltd v Office of Communications* [2020] EWCA Civ 183; [2020] Q.B. 857.
153b [1993] A.C. 70.

(2) Proprietary Remedies

14–125 *At the end of footnote 160, add:*

The position that subrogation is a remedy for unjust enrichment is not universally accepted by academics: see, for example, Virgo, *Principles of the Law of Restitution* (2015) at p.637. There are indications that the availability of subrogation as a remedy for unjust enrichment is falling out of favour in recent times: see *Menelaou v Bank of Cyprus UK Ltd* [2015] UKSC 66; [2016] A.C. 176, per Lord Carnwath at [108] and Lord Neuberger at [59]; *Swynson Ltd v Lowick Rose LLP* [2017] UKSC 32; [2018] A.C. 313, per Lord Sumption at [30]; *Prudential Assurance Co Ltd v Revenue and Customs Commissioners* [2018] UKSC 39; [2019] A.C. 929, per Lords Mance, Reed and Hodge at [68]. See also Gregson, *Is subrogation a remedy for unjust enrichment?* LQR 2020, 136 (July) 481–505.

CHAPTER 15

UNDUE INFLUENCE AND DURESS

A. INTRODUCTION

(2) The Difference Between the Two Types of Claim

Replace footnote 2 with: **15–005**

[2] See generally, N. Enonchong, *Duress, Undue Influence and Unconscionable Dealing*, 3rd edn (London: Sweet & Maxwell, 2018).

At end of the paragraph, add:

The crossover between the two types of claim has been stressed by the Supreme Court in its recent decision in *Pakistan International Airline Corp v Times Travel (UK) Limited*,[2a] where the Court explained that lawful act duress has its origins in equitable doctrines such as those applied in undue influence cases, and that many cases that were decided under the auspices of undue influence were in fact instances of duress.[2b]

[2a] [2021] UKSC 40; [2021] 3 W.L.R. 727.
[2b] See *Pakistan International Airline*, above, per Lord Hodge DPSC at [4]–[9], concerning cases decided by the courts of equity before the development of the common law doctrine of lawful act duress, in the context where a defendant uses his knowledge of criminal activity by the claimant or a member of the claimant's close family to obtain a personal benefit from the claimant by the express or implicit threat to report to crime or initiate a prosecution.

B. UNDUE INFLUENCE

(2) Actual Undue Influence

15–012 *At the end of the third sentence in sub-paragraph (1), add footnote 12a:*

[12a] See Enonchong, *Duress, Undue Influence and Unconscionable Dealing* (2018), para.10–044.

At the end of the first sentence in sub-paragraph (4), add footnote 19a:

[19a] It seems that unconscionable conduct requires a "conscious act of wrongdoing", though this need not amount to a subjective appreciation by the influencing party that he is acting wrongly: see *YS GM Marfin II LLC v Lakhani* [2020] EWHC 2629 (Comm), at [92]–[93].

(3) Presumed Undue Influence

15–019 *At the end of the first sentence in sub-paragraph (2), add footnote 30a:*

[30a] This relationship must arise before the impugned transaction. If the claimant reposes trust and confidence in the defendant during the transaction, but not beforehand, no presumption arises and the claimant must show actual undue influence. See *Perwaz v Perwaz* [2018] UKUT 325 (TCC), at [72]: "To allow the presumption to be raised purely as a result of what happened in the transaction itself would simply lower the bar for the proof of actual undue influence. The evidential presumption arises only where something that was already established prior to the transaction makes the claimant vulnerable at its outset."

15–020 *At the end of footnote 35, add:*

In *Lennon v Englefield* [2021] EWHC 1473 (QB), at [84]–[85], the Court held that a transaction whereby a solicitor had misappropriated funds by procuring that they be transferred to the relevant family's client account was not manifestly disadvantageous for the simple reason that the account into which the money had been paid was a client account, i.e. held by him as agent for the family. Had it been his own account, the position would have been different. The transaction in question has to be looked at in all the circumstances of the particular case: see for example *Re Seale (dec'd)* [2021] EWHC 1458 (Ch), where the Court held that it was wrong to say that the severance of a joint tenancy could never be a 'transaction' for the purposes of a claim in undue influence.

At the end of footnote 40, add: **15–021**

Similarly, see *Bird v Lantern Recovery LLP* [2021] EWHC 1379 (Ch), where the Court set aside a series of dividend waivers by an elderly lady, and gifts for the purchase of multi-million pound properties for her grandchildren, on the grounds of presumed undue influence by her son.

(4) Causation

At the end of the third sentence, add footnote 41a: **15–022**

[41a] See, for example, *Syndicate Bank v Dansingani* [2019] EWHC 3439 (Ch), at [96].

(6) Rescission Against Third Parties on Notice

Replace footnote 48 with: **15–028**

Enonchong, *Duress, Undue Influence and Unconscionable Dealing* (2018), para.24–001.

At end of paragraph, add: **15–029**

This situation was recently further examined in *Syndicate Bank v Dansingani*,[52a] where the Court held that the wife was not bound by a personal guarantee and mortgage that she had granted to a bank to secure the company's liabilities, notwithstanding that the husband remained bound by the same mortgage and guarantee, and that the wife was both a director and a shareholder of the company.

[52a] [2019] EWHC 3439 (Ch). (For further proceedings in the Court of Appeal, see *Dansingani v Canara Bank* [2021] EWCA Civ 714).

Replace footnote 48 with: **15–031**

Enonchong, *Duress, Undue Influence and Unconscionable Dealing* (2018), para.24–010.

At end of footnote 65, add: **15–033**

In the recent decision in *Dansingani*, above, the Court found that the bank had not taken reasonable steps, as it had not communicated directly with the wife, and did not suggest that she take independent legal advice, and there was no evidence that the wife had a full understanding of the guarantee or the underlying transaction, or that a faxed confirmation that she fully understood the implications of the guarantee was provided free from the influence of her husband. Procuring a letter signed by the wife *after* the transaction had been executed, to the effect that she understood the guarantee and did not need to obtain further legal advice, was held to be insufficient, as it had been drafted by her husband or her brother and simply placed in front of her to sign.

C. DURESS

(1) Introduction

In footnote 69, add to citation: **15–034**

; [2018] 1 C.L.C. 216

In footnote 71, add to citation for Al Nehayan v Kent: **15–036**

; [2018] 1 C.L.C. 216

(2) The Legal Consequences of Duress

15–037 *In footnote 72, add to citation for Al Nehayan v Kent:*

; [2018] 1 C.L.C. 216

(4) Elements of Duress

Replace paragraph with:

15–039 In *Pakistan International Airline Corp v Times Travel (UK) Limited*,[77] the Supreme Court clarified that there are two (or in the case of economic duress, three) essential elements that a claimant needed to establish in order to succeed in a claim for rescission of the contract:

(1) First, a threat (or pressure exerted) by the defendant that was illegitimate;
(2) Second, that that illegitimate threat (or pressure) caused the claimant to enter into the contract;
(3) Third, in the context of 'economic duress', that the claimant must have had no reasonable alternative to giving in to the threat or pressure.

We will consider these three elements below primarily as they are to be interpreted in claims for economic duress, which is, in the context of this book the most significant manifestation of the law of duress.

[77] See *Pakistan International Airline*, above, per Lord Burrows JSC at [77]–[80].

(i) Illegitimate Pressure

15–041 *Delete footnote 85*

At end of paragraph, add:

The law in relation to 'lawful act economic duress' was recently restated by the Supreme Court in *Pakistan International Airline*.[85] The Court reiterated that the boundaries of the doctrine were not fixed, and that the courts should approach any extension with caution, particularly in the context of contractual negotiations between commercial entities. The Court explained that there are two circumstances in which the English courts have recognised lawful act duress:

(1) Where a defendant used his knowledge of the claimant's criminal activity, or that of a person close to the claimant, to obtain a personal benefit from the claimant by the use of express or implicit threat. As noted above, this has historically been viewed as an example of undue influence, but is now seen as lawful act duress.
(2) Where the defendant, having exposed himself to a civil claim by the claimant, deliberately manoeuvred the claimant into a position of vulnerability by illegitimate means and so forced him to waive his claim.[85a]

[85] *Pakistan International Airline*, above, at [4].

[85a] The Court in *Pakistan International Airline* was concerned with this situation. Specifically, an airline had entered into a contract with a travel agency, pursuant to which it would act as ticketing agent to the airline. The agent's business was largely dependent on its ability to sell the airline's tickets. The

airline came under pressure from many of its agents in relation to unpaid commission. As regards the claimant, the airline threatened to refuse to renew its agency contract unless the agent agreed to terms waiving its claims to commission. The agent agreed, but subsequently brought proceedings seeking to rescind the new contract for lawful act duress. The court found that the reduction of the ticket allocation was a "hard-nosed exercise of monopoly power" which, in the absence of a doctrine of unequal bargaining power, could not amount to illegitimate pressure for the purposes of a claim of duress (at [57]).

Add new paragraphs 15–041A and 15–041B after para.15–041:

As the Court noted, there is no general doctrine of inequality of bargaining power and no general principle of good faith in English contract law, although inequality can sometimes be a relevant feature in cases of undue influence.[85b] A commercial party in negotiation with another commercial party is entitled to use its bargaining power to obtain by negotiation that which it did not have until the contract was signed, and a more powerful commercial party could impose onerous terms as a condition of the contract being entered into. **15–041A**

[85b] *Pakistan International Airline*, above, at [26]–[27] and [44].

Although the Court was unanimous as to the disposal of the appeal and the basic law of and requirements for duress, Lord Burrows disagreed with the majority as to the relevance of good faith. The majority view was that the absence of good faith, i.e. a lack of belief on the part of the defendant that it had a good defence to the claimant's claims against it, was not a sufficient criterion for establishing duress.[85c] Rather it had to be shown that the defendant had acted reprehensibly.[85d] Lord Burrows' view was that bad faith should be the relevant criterion.[85e] **15–041B**

[85c] *Pakistan International Airline*, above, at [45]–[52]

[85d] *Pakistan International Airline* has since been applied in *Heritage Travel and Tourism Ltd v Windhorst* [2021] EWHC 2380 (Comm) and *Al-Subaihi v Al-Sanea* [2021] EWHC 2609 (Comm), in each of which the Court found that the facts involved commercial bargaining of the sort which the Supreme Court had held did not suffice for the purposes of a claim in lawful act duress.

[85e] *Pakistan International Airline*, above, at [136]: "lawful act economic threat is illegitimate, where, first, the threatening party has deliberately created, or increased, the threatened party's vulnerability to the demand and, secondly, the "bad faith demand" requirement is satisfied. The demand is made in bad faith where the threatening party does not genuinely believe that it has any defence (and there is no defence) to the claim being waived." See further at [96]–[136].

(iii) Causation

In the third sentence of footnote 93, replace the text in parentheses with the following, and delete the words "and following" after that parenthesis: **15–043**

in *Duress, Undue Influence and Unconscionable Dealing* (2018), para.4–021 and following

At the end of footnote 96, add: **15–044**

For recent confirmation that coercion is an essential ingredient of economic duress, see *Morley v The Royal Bank of Scotland Plc* [2021] EWCA Civ 338, at [52]. On the facts of that case the Court found that there was no coercion because the claimant had continued to negotiate the terms of the relevant contract after the threat that was the subject of the allegation: see [53]–[58].

At the end of footnote 105, add: **15–047**

See now Enonchong, *Duress, Undue Influence and Unconscionable Dealing* (2018), at para.4.16 and following.

In footnote 106 add to citation for Al Nehayan v Kent:

; [2018] 1 C.L.C. 216

15–050 *Replace footnote 112 with:*

See also J. McGhee, *Snell's Equity*, 34th edn (London: Sweet & Maxwell, 2020), paras 8–040 and following.

15–055 *At the end of footnote 127, add:*

; *Adare Finance DAC v Yellowstone Capital Management SA* [2020] EWHC 2760 (Comm), at [69].

CHAPTER 16

STATUTORY CLAIMS

A. INTRODUCTION

(3) Other Statutory Provisions

In footnote 5, replace the citation with: **16–009**

[1978] Ch. 262

B. TRANSACTIONS DEFRAUDING CREDITORS

(1) Introduction

At the end of footnote 16, add: **16–014**

The Court will carefully consider the effect of an order under s.423 on the foreign proceedings: *New Media Distribution Co SEZC Ltd v Kagalovsky* [2018] EWHC 2876 (Ch). For an example of a case where the sufficient connection test was not satisfied but the claim was permitted to continue nonetheless, because the parties would be involved in litigation in the jurisdiction in any event, see *Suppipat v Narongdej* [2020] EWHC 3191 (Comm).

At the end of footnote 17, add:

Kea Investments Ltd v Ivory Castle Ltd [2019] EWHC 309 (Ch).

(2) Time within which Claim to be Brought

16–015 *In footnote 17, after the existing citation add:*

; [2018] 1 W.L.R. 4847

(3) The Requirement of a Transaction at an Undervalue

16–020 *Replace the final 3 sentences of the paragraph, from "But if.." to the end, with:*

Following the decision of Zacaroli J in *Burnden Holdings (UK) Ltd v Fielding*,[28] it appears as though the principle in *Re MC Bacon Ltd* should be treated as of general application. The judge effectively applied the principle directly in the same terms, notwithstanding any inconsistency with the language of the statute itself. He considered that the grant of security "involved no transfer of value" from the company because the question of the value of the assets had to be judged from the perspective of the company itself and, even if the creditor to whom security was granted received more than he gave, that was "irrelevant".[28a] Accordingly, the grant of security cannot fall within subsection (c) and it is doubtful whether the grant of security could fall within s.423 at all on the basis that it could never be established that the transaction was at an undervalue.

[28] [2019] EWHC 1566 (Ch), declining to follow the obiter dicta in *Hill v Spread Trustees* [2007] 1 W.L.R. 2404.
[28a] *Burnden Holdings*, above, at [504].

16–021 *In footnote 29 replace "(the point is to be considered in a pending appeal)" with:*

. The decision was upheld on appeal: see [2019] EWCA Civ 112; [2019] 2 All E.R. 784. The Court of Appeal (the sole reasoned judgment being that of David Richards LJ) rejected an argument that dividends were gifts (see [37–41]). The Court of Appeal further held: (i) that the payment of a dividend was a transaction for 'no consideration', notwithstanding that payment of a dividend arises out of rights acquired by the shareholder on acquisition of the shares, including the right to receive a dividend if declared. The crucial point is that the payment of a dividend "involves the payment of funds beneficially owned by a company to its shareholders" as a result of the discretionary process of the directors deciding to declare a dividend (see [50]). That was quite different from, for example, the right to interest under a loan note, where there was no discretion as to whether the payment should be made; and (ii) that the payment of a dividend was a 'transaction' within the scope of s.423. It also held at [59] that the language of s.423 did not preclude a unilateral act from being a 'transaction' for the purposes of s.423; that payment of a dividend was in any event not a unilateral act; and that there was no tension between s.423 and Part 23 of the Companies Act 2006 which would prevent a dividend from being such a transaction. There was "no conceptual difficulty in an otherwise lawful dividend being paid for the purpose of putting assets beyond the reach of actual or potential claimants"; see [62].

16–023 *At the end of the paragraph, add:*

As was noted in *Payroller Ltd (In Liquidation) v Little Panda Consultants Ltd*,[31a] there is no authority as to whether payments by a debtor for the purposes of discharging bona fide liabilities to a third party could be 'transactions' for the purposes of s.423, the point having been left open in *Re Hampton Capital Ltd*. An application to strike out the claim on that basis was dismissed. It is suggested that it would be inconsistent with the purpose of s.423 if such transactions were excluded from the scope of s.423. As has been noted, s.423 is drafted in wide terms to protect creditors from assets being moved from the potential debtor out of their reach.[31b] That consideration applies with equal force to a transaction which benefits third parties as to one which (in the more usual scenario) benefits the company's directors: the end result is the same, namely that the creditors' interests are damaged.

[31a] [2018] EWHC 3161 (QB).
[31b] See *Sequana* [2019] EWCA Civ 112; [2019] 2 All E.R. 784, at [43].

(4) The Improper Purpose Requirement

At the end of footnote 32, add: **16–025**

For a recent example, see *Re Cartwright (a bankrupt)* [2020] EWHC 2655 (Ch).

At the end of footnote 33, add:

See also *Integral Petroleum SA v Petrogat FZA* [2021] EWHC 1365 (Comm).

At the end of the paragraph, add: **16–030**

For another example where a seemingly strong case under s.423 was dismissed on the facts, see *Fox v Mohammed*.[41a] Notwithstanding that the debtor had made a number of transactions by which he divested himself of the beneficial interests in properties in quick succession for no consideration, the Court declined on the facts to draw the inference that the statutory purpose formed a substantial part of the debtor's intention. The finding was upheld on appeal in the High Court.

[41a] [2019] EWHC 3409 (Ch).

(5) The "Victim"

At the end of the paragraph, add: **16–033**

If a party is a victim of the transaction at the time it takes place, subsequent events do not, or do not necessarily, alter that status. In *Gordian Holdings Ltd v* Sofroniou,[46a] a Cypriot bank had obtained judgment against a debtor. Shortly thereafter the debtor transferred his shareholding in a company to his wife. The bank was plainly a 'victim' for the purposes of s.423 following the transfer. The return of the shareholding to the husband did not deprive the bank of victim status, and an application to strike out the bank's claim failed. The Court could not be sure that further relief would not be granted, including payment of a sum of money if the value of the shareholding had been affected, for example.

[46a] [2021] EWHC 235 (Comm).

(6) The Claim and the Relief

16–040 *At the end of footnote 54, add:*

And see *Gordian Holdings Ltd v Sofroniou*, above.

16–041 *At the end of the paragraph, add:*

For an example of how an order under s.423 can interplay with a property adjustment order within the Matrimonial Causes Act 1973 s.24, and the approach the Court will take in such hybrid situations, see *Akhmedova v Akhmedov.*[55a]

[55a] [2020] EWHC 2235 (Fam).

16–044 *At the end of the paragraph, add:*

The decision was upheld on appeal.[59a] The Court of Appeal held "it was for the Judge to fashion the remedy that, in her discretion, she considered would best restore the position to what it would have been if the May dividend had not been paid and best protect the interests of the victims."

[59a] [2019] EWCA Civ 112; [2019] 2 All E.R. 784, at [88].

C. FALSE OR MISLEADING LISTING PARTICULARS OR PROSPECTUSES

(4) Potential Claimants

16–061 *At the end of the paragraph, add:*

It includes an investor who held securities through a chain of intermediaries, who can be a claimant, even though he would not have any direct proprietary interest in the underlying security: the "'right to the right' which the investor has via the custody chain is, or can be equated to, an equitable property right in respect of the securities, and this is sufficient."[86a]

[86a] *SL Claimants v Tesco plc* [2019] EWHC 2858 (Ch), per Hildyard J at [79].

Chapter 17

AN INTRODUCTION TO THE KEY CONCEPTS

B. The Key Principles Distinguished

(1) Attribution

At the end of footnote 2, add: **17–005**

and, to a lesser extent, in *Singularis Holdings Ltd (In Liquidation) v Daiwa Capital Markets Europe Ltd* [2019] UKSC 50; [2020] A.C. 1189 (both building on and explaining the leading case: *Meridian Global Funds Management Asia Ltd v The Securities Commission* [1995] 2 A.C. 500).

(3) Piercing the Corporate Veil

At the end of footnote 8, add: **17–007**

The clarity provided by *Prest* has—to some extent—been undermined by the Supreme Court's subsequent decision in *Rossendale Borough Council v Hurstwood Properties (A) Ltd* [2021] UKSC 16; [2021] 2 W.L.R. 1125, in which the Court has called into question (for the future, but without deciding the point now) whether the doctrine really exists, notwithstanding the very recent conclusion in *Prest* that it does. Nevertheless for the present, at least, *Prest* remains good law: the doctrine does exist and is defined and confined as the Supreme Court held in that case.

CHAPTER 18

PIERCING THE CORPORATE VEIL

A. INTRODUCTION

(1) What is "Piercing the Corporate Veil"?

Add new paragraphs 18–003A to 18–003C after 18–003:

It is nevertheless necessary to note at the outset of this chapter that the clarity provided by *Prest* has—to some extent—been undermined by the Supreme Court's subsequent decision in *Rossendale Borough Council v Hurstwood Properties (A) Ltd.*[11a] Perhaps somewhat unhelpfully, that case has called into **18–003A** question (for the future, but without deciding the point now) whether the doctrine really exists, notwithstanding the very recent conclusion in *Prest* that it does.

[11a] *Rossendale Borough Council v Hurstwood Properties (A) Ltd* [2021] UKSC 16; [2021] 2 W.L.R. 1125.

18–003B In *Rossendale*,[11b] Lord Briggs and Lord Leggatt—giving a judgment with which the remainder of the Court agreed—referred to the brief judgment of Lord Walker of Gestingthorpe in *Prest*, in which he effectively declined to endorse the majority's analysis and said:

> "for my part I consider that piercing the corporate veil is not a doctrine at all, in the sense of a coherent principle or rule of law. It is simply a label often, as Lord Sumption JSC observes, used indiscriminately to describe the disparate occasions on which some rule of law produces apparent exceptions to the principle of the separate juristic personality of a body corporate reaffirmed by the House of Lords in *Salomon v A Salomon & Co Ltd* [1897] AC 22. These may result from a statutory provision, or from joint liability in tort, or from the law of unjust enrichment, or from principles of equity and the law of trusts... They may result simply from the potency of an injunction or other court order in binding third parties who are aware of its terms. If there is a small residual category in which the metaphor operates independently no clear example has yet been identified."[11c]

Of that passage, Lords Briggs and Leggatt observed: "[a]lthough this is not the occasion for reaching any final view, we are inclined to share Lord Walker's doubts".[11d] Having done so, the Court then proceeded both to give some further guidance on the *Prest* test and to apply the *Prest* analysis to the case at hand.

[11b] *Rossendale*, above, at [71].
[11c] *Prest*, above, at [106].
[11d] *Rossendale*, above, at [71].

18–003C Accordingly, for the present, at least, *Prest* remains good law: the doctrine does exist and is defined and confined as the Supreme Court held in *Prest*. But it is fair to say that the warning note struck by the Court in *Rossendale* introduces unwanted uncertainty for litigators, who will be left wondering in any given case in which the doctrine is relied upon whether it will turn out to be the case in which the Supreme Court may choose—in the end—to abolish the doctrine altogether. There is no help for that, other than to be aware of the position and the risks it creates for litigants.

C. PIERCING THE CORPORATE VEIL: THE PRINCIPLES AND ITS ELABORATION

(1) The Basic Principle: The "Evasion Principle"

18–015 *After the first sentence, add:*

That is the approach which the lower courts—and indeed the Supreme Court in *Rossendale*—have taken: treating Lord Sumption's exegesis as representing the current state of the law.

(2) The Critical Distinction: Evasion vs. Concealment

Add new paragraph 18–029A after para.18–029:

As the Supreme Court observed in *Rossendale*,[59a] one consequence of the points in the preceding two paragraphs is that there is apparently no room for reliance on the "evasion principle" to impose upon the shareholder controller of a company a fresh liability incurred by a company (as distinct from its shareholder controller). That is: whilst the evasion principle may justify holding a company to, or liable for breach of, an obligation owed by its controlling shareholder, there appears to be no scope for applying the principle "in the opposite direction" so as to hold a person who owns or controls a company liable for breach of an obligation which has only ever been undertaken by the company itself. **18–029A**

[59a] *Rossendale*, above, at [68]–[73].

After sub-paragraph (4), insert new sub-paragraph (4a): **18–031**

(4a) It follows that there appears to be no scope for applying the principle "in the opposite direction" so as to hold a person who owns or controls a company liable for breach of an obligation which has only ever been undertaken by the company itself.

*Replace the heading "**(3) Other Examples of the Principles in Practice: The Decision in Prest and VTB v Nutritek**" with:*

(3) Other Examples of the Principles in Practice: The Decisions in Prest, VTB v Nutritek and Rossendale

At the end of footnote 68, add: **18–035**

Alvarez v Moor [2019] EWHC 1774 (QB) (at [117]–[119]) offers another example of the same type.

Add new paragraphs 18–035A to 18–035C after para.18–035:

Rossendale Borough Council v Hurstwood Properties (A) Ltd[68a] concerned defendants who were the registered owners of unoccupied commercial properties on which non-domestic rates were payable, under relevant legislation, by the "owner of the hereditament", statutorily defined as "the person entitled to possession" of the hereditament. In order to avoid liability for such rates, the defendants leased the hereditaments to special purpose vehicle companies, without any assets or business, which were then voluntarily wound up, so as to trigger the winding-up exemption to non-domestic rates, or allowed to be struck off the register of companies as dormant companies and thus dissolved, so that the leases and liability for rates passed as bona vacantia to the Crown. The leases were not shams, so that as a matter of real property law they conferred an entitlement to possession upon the SPVs. The claimant local authorities brought claims seeking recovery of non-domestic rates from the defendants, contending that: (i) the legislation should be given a purposive interpretation so that "owner" meant someone with a "real" entitlement to possession, which in the present cases would be the defendants; and (ii), alternatively, the court could pierce the **18–035A** corporate veil of the SPVs so that the defendants would be treated as the true owners of the hereditaments for the purposes of the statute.

[68a] *Rossendale Borough Council v Hurstwood Properties (A) Ltd* [2021] UKSC 16; [2021] 2 W.L.R. 1125.

18–035B The Supreme Court disposed of the case by finding for the claimant local authorities on ground (i)—i.e. the question of statutory interpretation—holding that "owner" did indeed mean something wider than simply the person with an immediate right to possession under the leases as a matter of real property law. But the Court also dealt with the alternative veil-piercing argument on the assumed basis—contrary to the Court's actual decision—that "owner" meant only the person with an immediate right to possession in property law: i.e., in this case (from the dates of the various leases), only the SPVs.

18–035C The argument ran as follows: on the assumed facts, the defendants interposed companies under their control solely in order to avoid a liability for business rates that would in each case, but for the company's separate legal personality, be a liability of the defendant; that was, it was argued, an abuse of the separate legal personality of the SPV which would justify the court in piercing the corporate veil to deprive the defendant of the advantage that it would otherwise have obtained by the SPV's separate legal personality in accordance with the evasion principle in *Prest*. Lords Briggs and Leggatt were scathing in their rejection of it,[68b] as being precisely the sort of case which Lord Sumption had stated in *Prest* did not engage the evasion principle: namely one where a shareholder/controller caused a liability to be incurred by a company in the first place, rather than seeking to evade a pre-existing liability of the shareholder/controller. Because liability for non-domestic rates accrues from day to day, from the date of the grant of the leases, all the defendants were doing was causing the liability for those rates (on the assumed basis as to the effect of the legislation) to be incurred by the SPVs rather than themselves. That was not the evasion of a pre-existing liability of the defendants;[68c] nor was it an abuse of the separate legal personality of the SPVs if that was the effect of the relevant legislation. What *was* abusive was the way in which the SPVs' liability for rates was subsequently sought to be frustrated (by the dissolution or liquidation of the SPVs), but—so said the Court—the law provides comprehensive remedies for such abusive behaviour which do not require piercing the corporate veil.

[68b] *Rossendale*, above, at [73]–[76].

[68c] Indeed, such pre-existing liability of the defendants as there was—i.e. their liability for rates for the days up until the granting of the leases of the SPVs—remained, under the legislation, exactly where it was and always had been: a liability of the defendants.

D. THE FUTURE POST-PREST IN THE FRAUD CONTEXT

(1) An Increasing Willingness to Apply the Concealment Principle?

18–036 *At the end of footnote 69, add*:

; *R v Forte (Michael)* [2020] EWCA Crim 1455; [2021] 4 W.L.R 26.

At the end of the first sentence, add new footnote 70a: **18–037**

[70a] If, following *Rossendale*, the Supreme Court were ultimately to abolish the veil-piercing doctrine, that would seem likely to encourage any such trend.

Add new paragraph 18–040A after para.18–040:

Since those two *Ablyazov* cases, time has indeed proved the concealment principle, and Lord Sumption's dictum at [52] in *Prest* in particular, popular tools in resolving fraud cases with issues as to the true ownership of assets: see, taking just the very recent examples, *National Bank Trust v Yurov*;[76a] *JSC VTB Bank v Shurikhin*;[76b] *Cobussen Principal Investment Holdings Ltd v Akbar*;[76c] *R v Forte (Michael)*;[76d] and *In re Smith: The Serious Fraud Office v Litigation Capital Limited*.[76e] **18–040A**

[76a] [2020] EWHC 100 (Comm) (especially at [1365] and following).
[76b] [2020] EWHC Civ 1337; [2021] 1 W.L.R. 434.
[76c] [2020] EWHC 2805 (QB).
[76d] [2020] EWCA Crim 1455; [2021] 4 W.L.R 26
[76e] [2021] EWHC 1272 (Comm) (especially at [604] and following).

CHAPTER 19

ATTRIBUTION

A. INTRODUCTION

(3) The Scope and Focus of this Chapter

At the end of the last sentence in the paragraph, add: **19–011**

And, in any event, the principles applicable to the company context provide guidance more generally: see e.g. *Sandham t/a Premier Metals Leeds v Revenue and Customs Commissioners*.[9a]

[9a] *Sandham t/a Premier Metals Leeds v Revenue and Customs Commissioners* [2020] UKUT 193 (TCC); [2020] STC 1682, a case relating to attribution in a partnership context, per Miles J at [14].

B. THE "RULES" OF ATTRIBUTION

(1) The Basic Principle

19–012 *At the end of the paragraph, add new footnote 9b*:

[9b] As to the precise relevance of "factual circumstances", see paras 19–025a and 19–025b below.

(2) The Leading Case: Meridian Global

19–015 *At the end of the first paragraph of the quotation from Meridian Global, add new footnote 14a*:

[14a] But note—as explained in *Julien v Evolving Tecknologies and Enterprise Development Co Ltd* [2018] UKPC 2; [2018] B.C.C. 376—the limits of this principle. It does not follow from this that the *knowledge* of all the shareholders (or even a sole shareholder) is automatically attributed to the company, even where there can be no attribution of the knowledge of the directors (because, e.g., the legal context in which the attribution question arises is one where the company is suing delinquent directors—see further Section C below).

19–016 *At the end of footnote 16, add*:

; *Julien v Evolving Tecknologies and Enterprise Development Co Ltd* [2018] UKPC 2; [2018] B.C.C. 376, per Lord Briggs at [46].

*Replace the heading "**(2) Understanding Meridian Global**" with the heading*:

(3) Understanding Meridian Global

Add new paragraphs 19–025A and 19–025B after para.19–025:

19–025A Accordingly, from *Meridian Global* emerges the cardinal importance of the legal context in which a question of attribution arises to the determination of that attribution question. The point was underlined by Miles J in *Sandham t/a Premier Metals Leeds v Revenue and Customs Commissioners*,[23a] a case relating to the rules of attribution to be employed when determining whether a partnership knew or should have known that certain transactions were connected to the fraudulent evasion of VAT for the purposes of liability under the *Kittel* principle.[23b] In rejecting a series of submissions relating to the general factual and procedural circumstances of the case said to bear on the attribution question, Miles J highlighted that Lord Hoffmann's analysis in *Meridian Global* focuses on the construction of the legal context in order to determine questions of attribution; and rejected the idea that the consideration of that question involves any kind of general analysis of overall "fairness".[23c] The cases do consider the factual circumstances when addressing attribution questions,[23d] but that consideration is directed not at an overall "what's fair in all the circumstances" type analysis, but at working out what, on the facts of the particular case, the legal context requires in terms of a rule of attribution.

[23a] *Sandham t/a Premier Metals Leeds v Revenue and Customs Commissioners* [2020] UKUT 193 (TCC); [2020] STC 1682.

[23b] *Kittel v Belgium, Belgium v Recolta Recycling SPRL (Joined cases C-439/04 and C-440/04)* EU:C:2006:446; [2006] E.C.R. I-6161; [2008] STC 1537: enshrining the principle that a person who enters into transactions that are connected with the fraudulent evasion of VAT either knowing, or having

the means of knowing, that the transactions are so connected, is not entitled to credit for associated input tax.

[23c] *Sandham*, above, at [14], [15] and [19].

[23d] A good example is to be found in *Re Bank of Credit and Commerce International SA (No 15), Morris v Bank of India* [2005] EWCA Civ 693; [2005] 2 B.C.L.C. 328, considered in detail in section B.(5) below.

Similarly to be rejected—it would appear—is the idea that context other than that extant or arising at the time the claim arose is relevant. In *Aquila Advisory Limited v The Crown Prosecution Service*,[23e] Mann J rejected the contention that the relevant "context" for determining attribution could include events subsequent to those giving rise to the claim, such as a subsequent prosecution, confiscation order, and the fact that the CPS now had an interest in the relevant property as well as the company etc. Were it otherwise, Mann J held, the answer to the attribution question in any given case might vary across time, which he did not consider could be correct.[23e] **19–025B**

[23e] *Aquila Advisory Limited v The Crown Prosecution Service* (*Crown Prosecution Service v Aquila Advisory Ltd*; sub nom. *Aquila Advisory Ltd v Faichney*) [2018] EWHC 565 (Ch).

[23e] *Aquila Advisory Ltd v The CPS*, above, at [56]. (Neither the Court of Appeal nor the Supreme Court directly addressed this point in these terms in their subsequent judgments in this case discussed further below.)

*Replace the heading "**(3) The General Rules of Attribution in the Law of Agency**" with the heading*:

(4) The General Rules of Attribution in the Law of Agency

*Replace the heading "**(4) The Interaction Between the Three Sources of "Rules of Attribution" Identified in Meridian Global**" with the heading*:

(5) The Interaction Between the Three Sources of "Rules of Attribution" Identified in Meridian Global

At the end of footnote 26, add: **19–029**

; *Financial Conduct Authority v Da Vinci* [2015] EWHC 2401 (Ch); [2016] 3 All E.R. 547, at [112]–[115].

At the end of footnote 31, add: **19–031**

In *Goyal v Florence Care Limited* [2020] EWHC 659 (Ch), Morgan J's treatment of this question presents as a little confused—but he did not, and did not need to, resolve the attribution question fully in order to dispose of the case, and it appears that he did not have very full assistance in relation to the case law on attribution, such that his very incomplete treatment of the question is probably best put to one side.

Add new paragraph 19–031A after para.19–031:

Another way of capturing this concept may be the idea—reflected in the judgment of Lords Toulson and Hodge in *Bilta*[36a] and very recently emphasised by Miles J in the *Sandham* case[36b]—that the legal context (i.e. the nature and subject matter of the relevant rule or duty in which the question of attribution arises) is relevant to all three of Lord Hoffmann's categories of rules of attribution (not just the third **19–031A** category, special rules of attribution). In that sense, there is an artificiality in suggesting that the process the Court goes through in seeking to identify the right rule of attribution is different in each of the three categories: in all cases the question is simply "whose act, knowledge or state of mind is for the relevant purpose to count as the act etc of the company (or other principal)"? It is just that, having been through the process, sometimes one of the "general" rules of attribution (either primary or agency-based principles) will meet the case, and other times a different "bespoke" rule will be needed to identify whose actions, knowledge or state of mind is relevant.

[36a] *Bilta*, above, at [191].
[36b] *Sandham*, above, at [15].

*Replace the heading "**(5) Examples of the Rules of Attribution in Fraud Claims**" with the heading:*

(6) Examples of the Rules of Attribution in Fraud Claims

19–035 *At the end of the second sentence, add new footnote 38a:*

[38a] Similar analysis can be discerned—in a criminal context—in *Serious Fraud Office v Barclays Plc* [2018] EWHC 3055 (QB); [2020] 1 Cr. App. R. 28. The question was whether Barclays Bank had the necessary *mens rea* for the commission of offences of conspiracy to commit fraud and unlawful financial assistance pursuant to s. 151 of the Companies Act 1985 arising out of large loans made by the bank to the State of Qatar, during the 2008 financial crisis, which had then been used to fund capital investment in the bank. The SFO's case was that certain senior officers of the bank had the required *mens rea* and that it should be attributed to the bank. In this case, the analysis of whose state of mind was to "count" for the relevant purpose in fact led to the application of the general rules of attribution (either the primary rules of attribution in the company context and/or those derived from the ordinary law of agency): the basic holding was that the guilty officers were not the directing mind and will for the purposes of the relevant transaction because they did not have unfettered authority, in form or in substance, "to do the deal". The decision to enter into the relevant transaction was—in essence—that of a sub-committee of the board; and it was that sub-committee's (innocent) state of mind which was to be attributed. Thus—in that sense—there was no need to fashion a "special" rule of attribution to deal with the case: the general rules of attribution relating to decision making by the board (or its sub-committee) sufficed to provide an answer. But, nevertheless, the Court still went through the process of identifying—in accordance with the guidance in *Meridian* and applying *Tesco v Nattrass* (as explained in *Meridian*)—who, in this legal context, was the relevant directing mind and will for the purpose of the relevant transaction. In that sense, the process involved the same analytical machinery as would identify a "special rule"—it is just that the answer to the question in this case was, in effect, an organ of the company to whom the general rules of attribution already applied. The case is good example of the point discussed in paras 19–031 and 19–031A above in operation. Another is provided by the decision of Snowden J in *Financial Conduct Authority v Da Vinci* [2015] EWHC 2401 (Ch); [2016] 3 All E.R. 547 at [112]–[115]. In that case, the question was what is the correct approach to attribution in the context of whether a company had been engaged in market abuse under s.118 of the Financial Services and Markets Act 2000. Having considered the nature of the legal test for *mens rea* under s.118, and in light of both the policy behind the Act and the nature of modern trading on regulated markets, the Judge concluded that the question could be answered simply by reference to the general rules of attribution which are derived from the laws of agency. He attributed the behaviour of the relevant individual traders (who were agents of the relevant company for the purposes of the relevant transactions) to the company accordingly.

C. HAMPSHIRE LAND AND THE "FRAUD EXCEPTION"

(1) Introduction and Origin

In the first sentence, replace the phrase "nor is not confined to fraud" with: **19–044**

nor is it confined to fraud

At the end of footnote 51, add:

See also *Sandham*, above, at [17].

At the end of footnote 61, add: **19–046**

(as Lady Hale has subsequently put it in *Singularis Holdings Ltd (In Liquidation) v Daiwa Capital Markets Europe Ltd* [2019] UKSC 50; [2020] A.C. 1189, at [34]).

(2) The Correct Approach: Moulin and Bilta

(i) Liability cases

At the end of the paragraph, add: **19–052**

Further examples post-*Bilta* are *Mobile Sourcing Ltd v Revenue and Customs Commissioners*[68a] and the *Sandham* case.[68b]

[68a] *Mobile Sourcing Ltd v Revenue and Customs Commissioners* [2016] UKUT 274 (TCC).
[68b] *Sandham*, above.

(ii) Redress cases

At the end of footnote 70, add: **19–054**

The same is true of a situation where the director's default was intended to, or did, benefit the company itself: see *The Crown Prosecution Service v Aquila Advisory Limited* [2021] UKSC 49, especially at [70]–[75].

After the penultimate sentence of footnote 71, add:

The Supreme Court in *Singularis* did not address the question of the definition of a "one man" company directly, although Lady Hale's exposition at [31]–[33] is consistent with the Court of Appeal's formulation. She nevertheless raised—but did not answer—difficulties about what was meant by "innocent" in this context.

Add new paragraphs 19–055A and 19–055B after para.19–055:

The post-*Bilta* case of *CPS v Aquila*[75a] is a further example. In this case, an attempt was made to distinguish *Bilta*. The CPS contended that it was entitled to enforce its claim under a confiscation order made against the fraudulent directors of a company in priority to the company's own proprietary claim against those same directors for breach of duty under the principles in *FHR European Ventures LLP v Makarious*.[75b] In order to do so, it was necessary to contend that the fraud of the directors should be attributed to the company so as to debar the company's claim under the illegality principle. That proposition, obviously unpromising in light of *Bilta*, was rejected on that basis: there was nothing which took the case outside the **19–055A** scope of the "redress" category of cases in the specific legal context at hand (i.e. the claim under *FHR* arising out of the breach of duty to the company).[75c] Neither the point that the company's claim sought to recover (at least in some sense) what might be characterised as "the proceeds of crime" or was connected to criminal activity, nor the more general *ex post facto* context of the prosecution and the confiscation order[75d] were sufficient basis on which to distinguish *Bilta*).[75e] More specifically, the Supreme Court firmly rejected the CPS's attempt to re-introduce the notion from the pre-*Bilta* case law that the "fraud exception" to attribution should only apply where the company was in some sense a "victim" of the director's wrong-doing. The central insight of the *Bilta* decision is that the attribution question in redress cases depends on the identity of the parties between whom that question arises (company and director) and the nature of the duty (owed by the director to his company), not on whether the company was intended to, or did, benefit from the dishonest conduct of the director.[75f] As Lord Stephens explained in *CPS v Aquila*: "[t]he purpose of the [director's duty] itself means that the company cannot be identified with its officers [in relation to claim by the company for breach of the director's duty]".[75g]

[75a] At first instance: *Aquila Advisory Limited v The Crown Prosecution Service* [2018] EWHC 565 (Ch); in the Court of Appeal: *The Crown Prosecution Service v Aquila Advisory Limited* [2019] EWCA Civ 588; in the Supreme Court: *The Crown Prosecution Service v Aquila Advisory Limited* [2021] UKSC 49.

[75b] *FHR European Ventures LLP v Makarious* [2015] A.C. 250; discussed generally in Ch.9, at paras 9–068—9–072.

[75c] Lord Stephens—with whom the rest of the Supreme Court agreed—specifically held that the reasoning in *Bilta* applied equally to a case where the company's claim against the defaulting director was for gains made by the director (as well as to the case where the claim was for losses suffered by the company): *The Crown Prosecution Service v Aquila Advisory Limited* [2021] UKSC 49, at [71].

[75d] See para.19–025b above.

[75e] *Aquila Advisory Limited v The Crown Prosecution Service* [2018] EWHC 565 (Ch), per Mann J at [38]–[57]; *The Crown Prosecution Service v Aquila Advisory Limited* [2019] EWCA Civ 588, per Patten LJ at [13]–[28]; *The Crown Prosecution Service v Aquila Advisory Limited* [2021] UKSC 49, per Lord Stephens at [63]–[81].

[75f] See *Bilta*, above, generally and, for example, at [93].

[75g] *The Crown Prosecution Service v Aquila Advisory Limited* [2021] UKSC 49, at [71].

19–055B The Privy Council case of *Julien v Evolving Tecknologies*[75e] was a redress case in which the key point was whether a company's claim against delinquent directors was time barred under the provisions of limitation statutes. That depended on when it could be said that the company had knowledge of the relevant breaches of duty by the directors, which in turn depended on attribution. It was agreed—following the basic model of a redress case—that the knowledge of the guilty directors could not be attributed to the company. But it was argued that the knowledge of the sole shareholder (who was not also a defendant director) should instead be attributed to the company, so as to defeat the claim on limitation grounds. The point was argued both as a general rule of attribution—i.e. that there is a general rule that, where there can be no attribution of the knowledge of the company's directors, then attribution of (sole) shareholder knowledge should follow automatically—and as a special rule of attribution in relation to sole shareholders in the context of the relevant provisions of the Limitation Act. In an illuminating discussion of the *Meridian* principles, Lord Briggs—writing for the Board—rejected the first basis: there is no such general rule of attribution.[75f] As to the second basis—the special rule of attribution in the context of the Limitation Act—there was no need to reach a conclusion on the evenly balanced arguments on the facts of the *Julien* case: but Lord Briggs indicated that the Board would have been inclined to hold that no such special rule of attribution existed, adhering to the simple rule that shareholder knowledge of a breach of duty owed to the company by its directors, or the ability to discover the facts relevant to that breach of duty, is not to be attributed to the company for the purposes of limitation, at least for so long as the delinquent directors retain control of it.[75g] Some of the reasons for that view were generally applicable to attribution of shareholder knowledge, but others were linked to the specific limitation context; so care must be taken when extrapolating from Lord Briggs' (provisional) view in the context of limitation to other possible scenarios.

[75e] *Julien v Evolving Tecknologies and Enterprise Development Co Ltd* [2018] UKPC 2; [2018] B.C.C. 376.
[75f] *Julien v Evolving Tecknologies*, above, at [43]–[55].
[75g] *Julien v Evolving Tecknologies*, above, at [57]–[62].

(iii) Other cases

At the end of footnote 78, add: **19–058**

and [91]; and per Lady Hale in *Singularis Holdings Ltd (In Liquidation) v Daiwa Capital Markets Europe Ltd* [2019] UKSC 50; [2020] A.C. 1189, at [36].

At the end of the paragraph, add: **19–059**

, a point which the Supreme Court considered significant in *Singularis Holdings Ltd (In Liquidation) v Daiwa Capital Markets Europe Ltd.*[81a]

[81a] See *Singularis Holdings Ltd (In Liquidation) v Daiwa Capital Markets Europe Ltd* [2019] UKSC 50; [2020] A.C. 1189, at [36].

Replace the passage after the quotation from Lord Sumption in Bilta, to the end of the paragraph, with: **19–060**

That dictum of Lord Sumption appears to be of general application—not limited to "one-man" cases,[83a] and not necessarily limited to auditor cases. Nevertheless, no other Justice specifically endorsed this view (even in the "one-man" context),[84] and attempts to suggest that it represents the law, outside the auditor context and even in the "one-man" company case, have already been rejected at first instance, in the Court of Appeal and, in the Supreme Court.[85] Indeed, in *Singularis*,[85a] the Supreme Court has expressly stated the general proposition that there is no principle of law that in any proceedings where the company is suing a third party for breach of a duty owed to it by that third party, the fraudulent conduct of a director is to be attributed to the company if it is a one-man company. Rather, in all such proceedings—including those in which the third party is an auditor—the position will depend on the exact legal and factual context. In the auditor context, that will include (as Lord Sumption himself conceded) exactly what the auditor undertook to do and what the scope of his legal duty was as a matter of law, a point which Lady Hale emphasised in *Singularis*.[85b]

[83a] Although his observations at [80], as summarised by Lord Neuberger at [26] (i.e. "the [illegality] defence is not available where there are innocent shareholders (or, it appears, directors)"), may have been intended to exclude cases not involving "one-man" companies.
[84] Indeed, other relevant Justices made it quite clear that they regarded attribution to be appropriate (and therefore the illegality defence to be available) in only *some* situations in which there were no

innocent shareholders or directors: see e.g. *Bilta*, above, at [26] and the discussion of this issue in *Singularis Holdings Ltd (in official liquidation) v Daiwa Capital Markets Europe Ltd* [2018] EWCA Civ 84, especially at [46] and [56]–[59], in the Court of Appeal; and [2019] UKSC 50; [2020] A.C. 1189, at [29]–[34], in the Supreme Court.

85 *Singularis*, above, discussed further below.

85a *Singularis*, above, at [34].

85b *Singularis*, above, at [36]: Lady Hale observed that, in general terms, "the auditor's duty is to report on the company's accounts to those having a proprietary interest in the company or concerned with its management and control. If the company already knows the true position (as in *Berg*) then the auditor's negligence does not cause the loss". Although that dictum might be said to confuse—or at least mingle—different lines of analysis, it would nevertheless appear that, in this auditor's negligence context, the distinction between "true" "one-man" companies (i.e. ones where there are no innocent shareholders or directors to whom an auditor might report) and other principals may continue to be a major factor in determining the outcome of cases.

Add new paragraph 19–064A after para.19–064:

19–064A As already canvassed above, in the Supreme Court,[96a] Lady Hale (with whom the rest of the Court agreed) concurred with Rose J and the Court of Appeal that Singularis was not a "one man" company in the relevant sense. But—more importantly—she agreed that, again "in any event",

> "there is no principle of law that in any proceedings where the company is suing a third party for breach of a duty owed to it by that third party, the fraudulent conduct of a director is to be attributed to the company if it is a one-man company";[96b]

and that

> "the answer to any question whether to attribute the knowledge of the fraudulent director to the company is always to be found in consideration of the context and the purpose for which the attribution is relevant".[96c]

Lady Hale affirmed Rose J's conclusion on attribution based on the legal context of the present case—the *Quincecare* duty—emphasising both (i) that the content of that duty was different from that owed by e.g. an auditor and (ii) that a company is a separate legal personality whose assets are not owned by its shareholders, and that it is possible for even a sole shareholder to steal from his own company.[96d]

96a *Singularis*, above

96b *Singularis*, above, at [34].

96c *Singularis*, above, at [34].

96d *Singularis*, above, at [35]–[37].

CHAPTER 20

JOINT LIABILITY IN TORT

A. INTRODUCTION

(1) Joint and Several Tortfeasors

Replace the final sentence with: **20–001**

A claimant should, therefore, give consideration to whether joint tortfeasorship allows the liability of one tortfeasor to be extended to a third party, and not only seek to employ causes of action, such as the tort of unlawful means conspiracy, that entail a form of primary, rather than secondary, wrongdoing. That being said, in many instances a claim to joint tortfeasorship will add little, if anything, to a claim in unlawful means conspiracy.

Replace the first sentence of footnote 1 with: **20–002**

See generally M.A. Jones and A.M. Dugdale (eds), *Clerk & Lindsell on Torts*, 23rd edn (London: Sweet & Maxwell 2020), para.4–02.

Replace footnote 3 with:

See M.A. Jones and A.M. Dugdale (eds), *Clerk & Lindsell on Torts*, 23rd edn (London: Sweet & Maxwell 2020), paras 4–07 and following. For example, a settlement agreement that discharges the liability of a tortfeasor, and does not only contain a covenant on the part of the victim not to sue, will also discharge the liability of a joint tortfeasor unless the victim has reserved the entitlement to sue the joint tortfeasor: see, e.g., *Gladman Commercial Properties v Fisher Hargreaves Proctor* [2013] EWCA Civ 1466, [2014] C.P. Rep. 13, in which the Court of Appeal declined to imply in the settlement agreement a reservation of the right to sue the joint tortfeasors.

Before "Civil Liability (Contribution) Act 1978" add "the".

(2) Types of Joint Tortfeasorship

20–003 *Insert at the beginning of the paragraph*:

The law of joint tortfeasorship is not peculiar to the tort of deceit; its principles are the same for all torts.

20–004 *Delete footnote 6.*

B. JOINT TORTFEASORSHIP THROUGH ASSISTANCE

(5) Types of Joint Tortfeasorship

20–019 *Delete the word "joint or" in the first sentence of the paragraph.*

CHAPTER 21

DAMAGES

B. GENERAL PRINCIPLES

(2) The Tortious and the Contractual Measure

21–004 *Replace the second and third sentences with:*

Whereas the purpose of an award of damages in tort is to restore the claimant's position to what it would have been absent the wrong, the law of contract seeks to place the claimant in the position he would have been in had the defendant fulfilled his contractual obligations. Damages in tort for fraudulent misrepresentation are not awarded on the counterfactual that the misrepresentation was, in fact, true.

C. THE POSITION IN DECEIT CLAIMS: THE BASIC MEASURE

(3) The Primary Measure: Price Paid Less Value Received

Add new paragraph 21–014A after para.21–014:

21–014A The onus of proving loss, so as to make out the claim to damages for deceit, lies on the claimant. However, where a defendant claims that credit for some benefit must be given in computing that loss, the burden lies on the defendant to prove both the amount of the credit and that it is a credit that is properly to be taken into account.[23a] Where the act induced by a misrepresentation or other tort is the entry into a contract, the *prima facie* loss suffered by the victim is the full purchase price paid by them under the contract.

[23a] *Parallel Imports (Europe) Ltd v Radivan* [2007] EWCA Civ 1373, per Wall LJ at [29], [34]–[35] (per curiam) (where the judge at first instance had wrongly held that the onus of proof lay on the innocent party to prove that the fraudster was not entitled to retain the purchase price that it was induced to pay for the purchase of motor vehicles). See also *OMV Petrom SA v Glencore International AG* [2017] 3 All E.R. 157, per Christopher Clarke LJ at [88] (Kitchin and Black LJJ agreeing); *Midco Holdings Limited v Piper* [2004] EWCA Civ 476, per Tuckey LJ at [24] (Peter Gibson LJ and Sir Martin Nourse agreeing); *Barker v Winter* [2018] EWHC 1785 (QB), per HHJ Rawlings at [26]–[28]. Compare *Hughes-Holland v BPE Solicitors* [2018] A.C. 599, per Lord Sumption at [53] (per curiam) (albeit a case of negligent misstatement rather than deceit).

(5) Sale of Assets

21–033 *At the end of the paragraph, add new footnote 60a:*

[60a] The reasoning of the Court of Appeal in this case has nonetheless been questioned: see Burrows, *Remedies for Torts, Breach of Contract, and Equitable Wrongs* (4th edn, OUP 2019) 224–5. The Court of Appeal has treated the judgment as binding, but suggested that it may be confined to its "very special facts": *Inter Export LLC v Townley* [2018] EWCA Civ 2068, per Arden LJ at [60], [65]–[67] (Kitchin LJ and Birss J agreeing).

D. FURTHER LIMITING PRINCIPLES

Add new heading and paragraphs 21–046A and 21–046B after para.21–046:

(4) No "Reflective Loss"

Where a company has been the victim of a wrong that depletes its assets, the consequent diminution in the value of a shareholder's shares or a reduction in the distributions that the company may make to a shareholder are not a form of loss for which the shareholder may obtain a remedy against the wrongdoer. In that instance, the shareholder's loss is merely "reflective" of the loss to the company and it is ordinarily the company that is the proper party to sue on a cause of action in respect of it. However, there may be loss suffered by a shareholder, distinct from the loss suffered by the company that a shareholder with a personal claim against a wrongdoer may sue to recover.[85a] **21–046A**

[85a] See, e.g., *Smith New Court Securities Ltd v Citibank N.A.* [1997] A.C. 254.

The ambit of the reflective loss principle had been uncertain until, in *Sevilleja v Marex Financial Ltd*, the Supreme Court restated the reflective loss principle in the narrow way described above.[85b] However, even this narrow statement of the reflective loss principle barely survived: a sizeable minority of three judges in that case considered that the reflective loss principle should be abandoned altogether in favour of a combination of valuation principles that avoid double-recovery and active case management by the Court.[85c] **21–046B**

[85b] [2020] UKSC 3; [2020] 3 W.L.R. 255, per Lord Reed at [79]–[89] (Lady Black and Lord Lloyd-Jones agreeing; Lord Hodge concurring). The facts of this case are described at para.4–035. The Supreme Court notably overruled a number of judgments of the Court of Appeal and part of the judgment of the House of Lords in *Johnson v Gore Wood & Co (a firm)* [2002] 2 A.C. 1.

[85c] *Sevilleja Marex*, above, per Lord Sales at [143] and [156] (Lord Kitchin and Lady Hale agreeing).

E. LOSSES OTHER THAN PURCHASE (OR SALE) PRICE

(5) Lost Profits on Alternative Transaction

Add new sub-heading "(i) The general principle" before paragraph 21–057

At the end of the paragraph, add: **21–058**

When the court assesses the loss that was suffered by the claimant, it does so on a "no-transaction" basis.

Delete paragraph. **21–061**

Delete the text "Another more recent example" and replace it with "A recent example". **21–062**

Add new sub-heading and paragraphs 21–062A to 21–062C after para.21–062:

(ii) Loss on alternative transaction where actual transaction profitable

21–062A A claimant that made a good bargain, despite the deceitful inducement to enter into the contract, may nonetheless suffer loss for which he may be awarded a remedy in damages. In *Clef Aquitaine SARL v Laporte Materials (Barrow) Ltd*,[105a] the Court of Appeal held that a claimant could recover their lost profit on a hypothetical alternative transaction even where the transaction entered into by reason of the defendant's deceit was itself profitable. In that case, the claimant was able to do so because it established that, but for the deceit, the claimant would have negotiated more favourable contractual terms than it in fact did and that those more favourable terms would have resulted in the claimant earning a greater profit.

[105a] [2001] Q.B. 488.

21–062B At first blush, the reasoning in this case may appear to re-write the traditional principles for measuring the loss that was suffered by the innocent claimant. However, once the substantive analysis of the court is broken down into its constituent parts, it is evident that the court merely applied traditional principles in a different but nonetheless correct way. In substance, the court began with the (usual) no-transaction measure to determine the loss suffered by the claimant as a result of entering into the transaction. Where a claimant makes a "good" bargain notwithstanding the deceit (as they had in that case), the claimant has suffered no loss and, in fact, is ordinarily required to give credit for the benefits that they have received as a result of entering into the transaction. It is the next step in the court's reasoning that involved a degree of novelty. The court may then go on to award damages on a hypothetical alternative transaction that the claimant would have entered into if the misrepresentation had not been made. In the more common case, the alternative transaction is with a third party, but in *Clef Aquitaine SARL v Laporte Materials (Barrow) Ltd*, the hypothetical alternative transaction was with the same counterparty (that is, the fraudster).

21–062C The reasoning of the Court of Appeal in this case should not, therefore, be misunderstood as an invitation to a fraudster to seek to argue that the claimant would have entered into the same transaction on different terms, so that the court need only ask: 'what are those different terms?' and award damages in a modest amount to account for the difference.[105b] To the contrary, as Lord Denning MR observed in *Doyle v Olby (Ironmongers) Ltd*:

> "The person who has been defrauded is entitled to say: 'I would not have entered into this bargain at all but for your representation."[105c]

That is to say, the claimant is always entitled to compensation for direct loss measured as the difference between what has been lost by the transaction itself and what has been gained. It is only if the claimant elects to pursue a claim for consequential losses—which is, of course, a decision for the claimant rather than the defendant—that questions as to what the claimant might have done if they had not entered into the fraudulent transaction arise and further damages may be awarded.

[105b] See *Glossop Cartons and Print Ltd v Contact (Print & Packaging) Ltd* [2021] EWCA Civ 639; [2021] 1 W.L.R. 4297.

[105c] [1969] 2 Q.B. 158, at 167, which was quoted with approval in *Smith New Court Securities Ltd v Citibank NA* [1997] AC 254, per Lord Browne-Wilkinson at 264 and per Lord Steyn at 281.

Add new sub-heading "(iii) Evidence of loss" before paragraph 21–063

Delete the second sentence, and add: **21–063**

The particular evidence that it will be necessary for a claimant to adduce to make out a claim to damages for the loss of an opportunity to enter into an alternative transaction will depend on the circumstances. However, in general terms, a claimant should seek to evidence both the specific alternative transaction or opportunities to transact that were lost and the reason why the claimant, having been induced by the representation, was unable to take up the alternative transaction.[105d] Where the claimant has committed capital as part of a transaction, it is relatively straightforward to infer that, if they had not entered into the induced transaction, they would have exploited the capital in another way for their own benefit. However, as described already, it is not necessary in all instances to identify a specific alternative transaction that the claimant would have entered into if the misrepresentation had not been made. Indeed, it may be the case that, although it is clear that a claimant would have entered into an alternative transaction of a similar kind, the alternative transaction that they would have entered into cannot be determined with any specificity.

[105d] *First Tower Trustees Ltd v CDS (Superstores International) Ltd* [2018] EWCA Civ 1396; [2019] 1 W.L.R. 637, per Lewison LJ at [34] (Colin Rimer agreeing).

(6) Loss of Income and Prospect of Capital Appreciation

Replace "made" with "make". **21–067**

In footnote 112, replace "47" with "477". **21–069**

(9) Aggravated and Exemplary Damages

At the end of the paragraph, add: **21–077**

In either case, a claimant who seeks such damages must specifically plead a claim to them in their Particulars of Claim and cannot seek to claim such damages as part of a general claim to "damages".[123a]

[123a] CPR 16.4(1)(c). Although a claimant should, as a matter of best practice, also identify a claim to damages of these kinds in the Claim Form where they are claimed, the Civil Procedure Rules do not require an express plea in the way that they do of the Particulars of Claim.

Before the full-stop at the end of footnote 124, add: **21–078**

, per Peter Pain J at 425–6. See also *Banks v Cox* [2002] EWHC 2166 (Ch), at [13] and [31], in which Lawrence Collins J awarded damages in a claim in deceit in the amount of £10,000 as compensation for a depressive illness. Compare *Barker v Winter* [2018] EWHC 1785 (QB), at [67]–[69], in which HHJ Rawlings declined to award aggravated damages for the "significant distress" caused by the tortfeasor because the claimant had contributed to the distress that she had suffered, as if there were a notion of contributory fault relevant to the decision to award aggravated damages.

21–079 *Replace the third sentence of the paragraph with:*

Awards of damages have recently been made in claims in deceit by an insurer against defendants involved in making fraudulent insurance claims in relation to fabricated road accidents.

At the beginning of footnote 127, add:

AXA Insurance UK plc v Financial Claims Solutions Ltd [2018] EWCA Civ 1330;

F. CONTRIBUTORY NEGLIGENCE

(1) Introduction

21–080 *At the beginning of the paragraph, add:*

Fraud claims are commonly pursued alongside claims that have a non-fraudulent basis. So, a director pursued for having acted fraudulently in misappropriating company property may also be pursued for having acted negligently. It is, therefore, worth digressing, briefly, into the law of contributory negligence, although it is not a defence or partial defence to the intentional wrongs that are the primary subject of this book.

CHAPTER 22

EQUITABLE REMEDIES: RESCISSION, ACCOUNT OF PROFITS, COMPENSATION & FORFEITURE

A. INTRODUCTION

(1) The Remedies Considered in this Chapter

22–003 *Replace the first sentence with*:

There are three other potentially relevant equitable remedies which deserve mention: (a) injunction, (b) specific performance; and (c) rectification.[2]

[2] Declarations are sometimes said to be equitable remedies, but they are probably better regarded as being a creature of statute; and they are in any event of limited relevance in the fraud context.

(3) Accounting as a "Remedy"

(i) *Accounting for funds*

22–009 *Replace footnote 10 with*:

[10] *Libertarian Investments Ltd v Hall* [2014] 1 H.K.C. 368 (CFA), per Lord Millett PJ at [168]. See also *Sinclair Investments (UK) Ltd v Versailles Trade Finance Ltd* [2011] EWCA Civ 347; [2012] Ch. 453, per Lord Neuberger MR at [45]; and *Auden McKenzie (Pharma Division) Ltd v Patel* [2019] EWCA Civ 2291; [2020] B.C.C. 316, at [34].

22–018 *At the end of the paragraph, insert new footnote 28a*:

[28a] As for example in *Auden McKenzie (Pharma Division) Ltd v Patel* [2019] EWCA Civ 2291; [2020] B.C.C. 316, at [36]. There was no need for the company to seek judgment on its claim for an account before seeking summary judgment on its claim for equitable compensation.

22–019 *At the end of footnote 30, add:*

; and *Fairford Water Ski Club Ltd v Cohoon* [2020] EWHC 290 (Comm), per HHJ Russen QC at [113]–[135], similarly suggesting that the principle applies whenever the fiduciary "held the purse strings".

(ii) *Account of profits*

At the end of the second sentence, insert new footnote 30a: **22–020**

[30a] An account of profits is a "true remedy for a breach of fiduciary duty" and not to be confused with the sort of account that sets up some other remedy: *Goyal v Florence Care Ltd* [2020] EWHC 659 (Ch), per Morgan J at [41].

(4) "Clean Hands"

Add new paragraph 22–027A after para.22–027:

Where a claimant sues as assignee of a claim, it is the conduct of the assignor that is relevant to the "clean hands" maxim, not that of the claimant.[42a] **22–027A**

[42a] *Davies v Ford* [2020] EWHC 686 (Ch).

B. RESCISSION

(1) Introduction: Rescission and Other Concepts Distinguished

Replace footnote 53 with: **22–031**

[53] See P.G. Watts (ed), *Bowstead and Reynolds on Agency*, 22nd edn (London: Sweet & Maxwell, 2021), art.23 and the comment on it (3–012).

At the end of footnote 57, add: **22–032**

But the voidness is only in equity; and so in the context of certain powers (e.g. those to create legal property, such as allotting shares in a company) an improper purpose will only render the exercise voidable: *Stobart Group Ltd v Tinkler* [2019] EWHC 258 (Comm), at [453]–[488].

(3) Grounds

Replace footnote 60 with: **22–036**

[60] See *BV Nederlandse Industrie Van Eiprodukten v Rembrandt Enterprises Inc* [2019] EWCA Civ 596; [2020] Q.B. 551; and, more generally, Ch.1, para.1–116 (in this supplement).

At the end of footnote 66, add:

(not considered on appeal at [2019] EWCA Civ 88); see also *Wood v Commercial First Business Ltd* [2021] EWCA Civ 471; [2021] 3 W.L.R. 395, at [99]–[101].

(4) Exercise of the Right to Rescind

At the end of footnote 76, add: **22–041**

The authorities on the question were said to be in "such a state of disarray that…only the Supreme Court can reconcile them" by Henderson LJ in *Revenue and Customs Commissioners v IGE USA Investments Ltd* [2021] EWCA Civ 534; [2021] 3 W.L.R. 313, at [91].

(5) Rescission Where Wrongdoing is not by a Party to the Transaction

22–046 *At the end of the first sentence, add new footnote 82a:*

[82a] The use of the term "fiduciary" in this context needs to be read in light of the Court of Appeal decision in *Wood v Commercial First Business Ltd* [2021] EWCA Civ 471; [2021] 3 W.L.R. 395. In short, for relief (such as rescission) with respect to a bribe or fully secret commission to lie, what is required is that the bribed "agent" should owe a duty to give disinterested information, advice or recommendations, and it is not necessary to go further and determine whether that is properly to be characterised as a fiduciary duty. Where the commission is only "half-secret", however, it seems that a fiduciary relationship is required for rescission to lie: *Hurstanger Ltd v Wilson* [2007] EWCA Civ 299; [2007] 1 W.L.R. 2351.

(6) Affirmation and Acquiescence

22–049 *At the end of footnote 88, add:*

As to knowledge of the facts giving rise to the right, what is needed is knowledge of the facts one would need to plead the case (but not all aspects of incidents of those facts). As to knowledge of the legal right, the law does not require certainty that the claim is a good one, but a "basis for belief in the claim". There is no rule that such knowledge will be inferred whenever a party has the benefit of legal advice; it is a fact sensitive question. See *Leeds City Council v Barclays Bank plc* [2021] EWHC 363 (Comm); [2021] 2 W.L.R. 1180, per Cockerill J at [173]–[175], [199], [207]–[208].

(7) Restitutio in Integrum

22–054 *At the end of footnote 100, add:*

It has been held that there is no requirement as such for *restitutio in integrum* to be possible for a voluntary disposition to be rescinded for mistake; rather, it is a consideration that goes towards the overall evaluation of whether it would be unjust, unfair or unconscionable to leave the disposition in place: *Rogge v Rogge* [2019] EWHC 1949 (Ch), at [162]–[175].

(8) Rescission and Title to Money and Property

22–064 *At the end of the first sentence of footnote 125, add:.*

; *Global Currency Exchange Network Ltd v Osage 1 Ltd* [2019] EWHC 1375 (Comm); [2019] 1 W.L.R. 5865, at [40]–[48].

(11) No Partial Rescission

22–073 *After the second sentence, add:*

This principle applies not just to single contracts, but also to commercially interdependent contracts which form part of an indivisible bargain: the underlying principle is that the rescinding party should not be allowed to rewrite the parties' bargain by picking which parts of the transaction to perform.[148a]

[148a] *Marme Inversiones 2007 SL v Natwest Markets Plc* [2019] EWHC 366 (Comm), per Picken J at [332]–[338].

At the end of footnote 149, add:

See also *MacKay v Wesley* [2020] EWHC 3400 (Ch).

C. ACCOUNT OF PROFITS

(1) Introduction and Bases

In the second sentence, after the semi-colon, insert footnote 149a: **22–074**

[149a] For this reason the remedies of an account of profits and equitable compensation are inconsistent and a claimant must elect between the two (where both are available against a given defendant): *Tang Man Sit v Capacious Investments* [1996] 1 A.C. 514, at 520–21. But that may not be so where the remedies are sought against different defendants, for different wrongs: *FM Capital Partners v Marino* [2018] EWHC 2905 (Comm), per Cockerill J at [88]–[92], and *Davies v Ford* [2021] EWHC 2550 (Ch), per David Holland QC at [227]–[229].

Replace footnote 154 with: **22–076**

[154] See paras 22–089—22–093.

(2) The Relationship Between Profit and Breach: As Against the Fiduciary

At the end of footnote 156, add: **22–078**

Note the caution about the second listed point sounded by the Court of Appeal in *Gray v Global Energy Horizons Corporation* [2020] EWCA Civ 1668; [2021] 1 W.L.R. 2264, at [125]–[127]: the remedy of an account of profits is a stringent one, intended to operate as a deterrent, and if an unauthorised profit falls within the scope of the fiduciary's duty, it does not matter that requiring him to account for it confers a benefit on the principal which he would not otherwise have been able to reap.

At the end of the paragraph, add: **22–080**

The benefits for which the fiduciary must account do not, however, extend to his agreed remuneration payable by the principal: if the fiduciary is to be precluded by reason of a breach of fiduciary duty from receiving or retaining that, it must be under the separate principles governing forfeiture of remuneration.[159a]

[159a] *HPOR Servicos de Consultoria LTDA v Dryships Inc.* [2018] EWHC 3451 (Comm). See Section E of this chapter.

In footnote 163, replace the reference to Global Energy Horizons with: **22–083**

Keystone Healthcare Ltd v Parr [2019] EWCA Civ 1246; [2019] 4 W.L.R. 99, per Lewison LJ at [18]; *Gray v Global Energy Horizons Corporation* [2020] EWCA Civ 1668; [2021] 1 W.L.R. 2264, at [128].

At the end of the first sentence of footnote 164, add:

; *Keystone Healthcare Ltd v Parr* [2019] EWCA Civ 1246; [2019] 4 W.L.R. 99, per Lewison LJ at [19].

Add new paragraph 22–084A after para.22–084:

Similarly, it is of course irrelevant that the profit which the fiduciary has made is not one which, but for the breach of duty, the principal would have made, and that the breach has caused the principal no loss.[166a] So, in one case, the Court of Appeal held it to be no bar to an account of profits that the profit which a defaulting director had made would, but for his breach, have been made by the claimant's holding company rather than the company of which he was a director.[166b] **22–084A**

[166a] See Ch.11, paras 11–095-11–096.

[166b] *Keystone Healthcare Ltd v Parr* [2019] EWCA Civ 1246; [2019] 4 W.L.R. 99.

Add new paragraph 22–086A after para.22–086:

22–086A Because an account of profits is a means of enforcing the fiduciary's duty of loyalty (it is properly a remedy, and not just—as with an account of funds—a means of ascertaining the quantum of some other remedy), it is something which is available to the beneficiary "virtually as of right" and should not be refused merely because (for example) it would be disproporitionate.[171a] That said, like any equitable remedy, it can be refused on the usual equitable grounds.

[171a] *Goyal v Florence Care Ltd* [2020] EWHC 659 (Ch), per Morgan J at [31]–[50]. The position is different where an account of profits is ordered against a non-fiduciary: see para.22–093 below.

(4) Account as Against Dishonest Assister/Knowing Recipient

22–092 *At the end of footnote 181, add:*

; *Tuke v Hood* [2020] EWHC 2843 (Comm), at [161]–[175].

(7) Deductions and Allowances

22–100 *At the end of footnote 195, add:*

See also *Davies v Ford* [2020] EWHC 686 (Ch), at [396]–[401].

D. EQUITABLE COMPENSATION

(1) Introduction

22–104 *At the end of footnote 203, add:*

; see also *Davies v Ford* [2021] EWHC 2550 (Ch), per David Holland QC at [92]–[110].

(2) The Decision in AIB Group and the Causation Requirement

Add new paragraph 22–113A after para.22–113:

22–113A In addition, it was held in *Giambrone* that for the solicitors to be liable to pay equitable compensation for their breach of trust the loss had to be "within the scope of" their duty and not excluded by the principles derived from *SAAMCO*[216a]—a transposition of a limitation from contract law, reflecting the fact that the fiduciary/trust obligations of the solicitors ran in tandem with their contractual obligations ("the trust was part of the machinery for the performance of the solicitors' contract of retainer").[216b] That test was satisfied, because the solicitors were guiding the claimants' whole decision-making process in relation to the transaction, and explained that the claimants would be protected by the guarantees, before paying the deposits away without the guarantees in place. In contrast, in *LIV Bridging Finance Ltd v EAD Solicitors LLP* it was held that *SAAMCO* / scope of duty principles did limit the equitable compensation payable, in a case where loan monies were paid away without a first charge, so as to exclude from recovery losses that the claimant would have suffered even had a first charge been obtained.[216c]

[216a] *Giambrone*, above, at [84]–[87]; for the *SAAMCO* principles, see the speech of Lord Sumption in *Hughes-Holland v BPE Solicitors* [2017] UKSC 21; [2018] A.C. 599 and see further *Manchester Building Society v Grant Thornton UK LLP* [2021] UKSC 20; [2021] 3 W.L.R. 81.
[216b] *Giambrone*, above, at [63].
[216c] [2020] EWHC 1590 (Ch), at [65].

(3) Application to Other Fiduciaries

Add new paragraph 22–114A after para.22–114:

The point came up for consideration by the Court of Appeal in the recent case of *Auden McKenzie (Pharma Division) Ltd v Patel*.[225a] There a director sought to resist summary judgment in the full amount of sums paid out to himself and associates under sham invoices (and so in breach of fiduciary duty), on the grounds that the payments could and would have been paid lawfully as dividends to the director and his associates as shareholders. The Court of Appeal accepted that *Target* and *AIB* were authority for the proposition that equitable compensation should put the beneficiary (i.e. the company) back into the position it would have been in had there been no breach, and so should take account of what the position would have been if the fiduciary had properly performed his duties. This could take into account actual events which had occurred and which established that the loss would have occurred even but for the breach (as in *Target*), as well as hypothetical events which would have occurred if the fiduciary had fully performed his obligations (as in *AIB*); but there was nothing in those authorities to justify going further and taking into account hypothetical alternative transactions (e.g. lawful dividends) that the fiduciary was under no obligation to effect.[225b] It was also held that the authorities on compensation for unlawful dividends (in the full amount paid away) could not be distinguished.[225c] Thus although the "but for" causation question did indeed have to be asked when assessing equitable compensation for the misapplication of company assets, in answering that question the court was constrained (at least on existing authorities) to focus on what would have happened had the fiduciary performed his duties, and not to stray further into hypotheticals. Nevertheless, the Court of Appeal reversed the summary judgment below and allowed the defence to proceed to trial: *Target* and *AIB* did at least demonstrate a willingness on the part of the courts "to develop the equitable remedies for breach of trust and breach of fiduciary duty and, where required to do what is practically just, to entertain some departure from the strict obligation of trustees and fiduciaries to restore the fund under their control." This was therefore a developing area of law and not one suitable for summary determination.[225d] **22–114A**

[225a] [2019] EWCA Civ 2291; [2020] B.C.C. 316.
[225b] *Auden McKenzie v Patel*, above, at [44]–[49].
[225c] *Auden McKenzie v Patel*, above, at [58].
[225d] *Auden McKenzie v Patel*, above, at [60]–[64].

In footnote 224, replace the reference to Gower with: **22–118**

P. Davies, S. Worthington and C. Hare, *Gower: Principles of Modern Company Law,* 11th edn (London Sweet & Maxwell, 2021), at para.10–106.

(5) Equitable Compensation and the "Core" Fiduciary Dealing Rules

22–126 *At the end of the paragraph, add new footnote 237a:*

[237a] See also *Davies v Ford* [2021] EWHC 2550 (Ch), a diversion of corporate opportunity case, where it was held that the award of equitable compensation should reflect the fact that in the counterfactual world (but for the breaches of fiduciary duty) the company to which the directors owed their duties would have ceased trading in any event by a certain point.

(8) Interest

22–130 *At the end of the first sentence, insert new footnote 243a:*

[243a] See paras 22–087—22–088.

At the end of the first sentence, insert new sentence:

Additionally, the Court has a well-established equitable jurisdiction to award compound rather than simple interest in any case where money has been obtained by fraud; but the jurisdiction should not be exercised outside these two categories of case.[243b]

[243b] *President of India v. La Pintada Compania Navigacion S.A.* [1985] A.C. 104, at 116; *Westdeutsche Landesbank Girozentrale v Islington LBC* [1996] AC 669, at 701C–702E; *LIV Bridging Finance Ltd v EAD Solicitors LLP* [2020] EWHC 1908 (Ch), at [7].

Add new paragraph 22–130A after para.22–130:

22–130A Where equitable compensation is awarded against a defaulting trustee (or person in an analogous position) with respect to losses to the trust fund, the principles applicable are not the same as those which apply against commercial or arms-length parties:[244a] the deprived fund would not have borrowed the missing monies to deploy in business, nor would it have placed them on deposit; it would have invested them. Accordingly, in such a case interest should be awarded at a rate which reflects an appropriate investment return (including capital return), rather than a borrowing or deposit rate.[244b] By contrast, where equitable compensation is awarded against a fiduciary other than for the misapplication of pre-existing trust or corporate assets, the *Carrasco* principles (which essentially look to the rate at which the claimant could have borrowed the amounts lost) are applicable.[244c]

[244a] As to which, *see Carrasco v Johnson* [2018] EWCA Civ 87, per Hamblen LJ at [17]–[18].
[244b] *Watson v Kea Investments Ltd* [2019] EWCA Civ 1759; [2019] 4 W.L.R. 145.
[244c] *Davies v Ford* [2021] EWHC 2550 (Ch), per David Holland QC at [211]–[212].

(9) Equitable Compensation and Dishonest Assistance/Knowing Receipt

Add new paragraph 22–132A after para.22–132:

22–132A Where equitable compensation is ordered against a knowing recipient, the principles concerning awards of interest in equity against defaulting trustees—including in particular the award of interest at an investment rate, rather than a borrowing or deposit rate—usually apply (since although a knowing recipient is not a trustee, he is accountable in equity as if he were).[249a] For the same reason, an award of compound interest in equity can be made against a knowing recipient or a dishonest assistant who is not himself a fiduciary.[249b]

[249a] *Watson v Kea Investments Ltd* [2019] EWCA Civ 1759; [2019] 4 W.L.R. 145, per McCombe LJ at [40]. See that case generally for an examination of the relevant principles.
[249b] *FM Capital Partners Ltd v Marino* [2019] EWHC 725 (Comm), per Cockerill J at [27]–[35], applying *Central Bank of Ecuador v Conticorp SA* [2015] UKPC 11, at [185].

E. FORFEITURE OF REMUNERATION

(2) The Basis for and Scope of the Remedy

At the end of footnote 256, add: 22–135

See also *Staechelin v ACLBDD Holdings Ltd* [2019] EWCA Civ 817, at [69]–[94] (although note the doubt that the non-disclosure in that case even amounted to a breach of fiduciary duty).

CHAPTER 23

EQUITABLE PROPRIETARY REMEDIES

B. What Property is Subject to the Claim?

(2) Following and Tracing

(i) Nature of following and tracing

23–006 *At the end of the paragraph, add:*

Indeed, it has been held that a judgment creditor with no proprietary interest may be able to invoke the principles of following and tracing in order to establish a rebuttable presumption as to the consequences of transactions between the judgment debtor and a third party in relation to property over which it seeks a charging order.[1a]

[1a] *National Bank Trust v Yurov* [2020] EWHC 1779 (Comm).

(ii) Equitable title to follow or trace in equity

23–009 *At the end of footnote 5, add:*

See *Scott v Bridge* [2020] EWHC 3116 (Ch), at [125]–[131], for an application of that principle to exclude a tracing remedy in circumstances where a payment had been received and invested in property in the mistaken belief it was a gift.

23–011 *At the end of the first sentence, add new footnote 7a:*

[7a] See the case of the outright thief, addressed at para.9–062 above.

(iv) Identification of property by following and tracing

23–014 *At the end of the first sentence, add new footnote 9a:*

[9a] For a case where a tracing claim (if otherwise sustainable) would have failed simply due to paucity of evidence to reconstruct the relevant transactions, see *Dhir v Flutter Entertainment plc* [2021] EWHC 1510 (QB), at [185] and following.

At the end of the paragraph, add:

Obviously (and as appears in detail from the principles set out below), the process of following or tracing may involve numerous elections by a claimant as to which asset to follow or trace into in each relevant transaction: the best view appears to be that such elections need only be made at the point of judgment and the claimant can keep its options open until then.[12a]

[12a] *Serious Fraud Office v Hotel Portfolio II UK Ltd* [2021] EWHC 1273 (Comm), at [49]–[52].

Replace footnote 13 with: **23–016**

[13] In the rarer situation where there is a physical mixture of tangible trust property with other tangible property (for examples two sets of fungibles placed in the same container or two sets of raw materials combined in manufacturing a finished product) the position is unclear; it may well be that similar principles would apply, but it may be that equity would in some instances follow the common law rules applicable to such mixtures: see the discussion in L.Tucker, N. Le Poidevin and J. Brightwell, *Lewin on Trusts*, 20th edn (London: Sweet & Maxwell, 2020), paras 44–094—44–097. Issues arising from the transfer and issuance of shares have received somewhat more attention in the authorities and are helpfully discussed in *Lewin* at 44–098.

At the end of the paragraph, add: **23–020**

In *Serious Fraud Office v Hotel Portfolio II UK Ltd*, a wholesale attack was made on the traditional rule and was rejected by Foxton J, who summarised the current state of the law as follows on the basis of an extensive review of the authorities:

> "I have concluded that present state of English law is that backwards tracing into assets acquired prior to the misuse of trust assets is not permitted, save in certain narrow (but, for all that, soft-edged and overlapping) exceptions where a strict insistence on chronological sequence would fail to reflect the substance of the position. For those who might object that this involves "break[ing] down the cases into different factual categories" and thereby "deconstruct[ing] the law into a fissiparous bundle of distinct rules" (cf. Lord Sumption's observation in *Belhaj v Straw* [2017] UKSC 3; [2017] A.C. 964, [227]), it can be said that while this approach might be deprecated when identifying and formulating rules, it is in the very nature of exceptions to an otherwise general rule, and that the recognition of such exceptions should not inexorably require the re-visiting of the rule.
>
> On the basis of the authorities to date, these exceptions include:
>
> i) cases where the payment of money through the banking network for the purpose of effecting a payment from A to B involves credits occurring before debits;
> ii) cases in which the debit of trust property and the credit to be traced into were effected as part of a single transaction intended to achieve that outcome through a series of co-ordinated elements, whatever the chronological ordering of those elements (indeed it might be suggested that the only difference between i) and ii) is that in the former, the chronological issues arise as a consequence of ministerial or administrative acts, whereas in the latter they may sometimes form part of what Lord Toulson JSC referred to as the "choreography");
> iii) cases of anticipatory substitution as discussed by Arden LJ in *Relfo*, where an asset is acquired on the basis of an undertaking that the trust property will be exchanged for it (as, in due course, it is); and
> iv) conventional bilateral exchange transactions where the respective transfers are not simultaneous (e.g. Professor Smith's example of the car sale where the price is payable after property in the car passes)."[29a]

[29a] [2021] EWHC 1273 (Comm), at [45]–[46].

(vi) *Creation of fresh constructive trust as an alternative to following/tracing*

Replace footnote 36 with: **23–024**

[36] See L. Tucker, N. Le Poidevin and J. Brightwell, *Lewin on Trusts*, 20th edn (London: Sweet & Maxwell, 2020), paras 44–018, 44–053—44–056.

(3) Loss of Beneficial Interest and Priorities

(iii) The bona fide purchaser for value of the legal estate without notice

23–029 *Replace footnote 41 with:*

[41] See discussion, for instances, in L. Tucker, N. Le Poidevin and J. Brightwell, *Lewin on Trusts*, 20th edn (London: Sweet & Maxwell, 2020), at paras 44–138 and following.

Replace footnote 47 with:

[47] *Barclays Bank v O'Brien* [1994] 1 A.C. 180, at 195–196, per Lord Browne-Wilkinson, as applied in *Bishopsgate v Homan*, above, at 1000. In the application of that test, a body of technical rules apply in relation to transactions in land (see L. Tucker, N. Le Poidevin and J. Brightwell, *Lewin on Trusts*, 20th edn (London: Sweet & Maxwell, 2020), paras 44–129 and following). In relation to other transactions, the test is applied by asking what a reasonable person in the recipient's position would have understood or done, taking into account their past experience, any expert advice available and any routine procedures followed in transactions of the type in question: *Sinclair Investments v Versailles* [2011] EWCA Civ 347; [2012] Ch 453, at [97]–[109]; *Credit Agricole Corp and Investment Bank v Papdimitriou* [2015] UKPC 13; [2015] 1 W.L.R. 4265. Until put on enquiry, he is entitled to assume that he is dealing with honest people: *Bishopsgate v Homan*, above, at 1014.

(vi) Foreign law priority rules in respect of foreign situated property

23–033 *At the end of footnote 52, add:*

But query whether this can be so where the property never became subject to a proprietary interest in the first place under the relevant foreign law, or where the applicable law would not allow of proprietary relief: see *Dhir v Flutter Entertainment plc* [2021] EWHC 1510 (QB), at [180] and [184].

At the end of footnote 53, add:

See also *Byers v Samba Financial Group* [2020] EWHC 60 (Ch) and *Dhir v Flutter Entertainment plc* [2021] EWHC 1510 (QB).

C. PURSUING EQUITABLE PROPRIETARY CLAIMS

(1) The Nature of the Proprietary Claim

(iv) What proprietary interest may the claimant assert?

23–045 *Replace footnote 67 with:*

[67] *Boscawen v Bajwa* [1996] 1 W.L.R. 328; *Banque Financiere de la Cite v Parc (Battersea) Ltd* [1999] 1 AC 221; *Cheltenham & Gloucester v Appleyard* [2004] EWCA Civ 291; *Menelaou v Bank of Cyprus plc* [2016] AC 176. For a fuller account of the law of subrogation, see (for example) chapter 39 of C. Mitchell, P. Mitchell and Watterson, *Goff & Jones: The Law of Unjust Enrichment* (2016) and C. Mitchell's *The Law of Subrogation* (Oxford: Clarendon Press, 1994). The recent reconsideration of that law by the Supreme Court in *Menelaou* may have reduced the need to rely upon a strict process of following / tracing in order to invoke the remedy.

(2) Defences

(ii) A defence of "change of position" or "windfall"

Replace footnote 69 with: **23–049**

[69] *Lipkin Gorman v Karpnale* [1992] A.C. 548. See more generally Ch.27 of C. Mitchell, P. Mitchell and Watterson, *Goff & Jones: The Law of Unjust Enrichment* (2016).

Replace footnote 70 with:

[70] See the academic controversy raging in Birks (2001) 54 CLP 231; Burrows (2001) 117 LQR 412; Smith (2000) 116 LQR 412; G. Virgo, *The Principles of the Law of Restitution*, 2nd edn (Oxford: OUP, 2006), p.569 and following; C. Mitchell, P. Mitchell and Watterson, *Goff & Jones: The Law of Unjust Enrichment* (2016), para.27–55; L. Tucker, N. Le Poidevin and J. Brightwell, *Lewin on Trusts*, 20th edn (London: Sweet & Maxwell, 2020), paras 44–060—44–061; C Mitchell, D.J. Hayton and P. Matthews, *Underhill & Hayton Law of Trusts and Trustees*, 19th edn (London: LNUK, 2016), paras 90.6–90.9; and G. Thomas and A. Hudson *The Law of Trusts* (Oxford: OUP), para.33.93 and following.

(iii) "Unclean hands" and the "ex turpi cause" / illegality doctrine

At the end of footnote 76, add: **23–051**

In *Ball v De Marzo* [2019] EWHC 1587 (Ch), at [36]–[53], the relationship between the two doctrines was considered but left open.

(v) Credit to the defendant trustee for his contributions to the property

Replace footnote 77 with: **23–053**

[77] *Re Johnson* (1880) 15 Ch.D. 548; *Smith v Dale* (1881) 18 Ch.D. 516, at 518; *Re Knott* (1887) 56 LJCH 318. See L. Tucker, N. Le Poidevin and J. Brightwell, *Lewin on Trusts*, 20th edn (London: Sweet & Maxwell, 2020), Ch.19 for a detailed commentary on the right to indemnity.

Replace footnote 78 with:

[78] *Rowley v Ginnever* [1897] 2 Ch 503; and see the analysis of the older cases in L. Tucker, N. Le Poidevin and J. Brightwell, *Lewin on Trusts*, 20th edn (London: Sweet & Maxwell, 2020), para.19–038.

Replace footnote 80 with: **23–054**

[80] *Re Duke of Norfolk's Settlement* [1982] Ch. 61; *Re Berkeley Applegate Ltd (No 2)* (1988) 4 BCC 279, and many other authorities. See the fuller analysis in L. Tucker, N. Le Poidevin and J. Brightwell, *Lewin on Trusts*, 20th edn (London: Sweet & Maxwell, 2020), para.20–049 and following.

Replace footnote 84 with: **23–055**

[84] See (briefly) Ch.22 and the summary of the relevant law in L. Tucker, N. Le Poidevin and J. Brightwell, *Lewin on Trusts*, 20th edn (London: Sweet & Maxwell, 2020), para.10–079 and following.

(3) Remedies

(ii) Consequential relief where the claimant(s) is (or are) entitled to the whole of the property

23–059 *Replace footnote 90 with:*

[90] The so-called rule in *Saunders v Vautier* (1841) 4 Beav 115. See the fuller treatment in Ch.22 of L. Tucker, N. Le Poidevin and J. Brightwell, *Lewin on Trusts*, 20th edn (London: Sweet & Maxwell, 2020).

23–064 *Replace footnote 105 with:*

[105] For a fuller consideration of vesting orders under the 1925 Act, see Ch.17 of L. Tucker, N. Le Poidevin and J. Brightwell, *Lewin on Trusts*, 20th edn (London: Sweet & Maxwell, 2020).

CHAPTER 24

ILLEGALITY

A. INTRODUCTION

(2) The 250 Years following Holman v Johnson

24–004 *Replace the first sentence with*:

That opportunity arose in *Patel v Mirza*;[12] and—subject to two increasingly minor caveats—the mess has now been tidied up by the Supreme Court.

[12] *Patel v Mirza* [2016] UKSC 42; [2017] A.C. 467.

(3) The Position Post-Patel: Summary

Replace paragraph 24–006 with:

24–006 The two caveats—considered in more detail in section C.(5) below—are, first, the extent to which pre-*Patel* case law is relevant to—and, crucially, the extent to which *Patel* is binding on—lower courts considering cases in which illegality issues arise; and, secondly, the extent to which there remains uncertainty in how, in any particular set of circumstances, the courts will apply the guidelines set out in *Patel*. In the immediate aftermath of the *Patel* decision, these were important caveats created by a faulty understanding of the *Patel* decision and its reach by lower courts, but the potential problems have diminished with subsequent interventions from the Supreme Court.

B. WHAT COUNTS AS AN "ILLEGAL OR IMMORAL" ACT?

(3) Conduct Illegal under Foreign Law

Replace paragraph 24–020 with:

24–020 There is a series of cases relating to the enforceability in England of contracts which are illegal under applicable foreign law, illegal under English law but legal under their applicable foreign law or which involve performance in a foreign country under whose law that performance would be illegal: see, in particular, *Ralli Bros v Compania Naviera Sotay Aznar*, [30a] *Foster v Driscoll*[30b] and *Regazzioni v KC Sethia*,[30c] as discussed recently in Hong Kong in *Ryder Industries Limited v Chan Shui Woo*[30d] (in the Hong Kong Court of Final Appeal), and in England at first instance in *Magdeev v Tsvetkov*[30e] and *Haddad v*

Rostamani.[30f] The cases in this long series do not always maintain clearly the distinction between (i) questions of what are the parties' substantive rights under the law applicable to their contractual relations; (ii) principles of public policy based on international comity as to the enforcement of contracts connected to illegality under foreign law; and (iii) the operation of the illegality principle with which we are here concerned. In general, it is suggested that this line of cases is best analysed in the context of discussion of the parties' substantive legal rights under applicable law and the principles of public policy based on international comity in this context: the reader is referred to works on the law of contract in this regard.

[30a] *Ralli Bros v Compania Naviera Sota y Aznar* [1920] 2 K.B. 287.
[30b] *Foster v Driscoll* [1929] 1 K.B. 470.
[30c] *Regazzioni v KC Sethia* [1958] A.C. 301.
[30d] *Ryder Industries Limited v Chan Shui Woo* (2015) 18 HKCFAR 544; [2016] 1 HKC 323.
[30e] *Magdeev v Tsvetkov* [2020] EWHC 887 (Comm).
[30f] *Haddad v Rostamani* [2021] EWHC 1892 (Ch).

Replace paragraph 24–021 with:

Nevertheless, it is right to observe that the illegality principle is a question of English public policy to be applied by the English courts. So, insofar as it can be said that enforcement of a contract with such international elements would engage the interests of the (British) state in the sense described by the Supreme Court in *Apotex*, then the illegality principle could, at least in theory and in appropriate circumstances, bar a relevant claim brought in England. An obvious possible example in the fraud context might be cases which involved the public interest in fighting international corruption (as reflected in the UK's international obligations and/or cooperation in the fighting of corruption) and there have been cases in this category: *Marlwood v Kozeny*[31] is an example. Indeed, *Apotex* itself was a case on the illegality principle involving alleged illegality under foreign law (although the Supreme Court held in the end that the allegedly illegal conduct (infringement of foreign patents) did not "count" for the purposes of the illegality principle, that was not because it was only illegal under foreign law but because patent infringement did not have the requisite quality of illegality or immorality to engage the principle). However, following the judgment of Lord Collins in the Hong Kong case of *Ryder*,[31a] and the two subsequent English cases which have considered it,[31b] it is not at present clear to what extent the Courts are likely in future to apply the analytical framework of the illegality principle to foreign law illegality, rather than that of the doctrine based on international comity flowing out of *Ralli Bros* and *Foster v Driscoll*.[31c] **24–021**

[31] *Marlwood v Kozeny* [2006] EWHC 872 (Comm) per Jonathan Hirst QC, at [133] ("whilst...Mr Kozeny [the claimant] committed no criminal offence in English law, it is abundantly clear that in civil law this corruption would be regarded as immoral and contrary to public policy"). See also *Barros Mattos Junior v. General Securities* [2005] 1 W.L.R. 247, where illegality under foreign law appears to have been enough to engage the illegality principle.
[31a] *Ryder Industries Limited v Chan Shui Woo* (2015) 18 HKCFAR 544; [2016] 1 HKC 323.
[31b] *Magdeev v Tsvetkov* [2020] EWHC 887 (Comm) and *Haddad v Rostamani* [2021] EWHC 1892 (Ch).
[31c] Although it may not make much practical difference. In light of the conclusions of Cockerill J in *Magdeev* at [332] (and [353]) and Zacaroli J in *Haddad v Rostamani* at [86]–[88], it may well be that the application of either line of authority—the illegality principle under *Patel v Mirza* or the *Ralli Bros/ Foster v Driscoll* line—leads to a very similar analytical exercise, and result, in any given set of circumstances.

(4) Post-Patel

24–023 *At the end of the paragraph, insert new footnote 35a:*

[35a] See also in this regard *Henderson v Dorset Healthcare University NHS Foundation Trust* [2020] UKSC 43; [2021] A.C. 563, at [112].

C. THE ILLEGALITY PRINCIPLE

(1) Introduction

24–024 *At the end of the paragraph, add:*

Indeed, as explained in section C.(5)(i) below, previous case law which is "*Patel* compliant" will retain precedential value in explaining how *Patel* "plays out" in certain types of cases.

(4) The New Law: Patel v Mirza

(ii) The reasoning and decision in Patel

24–040 *At the end of footnote 54, add:*

, as subsequent Supreme Court decisions appear to acknowledge is correct: see *Singularis Holdings Ltd (In Liquidation) v Daiwa Capital Markets Europe Ltd* [2019] UKSC 50; [2020] A.C. 1189, at [14] and *Henderson v Dorset Healthcare University NHS Foundation Trust* [2020] UKSC 43; [2021] A.C. 563, at [63].

Add new heading after paragraph 24–049:

(iv) Subsequent Supreme Court decisions: further guidance on the application of Patel

Add new paragraphs 24–049A to 24–049C after para.24–049:

24–049A Unsurprisingly, *Patel v Mirza* has been followed by a number of cases in which the new law has been explored and applied. Several of those cases have risen to the Supreme Court in order that further clarification or guidance could be given as to the application of the *Patel* test. Two are particularly worthy of consideration in that regard here: *Stoffel & Co v Grondona*[66a] and *Henderson v Dorset Healthcare University NHS Foundation Trust.*[66b]

[66a] *Stoffel & Co v Grondona* [2020] UKSC 42; [2021] A.C. 540.
[66b] *Henderson v Dorset Healthcare University NHS Foundation Trust* [2020] UKSC 43; [2021] A.C. 563.

24–049B In each of these cases, the Supreme Court provided additional general guidance on the application of the *Patel v Mirza* test, which may be summarised as follows:

(1) It is important to bear in mind that Lord Toulson's "trio of necessary considerations" are relevant not because it may be considered desirable that a given policy should be promoted, but because of their bearing on

determining whether to allow a claim would damage the integrity of the law by permitting incoherent contradictions: that is where the inquiry is directed (and considerations which go to coherence in the law, and the allied point that a person should not be allowed to profit from his own wrong, will be of very great weight).[66c]

(2) The evaluation of policy considerations, while necessarily structured, must not be permitted to become either another mechanistic process or a mini-trial. In particular, the relevant policy questions should usually be addressed at a level of generality which does not require evidence. The court is not concerned to evaluate the policies in play or to carry out a policy-based evaluation of relevant laws. It is simply seeking to identify the relevant policies to which the law gives effect in general, and then to ascertain whether to allow the claim would be inconsistent with those policies or, where policies compete, where the overall balance lies.[66d]

(3) In considering the key issue of consistency and coherence in the law, the closeness of the connection between the claim and the illegal act may be of relevance. The closer that connection is, the greater and more obvious may be the inconsistency and consequent risk of harm to the integrity of the legal system. Although *Patel* rejected the reliance test, that does not mean that reliance was thereby rendered irrelevant to the policy-based approach: it will still often be a relevant factor.[66e]

(4) The first of Lord Toulson's "trio of considerations" (considering the underlying purpose of the prohibition which has been transgressed) is not limited—in terms of the policy considerations at play—to the specific aim of the particular prohibition in issue. Whilst that is of great importance, other general policy considerations that impact on the consistency of the law and the integrity of the legal system also fall to be taken into account as part of the "underlying purpose" of the relevant prohibition: that is what is required by the policy balancing exercise outlined in Lord Toulson's first two considerations (which are meant to operate "conversely" to one another). So, for example, preventing someone from profiting from his own wrong is a policy going to the coherence of the law which is of great importance, even though it may not be directly engaged by the prohibition transgressed in any particular case: it is nevertheless to be taken into account.[66f]

(5) It may not be necessary in every case to complete an exhaustive examination of all stages of the trio of considerations. If, on an examination of the relevant policy considerations (the first two stages), the clear conclusion emerges that the defence should not be allowed, there will be no need to go on to consider proportionality–Lord Toulson's third consideration: that is because the third consideration is designed to prevent the possibility of "overkill"[66g]; as Lord Hamblen put in *Henderson v Dorset Healthcare*, the third consideration is a disproportionality check on a decision to bar a claim under the illegality principle, not a proportionality requirement that must be satisfied in all cases, either way.[66h]

(6) In considering proportionality at stage (c), by contrast with the policy-based considerations in the first two stages, it is likely that the court will have to give close scrutiny to the detail of the case in hand—which will require evidence. In balancing the range of factors which are relevant to the proportionality limb, the centrality of the illegal conduct to the transaction under consideration will often be a factor of particular importance.

Relatedly, whether there is a causal link between the illegality and the claim, and the closeness of that causal connection, will often be important considerations.[66i]

[66c] *Stoffel*, above, at [26]; *Henderson v Dorset Healthcare*, above, at [121].
[66d] *Stoffel*, above, at [26]; *Henderson v Dorset Healthcare*, above, at [115].
[66e] *Henderson v Dorset Healthcare*, above, at [120].
[66f] *Henderson v Dorset Healthcare*, above, at [116]–[119].
[66g] *Patel*, above, at [101].
[66h] *Stoffel*, above, at [26]; *Henderson v Dorset Healthcare*, above, at [123].
[66i] *Stoffel*, above, at [26]; *Henderson v Dorset Healthcare*, above, at [124].

24–049C In addition to the points of principle distilled above, the last section of *Stoffel* repays careful reading as a "worked example" of the application of the principles in action.[66j]

[66j] *Stoffel*, above, at [27]–[46].

(5) The Caveats

24–050 *At the end of the paragraph, add*:

When they emerged, each of these caveats threatened seriously to undermine the Supreme Court's obvious intention to clarify and simplify the law in this difficult area; but the Supreme Court has either already ironed out these teething problems (in the case of the first caveat), or looks likely shortly to do so (in the case of the second).

Replace the section entitled "(i) To what extent is the Patel approach binding?" (paragraphs 24–051 to 24–054 and footnotes 67 to 71) with:

(i) The extent to which the Patel approach is binding and the relevance of prior authority

24–051 The question of whether the *Patel* approach to the illegality principle is binding might seem a surprising one to raise so soon after the Supreme Court has so plainly sought to re-state the law, sitting as a panel of nine specifically in order to resolve the 250 year controversy as to the proper approach to this difficult area of law. But it was necessitated by the first instance decision in the *Henderson v Dorset Healthcare* case,[67] in which Jay J took a particularly strict view of the doctrines of precedent and stare decisis (what he called giving "full weight" to Lord Halsbury's dictum in *Quinn v Leathem*[68]), limiting (or at least potentially limiting) the application of the new *Patel* approach in cases which gave rise to illegality issues which had previously been considered by the Courts under the old law.

[67] *Henderson v Dorset Healthcare University NHS Foundation Trust* [2016] EWHC (QB) 3275; [2017] 1 W.L.R. 2673.
[68] *Quinn v Leathem* [1901] A.C. 495: "... every judgment must be read as applicable to the particular facts proved, or assumed to be proved, since the generality of the expressions which may be found there are not intended to be expositions of the whole law, but governed and qualified by the particular facts of the case in which such expressions are to be found. The other is that a case is only an authority for what it actually decides. I entirely deny that it can be quoted for a proposition that may seem to follow logically from it" (at 506).

However, as foreshadowed in the first edition of this work, the Supreme Court has acted—quickly but with tact—to steer away from so strict a course. In the appeal in *Henderson v Dorset Healthcare* itself, Lord Hamblen (with whom all 6 other members of the Supreme Court agreed) addressed the application of *Patel*[69] and drew out two critical points in this regard. **24–052**

[69] *Henderson v Dorset Healthcare,* above, at [73]–[78].

First, he made it clear that *Patel* sets the test for the common law illegality principle across civil law generally.[70] **24–053**

[70] *Henderson v Dorset Healthcare,* above, at [76]. This is consistent with the approach taken to the *Patel* decision by the higher courts more generally: see, for example, *Stoffel*, above, at [1]; *Bank St Petersburg PJSC v Arkhangelsky* [2020] EWCA Civ 408; [2020] 4 W.L.R. 55, at [87]; and *Okedina v Chikale* [2019] EWCA Civ 1393; [2019] I.C.R. 1635, at [12].

But, secondly, he explained—again unsurprisingly—that that does not mean that previous case law is entirely redundant. *Patel* is not "year zero", as he put it. Decisions built up in various areas of law to address particular factual situations giving rise to the illegality principle "remain of precedential value unless it can be shown that they are not compatible with the approach set out in *Patel* in the sense that they cannot stand with the reasoning in *Patel* or were wrongly decided in the light of that reasoning."[71] Accordingly, there will be examples of "*Patel* compliant" analysis in previous case law which show "how *Patel v Mirza* plays out in that particular type of case."[71a] **24–054**

[71] *Henderson v Dorset Healthcare*, above, at [77]–[78].
[71a] Per Underhill LJ in *Okedina v Chikale* [2019] EWCA Civ 1393; [2019] I.C.R. 1635, at [62], quoted with approval by Lord Hamblen in *Henderson v Dorset Healthcare,* at [78] (although, even so, it is important to note the qualification as to the proper understanding of Underhill LJ's dictum in the context of the facts of the *Okedina* case, as expressed by Singh LJ in *Robinson v Al-Qasimi* [2021] EWCA Civ 862, at [42]–[57] and then further explained in the context of *Robinson,* at [58]–[70]: Singh LJ's treatment makes it clear that prior authority must be carefully scrutinised for "*Patel* compliance" and to ensure that only those propositions which truly are consistent with the new law are taken from previous decisions in a particular area).

(ii) Does the Patel approach amount to an arbitrary discretion?

At the end of footnote 73, add: **24–056**

; and *Victus Estates (2) Ltd v Munroe* [2021] EWHC 2411 (Ch), at [103], where Morgan J referred to "public morality" as part of the policy consideration mandated by *Patel.*

Replace the final two sentences with: **24–057**

The point was not contested (it was the test put forward by both parties) and, for an evaluative exercise which includes at its heart issues of public policy, it might be thought to be a surprising result. Not wholly unexpectedly, therefore, the point was expressly queried—though not finally determined—by the Supreme Court in the appeal in the *Singularis* case: Lady Hale said that it was not necessary to decide the point in *Singularis*, but that there were cases pending before the Supreme Court in which it "should not be assumed that this Court will endorse the approach of the Court of Appeal". Since then the Court of Appeal has ducked the issue twice (in both *Bank St Petersburg PJSC v Arkhangelsky*[76a] and *Robinson v Al-Qasimi*[76b]); and (as was observed in the latter case) the Supreme Court did not touch on the point in the two illegality cases it has subsequently heard[76c] (which may have been the ones Lady Hale had in mind). Unhelpfully, therefore, the point remains open, in a sense (i.e. even though formally the subject of a decision of the Court of Appeal). The authors venture that the better view, contrary to the concession adopted by the Court of Appeal in *Singularis*, is that the *Patel v Mirza* test does not involve a "discretion" "in law".

[76a] See *Bank St Petersburg PJSC v Arkhangelsky* [2020] EWCA Civ 408; [2020] 4 W.L.R. 55, at [88]–[92].
[76b] See *Robinson v Al-Qasimi* [2021] EWCA Civ 862, at [71]–[74].
[76c] *Stoffel* and *Henderson v Dorset Healthcare*, above.

24–058 *At the end of the paragraph, add:*

Indeed, the (unsurprising) fact—considered above—that prior case law which is "*Patel* compliant", and which represents a "working out" of how the *Patel* approach should apply to particular factual and legal circumstances, is still of precedential value provides further assistance in predicting what the outcome of any individual case might be.

(6) The General Impact of Patel

24–059 *At the end of the last sentence of sub-paragraph 3, insert a new footnote 78a:*

[78a] As a handful of the more high profile decisions on the illegality principle since *Patel* have demonstrated. First, in *Bank St Petersburg PJSC v Arkhangelsky* [2020] EWCA Civ 408; [2020] 4 W.L.R. 55, Dr Arkhangelsky counterclaimed for damages in respect of an alleged conspiracy to raid and seize the assets of two of his main businesses in Russia, in respect of which he admitted he had paid substantial bribes to obtain licences for their acquisition and development. The Court of Appeal had no hesitation in rejecting the suggestion that these counterclaims were barred by reason of the illegality principle, holding, at [91], that (i) barring the counterclaims would do nothing to prevent or discourage bribery—the bribery and the subsequent claim for dishonest conspiracy were not closely linked; (ii) there is a strong public policy in favour of allowing the victims of dishonest conspiracies to vindicate their rights; and (iii) the denial of the counterclaims would not be proportionate, bearing specifically in mind that punishment for bribery is generally a matter for the criminal courts. Similarly, in *Medsted Associates Ltd v Canaccord Genuity Wealth (International) Ltd* [2019] EWCA Civ 83; [2019] 1 W.L.R. 4481, it was suggested (without deciding the point) that a claim for damages representing commissions of which a broker had been deprived when the third party contracted directly with the clients might not be barred on public policy grounds by reason of the commissions having been kept secret from the clients. The Court of Appeal would, had it been necessary to decide the point, have given more weight to the considerations that the third party was aware of the non-disclosure and that to deprive the broker of damages entirely would be disproportionate, since it had reasonably earned at least some commission: see per Longmore LJ at [48]–[51]. Thirdly, in *Rashid v Nasrullah* [2018] EWCA Civ 2685; [2020] Ch. 37, the Court of Appeal considered if the illegality principle could avail the victim of a fraud in these circumstances: the original registered proprietor of land was deprived of his title by way of a series of forged documents; the land was then transferred to another who was complicit in the fraud and who entered into occupation; over 20 years later, the original proprietor applied for rectification of the register to undo the fraud; but the current registered owner and occupier asserted his adverse possession in an attempt to defeat the rectification claim (i.e. in essence, a plea of limitation). The question was whether the illegality principle stopped him from doing so. The answer—according to the Court of Appeal at [68]–[75] and [83]—was: no, it did not. The Court accepted that *Patel v Mirza* was in principle applicable to cases based on a plea of limitation, but that in applying the "range of factors" test in *Patel*, great weight had to be given to the fact that the whole point of limitation is to limit the time in which even good claims could be brought and that the limitation regime is a carefully calibrated statutory regime, balancing all the competing interests which exist in such circumstances. With the possible exception of "extreme examples of illegality not encompassed within the structure of the Limitation Act", it would be wrong to upset that balance. Fourthly, and finally, see also Lord Lloyd-Jones' examination of the factual case, and the application of the *Patel* test, in the context of a mortgage fraud in *Stoffel* at [27]–[46].

D. THE POSITION POST-PATEL: COMMON CASES RELEVANT TO FRAUD LITIGATION

(4) Claims by Companies (or Other Principals) Against Fraudulent Agents

Replace footnote 104 with: 24–082

[104] In both the Court of Appeal: *Singularis Holdings Ltd (in official liquidation) v Daiwa Capital Markets Europe Ltd* [2018] EWCA Civ 84; [2018] 1 W.L.R. 2777; and the Supreme Court: *Singularis Holdings Ltd (in official liquidation) v Daiwa Capital Markets Europe Ltd* [2019] UKSC 50; [2020] A.C. 1189.

At the end of the second sentence, add:

, in terms endorsed by both the Court of Appeal[104a] and the Supreme Court.[104b]

[104a] *Singularis Holdings Ltd (in official liquidation) v Daiwa Capital Markets Europe Ltd* [2018] EWCA Civ 84; [2018] 1 W.L.R. 2777, at [66].
[104b] *Singularis Holdings Ltd (in official liquidation) v Daiwa Capital Markets Europe Ltd* [2019] UKSC 50; [2020] A.C. 1189, at [21].

CHAPTER 25

LIMITATION

A. INTRODUCTION

Replace footnote 1 with: **25–002**

A full discussion of such matters may be found in A. McGee, *Limitation Periods*, 8th edn (London: Sweet & Maxwell, 2018).

B. PRIMARY LIMITATION PERIODS

(1) Claims in Tort Generally

Replace footnote 6 with: **25–005**

See generally, McGee, *Limitation Periods* (2018), Ch. 5.

(4) Claims under Statute

25–009 *At the end of footnote 9, add:*

In another case brought by a creditor under s.423, s.8, and not s.9, was held to be applicable because the initial remedy sought was a challenge to the validity of a property transfer rather than to recover a sum of money; and the cause of action was held to accrue when the creditor became a victim, which was when he became "capable of being prejudiced" by the transfer: *Giles v Rhind* [2007] EWHC 687 (Ch); [2007] Bus LR 1470; affirmed [2008] EWCA Civ 118; [2009] Ch 191.

(5) Claims for Breach of Trust or the Recovery of Trust Property and Claims against Fiduciaries

25–016 *Replace the reference in the first clause of footnote 22 with:*

L. Tucker, N. Le Poidevin and J. Brightwell, *Lewin on Trusts* 20th edn (London: Sweet & Maxwell, 2020), para.50–080.

25–020 *At the end of footnote 26, replace the words in the final sentence after the comma with the following:*

and whereas it might have had another opportunity to consider the point on the appeal in *First Subsea Ltd v Balltec Ltd* [2017] EWCA Civ 186; [2018] Ch 25, permission to appeal having been granted by Lords Neuberger, Wilson and Hodge on 18 July 2017 (*First Subsea Limited (Formerly BSW Limited) (Respondent) v Emmett (Appellant)* UKSC 2017/0081), the case settled shortly before the hearing in the Supreme Court took place.

(6) Claims for Equitable Remedies and Section 36 of the 1980 Act

25–024 *In footnote 30, replace the reference with:*

Lewin on Trusts (2020), para.50–055.

(i) Is the claim for an equitable remedy?

25–027 *In footnote 35, replace the reference with:*

M. Jones and A. Dugdale (ed), *Clerk & Lindsell on Torts*, 23rd edn (London: Sweet & Maxwell, 2020), para.27–150.

(ii) Will the court apply a limitation period under the 1980 Act by analogy?

25–030 *At the end of footnote 40, add:*

For recent confirmation of this principle, see *Claimants in the Royal Mail Group Litigation v Royal Mail Group Ltd* [2021] EWCA Civ 1173, at [182].

At the end of footnote 44, add:

In *Commissioners for HMRC v IGE USA Investments Limited* [2020] EWHC 2121 (Ch); [2021] Bus L.R. 424, Zacaroli J refused to draw any such inference because the point had been very briefly dealt with by Asplin J, in such a way as to render it impossible to discern whether, and if so on what basis, she considered *Molloy* could be distinguished.

At the end of the paragraph, add:

This can be contrasted with the Court of Appeal's recent clarification of the issue in *Commissioners for HMRC v IGE USA Investments Limited.*[46a] In 2005 the taxpayers entered into a settlement agreement with HMRC in which HMRC agreed not to issue a notice. In 2018, HMRC purported to rescind the settlement agreement on the basis that the taxpayers had misrepresented the transaction. HMRC issued a claim seeking a declaration that the rescission was valid. It later sought permission to amend its Particulars of Claim to introduce a new claim for equitable rescission based on fraudulent misrepresentation. The taxpayers opposed the application on the ground that, pursuant to section 36(1) of the 1980 Act, the six-year limitation period for claims in the tort of deceit should be applied to such a claim. The appeal turned on the interpretation of the *ratio* of *Molloy*, which the court concluded was "that any claim for equitable rescission of a contract on the ground of fraudulent misrepresentation is subject to a six-year limitation period by analogy to a claim for damages in the tort of deceit, where the facts as pleaded would allow either claim." [46b] The Court of Appeal held that the lower court was not free to depart from that *ratio* in the present case[46c] and that the decision in *P&O Nedlloyd BV* was not directly inconsistent with *Molloy.*[46d] As such, the lower court had erred in finding that it was decisive that HMRC did not seek property or money as a consequence of recission and that the only remedy sought was declaratory relief.[46e] The Court of Appeal held that:

> "it was enough that HMRC seek rescission of the Settlement Agreement on the ground of fraudulent misrepresentation, in circumstances where they could in principle have relied upon the same facts to bring an action for damages in deceit. Such an action would not have involved setting aside the Settlement Agreement, but the damages would have been calculated on essentially the same basis as HMRC now seek to achieve by rescinding the Settlement Agreement and relying on their statutory power to make discovery assessments within a twenty year period. It is that similarity in the relief claimed which is sufficient, on the authority of *Molloy*, to justify and require application of the statutory six-year limit by way of analogy."[46f]

The Court of Appeal made clear that the relief sought in the common law claim did not have to be identical to that sought in equity: it was enough that it was "similar."[46g] The court also emphasised that it is in the public interest that there should be an end of litigation.[46h] Authoritative guidance will be offered by the Supreme Court in due course as an application for permission to appeal has been granted.[46i]

[46a] *Commissioners for HMRC v IGE USA Investments Limited* [2021] EWCA Civ 534; [2021] 2 W.L.R. 534.
[46b] *HMRC v IGE Investments*, above, per Henderson LJ at [59].
[46c] *HMRC v IGE Investments*, above, per Henderson LJ at [98].
[46d] *HMRC v IGE Investments*, above, per Henderson LJ at [74].
[46e] *HMRC v IGE Investments*, above, per Henderson LJ at [60], [64]. See also *Commissioners for HMRC v IGE USA Investments Limited* [2020] EWHC 2121 (Ch), at [130]–[131].
[46f] *HMRC v IGE Investments*, above, per Henderson LJ at [60].
[46g] *HMRC v IGE Investments*, above, per Henderson LJ at [54].
[46h] *HMRC v IGE Investments*, above, per Henderson LJ at [56].
[46i] Permission to appeal granted on 8 July 2021.

(iii) *Is the claim barred by laches or acquiescence?*

25–032 *In footnote 48, replace the reference with:*

L. Tucker, N. Le Poidevin and J. Brightwell, *Lewin on Trusts* (2020), para.41–123.

In footnote 49, replace the reference with:

J. McGhee, *Snell's Equity*, 34th edn (London: Sweet & Maxwell, 2020), para.18–041.

25–033 *In footnote 52, replace both references with:*

L. Tucker, N. Le Poidevin and J. Brightwell, *Lewin on Trusts* (2020), para.41–113; McGhee, *Snell's Equity*, (2020), para.5–011.

C POSTPONEMENT OF RUNNING OF TIME

(1) Introduction

25–038 *At the end of the paragraph, add:*

See, for example, *Cave v Robinson Jarvis and Rolf (a Firm).*[56a]

[56a] [2003] 1 A.C. 384, per Lord Scott at [60].

(3) Deliberate concealment

(i) *Concealment*

25–040 *At the end of footnote 60, add:*

This is referred to as the "statement of claim test": see *Williams v Lishman, Sidwell, Campbell & Price Ltd* [2010] EWCA Civ 418; [2010] PNLR 25, per Elias LJ at [62]. In *Davy v 01000654 Ltd* [2018] EWHC 353 (QB), HHJ Russen QC (sitting as a Judge of the High Court) observed, at [53], that it necessarily follows from the statement of claim test that an allegation of prior deliberate concealment will fall to be considered by what the claimant in due course pleads as a necessary and proper element of his claim, once known.

25–041 *At the end of footnote 64, add:*

See *Canada Square Operations Ltd v Potter* [2020] EWHC 672 (QB); [2020] 2 All E.R. (Comm) 984, per Jay J at [28]: "The case law has expanded section 32(1)(b) to cover instances of non-disclosure but not, as we shall see, across the board."

In the fourth sentence, delete the text following the reference to footnote 66 to the end of the sentence and replace with:

It was previously thought that intentional concealment by omission to speak (as opposed to taking active steps) would only constitute deliberate concealment for the purposes of the sub-section where the defendant "knew himself to be under a duty to disclose."[66a] That is no longer the case. In *Canada Square Operations v Potter*,[66b] the Court of Appeal held that there need be no free-standing legal duty to disclose. Section 32(1)(b) does not refer to a "duty" (whereas s.32(2) does). Rather, s.32(1)(b) refers only to "concealment". Inherent in the concept of "concealing" something is the existence of an "obligation" to disclose it. To construe s.32(1)(b) as being satisfied only if there is a pre-existing legal duty to disclose would add an unwarranted gloss to the statute.[66c] The "obligation" need only be one arising from "a combination of utility and morality". The Court need not undertake a detailed analysis of implied contractual terms or the scope of tortious duties of care when considering whether s.32(1)(b) applied. Rather, the focus should be on the conduct alleged to amount to the concealment and on whether the defendant was, at that point, under a "sufficient obligation to disclose" for its failure to amount to concealment.[66d] The failure to disclose must be deliberate, in the sense that the defendant realised he should tell the claimant something, and decided not to do so;[66e] but this also includes recklessness, where the defendant realised that there was a *risk* that he had a duty to tell the claimant something and nevertheless decided not to.[66f]

[66a] *AIC Ltd v ITS Testing Services (UK) Ltd* [2006] EWCA Civ 1601; [2007] 1 All E.R. (Comm) 667.
[66b] *Canada Square Operations v Potter* [2021] EWCA Civ 339; [2021] 3 W.L.R. 777, at [77].
[66c] *AIC v ITS Testing*, above, at [75].
[66d] *AIC v ITS Testing*, above, at [76].
[66e] *AIC v ITS Testing*, above, at [85].
[66f] *AIC v ITS Testing*, above, at [137], and, further, the discussion about the term "deliberate" in the context of s.32 in the update to para.25–046 below.

At the end of footnote 67, add:

If the defendant's retainer is a continuing one to provide investment advice there is generally no obligation upon the adviser to exercise continuing vigilance to discover any past mistakes and to put them right: *Capita (Banstead 2011) v RFIB Group Ltd* [2016] QB 835 per Longmore L J at [19] (an observation made in the context not of section 32 concealment but an argument that such a continuing retainer meant that the cause of action in respect of the initial mistake continued to accrue day by day). The presumption is that investment advice is forward not backward looking; thus it follows that any allegation that some later advice involves deliberate concealment of negligent advice in the past is one that must be grounded in fact, rather than any duty of care to second guess the correctness of previous advice: *Davy v 01000654 Ltd* [2018] EWHC 353 (QB), HHJ Russen QC (sitting as a Judge of the High Court), at [56].

At the end of footnote 70, add: **25–044**

Applied by Fraser J in *RG Securities (No. 2) Ltd v Allianz Global Corporate and Speciality CE* [2020] EWHC 1646 (TCC), 191 Con. L.R. 1.

At the end of footnote 71, add: **25–045**

The rule in *Ezekiel v Lehrer* applies to corporations as well as to individuals, see *Libyan Investment Authority v Credit Suisse International* [2021] EWHC 2684 (Comm), per HHJ Pelling QC at [37]: "there is no reason for applying a different rule for loss of memory depending on whether a court is concerned with the memory of that individual *qua* individual or in his capacity as repository of the memories of a corporation of which he is or was an agent."

(ii) Section 32(2)

At the end of footnote 72, add: **25–046**

The ratio is contained in [36]–[39]: s.32(2) should be interpreted widely so as to cover "legal wrongdoing of any kind, giving rise to a right of action". See also the analysis of Jay J in *Canada Square Operations Ltd v Potter* [2020] EWHC 672 (QB); [2020] 2 All ER (Comm) 984. Whilst the language of s.32(2) does not precisely track that of s.32(1)(b), because the former uses the term "breach of duty", whereas the latter uses "right of action", the two concepts "must be the two sides of the same coin: in Hohfeldian terms, "juridical correlates". S.32(1)(b) considers the matter from the perspective of a claimant; section 32(2) from the perspective of a defendant. The breach of duty must constitute "some form of legal wrongdoing as stigmatised by statute; and it follows that the act or omission in question involves a "breach of duty" even if the "right of action" is not for a breach of duty and, outside of the statutory scheme, there is no independent duty". See also the Court of Appeal's approval of Arden LJ's reasons in *Canada Square Operations Ltd v Potter* [2021] EWCA Civ 339, at [62]–[63]. The term breach of duty is to be interpreted expansively, to encompass "legal wrongdoing of any kind" (at [62]).

At the end of the first sentence, add footnote 74a:

[74a] "S.32(2) is in the nature of a deeming provision: it treats for these purposes s.32(1)(b) as fulfilled if its own self-contained criterion is met": *Canada Square Operations Ltd v Potter* [2020] EWHC 672 (QB), per Jay J at [29].

At the end of footnote 75, add:

See also *Siddiqui v University of Oxford* [2018] EWHC 184 (QB), at [232].

At the end of the paragraph add:

In *Canada Square Operations Ltd v Potter*,[75a] Jay J considered the interplay between *Cave v Robinson Jarvis and Rolf (a Firm)*[75b] and *Giles v Rhind*.[75c] He was concerned to assess whether the application of Arden LJ's three stage approach in *Giles v Rhind* might lead to the conclusion that, for the purposes of the right of action under s.423, all that is required is proof of a deliberate act which amounts to a breach of duty without proof that the actor knew that it was a breach of duty. He posited that an individual might enter into a transaction which contravened s.423 without having any idea that the transaction might be impugned under that provision. All that is required is proof of an action carried out with the purpose of placing assets out of reach of creditors, by a person who might be oblivious to the legal consequences of that act. Jay J held that Arden LJ's reasoning "was premised on the concept of unconscionable conduct"—the deliberate placing of assets beyond the reach of creditors "is not morally neutral". He relied on Arden LJ's invocation of the concepts of "some degree of blameworthiness" and "unconscionable conduct" in *Giles v Rhind*. In the case before him, which concerned non-disclosure of a commission said to be "unfair" within the meaning of ss.140A-D of the Consumer Credit Act 1974, Jay J held that the appellant "must be taken to have known that it was under a duty to act fairly, and also must be taken to have decided that the commission would not be disclosed. In that critical respect, the Appellant acted deliberately; it did not act negligently or inadvertently." It followed that the Appellant "must be treated as apprehending that there was a risk that legal wrongdoing would be found by the court even if it cannot be deemed to have predicted what the courts might say...there being no legal certainty in that respect." It followed that there was "some degree of blameworthiness" and "unconscionable conduct" such that the mental element of s.32(2) was fulfilled. The Court of Appeal upheld his decision.[76d] As Rose LJ explained, the decision of the House of Lords in *Cave v Robinson Jarvis and Rolf* establishes that the breach of duty must have been "deliberate" in the sense that the defendant had the "necessary mental element in respect of the fact that their conduct gave rise to a breach of duty". The court identified four possibilities for the necessary mental element: (i) subjective knowledge or actual awareness; (ii) wilful blindness; (iii) recklessness with both an objective and subjective element (in that a person is subjectively aware of a risk and it is objectively unreasonable to take that risk); and (iv) recklessness with only a subjective element. The court considered that there was no clear, natural meaning of the term "deliberate" in this context, and that the case law construing the term in the context of s.32 was inconclusive. However, the pre-1980 case law established that recklessness was a sufficient mental element for liability under s.26 of the Limitation Act 1939 (the precursor to s.32), and Parliamentary materials established that the test under s.32 was not intended to be more difficult for a claimant to overcome. The Court of Appeal held that Mrs Potter could rely on s.32(2) because the defendant realised that there was a risk that their failure to disclose the commission resulted in the relationship being unfair under s.140A, and it was not reasonable for them to take that risk.

[75a] *Canada Square Operations Ltd v Potter* [2020] EWHC 672 (QB); [2020] 2 All E.R. (Comm) 984, at [61]–[63].
[75b] *Cave v Robinson Jarvis and Rolf (a Firm)* [2002] UKHL 18; [2003] 1 A.C. 384.
[75c] *Giles v Rhind* [2008] EWCA Civ 118; [2009] Ch 191.
[76d] *Canada Square Operations Ltd v Potter* [2021] EWCA Civ 339; [2021] 3 W.L.R. 777, at [85]–[89].

(5) Discovery of the Fraud/Concealment/Mistake

(i) Discovery

At the footnote 79, add: **25–050**

For a recent reiteration of this principle, see *Boyse (International) Ltd v Natwest Markets Plc* [2021] EWHC 1387 (Ch), at [29].

At the end of the second sentence, insert footnote 79a:

[79a] While investigating the claimant's state of mind, the court will not draw a bright line between events, communications and things known by the claimant before and after the accrual of the cause of action, see *European Real Estate Debt Fund (Cayman) Ltd v Treon* [2021] EWHC 2866 (Ch), per Miles J at [775]: "If a claimant could reasonably have discovered the fraud by virtue of events and circumstances occurring before it actually suffered a loss, there was no principled rationale for allowing it the indulgence of more than the normal six years' period to bring its claim."

At the end of footnote 80, add:

Applied in *Boyse (International) Ltd v Natwest Markets Plc* [2020] EWHC 1264 (Ch), per Chief Master Marsh at [40].

Add new paragraph 25–050A after para.25–050:

The formulation of the test to determine the time of discovery has shifted in different cases, although the various iterations appear to operate in the same way for the most part.[80a] The most frequently applied test is the "statement of claim" test, that is that "a claimant must have sufficient knowledge to enable it to plead a claim."[80b] However, in the context of mistake, the Supreme Court has recently clarified that a different time is applicable. In such cases, time should run from when the claimant knows, or could with reasonable diligence know, that he made such a mistake "with sufficient confidence to justify embarking on the preliminaries to the issue of a writ."[80c] This test is "less stringent"[80d] and uses a "slightly earlier date"[80e] than the "statement of case" test. It is currently unclear whether this analysis may be extended beyond the context of mistake were an appropriate case to arise for consideration.[80f] **25–050A**

[80a] See, for example, *Cunningham v Ellis* [2018] EWHC 3188 Comm, Teare J put the test somewhat differently, at [87]: discovery of the alleged fraud means knowledge of the "essential facts constituting the alleged fraud" is required. There is no difference of substance between the two formulations: *Boyse (International) Ltd v Natwest Markets Plc* [2020] EWHC 1264 (Ch), per Chief Master Marsh at [40].
[80b] See *OT Computers Ltd (In Liquidation) v Infineon Technologies AG* [2021] EWCA Civ 501, [2021] Q.B. 1183, per Males LJ at [26]. See further *Law Society v Sephton &Co* [2004] EWCA Civ 1627; [2005] Q.B. 1013; *The Kriti Palm* [2006] EWCA Civ 1601; [2007] 1 All E.R. (Comm) 667; and *DSG Retail Ltd v Mastercard Inc* [2020] EWCA Civ 671; [2020] Bus L.R. 1360.
[80c] *Test Claimants in the Franked Investment Income Group Litigation v Revenue and Customs Commissioners* [2020] UKSC 47; [2020] 3 W.L.R. 1369, per Lord Reed and Lord Hodge at [209], [213].
[80d] *Libyan Investment Authority v Credit Suisse International* [2021] EWHC 2684 (Comm), per HHJ Pelling QC at [29].
[80e] *Allianz Global Investigators Investors GmbH v RSA Insurance Group (Ltd)* [2021] EWHC 2950 (Ch), per Miles J at [31].
[80f] The point was argued in *Libyan Investment Authority v Credit Suisse International* [2021] EWHC 2684 (Comm), but it was held to be "entirely inappropriate" to determine that issue on an application for summary judgment, per HHJ Pelling QC at [32].

(ii) Reasonable diligence

25–052 *At the end of footnote 81, add:*

Cited with approval by the Supreme Court in *Test Claimants in the Franked Investment Income Group Litigation v Revenue and Customs Commissioners* [2020] UKSC 47; [2020] 3 W.L.R. 136, at [203].

Replace paragraphs 25–053 and 25–054 with:

25–053 The rigorous approach disclosed by this passage, which has been much quoted in later cases, should not be taken to constitute a general statement of the legal position. In reality, the concept of reasonable diligence is vitally dependent on the context[82] and has given rise to a number of different approaches.[83] In *OT Computers Ltd (In Liquidation) v Infineon Technologies AG*,[84] the Court of Appeal attempted to draw together the various strands of reasoning that have developed in this area and to provide a coherent approach for assessing reasonable diligence:

> "although the question what reasonable diligence requires may have to be asked at two distinct stages, (1) whether there is anything to put the claimant on notice of a need to investigate and (2) what a reasonably diligent investigation would then reveal, there is a single statutory issue, which is whether the claimant could with reasonable diligence have discovered (in this case) the concealment. Although some of the cases have spoken in terms of reasonable diligence only being required once the claimant is on notice that there is something to investigate (the "trigger"), it is more accurate to say that the requirement of reasonable diligence applies throughout. At the first stage the claimant must be reasonably attentive so that he becomes aware (or is treated as becoming aware) of the things which a reasonably attentive person in his position would learn. At the second stage, he is taken to know those things which a reasonably diligent investigation would then reveal. Both questions are questions of fact and will depend on the evidence."[85]

This two-stage test has already been adopted in subsequent cases[86] and appears to provide much-needed clarification as to the correct approach to reasonable diligence.[87]

[82] In *Paragon*, a claim which arose out of a mortgage fraud, there were numerous pointers which suggested that the claimant might have been the victim of such a fraud. However, in the later decision in *Barnstaple Boat Co Ltd v Jones*, which was a claim in deceit, one detects a more lenient approach to the question of reasonable diligence. See also *Peco Arts Inc v Hazlitt Gallery Ltd* [1983] 1 W.L.R. 1315 (QBD) a work of art believed to be by Ingres (and sold by the defendant on that basis) was subsequently discovered to be a reproduction; "reasonable diligence" did not mean the doing of everything

possible nor necessarily the use of any means at the claimant's disposal nor even necessarily the doing of anything at all, but simply the doing of that which the ordinarily prudent buyer and possessor of a valuable work of art would do having regard to all the circumstances. In *Collins v Brebner* [2000] Lloyd's Rep. PN 587, the Court of Appeal held that where the defendant (solicitor) was falsely asserting to the claimant the relevant position, the claimant could not be said to have been able with reasonable diligence to have discovered the true position.

[83] See, for example, the notion of "trigger for an investigation" in *JD Wetherspoon v Van de Berg & Co Ltd* [2007] EWHC 1044 (Ch); [2007] P.N.L.R. 28, at [42]; *Granville Technology Group Limited (in liquidation) v Infineon Technologies AG* [2020] EWHC 415 (Comm), per Foxton J at [45]–[46]; and *DSG Retail Ltd v Mastercard Inc* [2020] EWCA Civ 671; [2020] Bus LR 1360, per Sir Geoffrey Vos at [64] and following. See also the notions of a statutory assumption that the claimant was on notice of something meriting investigation in *Gresport Finance Ltd v Battaglia* [2018] EWCA Civ 540, per Henderson LJ at [49] or the assumption that the claimant desires to discover whether or not there has been a fraud in *Law Society v Sephton* [2004] EWCA Civ 1627; [2005] QB 1013, per Neuberger LJ at [112], [116].

[84] [2021] EWCA Civ 501; [2021] QB 1183.

[85] *OT Computers Ltd (In Liquidation) v Infineon Technologies AG* [2021] EWCA Civ 501, [2021] QB 1183, per Males LJ at [47].

[86] See *Allianz Global Investigators Investors GmbH v RSA Insurance Group (Ltd)* [2021] EWHC 2950 (Ch), at [36]–[37] and at [82] and following; *The ECU Group PLC v HSBC Bank PLC* [2021] EWHC 2875 (Comm), at [462]; *Boyse (International) Ltd v Natwest Markets Plc* [2021] EWHC 1387 (Ch), at [39]; and *European Real Estate Debt Fund (Cayman) Ltd v Treon & Ors* [2021] EWHC 2866 (Ch), per Miles J at [806].

[87] Whether there was something to put the claimant on notice must be determined on an objective basis: *OT Computers Ltd (In Liquidation) v Infineon Technologies AG* [2021] EWCA Civ 501; [2021] Q.B. 1183, per Males LJ at [48]. See also *DSG Retail Ltd v Mastercard Incorporated* [2020] EWCA Civ 671; [2020] Bus LR 1360, at [66], [112], [113]. This test leaves open to argument the extent to which the personal characteristics of the claimant are to be taken into account when deciding what diligence he could reasonably have been expected to have shown: *Peconic Industrial Development Ltd v Lay Kowk Fai* [2009] HKCFA 17, at [30]. However, the Court of Appeal has made clear that "personal traits or characteristics bearing on the likelihood of the particular claimant discovering facts which a person in his position could reasonably be expected to discover, such as whether the claimant is slothful, naïve, shy, nervous, uncurious or ill informed, are not relevant. But it does not necessarily follow, as Lord Hoffmann said in *Peconic*, that the claimant must be assumed to be someone or something which he is not": *OT Computers,* per Males LJ at [38]. It has been suggested that whether or not a characteristic can be taken into account turns "on the level of abstraction of description of characteristics of the claimant": *Allianz Global Investigators Investors GmbH v RSA Insurance Group (Ltd)* [2021] EWHC 2950 (Ch), per Miles J at [41]. See also *Hussain v Mukhtar* [2016] EWHC 424 (QB), at [43], applied in *Boyse (International) Ltd v Natwest Markets Plc* [2020] EWHC 1264 (Ch), per Chief Master Marsh at [40]; whose decision was upheld on appeal by Trower J at [2021] EWHC 1387 (Ch).

CHAPTER 26

THE COURT'S POWERS TO GRANT INTERIM RELIEF

A. INTRODUCTION

(1) The Subject Matter of this Chapter

Delete the words "(which it would not otherwise have)" **26–004**

(2) Jurisdiction, Proper Exercise of it and Discretion Contrasted

26–013 *Replace "It is important to distinguish" in the eighth line with:*

As explained below, it is doubtful whether precisely the same reasoning would be followed today. However, it remains important to distinguish

26–014 *After "identifying a principle" in the third and fourth lines, insert:*

(or an aspect of the Court's practice)

At the end of footnote 14, insert:

In *Broad Idea International Ltd v Cho Kwai Chee* [2021] UKPC 24, at [75]–[102] and [114]–[121], the majority of the Privy Council held, obiter, that the Court could grant injunctions in support of foreign proceedings in exercise of its equitable jurisdiction, without reliance upon s. 25 of the Civil Jurisdiction and Judgements Act 1982. (Albeit it may be necessary to rely upon that provision, together with paragraph 3.1(5) of Practice Direction 6B, in order to serve the respondent out of the jurisdiction.)

Add new paragraph 26–014A after para.26–014:

26–014A The *Siskina* requirement was the subject of extensive re-consideration in the recent Privy Council case, *Broad Idea International Ltd v Cho Kwai Chee*. In that case, and as explained in further detail below, the majority held (obiter) that it is consistent with principle and good practice for the Court to grant relief whether or not the substantive relief sought was relief which it had jurisdiction to grant.[14a]

[14a] See [2021] UKPC 24, at [75]–[102] and [114]–[121].

(3) Human Rights Considerations

26–017 *Replace "is generally thought not to be" in the sixth and seventh lines, with:*

is ordinarily not

At the end of the paragraph, add:

Micallef was applied by the employment appeal tribunal in *Queensgate Investments LLP v Millet*, in which an application was made under section 128 of the Employment Rights Act 1996 for payment of the claimant's salary pending determination of his claim for unfair dismissal. The tribunal concluded that, notwithstanding that the application was interim in nature, it would amount to a determination of a civil right or obligation to which article 6 applied.[18a]

[18a] [2021] I.C.R 863, at [55].

B. THE JURISDICTIONAL PLATFORMS RELEVANT TO PROCEEDINGS BEFORE THE ENGLISH COURTS

(1) Section 37 of the Senior Courts Act 1981

At the end of the paragraph, add: 26–024

The most significant recent development is the re-consideration of the *Siskina* requirement in *Broad Idea International Ltd v Cho Kwai Chee*. As mentioned above, the majority held, obiter:

> "a court with equitable and/or statutory jurisdiction to grant injunctions where it is just and convenient to do so has power—and it accords with principle and good practice—to grant a freezing injunction against a party (the respondent) over whom the court has personal jurisdiction provided that:
> i) the applicant has already been granted or has a good arguable case for being granted a judgment or order for the payment of a sum of money that is or will be enforceable through the process of the court;
> ii) the respondent holds assets (or, as discussed below, is liable to take steps other than in the ordinary course of business which will reduce the value of assets) against which such a judgment could be enforced; and
> iii) there is a real risk that, unless the injunction is granted, the respondent will deal with such assets (or take steps which make them less valuable) other than in the ordinary course of business with the result that the availability or value of the assets is impaired and the judgment is left unsatisfied.
>
> Although other factors are potentially relevant to the exercise of the discretion whether to grant a freezing injunction, there are no other relevant restrictions on the availability in principle of the remedy. In particular:
> i) There is no requirement that the judgment should be a judgment of the domestic court—the principle applies equally to a foreign judgment or other award capable of enforcement in the same way as a judgment of the domestic court using the court's enforcement powers.
> ii) Although it is the usual situation, there is no requirement that the judgment should be a judgment against the respondent.
> iii) There is no requirement that proceedings in which the judgment is sought should yet have been commenced nor that a right to bring such proceedings should yet have arisen: it is enough that the court can be satisfied with a sufficient degree of certainty that a right to bring proceedings will arise and that proceedings will be brought (whether in the domestic court or before another court or tribunal)."[28a]

As made clear by (iii) above, the majority were of the firm view that the aspect of the *Siskina* principle which required—absent specific statutory authority—that injunctions would only be granted in support of proceedings which could be commenced before the English courts should no longer be applied. What matters is that a judgment may require enforcement in the English (or in this case BVI) courts, not the identity of the court which might issue that judgment.

[28a] See [2021] UKPC 24, at [101]–[102].

(4) CPR 25.1

At the end of footnote 42, insert: 26–041

It is respectfully suggested that, to the extent that HHJ Hodge QC regarded CPR 25.1 as conferring jurisdiction to make an order upon the court (in the strict sense of conferring power upon the court to make the order) he fell into error. Rules of the Court regulate its practice and procedure, but do not confer powers upon it which it did not previously have unless expressly authorised to do so by statute—see *GFN SA v Bancredit Cayman Ltd* [2009] UKPC 39; [2010] Bus. L.R. 587, at [14] and

Dunhill v Burgin (Nos 1 and 2) [2014] UKSC 18; [2014] 1 W.L.R. 933, at [27]. The distinction is often overlooked in practice and is usually academic. While the CPR do not generally alter the limits of the court's power, they do alter the extent to which, and manner in which, that power is utilised. In most circumstances, this amounts to the same thing in practical terms.

(5) Miscellaneous Statutory Provisions

26–046 *After each reference to the Financial Conduct Authority in the first and sixth lines insert:*

(or the Prudential Regulation Authority, as appropriate)

26–051 *In footnote 57, replace "[2008] EWCA Civ 1443" with:*

[2008] EWCA Crim 1443

C. JURISDICTION IN SUPPORT OF FOREIGN PROCEEDINGS

26–053 *At the end of the paragraph, add:*

As explained above, in light of the obiter views expressed by the majority of the Privy Council in *Broad Idea International Ltd v Cho Kwai Chee*, it appears that the court would be prepared to grant an injunction in support of foreign proceedings in exercise of its powers recorded in s.37 of the SCA, without reliance upon the CJJA, provided that one satisfies the requirements for relief articulated and glossed in [101]–[102] of that judgment (quoted above). It will, however, remain necessary to rely on the CJJA in circumstances in which one needs to invoke para.3.1(5) of Practice Direction 6B in order to obtain permission to serve a respondent out of the jurisdiction.

26–054 *Replace each instance of "such relief" in the first and second lines with:*

relief pursuant to the CJJA

At the end of the paragraph, add:

To the extent that the court begins granting injunctions in support of foreign proceedings in exercise of its powers set out in s.37 of the SCA as opposed to the CJJA, it remains to be seen whether the Court will apply the same or similar guidelines to those which it has hitherto utilised when granting relief pursuant to the CJJA.

(1) The Scope of Section 25 of the CJJA 1982

26–056 *Replace the quoted text with:*

"(1) The High Court in England and Wales or Northern Ireland shall have power to grant interim relief where—

(a) proceedings have been or are to be commenced in a 2005 Hague Convention State other than the United Kingdom or in a part of the United Kingdom other than that in which the High Court in question exercises jurisdiction; and

(b) they are or will be proceedings whose subject-matter is within scope of the 2005 Hague Convention as determined by Articles 1 and 2 of the 2005 Hague Convention (whether or not the 2005 Hague Convention has effect in relation to the proceedings).

(2) On an application for any interim relief under subsection (1) the court may refuse to grant that relief if, in the opinion of the court, the fact that the court has no jurisdiction apart from this section in relation to the subject-matter of the proceedings in question makes it inexpedient for the court to grant it.

(3) Her Majesty may by Order in Council extend the power to grant interim relief conferred by subsection (1) so as to make it exercisable in relation to proceedings of any of the following descriptions, namely—

(a) proceedings commenced or to be commenced otherwise than in a 2005 Hague Convention State;

(b) proceedings whose subject-matter is not within the scope of the 2005 Hague Convention as determined by Articles 1 and 2 of the 2005 Hague Convention.[61]

...

(7) In this section "interim relief", in relation to the High Court in England and Wales or Northern Ireland, means interim relief of any kind which that court has power to grant in proceedings relating to matters within its jurisdiction, other than—

(a) a warrant for the arrest of property; or

(b) provision for obtaining evidence."

Replace the quoted text with: **26–057**

"2. The High Court in England and Wales or Northern Ireland shall have power to grant interim relief under section 25(1) of the Civil Jurisdiction and Judgments Act 1982 in relation to proceedings of the following descriptions, namely—

(a) proceedings commenced or to be commenced otherwise than in a 2005 Hague Convention State;

(b) proceedings whose subject-matter is not within scope of the 2005 Hague Convention as determined by Articles 1 and 2 of that Convention"

Replace paragraph 26–058 with:

As noted earlier, the effect of the Order, which in its original form came into effect on 1 April 1997, is to extend this ancillary jurisdiction to grant interim relief in relation to proceedings taking place in any jurisdiction. **26–058**

Delete ", and not just those proceeding in a state within the European Union,", in the second and third lines **26–060**

(2) The Need for Foreign Substantive Proceedings

At the end of the paragraph, add: **26–064**

Similarly, in *Re Derev*, the court declined to continue a freezing order obtained against a Russian bankrupt by his bankruptcy manager (the Russian analogue to a trustee in bankruptcy) in support of Russian bankruptcy proceedings, in part because bankruptcy proceedings are not "substantive" in the sense of vindicating private law rights in a litigation context.[71a]

[71a] *In re Derev* [2021] EWHC 392 (Ch); [2021] Bus. L.R. 685, at [41].

D. JURISDICTION IN SUPPORT OF ARBITRAL PROCEEDINGS

(1) The Scope of Section 44 of the AA 1996

26–084 *At the end of the paragraph, add:*

The position has been further complicated by the decision of the Court of Appeal in *A v C*, in which it was held that s.44(2)(a) *does* confer jurisdiction to make orders in respect of the taking of evidence of witnesses against non-parties to the relevant arbitration agreement, while declining to comment on whether that meant that *Cruz City* and *Dtek* (which related to other parts of section 44(2)) were incorrectly decided.[94a]

[94a] [2020] EWCA Civ 409; [2020] 1 W.L.R. 3504, at [35] and [57].

CHAPTER 27

THE WITHOUT NOTICE APPLICATION

A. THE BASIS FOR APPLYING WITHOUT NOTICE

(1) Deciding to Apply Without Notice

(iii) Urgency

At the end of footnote 6, add: **27–009**

See also the comments of Warby J in *Birmingham City Council v Afsar* [2019] EWHC 1560 (QB), at [53]: "Urgency can only be a compelling reason for applying without notice if there is simply no time at all in which to give notice. Modern methods of communication mean that will rarely, if ever, be the case, and it was not the position here. You do not justify applying in secret by showing that your case has merit, or by saying that the relief sought is limited in scope and time, and will have only limited impact on the respondents. These are not relevant considerations, let alone compelling reasons for proceeding without notice."

(2) An Exceptional Remedy

27–013 *At the end of footnote 11, add:*

See also *Birmingham City Council v Afsar* [2019] EWHC 1560 (QB), at [49]–[56].

B. PRACTICALITIES OF APPLYING WITHOUT NOTICE

(2) Private Hearings

Add new paragraph 27–026A after para.27–026:

27–026A It is sometimes assumed that an order that the Court sit in private at any given hearing necessarily carries with it an implied prohibition, enforceable by contempt proceedings, on the publication of information relating to that hearing. It does not. The Court of Appeal in *A F Noonan (Architectural Practice) Ltd v Bournemouth and Boscombe Athletic Community Football Club Ltd* confirmed that publication of information relating to proceedings before any court sitting in private is not a contempt of court unless one or more of the circumstances identified in section 12 of the Administration of Justice Act 1960 applies, of which civil fraud practictioners are most likely to encounter section 12(1)(e) in practice: "where the court (having power to do so) expressly prohibits the publication of all information relating to the proceedings or of information of the description which is published".[28a] The mere fact that a court has ordered that it shall sit in private does not amount to such a prohibition.[28b] While the judgment in *Noonan* leaves open the possibility that publication of information relating to a hearing heard in private might be actionable in some other way, such as (perhaps) an action for breach of confidence,[28c] an applicant seeking a hearing in private will often be well advised to seek an express prohibition on publication of information relating to that hearing.

[28a] *AF Noonan (Architectural Practice) Ltd v Bournemouth and Boscombe Athletic Community Football Club Ltd* [2007] EWCA Civ 848; [2007] 1 W.L.R. 2614, at [6]–[15].
[28b] This is perhaps surprising, given that the Court of Appeal had, in an earlier judgment, held that an order that proceedings be held in private under CPR 39.2 was to be equated to an order that proceedings be held—in pre-CPR terminology–*in camera* (i.e. secretly) as opposed to "in chambers" (i.e. outside the public forum, but not secretly), and one might have therefore regarded it as amounting to an express prohibition on the publication of information; see *Department of Economics, Policy and Development of the City of Moscow v Bankers Trust Co* [2004] EWCA Civ 314, [2005] Q.B. 207, at [28]. Nevertheless, the *Department of Economics* case was cited to the Court of Appeal in *Noonan*, and the Court was dismissive of an argument (presumably supported by that case) that an order that a hearing be conducted in private amounted to an express prohibition on the publication of information (see *Noonan* at [11] and [12]).
[28c] See *Noonan* at [1], [15] and [19].

Add new paragraph:

Finally, it should be noted that, generally speaking, if the Court determines it must sit in private or order that the identity of any party or witness shall not be disclosed, it will (or, at least, should) publish an order to that effect on the judiciary's website pursuant to CPR 39.2(5). In an appropriate case, an applicant for a without notice order may wish to consider applying for such publication to be postponed to the return date, so as to avoid an order that a hearing be held in private triggering the very tipping-off it was intended to avoid. **27–026B**

(5) After the Hearing

After "subsequent committal application", insert: **27–030**

(at least in circumstances in which the respondent is unrepresented).

Replace footnote 38 with:

CPR 81.5. As set out in CPR 81.5(2) (as amended with effect from October 2020), service may now ordinarily be served on a respresented respondent's legal respresentatives (as defined by CPR 2.3(1)), unless those representatives object to that course. CPR 81.5(1) provides that personal service on unrepresented litigants may be dispensed with in an appropriate case, although this is only likely to arise in circumstances in which the Court is satisfied that the respondent is deliberately taking steps to evade service, or that the respondent is fully aware of the contempt proceedings; see the consultation document prepared as part of the process of amending Part 81: *Proposed rule changes relating to contempt of court; redraft of CPR Part 81* (2020), at page 14.

In each instance of the words "personally served" *delete the word* "personally". **27–031**

C. THE CROSS-UNDERTAKING IN DAMAGES

(2) Discretion to Waive or Limit the Cross-Undertaking

After "not require an unlimited one", insert new footnote 54a: **27–042**

[54a] For examples of exceptional cases in which the Court has not required any cross-undertaking on interim injunctions (sought on notice), see *Gould v Kay* [2020] 7 WLUK 221 and *Travelodge Hotels Limited v Prime Aesthetics Limited* [2020] EWHC 1217 (Ch). Neither case is unproblematic.

Analysis of *Gould* is hampered by the fact that there does not appear to be a publically available copy of HHJ Simpkiss's judgment. However, according to the Westlaw summary, the applicant claimed that as a result of the fraud which the respondents had committed or facilitated against her, she had no money to give a cross-undertaking. HHJ Simpkiss considered that this was a relevant factor in the exercise of his discretion as to whether to require a cross-undertaking (referring to *Allen v Jambo Holdings Ltd* [1980] 1 WLR 1252), as was the respondents' refusal to explain what had happened to the claimant's money and the fact that the history of the case had involved delay and obfuscation. In all the circumstances, he decided not to require a cross-undertaking in damages. This appears to be the latest manifestation of a persistent myth that *Jambo* is authority for the proposition that an impecunious (or legally aided) applicant need not (or, at any rate, may not be required to) offer a cross-undertaking in damages to obtain interim relief. It is not authority for any such proposition. As Burton J (who was counsel for the applicant in *Jambo*) explained in *R (ex p. Ellson) v London Borough of Greenwich* [2006] EWHC 2379 (Admin), at [12]–[13], the fact that an applicant is impecunious may justify the Court in accepting a cross-undertaking which is very unlikely to be of any worth; it is not a reason to excuse them from offering a cross-undertaking at all.

In *Travelodge*, Birss J granted an interim injunction restraining the presentation of a winding up petition for 14 days. He declined to make the injunction conditional upon a cross-undertaking in damages because the respondents could not identify any loss which the injunction was likely to cause them (see [42]–[43]). This was, it is suggested, an error of principle. It is fairness to the respondent, and not likelihood of the respondent suffering loss, which underpins the practice of requiring an applicant for an interim injunction to give a cross-undertaking (see e.g. *JSC Mezhdunarodniy Promyshlenniy Bank v Pugachev* [2015] EWCA Civ 139, [2016] 1 W.L.R. 160, at [75]–[78]). For this reason, Morgan J declined to follow *Travelodge* and required a cross-undertaking in damages from an applicant on the very similar facts of *Re: A Company (Injunction to Restrain Presentation of Petition)* [2020] EWHC 1406 (Ch), at [28]–[31].

27–045 *At the end of footnote 61, insert:*

A well advised respondent seeking fortification would—wherever possible—either make the application at the return date, or seek directions at the return date for the making of such an application at a future date. If the matter is not raised at the return date, the respondent runs the risk of having his delay successfully raised against him as a reason not to grant fortification; see e.g. *Apollo Ventures Co. Limited v Manchanda* [2020] EWHC 2206 (Comm), at [35], in which it was said that "The appropriate time . . . for making ths application [for fortification] would have been at the time of the return date" (albeit, the delay in that case having run to three to four years, the Court may be more forgiving in a less extreme case).

27–047 *Replace footnote 64 with:*

[64] It might be wondered why the assets need to be in the jurisdiction, in circumstances where assets available in other jurisdictions might be equally readily amenable to execution. Compare the position with respect to security for costs, where residence outside the jurisdiction is not sufficient to establish the condition in CPR 25.13(2)(a) unless the claimant is also not resident in a State bound by the 2005 Hague Convention as defined in section 1(3) of the Civil Jurisdiction and Judgments Act 1982.

27–051 *After "Where the freezing order was widely cast (rather than directed to specific assets) it will be easier to infer a risk of loss from the existence of the freezing order", insert new footnote 71a:*

[71a] Of course, this will not invariably be the case. If a specific asset is frozen, and that asset has a highly volatile price, the respondent may well find himself unable to sell the asset (or unable to sell the asset without waiting for consent from the applicant) so as to protect himself from sudden collapses in the asset's value. This situation arose in *Adeem Investment Holding Company KSCH v Al-Humaidhi* [2021] EWHC 1483 (Ch), in which fortification was ordered; see [15]–[28].

And after "showing a sufficient level of risk of loss to require fortification is synonymous with showing a good arguable case to that effect.", insert new footnote 71b:

[71b] An interesting example of just how low this bar can—in certain circumstances—be is afforded by *The Claimants Set Out in Schedule 1 to the Claim Form v Spence* [2021] EWHC 925 (Comm). In that case, the respondent to a freezing order was a debtor under an on-demand facility with Coutts, and was able to successfully obtain fortification in respect of the damage which he would suffer if the grant of the freezing order prompted Coutts to call in his loans under the facility, notwithstanding the absence of any evidence that Coutts intended to do so, or the fact that Coutts would have been at liberty to do so at any time in any event (see [16]–[28]).

And after "As to the test of causation (in relation to the anticipated claim under the cross-undertaking) it was sufficient for the court to be satisfied that the making of the order is or was a cause without which the relevant loss would not be suffered.", insert new footnote 71c:

[71c] There are conflicting dicta on the question of whether one can seek fortification for losses suffered as a result of an order, but prior to the application for fortification. In *Standing v Power* [2020] EWHC 1173 (Ch), Mr Michael Green QC (sitting as a Deputy High Court Judge) expressed the view that one could only apply for fortification of prospective loss (see [38]). However, in *Alfa Trading UK Ltd v*

Bosworth [2021] EWHC 1126 (Comm), [2021] 4 WLR 72, at [30]–[33], Mr Peter MacDonald Eggers QC (sitting as a Deputy High Court Judge), having noted the comments in *Standing*, took the view that fortification could be awarded in respect of past and well as prospective loss. It is suggested that the approach in *Alfa* is to be preferred.

And after "The quantum of the anticipated claim was a matter for an intelligent estimate by the defendant.", insert new footnote 71d:

[71d] The defendant must be able to properly evidence an intelligent estimate, and a failure to do so will justify the refusal of fortification; see e.g. *PJSC National Bank Trust v Mints* [2021] EWHC 1089 (Comm) at [75]–[77], where a failure to provide an intelligent estimate in respect of one alleged loss amounted to an independent (and sufficient) ground on which to refuse fortification in respect of it. However, the Court is mindful that—given that one is typically considering some element of prospective loss—it will usually be impossible to avoid some element of imprecision; see *The Claimants Set Out in Schedule 1 to the Claim Form v Spence* [2021] EWHC 925 (Comm), at [40].

At the end of footnote 77, insert: **27–054**

This standard practice probably also extends to proprietary injunctions. This is the view of Steven Gee QC, *Commercial Injunctions* (7th Ed) at para.11–031, which Cockerill J appeared to regard as accurately reflecting the law in *McAfee Ireland Ltd v DSG Retail Ltd* [2019] EWHC 2797 (Comm), at [28].

D. THE DUTY OF FULL AND FRANK DISCLOSURE

(1) Introduction

After "is not before the court to put his case", insert: **27–059**

The duty is necessary to enable the Court to fulfil its own obligations to ensure fair process under Article 6 of the European Convention on Human Rights. It is the necessary corollary of the Court being prepared to depart from the principle that it will hear both sides before reaching a decision, which is a basic principle of fairness.[82a]

[82a] *Fundo Soberano de Angola v Dos Santos* [2018] EWHC 2199 (Comm), at [51].

(2) When the Duty Arises

After "notice to the respondent", insert new footnote 82b: **27–060**

[82b] At least, where the application is one for an injunction. The position may be different where the application is to vary an existing order which was made on notice—see *PJSC National Bank Trust v Mints* [2020] EWHC 3253, at [8].

And, after "deploy them before the court", insert new footnote 82c:

[82c] If the Court can be persuaded to abridge the period of notice, then it may be possible to give fewer than three days' notice without becoming subject to the duty of full and frank disclosure. However, an order abridging the period of notice will often be made on the condition that it does not stop the duty of full and frank disclosure arising—see, e.g. *In re Rigil Kent Acquisitions Limited* [2017] EWHC 3636 (Ch), at [10].

Add new paragraph 27–060A after para.27–060:

It is important to note that the duty of full and frank disclosure does not conclude with the end of an *ex parte* hearing, but continues until (at least) the first hearing **27–060A** on notice, combined with a continuing duty to correct the position if it transpires that information given at an *ex parte* hearing was materially inaccurate or misleading.[83a]

[83a] *Valbonne Estates Limited v Cityvalue Estates Limited* [2021] EWHC 554 (Ch), at [31]–[32].

(3) Incidents of the Duty

Add new paragraph 27–062A after para.27–062:

27–062A The principles applicable to the duty of full and frank disclosure have recently been usefully summarised by Carr J as follows:

> "The law is non-contentious. The following general principles can be distilled from the relevant authorities by way of summary as follows:
>
> i) The duty of an applicant for a without notice injunction is to make full and accurate disclosure of all material facts and to draw the court's attention to significant factual, legal and procedural aspects of the case;
>
> ii) It is a high duty and of the first importance to ensure the integrity of the court's process. It is the necessary corollary of the court being prepared to depart from the principle that it will hear both sides before reaching a decision, a basic principle of fairness. Derogation from that principle is an exceptional course adopted in cases of extreme urgency or the need for secrecy. The court must be able to rely on the party who appears alone to present the argument in a way which is not merely designed to promote its own interests but in a fair and even-handed manner, drawing attention to evidence and arguments which it can reasonably anticipate the absent party would wish to make;
>
> iii) Full disclosure must be linked with fair presentation. The judge must be able to have complete confidence in the thoroughness and objectivity of those presenting the case for the applicant. Thus, for example, it is not sufficient merely to exhibit numerous documents;
>
> iv) An applicant must make proper enquiries before making the application. He must investigate the cause of action asserted and the facts relied on before identifying and addressing any likely defences. The duty to disclose extends to matters of which the applicant would have been aware had reasonable enquiries been made. The urgency of a particular case may make it necessary for evidence to be in a less tidy or complete form than is desirable. But no amount of urgency or practical difficulty can justify a failure to identify the relevant cause of action and principal facts to be relied on;
>
> v) Material facts are those which it is material for the judge to know in dealing with the application as made. The duty requires an applicant to make the court aware of the issues likely to arise and the possible difficulties in the claim, but need not extend to a detailed analysis of every possible point which may arise. It extends to matters of intention and for example to disclosure of related proceedings in another jurisdiction;
>
> vi) Where facts are material in the broad sense, there will be degrees of relevance and a due sense of proportion must be kept. Sensible limits have to be drawn, particularly in more complex and heavy commercial cases where the opportunity to raise arguments about non-disclosure will be all the greater. The question is not whether the evidence in support could have been improved (or one to be approached with the benefit of hindsight). The primary question is whether in all the circumstances its effect was such as to mislead the court in any material respect;
>
> vii) A defendant must identify clearly the alleged failures, rather than adopt a scatter gun approach. A dispute about full and frank disclosure should not be allowed to turn into a mini-trial of the merits;
>
> viii) In general terms it is inappropriate to seek to set aside a freezing order for non-disclosure where proof of non-disclosure depends on proof of facts which are themselves in issue in the action, unless the facts are truly so plain that they can be readily and summarily established, otherwise the application to set aside the freezing order is liable to become a form of preliminary trial in which the judge is asked to make findings (albeit provisionally) on issues which should be more properly reserved for the trial itself;

ix) If material non-disclosure is established, the court will be astute to ensure that a claimant who obtains injunctive relief without full disclosure is deprived of any advantage he may thereby have derived;

x) Whether or not the non-disclosure was innocent is an important consideration, but not necessarily decisive. Immediate discharge (without renewal) is likely to be the court's starting point, at least when the failure is substantial or deliberate. It has been said on more than one occasion that it will only be in exceptional circumstances in cases of deliberate non-disclosure or misrepresentation that an order would not be discharged;

xi) The court will discharge the order even if the order would still have been made had the relevant matter(s) been brought to its attention at the without notice hearing. This is a penal approach and intentionally so, by way of deterrent to ensure that applicants in future abide by their duties;

xii) The court nevertheless has a discretion to continue the injunction (or impose a fresh injunction) despite a failure to disclose. Although the discretion should be exercised sparingly, the overriding consideration will always be the interests of justice. Such consideration will include examination of i) the importance of the facts not disclosed to the issues before the judge ii) the need to encourage proper compliance with the duty of full and frank disclosure and to deter non-compliance iii) whether or not and to what extent the failure was culpable iv) the injustice to a claimant which may occur if an order is discharged leaving a defendant free to dissipate assets, although a strong case on the merits will never be a good excuse for a failure to disclose material facts;

xiii) The interests of justice may sometimes require that a freezing order be continued and that a failure of disclosure can be marked in some other way, for example by a suitable costs order. The court thus has at its disposal a range of options in the event of non-disclosure."[86a]

[86a] *Tugushev v Orlov* [2019] EWHC 2031 (Comm), at [7]. This summary has subsequently been referred to with approval in *Manek v IFL Wealth (UK) Limited* [2021] EWCA Civ 625, at [57], *Valbonne Estates Limited v Cityvalue Estates Limited* [2021] EWHC 544 (Ch), at [28], and *The World LLC v Dalal* [2019] EWHC 2993 (Comm), at [53]. Similar summaries have been given by Popplewell J in *Fundo Soberano De Angola v Dos Santos* [2018] EWHC 2199 (Comm), at [50]–[53], Cockerill J in *Petrocceltic Resources Limited v Archer* [2018] EWHC 671 (Comm), at [78]–[79], and Saini J in *Qatar Airways Group Q.C.S.C v Middle East News FZ LLC* [2020] EWHC 2975 (QB), at [383].

At the end of footnote 90, insert: **27–066**

And see *Tugushev v Orlov* [2019] EWHC 2031 (Comm), at [7(v)] and [23] to [32]. In *Tugushev* a failure to make proper enquiries into matters relating to a transfer of shares 15 years previously led to the discharge of a worldwide freezing order.

Add new paragraph 27–071A after para.27–071:

While a well advised litigant is likely to err on the side of caution, the duty to raise legal points must be kept within sensible limits. It is a duty to "identify arguments which it is reasonably anticipated that the absent party might wish to make, rather than to attempt an exhaustive trawl through every possible legal objection that might be taken."[99a] **27–071A**

[99a] As it was put by Bacon J in *WWRT Ltd v Tyschenko* [2021] EWHC 939 (Ch), [2021] Bus LR 972, at [122].

CHAPTER 28

FREEZING AND PROPRIETARY INJUNCTIONS

A. OVERVIEW

(3) Practical Questions

28–005 *At the end of footnote 7, add:*

The burden also extends beyond facts and matters of which the applicant is actually aware, encompassing facts and matters of which he would have been aware, had he made reasonable enquiries: see *Bank Mellat v Nikpour* [1985] F.S.R. 87, at 89–90 and 93. In *Tugushev v Orlov* [2019] EWHC 2031 (Comm), a failure to investigate matters raised by the respondent to a freezing order was deemed sufficiently serious to justify the discharge of a worldwide freezing order, notwithstanding that it was accepted that there was a good arguable case that the respondent had engaged in two dishonest conspiracies to defraud the applicant of interests in corporate groups worth hundreds of millions of dollars: see [7], [30]–[32] and [44].

B. REQUIREMENTS FOR A FREEZING INJUNCTION

(1) Introduction

28–012 *After "grant the order", insert new footnote 8a:*

[8a] See now the re-formulation of these principles by the majority of the board in *Broad Idea International Ltd v Convoy Collateral Ltd* [2021] UKPC 24, at [101]: "a court with equitable and/or statutory jurisdiction to grant injunctions where it is just and convenient to do so has power—and it accords with principle and good practice—to grant a freezing injunction against a party (the respondent) over whom the court has personal jurisdiction provided that:

i) the applicant has already been granted or has a good arguable case for being granted a judgment or order for the payment of a sum of money that is or will be enforceable through the process of the court;

ii) the respondent holds assets (or, as discussed below, is liable to take steps other than in the ordinary course of business which will reduce the value of assets) against which such a judgment could be enforced; and

iii) there is a real risk that, unless the injunction is granted, the respondent will deal with such assets (or take steps which make them less valuable) other than in the ordinary course of business with the result that the availability or value of the assets is impaired and the judgment is left unsatisfied."

One significance of this re-formulation is that it encapsulates both *Mareva* and *Chabra* freezing orders, rather than treating them as conceptually distinct.

(2) Good Arguable Case

Replace paragraph 28–013 with:

Any applicant for a freezing injunction must show that he has been granted, or has a good arguable case for being granted a judgment or order for the payment of a sum of money that is or will be enforceable through the process of the court.[9] The initial edition of this work added the additional qualification that, unless reliance was placed on s. 25 of the CJJA 1982, the claim against the defendant must be justiciable in the courts of England and Wales,[9a] however, the (obiter) view reached by the majority of the board in *Broad Idea International Ltd v Convoy Collateral Ltd*, was that there was no such qualification: "There is no requirement that the judgment should be a judgment of the domestic court—the principle applies equally to a foreign judgment or other award capable of enforcement in the same way as a judgment of the domestic court using the court's enforcement powers."[9b] **28–013**

[9] *Broad Idea International Ltd v Convoy Collateral Ltd* [2021] UKPC 24, at [101].

[9a] The footnotes to the initial edition of this work gave further information and context relating to this ostensible requirement. Given that there is room for doubt as to the extent to which the obiter comments in *Broad Idea* will be applied by the courts, this text is reproduced here:

> "This is the so-called "*Siskina* requirement": see Ch.26, para.26–013. In cases of extreme urgency an injunction can be granted in advance of the issuing of a claim form (see para.28–019 below; and Ch.27, at para.27–010. But unlike quia timet injunctions, a freezing order cannot be granted prior to the accrual of a cause of action. This requirement of an accrued cause of action has been applied in various cases: see *Steamship Mutual v Thakur Shipping Co Ltd* [1986] 2 Lloyds's Rep. 439 and *Veracruz Transportation Inc v VC Shipping Co Inc* [1992] 1 Lloyd's Rep. 353. However it is a rule which creates a real risk of injustice, for example, if A has a right to a monetary sum from B which falls due in the (near) future and is concerned that B is taking steps to divest itself of assets so as to make himself judgment-proof. Accordingly various creative inroads have been made into the principles to meet such potential injustice: see e.g. *Rowland v Gulfpac Ltd (No.1)* [1999] Lloyd's Rep. Bank 86, a case where the claimant had a right of indemnity against the defendant which had not yet crystallised, but Rix J held that he could grant relief on a quia timet basis to preserve the fund against which the indemnity could be asserted. His decision was more recently followed by Burton J in *Starlight Shipping Co v Allianz Marine & Aviation Versicherungs AG (The "Alexandros T")* [2011] EWHC 3381 (Comm); [2012] 1 Lloyd's Rep. 162, at [37]–[38]); and in *Zurich Insurance PLC UK Branch v International Energy Group Ltd* [2015] UKSC 33; [2016] A.C. 509 Lord Mance referred to these cases with apparent approval, at [87]. See also *Re Q's Estate* [1999] 1 Lloyd's Rep. 931; *Papamichael v National Westminster Bank Plc (No.1)* [2002] 1 Lloyd's Rep. 332 and *HM Revenue and Customs Commissioners v Ali* [2011] EWHC 880 (Ch). In *Kazakhstan Kagazy v Zhunus* [2016] EWCA Civ 1036; [2017] 1 W.L.R. 1360, at [23]–[27] the Court of Appeal confirmed that the *Siskina* requirement did not mean that a freezing injunction was unavailable in support of a contribution claim, even though strictly speaking the cause of action was contingent and had yet to accrue: it was sufficient that the defendant had the right to commence proceedings claiming the substantive relief."

[9b] [2021] UKPC 24, at [101]. Notwithstanding that this is the clear view of the majority of the board of the Judicial Committee of the Privy Council, there is some doubt as to whether it can yet be said to represent the law of England, or of any other jurisdiction. The views expressed were obiter dicta (albeit extremely powerful obiter dicta), and are not strictly binding on the lower courts of the BVI (which is where the appeal was from), let alone England. This is one reason why the minority did not join them—see the comments of Sir Geoffrey Vos, at [221]: "*the majority's ground-breaking exposition of the law of injunctions will not, as a matter of precedent, be binding on lower courts, but will be powerful obiter dicta. That, in my judgment is an unsatisfactory way to change the law in such an important area. I understand that, in one sense, the importance of the subject is precisely the reason why the majority feel so strongly that they should subscribe to the views expressed by Lord Leggatt. But I am concerned that the result will be a lack of clarity in many jurisdictions as to the consequences of such obiter dicta.*"

28–016 *At the end of the paragraph, add:*

Following consideration of the "good arguable case" test within the context of jurisdictional disputes in *Kaefer Aislamientos SA de CV v AMS Drilling Mexico SA de CV,*[18a] it has been remarked that the central concept at the heart of the test in both that context and in the context of worldwide freezing orders is that there must be "a plausible evidential basis" for the allegations made.[18b]

[18a] [2019] EWCA Civ 10; [2019] 1 W.L.R. 3514.
[18b] *Lakatamia Shipping Company Limited v Morimoto* [2019] EWCA Civ 2203, at [38], and *Blockchain Optimization S.A. v LFE Market Ltd* at [2020] EWHC 2027 (Comm), at [33].

28–021 *At the end of footnote 27, add:*

As remarked by Spencer J in *DBI Innovations (UK) Ltd v The May Fair Avenue General Trading LLC* [2019] EWHC 2235 (QB) at [47], the fact that the return date for a freezing order must not be turned into a "mini trial" does not provide a claimant with a "full stop" argument against consideration of the merits in all circumstances. A defendant may put material before the court which presents such a different picture, and presents the case in such a different light, to that portrayed by the claimant that the court must take a view about the alternative pictures presented. In such circumstances, doubts about the merits of a claimant's case may justify the discharge of a freezing order notwithstanding the fact that proceedings are only at an interlocutory stage, and no trial of the issues has yet occurred.

28–027 *Replace the quoted text with:*

> "In our view the test is whether, on the assumption that the plaintiffs have shown at least "a good arguable case," the court concludes, on the whole of the evidence then before it, that the refusal of a Mareva injunction would involve a real risk that a judgment or award in favour of the plaintiffs would remain unsatisfied."

(3) Real Risk of Dissipation

(i) Generally

28–028 *After "PJSC Tatneft v Bogolyubov[38]", insert:*

And, more recently, in *Les Ambassadeurs Club Limited v Albuewi.*[38a]

[38a] [2020] EWHC 1313 (QB), at [34].

At the end of the paragraph, add:

The principles articulated in this paragraph are conveniently set out by the Court of Appeal in *Organic Grape Spirit Limited v Nueva IQT, S.L.*[41a]

[41a] [2020] EWCA Civ 999, at [14]–[24].

Replace footnote 47 with: 28–030

[47] *Laemthong International Lines Co Ltd v Artis* [2004] EWHC 2226 (Comm); [2005] 1 Lloyd's Rep. 100, per Colman J at [61].

(ii) Specific factors relevant to assessing a real risk of dissipation

At the end of footnote 49, add: 28–031

See also *Tugushev v Orlov* [2019] EWHC 2031 (Comm), at [49], *Ivy Technology v Martin* [2019] EWHC 2510 (Comm), at [43]–[45], *Arcelormittal USA LLC v Ruia* [2020] EWHC 740, at [216]–[219], and *Les Ambassadeurs Club Limited v Albuewi* [2020] EWHC 1313 (QB), at [30]–[38].

At the end of footnote 51, add: 28–032

See also *State of India v Mallya* [2018] EWHC 1084 (Comm), at [169]–[170], and *Taylor v Khodabaksh* [2021] EWHC 655 (Ch), at [108]–[[113].

At the end of the paragraph, add: 28–034

It is therefore necessary for any defendant opposing the grant or continuation of a freezing order and seeking to rely upon a claimant's delay to focus on what argument he is using the delay to substantiate. An argument to the effect that, following the delay, any dissipation which the defendant was going to make (assuming, no doubt contrary to the defendant's primary case, that he was minded to dissipate his assets) will already have happened is—absent an extreme case—unlikely to be successful, for obvious reasons. On the other hand, an argument to the effect that the defendant has been on notice of a potential claim for a substantial amount of time and yet has not taken any steps to dissipate his assets may—depending on the circumstances—have more success.[55a]

[55a] See e.g. *Tugushev v Orlov* [2019] EWHC 2031 (Comm), at [80]–[82], and *Arcelormittal USA LLC v Ruia* [2020] EWHC 740 (Comm), at [223].

At the end of the paragraph, add new footnote 56a: 28–035

[56a] *Arcelormittal USA LLC v Ruia* at [2020] EWHC 740 (Comm), at [263].

Add new paragraph 28–042A after para.28–042:

The same sentiment was recently approved by the Court of Appeal in *Lakatamia Shipping Company Limited v Morimoto*, in which Haddon-Cave LJ endorsed the following statement of principle: 28–042A

> "It is not enough to establish a sufficient risk of dissipation merely to establish a good arguable case that the defendant has been guilty of dishonesty; it is necessary to scrutinise the evidence to see whether the dishonesty in question points to the conclusion that assets may be dissipated. It is also necessary to take account of whether there appear at the interlocutory stage to be properly arguable answers to the allegations of dishonesty."[64a]

[64a] [2019] EWCA Civ 2203, at [34]. Haddon-Cave LJ took the above statement of principle from the judgment of Popplewell J in *Fundo Soberano de Angola v dos Santos* [2018] EWHC 2199 (Comm), at [86]. However, he changed Popplewell J's formulation of "assets are likely to be" to "assets may be".

At the end of footnote 65, add: 28–043

Although—absent special circumstances—morally dubious behaviour falling short of dishonesty will tend to be weaker evidence of a risk of dissipation than actual dishonesty would have been. See e.g. the comments of Freedman J in *Les Ambassadeurs Club Limited v Albluewi* [2020] EWHC1313 (QB), at [43]: "Just as dishonesty does not necessarily prove a real risk of dissipation, how much more so where the case is some lack of commercial probity falling short of dishonesty. The further removed one is from dishonesty in terms of a low commercial morality, the more difficult it will be for a claimant to rely upon the instant conduct falling short of dishonesty as giving rise to the inference of real risk of dissipation."

At the end of footnote 66, add:

However, a refusal to engage with a prospective claimant in the absence of any obligation to do so will not, taken in isolation, be sufficient to establish a risk of dissipation; see *Trans-Oil International SA v Savoy Trading LP* [2020] EWHC 57 (Comm), at [50].

28–044 *At the end of the second sentence, add new footnote 66a:*

[66a] See, e.g. *Tugushev v Orlov* [2019] EWHC 2031 (Comm), at [61]–[92]: the bulk of a defendant's assets consisted of shares in a company which owned large physical assets (such as fishing ships and real estate), which shares were subject to statutory controls on transfer and security interests granted to a large multi-national bank. Carr J was not persuaded that there was a real risk of dissipation of these assets notwithstanding the defendant's concession that there was a good arguable case of serious dishonesty against him. Of course, the fact that assets are of a nature that they can be easily dissipated does not necessarily amount to evidence that there is a real risk that they will be dissipated—see e.g. *Arcelormittal USA LLC v Ruia* [2020] EWHC 740 (Comm), at [221]–[229], in which Henshaw J accepted that a respondent's assets could be easily dissipated given sufficient planning and professional advice but, in the circumstances, the respondent did not appear to be intending, or able, to effect that dissipation.

At the end of footnote 67, add:

Tugushev v Orlov [2019] EWHC 2031 (Comm), at [86]; *Gulf International Bank BSC v Aldwood* [2019] EWHC 1666 (QB), at [181]–[182].

Replace the final sentence of the paragraph with the following:

It is suggested that the proper approach to the question of whether the use of complex corporate structures gives rise to or demonstrates a risk of dissipation is to be found in Gloster LJ's judgment in *Candy v Holyoake*:

> "... if the [claimants] had shown that there was a risk of the defendants dissipating their assets—the defendants' links to complex and offshore corporate structures and the potential to transfer value rapidly and invisibly through corporate reorganisation could contribute to that risk. That is because a complex corporate structure or corporate reorganisation could enable a party who is minded to dissipate assets to do so ... However, the mere possibility of a party using a complex corporate structure or corporate reorganisation to dissipate assets, without more, does not equate to a risk of dissipation. Otherwise, the burden of proof would be reversed: parties subject to a freezing order application would be compelled to show that they would not dissipate assets in that way ... This emphasis is important. An applicant must show a risk of dissipation as opposed to it merely being possible (without more) that the claimant could dissipate in that way."[67a]

Finally, there are cases in which a claimant has a high degree of control over parts of the defendant's assets or income. This may, depending on the facts of the case, militate against the grant of a freezing order.[67b]

[67a] [2017] EWCA Civ 92; [2018] Ch. 297, at [59].
[67b] *Rogachev v Goryainov* [2019] EWHC 1529 (QB), at [103].

(4) Existence of Assets

At the end of the paragraph, add: 28–054

Orders of this type are, however, exceptional, and—if granted—may only be granted so as to enable the relevant insolvency practitioner to make their own application.[80a]

[80a] *The New York Laser Clinic Limited v Naturastudios Limited* [2020] EWHC 560 (QB), at [152]–[161].

(5) Just and Convenient

At the end of footnote 84, add: 28–059

See also *Arcelormittal USA LLC v Ruia* [2020] EWHC 740 (Comm), at [233]–[242] and [267], in which a freezing order was refused for a number of reasons, including the damage which it would cause to the business of one of the respondents. However, a mere assertion that a freezing order will cause a respondent reputational damage is—obviously—not a strong basis on which to resist it or seek its discharge; see e.g. *Vestey Foods UK Limited v Cox* [2018] EWHC 3466 (Ch), at [63].

At the end of paragraph 28–059(5), add:

Similarly, if a respondent could show that a freezing order was being sought in order to place pressure upon him to concede a claim, that may well—theoretically—be a basis on which such an order would be refused or discharged. However, the mere fact that a freezing order might have this effect will not be a reason for its refusal or discharge, and—if the applicant has shown a good arguable case and a real risk of dissipation—it is suggested that the Court is unlikely (absent exceptional circumstances) to find that the collateral advantages which a freezing order might confer upon an applicant would disqualify him from protection to which he would otherwise be legitimately entitled.[90a]

[90a] See e.g. *Ivanhoe Mines Limited v Gardner* [2020] EWHC 144 (Comm), at [25]–[26].

At the end of the paragraph, add:

(6) The potential effect of the freezing order on third parties, such as creditors, suppliers and purchasers. In *Arcelormittal USA LLC v Ruia*, a freezing order was refused for a number of reasons, including the effect that it would have upon the respondent's lender.[90b]

(7) Whether the applicant is prepared to give a cross-undertaking in damages.[90c] It would only be in the rarest cases that the Court would be prepared to grant a freezing order without a cross-undertaking in damages being proffered by the applicant.[9]

[90b] [2020] EWHC 740 (Comm), at [243]–[261] and [267].
[90c] *Bravo v Amerisur Resources Plc* [2020] EWHC 125 (QB), at [22].
[90d] See further, Ch.27.

C. INTERNATIONAL ASPECTS: WORLDWIDE FREEZING ORDERS AND APPLICATIONS UNDER SECTION 25 CJJA

(2) Principles which the Court will Apply in Deciding Whether to Grant a Worldwide Freezing Order

28–073 *At the end of the paragraph, add:*

For this reason, an applicant for a world-wide freezing relief would be well advised to explain in evidence to the Court whether he intends to seek similar relief and/or domesticate the English Court's order in other jurisdictions, why he intends / does not intend to pursue such a course and, if he does, his intended timing and method.[102a]

[102a] See e.g. the criticisms made of the applicant for WFO relief in *Les Ambassadeurs Club Limited v Albuewi* [2020] EWHC 1313 (QB), at [63]–[65].

Add new section after para.28–076:

(4) Orders under Section 37 of the Senior Courts Act 1981?

28–076A In *Broad Idea International Ltd v Convoy Collateral Ltd*, the majority reached the obiter conclusion that the BVI court had jurisdiction to grant freezing orders over a defendant within its jurisdiction to assist in the prospective enforcement of a judgment which might be entered in foreign proceedings, pursuant to section 24(1) of the Eastern Caribbean Supreme Court (Virgin Islands) Act.[105a] The same reasoning is equally applicable to section 37 of the Senior Courts Act 1981. Assuming that the English court follows these powerful obiter dicta, it remains to be seen whether (as seems likely) it will approach applications for such freezing orders in the same way as it has approached applications under section 25 of the CJJA.

[105a] [2021] UKPC 24, at [101]–[102].

D. PRINCIPAL FEATURES OF THE STANDARD FORMS OF FREEZING INJUNCTIONS

(6) The Subject Matter and Scope of the Freezing Injunction

(ii) "Dispose of, deal with or diminish the value of"

28–097 *After "...overall indebtedness).[137]", insert:*

Further, in *Podstreshnyy v Pericles Properties Limited*, Falk J was not persuaded that merely marketing property constituted "dealing" with it.[137a]

[137a] [2019] EWHC 469 (Ch), at [24]. In the same case, Falk J accepted that incorporation of a company may be a breach of a freezing order, albeit—on the facts of that case—it was a trivial one: see at [25]. It would presumably have been regarded as a more substantial breach if the respondent had paid for substantial amounts of share capital.

At the end of the paragraph, add:

For an example of the complexities which can arise, see *JSC VTB Bank v Skurikhin*. In that case, the respondent to a freezing order (S) had the power to direct the decisions of a Liechtenstein Foundation (B) which held assets for him and others on a discretionary trust. Because S had that power so long as he was a beneficiary of B, B's decision to exclude him as a beneficiary amounted to a disposal of S's assets, and was made in breach of the freezing order.[138a]

[138a] [2020] EWCA Civ 1337; [2021] 1 W.L.R. 434, at [65]–[67]. The Court of Appeal expressly left open the "interesting but difficult" question of whether, taken in isolation (i.e., without the additional element of S being able to direct the decisions of B), excluding a discretionary beneficiary is a breach of a freezing order on the standard Commercial Court Form.

Replace footnote 138 with:

[138] However, note should be taken of *R. (on the application of Revenue and Customs Prosecutions Office) v R* [2007] EWHC 2393 (Admin), in which McCombe J held that the transfer of funds between two accounts held at a bank constituted "dealing" with those funds in breach of a restraining order: see [18]–[21]. On the facts of that case, the transfer between two accounts was found to make enforcement potentially more difficult. It is possible that a different decision would have been reached were that not the case. See also *Aspinalls Club Limited v Lim* [2019] EWHC 2379 (QB), at [61]–[62], in which the use of funds to purchase a building within the jurisdiction pursuant to a contractual obligation to do so (which pre-dated the freezing order) was held to be a substantive, and not merely technical, breach of a freezing order.

(iii) "... up to the value of ...": Maximum sum orders

At the end of the paragraph, add: **28–098**

The "value" of an asset for these purposes is its realisable value—i.e. the amount that the applicant could realise from the asset if he were to enforce against it.[138a]

[138a] *Aspinalls Club Limited v Lim* [2019] EWHC 2379 (QB), at [56].

Replace footnote 141 with: **28–099**

[141] See Gee, *Commercial Injunctions* (7th ed, 2020), para 4–009.

At the end of footnote 143, add: **28–100**

Another is the unusual case of *Bravo v Amerisur Resources Plc* [2020] EWHC 125 (QB), in which £552,000 was frozen in respect of damages and £2.5 million was frozen in respect of costs.

(vi) What constitutes "his" assets

At the end of footnote 157, add: **28–114**

See also the bespoke wording used in *Russian Commercial Bank (Cyprus) Limited v Khoroshilov* [2020] EWHC 1164 (Comm), at [7]–[11].

At the end of the paragraph, add: **28–117**

This tension was considered in *FM Capital Partners Ltd v Marino*. In that case, Mr Peter MacDonald Eggers QC (sitting as a Deputy High Court Judge) held that the effect of the Supreme Court's judgment in *Ablyazov* was that the extended definition of a respondent's assets inserted by the 2002 amendments to the standard form wording applies to assets over which the respondent has control but which the respondent does not legally or beneficially own and that, insofar as the Court of Appeal held otherwise in *Lakatamia*, that decision cannot stand given the decision in *Ablyazov*.[164a]

[164a] [2018] EWHC 2889 (Comm); [2019] 1 W.L.R. 1760, at [51]–[53]

Replace paragraph 28–120 with:

28–120 As noted above, some doubt had been expressed on this part of the reasoning by the Supreme Court decision in *Ablyazov*, insofar as it suggests that the post-2002 standard form language relating to the respondent having the power, directly or indirectly, to dispose of or deal with assets as if they were his own *does* in itself (and without the post-2009 Commercial Court addition) extend the scope of the order to assets that do not belong beneficially to him. These doubts seem to have been resolved by the decision in *FM Capital Partners Ltd v Marino*. The position now appears to be as follows. Insofar as the decision of the Court of Appeal in *Lakatamia* was founded on the proposition that the post 2002 extended definition of assets did not extend to assets which were not beneficially owned by the respondent, that can no longer be regarded as good law, following *Ablyazov*. However, that does not mean that the assets of a company with only one shareholder and director will be treated as the assets of its shareholder/director for the purposes of that definition. The fact that a sole shareholder/director will tend to deal with the assets of his company as an agent rather than on his own behalf will still mean that he will not (without more) ordinarily be regarded as having the power to dispose of or deal with the company's assets "as his own".[169a]

[169a] *FM Capital Partners Ltd v Marino* [2018] EWHC 2889; [2019] 1 W.L.R. 1760, at [51]–[53].

28–125 *After "in Ablyazov", insert:*

and the decision in *FM Capital Partners Ltd v Marino*

After "at [35]" in footnote 176, insert:

and *JSC VTB Bank v Skurikhin* [2019] EWHC 1407 (Comm), at [15].

(7) Permitted Exceptions

28–129 *At the end of footnote 179, add:*

One should note in this regard that the Commercial Court Guide stipulates in footnote 4 to Appendix 11 that this wording should only be included where "really necessary", so the onus will be on the applicant to articulate and evidence some reason why the bracketed wording should be included. One would have thought that, if the applicant is able to show the requisite risk of dissipation necessary to obtain *Mareva* relief, it will be relatively straightforward to identify such a reason, but the Commercial Court Guide appears to envisage situations in which there is a real enough risk of dissipation to justify a freezing order (with its associated asset disclosure obligations), but not enough of such a risk to justify advance notice of the sources of funds to be spent on legal costs.

(9) Disclosure of Assets

At the end of footnote 182, add: **28–137**

That said, where a domestic *Mareva* injunction is made, it will usually be inappropriate to order disclosure of assets on a worldwide basis—see *Motorola Solutions, Inc. v Hytera Communications Corporation Ltd* [2020] EWHC 980 (Comm), at [119] (reversed on appeal, but not on this point).

At the end of footnote 184, add: **28–139**

See, too, *Aspinalls Club Limited v Lim* [2019] EWHC 2379 (QB), at [20]–[21] and [56]–[57].

After "per Vos J." in footnote 192, add: **28–143**

supplemented by Trower J in *JSC Commercial Bank Privatbank v Kolomoisky* [2021] EWHC 403 (Ch), at [41].

E. THE "CHABRA" JURISIDICTION

(1) The Basis and Nature of "Chabra" Relief

At the end of footnote 211, insert: **28–165**

Generally speaking, relief could not be obtained against the *Chabra* defendant which extends further than the amount by which the *Chabra* defendant is accountable to the substantive defendant: if the claimant has a claim against the substantive defendant for £100 million, and can demonstrate good reason to suppose that the *Chabra* defendant is accountable to the substantive defendant for no more than £50 million, there is no obvious basis on which to freeze more than £50 million of the *Chabra* defendant's assets. That said, there will be occasions on which the claimant is able to demonstrate that the *Chabra* defendant is accountable to the substantive defendant for *some* substantial amount, but is unable to quantify it. In such circumstances, it may be appropriate to freeze the *Chabra* defendant's assets to the maximum value of the claimant's claim—see *The New York Laser Clinic Limited v Naturastudios Limited* [2020] EWHC 560 (QB), at [95]–[97].

Add new paragraph 28–166A after para.28–166: **28–166A**

The nature and basis of the *Chabra* jurisdiction was further considered by the Judicial Committee of the Privy Council in *Broad Idea International Ltd v Convoy Collateral Ltd*, in which the majority, in obiter remarks, incorporated both *Mareva* and *Chabra* freezing orders into one, holistic, rationalisation of the jurisdiction to restrain the ability of a person (whether or not they are a defendant) to deal with their assets, so as to preserve them for satisfaction of an actual or anticipated judgment. In all such cases, the court is exercising its jurisdiction to grant injunctions where it is just and convenient to do so to prevent steps (other than in the ordinary course of business) being taken which would result in an actual or prospective judgment being left unsatisfied.[214a]

[214a] [2021] UKPC 24, at [52]–[61], and [75]–[102].

(3) Jurisdictional Considerations

At the end of the paragraph, add: **28–170**

(insofar as it has continuing effect pursuant to Article 67 of the EU-UK Withdrawal Agreement).

28–171 *At the end of footnote 219, add:*

The view of Nugee J in *Kea Investments Limited v Ivory Castle Limited* [2019] EWHC 309 (Ch), at [46]–[50], was that the reasoning of Males J is now to be followed by the High Court.

At the end of footnote 221, add:

However, *Dtek* must now be open to doubt following the decision of the Court of Appeal in *A v C* [2020] EWCA Civ 409; [2020] 1 W.L.R. 3504. In the latter case, the Court of Appeal held that section 44(2)(a) of the Arbitration Act 1996 *did* confer jurisdiction to make orders in respect of the taking of the evidence of witnesses against non-parties to the relevant arbitration agreement, while declining to comment on whether that meant that *Dtek* (which related to section 44(2)(e) of the Act) was incorrectly decided: see [35] and [57].

(4) Established Chabra Situations

28–178 *At the end of the paragraph, add:*

"[T]he jurisdiction is not confined to cases where the non-cause of action defendant … is a nominee or trustee for the [cause of action defendant, or "CAD"]. Rather … the ultimate test is always whether there is good reason to suppose that the assets would be amenable to execution of a judgment obtained against the CAD."[230a]

[230a] *Per* Jacobs J in *Motorola Solutions, Inc. v Hytera Communications* [2020] EWHC 980 (Comm), at [96]. This judgment was reversed on a different point on appeal (see [2021] EWCA Civ 11).

F. PROPRIETARY INJUNCTIONS

(3) The Requirements for a Proprietary Injunction

(i) Serious issue to be tried

28–205 *At the end of the paragraph, add:*

That said, it follows from the nature of a proprietary injunction that the serious issue to be tried must—at least usually—be in respect of allegations which, if proven, would afford the claimant a proprietary remedy. Two interesting recent cases in this regard are *Taylor v Khodabaksh* and *AA v Persons Unknown. Taylor v Khodabaksh* concerned allegations that a judgment had been procured by fraud. Falk J refused to grant a proprietary injunction in respect of monies which had been paid pursuant to that judgment, ruling that—until the judgment was set aside—there could be no question of any alleged fraud giving rise to a constructive trust over the monies paid (and, even if the judgment was set aside, the consequences of that recission would probably be determined by the order effecting the recission, not the rules of equity).[263a] In *AA v Persons Unknown,* Bryan J had to consider the question of whether Bitcoin is a form of property over which one could obtain a proprietary injunction. He held that it was (albeit only on an interim and without notice basis).[263b] We say "at least usually" because, in the corporate context, the Court has demonstrated a willingness to grant injunctions in favour of a shareholder to preserve company assets, notwithstanding the fact that the shareholder has no direct proprietary interest in the assets in question, and asserts no direct claim against the company.[263c]

[263a] *Taylor v Khodabakhsh* [2021] EWHC 655 (Ch), at [84]–[99].
[263b] *AA v Persons Unknown* [2019] EWHC 3556 (Comm), at [55]–[61]. Cryptocurrency was subsequently held to be property for the purposes of priorities in a liquidation in the New Zealand case of *In re Cryptopia Limited* [2020] NZHC 728.
[263c] See *Koza Ltd v Koza Altin Isletmeleri AS* [2020] EWCA Civ 1018; [2021] 1 WLR 170, at [83]–[96] and [107]

(ii) Balance of Convenience

At the end of the paragraph, add: **28–208**

It is, however, important to recognise that "more readily" does not mean "will".[267a] It is still necessary to consider the balance of convenience. If, for example, a claimant has a proprietary claim to fungible and readily available assets, the fact that the defendant is highly likely to be able to satisfy any money judgment made against him may well weigh heavily against the grant of an injunction.[267b] Similarly, even if the claimant claims a proprietary interest in unique property, the fact that the claimant only intends to sell the property in question will weigh against the grant of an injunction at least in the case of a deep-pocketed defendant.[267c]

[267a] See e.g. *Rogachev v Foryainov* [2019] EWHC 1529 (Ch), at [125].
[267b] See e.g. *Toma v Murray* [2020] EWHC 2295 (Ch), in which an application to continue a proprietary injunction over bitcoins was dismissed on the basis that the defendant would be able to meet any judgment made against them, and the claimant might have difficulty meeting any claim under his cross-undertaking. Similarly, a proprietary injunction was refused in *Dodoun v Collings* [2019] EWHC 2008 (Ch) on the basis that, if it were granted, the defendant faced a very real risk of bankruptcy.
[267c] See e.g. *Rogachev v Forainov* [2019] EWHC 1529 (Ch), at [125].

(4) The Form of Order

At the end of the paragraph, add: **28–213**

An applicant for a proprietary injunction might be tempted to make the terms of a proprietary injunction as wide as possible, so as to maximise his protection. That temptation must be tempered by the need to ensure that the terms of the injunction are clear and workable. Extensive reference to "traceable proceeds" and the like might seem like a good idea, but if a respondent cannot practically judge what constitutes traceable proceeds of property and what does not, that will constitute an independent basis on which to oppose the injunction or its continuation.[274a]

[274a] See *Vestey Foods UK Limited v Cox* [2018] EWHC 3466 (Ch), at [78]–[88], in which a proprietary injunction was discontinued, in part because it forbade the respondent from dealing with money or assets "derived" from certain monies. On the facts, it was not practicably possible to identify which money or assets were so derived.

CHAPTER 29

DISCLOSURE ORDERS

A. INTRODUCTION

(2) Procedural Bases for Ordering Disclosure

29–004 *In sub-paragraph (1), replace the penultimate sentence with:*

There is a substantial body of authority which has now accreted around both sub-rules, which are analysed in depth in the most recent edition of "The White Book" (Sir Geoffrey Vos (editor-in-chief), *Civil Procedure*, 2020 edn (London: Sweet & Maxwell, 2020)) as well as the standard texts on disclosure.[4a]

[4a] For example, P. Matthews and H. Malek QC, *Disclosure*, 5th edn (London: Sweet & Maxwell, 2016), with supplement published 27 October 2020.

Replace sub-paragraph (2) with:

Of course, the general disclosure provisions contained in the CPR apply to fraud proceedings. For cases in the Business and Property Courts (the likely venue for most civil fraud claims), the provisions of the disclosure pilot scheme in CPR Practice Direction 51U apply. The pilot was introduced on 1 January 2019 without transitional provisions, and applies to all existing proceedings, including proceedings where an initial disclosure order had already been made before that date.[5] It was originally introduced for two years, but has since been extended to apply for four years from 1 January 2019 (see paragraph 1.2 of Practice Direction 51U). The scheme was intended to remedy various perceived problems with CPR Pt 31 disclosure, and to ensure a new, proportionate culture of disclosure in litigation with a better balance between wide disclosure, where (and only where) that is appropriate, and the reduction of unnecessary documentary disclosure. Where the pilot applies, CPR Pt 31 is disapplied and issues of disclosure and inspection are governed by Practice Direction 51U instead, save that, by reason of Practice Direction 51U paragraphs 1.9 and 1.10, CPR rr.31.16, 31.17, 31.18, 31.19 and 31.22, and the related provisions of Practice Directions 31A and 31B, continue to apply in proceedings falling within the pilot. Specific disclosure orders may be particularly useful in fraud claims and, despite the disapplication of CPR 31.12 ("Specific disclosure or inspection") in claims to which the pilot applies, similar provision is made in paragraphs 17 and 18 of Practice Direction 51U.[5a] The pilot is considered in detail in "The White Book" as well as the standard texts on disclosure,[6] and is not considered further in this book.

[5] *UTB LLC v Sheffield United Ltd* [2019] EWHC 914 (Ch) at [16]–[17], per Vos C.
[5a] *BDW Trading Ltd v Fitzpatrick* [2015] EWHC 3490 (Ch) is an example of an order under CPR r.31.12 being made as part of an ex parte freezing order.
[6] For example, P. Matthews and H. Malek QC, *Disclosure*, 5th edn (London: Sweet & Maxwell, 2016), with supplement published 27 October 2020.

Add new sub-paragraph (9):

An unusual application was made at the return date of a without notice application for a freezing order in *Barfoot Farms Ltd v Revuckas*[10a] for an order permitting the registrar of the Land Registry to carry out a search of the index of proprietors' names against the names of each respondent to a freezing order and to report on its outcome in order to assist the applicant to enforce its legal rights. The application was not resisted and so full argument was not heard, but the applicant relied on *Parkinson v Hawthorne*[10b] in arguing that the Court had an inherent jurisdiction to make the order sought. The order was granted on terms that the applicant should use the information obtained from the registrar for the sole purpose of assisting in the recovery of monies claimed in the proceedings.

[10a] [2021] EWHC 2423 (QB).
[10b] [2009] 1 W.L.R. 1665.

B. Disclosure Orders Relating to the Defendant's Assets

Replace footnote 12 with:

[12] See *Nigel Upchurch Associates v Aldridge Estates International Co Ltd* [1993] 1 Lloyd's Rep. 535 and the interesting discussion thereon in S. Gee, *Commercial Injunctions*, 7th edn (London: Sweet & Maxwell, 2020) at paras 23–005 to 23–013.

At the end of the paragraph, add: **29–006**

The notification injunction decision of Nugee J in *Holyoake v Candy* was appealed.[13a] The Court of Appeal confirmed that risk of dissipation had to be established before a notification injunction could be granted, but set aside the notification injunction granted by Nugee J because: (i) the judge had applied the wrong test to risk of dissipation; and (ii) on the application of the correct test to the evidence, the notification injunction was not justified. As to the test for establishing risk of dissipation, the Court of Appeal held that there must be a real risk, judged objectively, that a future judgment would not be met because of unjustifiable dissipation of assets. This is the same test as is applied in relation to risk of dissipation on an application for a conventional freezing injunction, which was held to be appropriate in *Holyoake v Candy* because of the wide terms of the notification injunction sought, rendering it in effect an application for a modified version of a conventional freezing order rather than for a separate species of injunction. However, the Court of Appeal commented that the position might well be different on an application for a simple order requiring notice to be given of the proposed disposition of a specific property.[13b]

[13a] *Holyoake v Candy* [2017] EWCA Civ 92; [2018] Ch 297.
[13b] *Holyoake v Candy* [2017] EWCA Civ 92; [2018] Ch 297, per Gloster LJ at [34]–[48].

(5) What Must the Respondent Do?

29–025 *At the end of the paragraph, add:*

The decision of Hildyard J in *Pugachev* was recently referred to by Jacobs J in *The Public Institution for Social Security v Al* Rajaan,[41a] which involved applications for: (i) further disclosure following (allegedly unsatisfactory) disclosure given pursuant to a worldwide freezing order; and (ii) disclosure to assist the applicant in tracing the proceeds of alleged secret commissions. The aspects of the *Al Rajaan* decision which relate to the proprietary claim over the proceeds of the alleged secret commissions are discussed in Section B below. In relation to the disclosure pursuant to the freezing order, Jacobs J said that the approach of Hildyard J was "instructive" and followed the test which Hildyard J had set out in *Pugachev*[41b] in relation to the ordering of further disclosure.

[41a] [2020] EWHC 1498 (Comm), at [24].
[41b] *The Public Institution for Social Security v Al Rajaan*, above, at [38]–[40].

(6) Information About the Source of Funds

29–026 *At the end of footnote 46, add:*

The approach of Birss J in the *Pugachev* proceedings was adopted by Patricia Robertson QC, sitting as a deputy judge of the High Court, in *JSC BTA Bank v Ablyazov* [2018] EWHC 1368 (Comm), at [14] and [16].

(7) Privilege Against Self-Incrimination

29–027 *At the end of footnote 47, add:*

For a decision where a defendant to a *Norwich Pharmacal* claim sought to rely on the privilege against self-incrimination, see *Rowland v Stanford* [2021] EWHC 988 (Ch), per Adam Johnson QC (sitting as a Deputy High Court Judge) at [57]–[82]. The decision contains an analysis of the applicable principles and engages with the detail of the drafting of an appropriate order in that case to protect the defendant.

C. DISCLOSURE ORDERS AGAINST RESPONDENTS IN SUPPORT OF PROPRIETARY CLAIMS

(1) The Court's Approach

29–030 *At the end of the paragraph, add:*

Despite the purpose of disclosure in a proprietary, as opposed to personal, claim identified in *A v C*, there remains a need for proportionality in the disclosure exercise ordered. The applicant must demonstrate a real prospect that the information may lead to the location or preservation of assets to which he is making a proprietary claim and the potential advantage of the order to the applicant must be balanced against the detriment to the respondent (including potential costs, invasion of privacy and requirements to breach obligations of confidence to others). Such a balancing exercise may more readily come down against disclosure in a case where an application is made for the exercise to be carried out by an innocent third party than when it is to be carried out by the alleged wrongdoer.[53a]

[53a] This analysis is clear from the judgment of Hoffmann J, as he then was, in *Arab Monetary Fund v Hashim (No.5)* [1992] 2 All E.R. 911 and other case law summarised in *BDW Trading Ltd v Fitzpatrick* [2015] EWHC 3490 (Ch), per HHJ Behrens at [49]–[55]. A recent example of the requirement for proportionality leading to a much-reduced disclosure application following an adjournment is found in the judgment of Jacobs J in *The Public Institution for Social Security v Al Rajaan* [2020] EWHC 1498 (Comm), which involved (inter alia) an application for disclosure to assist the applicant in tracing the proceeds of alleged secret commissions.

E. CONFIDENTIALITY CLUBS

Before the semi-colon in the first sentence, add new footnote 71a: **29–042**

[71a] [2015] EWHC 550 (QB), at [20]–[22].

G. ORDERS AGAINST THIRD PARTIES, INCLUDING NORWICH PHARMACAL, BANKERS TRUST AND BANKERS' BOOKS ACT ORDERS

(1) Norwich Pharmacal Orders

(i) The basis of the jurisdiction

At the end of the paragraph, add a new footnote 80a: **29–052**

[80a] This paragraph was cited in *K and S v Z and Z* (BVIHCM 2020/0016) by the BVI Commercial Court on a *Norwich Pharmacal* application on 10 March 2020, per Wallbank J.

(ii) Types of relief granted

At the end of footnote 86, add: **29–056**

These paragraphs in *AB Bank* were referred to, with apparent support for the analysis, by Bryan J in *AA v Persons Unknown* [2020] 4 W.L.R. 35, at [46]–[48]. However, it seems likely that *AB Bank* will have to be considered by a higher court. There are already examples of submissions (albeit only on interim applications) that it was wrongly decided: see *Ion Science v Persons Unknown,* unreported, 21 December 2020 (Butcher J, at [20]–[21]) and *Fetch.ai Ltd v Persons Unknown* [2021] EWHC 2254 (Comm) (HHJ Pelling QC, sitting as a High Court Judge, at [28]–[30]).

At the end of footnote 87, add:

The requirement to seek *Norwich Pharmacal* relief under CPR Pt 8, with a supporting witness statement given under r.8.5, technically brings a claimant within the scope of the definition of "trial witness statements" in PD 57AC (which applies to witness statements for trial signed on or after 6 April 2021). Bearing in mind the purpose of a "trial witness statement" (as explained at paragraph 2 of PD 57AC), the provisions are not likely to be appropriate for all claims for *Norwich Pharmacal* relief. Consideration should be given to seeking a dispensation from certain requirements in PD 57AC (which can be done by an application on paper without notice under PD 57AC itself—see paragraphs 4.2 and 4.4 thereof).

At the end of footnote 89, add: **29–057**

For an example of the granting of a *Norwich Pharmacal* order in connection with a proprietary claim (over a stolen Paul Signac artwork), see *Hickox v Dickinson* [2020] EWHC 2520 (Ch)

(iii) The requirements for exercising the jurisdiction

29–060 *At the end of footnote 104, add:*

Although slightly differently expressed, the three threshold conditions described in paragraph 29–060 and the point that, if those threshold conditions are met, the court still has to decide whether to exercise its discretion to grant the order or not were re-stated in the recent decision of Saini J in *Collier v Bennett* [2020] 4 W.L.R. 115 at [35]–[41], and relied on in *Hickox v Dickinson* [2020] EWHC 2520 (Ch), *Oldknow v Evans* [2021] EWHC 1028 (QB) (at the time of writing, the subject of an outstanding appeal) and *Rowland v Stanford* [2021] EWHC 988 (Ch).

29–061 *At the end of footnote 105, add:*

Whilst it has now been established that it is not necessary for the *Norwich Pharmacal* claimant to intend to bring civil proceedings against any underlying wrongdoer whose identity might be revealed (see discussion at paragraphs 29–067 to 29–070), there remains some debate as to whether it is necessary for the alleged wrongdoing (if proved) to involve a private law (civil) cause of action vested in the *Norwich Pharmacal* claimant against the wrongdoer. This issue was considered by Andrew Baker J in *Burford Capital Ltd v The Stock Exchange Group plc* [2020] EWHC 1183 (Ch); [2021] 1 B.C.L.C. 122. He stated that, whilst the "wrong" may be a crime, tort, breach of contract, equitable wrong or contempt of court, he had not been shown by counsel any case in which *Norwich Pharmacal* relief had been granted in respect of alleged wrongdoing that would not invest in the claimant a right of action against the alleged wrongdoer. The specific point did not require determination in that case, but Andrew Baker J indicated that, had he had to decide it, the authorities which he had reviewed pointed towards a conclusion that it would be necessary for the alleged wrongdoing (if proved) to give the *Norwich Pharmacal* claimant a civil cause of action against the wrongdoer. It is suggested that this obiter conclusion is open to question.

29–064 *At the end of the paragraph, add:*

In *FHL v LTC*,[119a] the BVI Commercial Court (Wallbank J) granted *Norwich Pharmacal* relief, requiring disclosure not only from several registered agents, but also a former voluntary liquidator and professional nominee director of BVI companies. The applicant, a BVI company, had obtained judgments in Russia against two Russian individuals and sought disclosure of documents and information in relation to a several BVI companies that were said to have been used by the two individuals in a complex scheme to hide and/or dissipate assets. Two of the BVI companies had been dissolved through voluntary liquidation. No wrongdoing was alleged against the voluntary liquidator of either company or their former corporate director, but Wallbank J granted the relief sought, accepting the applicant's argument that the voluntary liquidator in fulfilling his functions of distributing assets and winding up the companies is innocently involved in the life or affairs of the company and is also likely to have the sort of information that the applicant seeks as to ownership and assets for the purposes of enforcement. Relief was granted against the company which had formerly provided directors of the same companies on the basis that such a corporate services company was innocently mixed up in the wrongdoing by being involved in the affairs of the companies and was likely to have information of the type sought.

[119a] BVIHC (COM) 2020/0048.

29–066 *At the end of the paragraph, add a new footnote 126a:*

[126a] This paragraph was cited in *K and S v Z and Z* (BVIHCM 2020/0016) by the BVI Commercial Court on a *Norwich Pharmacal* application on 10 March 2020, per Wallbank J.

At the end of footnote 130, add: 29–069

See also *Rowland v Stanford* [2021] EWHC 988 (Ch), per Adam Johnson QC (sitting as a Deputy High Court Judge).

Add new paragraph 29–082A at the end of para.29–082:

A further matter to be taken into account in the exercise of the Court's discretion is whether bank account information which the applicant seeks is held by the defendant bank or by a foreign branch of the defendant bank. A recent decision of the Hong Kong Court of First Instance (16 March 2021) involved an application for a *Norwich Pharmacal* order by limited partners of a Cayman Islands fund (which was allegedly the subject of a large-scale fraud) against two Hong Kong-incorporated banks in relation to four bank accounts, two of which were held in Hong Kong and two of which were held with Macau branches of the two banks. The HKCFI held that there was no reason why *Norwich Pharmacal* relief should not be granted by the Hong Kong Court in relation to the accounts held with the Macau branches and, on the facts, considered that the order sought should be granted.[160a] In his judgment, the Judge explained that there did not appear to be any English authority (or any Hong Kong authority) directly addressing the situation where an applicant seeks information from a foreign branch of a bank incorporated within the Court's jurisdiction. He referred to the (very brief) English High Court decision of *Credit Suisse Trust v Intesa San Paulo Spa & Banca Monte Dei Pasche Di Siena*[160b] in which HHJ Waksman QC, sitting as a Judge of the High Court, granted relief against two Italian-incorporated banks in relation to accounts held with their London branches (i.e. the reverse situation). He then stated that he was satisfied that there was nothing to prevent him from making an order where the information sought was held by a foreign branch of the Hong Kong-incorporated bank and that it appeared to him that the grounds for making such an application might be thought stronger than in a situation where the main bank was overseas and the branch was local to the Court determining the application. No authority giving the issue any detailed consideration was cited in either *Credit Suisse v Banca Monte Dei Pasche di Siena* or *A1 v R1* and the defendant banks did not contest the applications, but factors which may be relevant to whether the Court will grant the relief sought include: (i) the regulatory requirements applicable to the defendant bank and its branches (eg whether there are regulatory requirements for banks or their branches to keep records for a particular period of time); (ii) the local law (especially in relation to confidentiality) in the jurisdiction in which the branches are situated; and (iii) whether there is evidence that, or the basis for an inference that, the defendant bank had power to access information held by the branches. 29–082A

[160a] *A1 v R1* [2021] HKCFI 650, per Hon Coleman J at [47].
[160b] [2014] EWHC 1447 (Ch).

(v) Form of order

At the end of the penultimate sentence of footnote 171, add: 29–088

See also *Stokoe Partnership Solicitors v Robinson* [2020] EWHC 3312 (QB) where the principles in both *Solodchenko* and *Kensington International v Congo* were discussed at [29]–[34] by William Davis J, whose decision was upheld on appeal: see *Stokoe Partnership Solicitors v Grayson* [2021] EWCA Civ 626; [2021] 4 W.L.R. 87.

(viii) *Applications for evidence or documents to be used in foreign proceedings*

29–101 *After the first sentence, add:*

This approach is reflected in *ArcelorMittal USA LLC v Essar Steel Ltd*,[193a] where Jacobs J held that *Norwich Pharmacal* relief would not be appropriate where the sole purpose was to facilitate enforcement proceedings abroad. However, in that case, the *Norwich Pharmacal* relief was justified because it was sought to support and make effective a WFO granted because of the risk that assets would be dissipated. The applicant could therefore rely on purposes for which they needed the information sought which did not involve foreign legal proceedings (in contradistinction to *Omar* and *Ramilos*, where no freezing orders were in place to justify the relief sought).

[193a] [2019] 2 All E.R. (Comm) 414, at [159].

Add new paragraphs 29–101A and 29–101B at the end of para.29–101:

29–101A A different approach has been taken recently in the Commercial Court in the BVI: in *K and S v Z and Z*,[193b] *Norwich Pharmacal* relief was granted by Wallbank J in support of intended foreign proceedings in applications brought against registered agents of BVI companies (which were alleged to be companies being used to hide assets) by applicants who already had non-BVI judgments or were awaiting non-BVI arbitration awards against the primary wrongdoer. Wallbank J relied on the Court's equitable jurisdiction to grant relief, despite the fact that the BVI has equivalent legislation to that which defeated the *Norwich Pharmacal* relief in *Ramilos*. Jack J also confirmed that such jurisdiction existed in *A Foreign Representative in Foreign Insolvency Proceedings v Five Registered Agents* in the BVI Commercial Court on 15 June 2020 and agreed with the reasoning of Wallbank J in *K and S*, stating that "in this jurisdiction *Ramilos* is not good law".

[193b] BVIHCM 2020/0016, 10 March 2020.

29–101B The Grand Court and the Court of Appeal of the Cayman Islands have, in contrast, followed the English Court's reasoning in *Ramilos*: in *ArcelorMittal USA LLC v Essar Global Fund Limited & Essar Capital Limited*,[193c] the Grand Court (subsequently upheld by the Court of Appeal) accepted that *if* adequate relief can be obtained under the Cayman Islands' statutory regime for obtaining evidence for use in foreign proceedings, the Court's equitable jurisdiction to grant corresponding *Norwich Pharmacal* relief falls away and is no longer available (see [64]). However, on the facts of that case, the Grand Court determined that the statutory remedy did not displace the *Norwich Pharmacal* jurisdiction because, although the information sought was likely to be deployed in proceedings abroad, the Court was satisfied that: (i) the party seeking the information did not yet have sufficient information to commence substantive remedial proceedings abroad; and (ii) having regard to the risk of information being destroyed, the statutory regime would not be an available effective alternative remedy for the party seeking the information to pursue (see [71]–[72] for discussion and analysis). The Court of Appeal of the Cayman Islands (Martin JA with whom Rix JA and Goldring P agreed) upheld the decision and gave reasons at [53]–[65]. In summary, the Court of Appeal's reasoning was as follows: (i) the Cayman Islands statutory regime only concerns the giving of evidence for the purposes of foreign proceedings, whereas the *Norwich Pharmacal* jurisdiction cannot as a matter of principle relate to evidence (because the basis of the jurisdiction is a duty to provide information about wrongdoing) and, accordingly, so long as care is taken to confine it to its proper scope, there can in principle be no overlap between the two regimes; and (ii) the Cayman Islands statutory regime is to be treated as impliedly excluding *Norwich Pharmacal* relief in support of foreign proceedings only where those proceedings are on foot or where the applicant has available to him in the relevant jurisdiction procedures for pre-action disclosure or the provision of non-documentary evidence.

[193c] The first instance decision of Kawaley J dated 29 March 2019 is reported as *ArcelorMittal USA LLC v Essar Global Fund Ltd and Essar Capital Ltd* [2019 (1) CILR 297]. The Cayman Islands Court of Appeal decision dated 3 May 2021 has the reference CICA (Civil) Appeal No.15 of 2019.

(ix) Service out

Replace footnote 199 with: **29–102**

See the discussion in the previous edition of Hollander, *Documentary Evidence*, 12th edn (2015) at para.4–18, which has since been updated to take account of the decision in *AB Bank Ltd v Abu Dhabi* in Hollander, *Documentary Evidence*, 13th edn (2018), para.4–19. It seems likely that *AB Bank* will have to be considered by a higher court. There are already examples of submissions (albeit only on interim applications) that it was wrongly decided: see *Ion Science v Persons Unknown,* unreported, 21 December 2020 (Butcher J at [20]–[21]) and *Fetch.ai Ltd v Persons Unknown* [2021] EWHC 2254 (Comm) (HHJ Pelling QC, sitting as a High Court Judge, at [28]–[30]).

Replace footnote 200 with:

To the same effect, see also S. Bushell and G. Milner-Moore, *Disclosure of Information: Norwich Pharmacal and Related Principles* (London: Bloomsbury, 2019) at p.223.

(2) Bankers Trust Orders

Replace footnote 218 with: **29–112**

Kyriakou v Christie Manson & Woods Ltd [2017] EWHC 487 (QB), per Warby J at [14]–[16]. The principles have been repeated and applied recently in two cases: (i) *Koenig v Credit Suisse (UK) Ltd*, Freedman J, unreported, 15 May 2020: the Court determined that it was appropriate to make the order on the application of an investor who, there were real grounds to suspect, had been the victim of a fraud; the evidence suggested that she owned the money that she was attempting to recover, and the information sought would lead to the discovery of the identity of the company with which her money had been invested and its recovery; and (ii) *Fetch.ai Ltd v Persons Unknown* [2021] EWHC 2254 (Comm): the Court granted a *Bankers Trust* order in case of an alleged fraud in which persons unknown were able to obtain access to cryptocurrency accounts and trade the assets credited to the accounts belonging to the claimant at significant undervalue leading to substantial losses; a number of heads of relief were sought on an interim basis, including a *Bankers Trust* order against a respondent incorporated in the Cayman Islands; the *Bankers Trust* order was granted and permission was given to serve that application out of the jurisdiction.

Replace footnote 224 with: **29–119**

Global Energy Horizons Corp v Gray [2014] EWHC 2925 (Ch), at [70]–[79]. The correctness of this decision on the test of "practical control" for the purposes of the separate power to order disclosure under CPR 31.17 was doubted by Males J in *Ardila Investments NV v ENRC* [2015] EWHC 3761 (Comm) but, in any event, Sales J indicated in *Global Energy Horizons Corp v Gray* at [70] that it would have been right to order disclosure of documents under the equitable jurisdiction. *Ardila* was of course a case under CPR Part 31 which, in large part, has been superseded in the Business and Property Courts by PD51U (see updates to paragraph 29–004 above). In *Pipia v BGEO Group Ltd* [2020] 1 W.L.R. 2582, Andrew Baker J referred to the limited instances in which the concept of "control" appears in PD51U and concluded that it was implicit that "control", as defined therein, fixes the universe from which a party's Extended Disclosure is to be generated (see [13]). He addressed the question of whether a "control arrangement" sufficient to bring documents within the document universe arose in that case by reference to the reasoning in *Schlumberger* and *Ardila* (see [14]–[21]) and explained at [50]–[54] that, when the court is considering whether a third party's documents or classes of documents are within the "control" of a party to the litigation by virtue of some standing consent given by the third party so as to be within that party's disclosure obligations under PD51U, of the three aspects of the consent (scope/subject matter, type and quality), the question of "control" is concerned with the quality of the consent: "The scope of the consent will define the documents over which the disclosed party has control by virtue of the consent (if it is of the right quality), so that its disclosure obligations extend to those documents. The type of consent will affect what the disclosing party can be expected and required to do so as to discharge any disclosure obligation to conduct a search for those documents (again, if the consent is of such a quality as to confer control)" (see [51]).

29–122 *At the end of footnote 227, add:*

The phrase "entries in" a banker's book in section 7, which, by section 9(2), include "other records used in the ordinary business of the bank", means transactional records and it does not include non-transactional records maintained for regulatory compliance: see *Meng v HSBC Bank plc* [2021] EWHC 342 (QB); [2021] 2 W.L.R. 1153, per Fordham J at [28].

29–124 *At the end of the paragraph, add:*

The words "a legal proceeding" in section 7 of the Bankers' Books Evidence Act 1879 mean "a legal proceeding in the United Kingdom" not "a legal proceeding anywhere in the world".[230a]

[230a] *Meng v HSBC Bank plc* [2021] EWHC 342 (QB); [2021] 2 W.L.R. 1153, per Fordham J at [11] and [20].

At the end of footnote 231, add:

However, for a recent example of an order being granted under s.7, see *Atkinson v Varma* [2019] EWHC 2054 (Ch) (also known as *Re Grosvenor Property Developers Ltd (in liquidation)*). There is a valuable discussion as to the exercise of the Court's discretion on such applications in *Meng v HSBC Bank plc* [2021] 2 W.L.R. 1153, per Fordham J at [29]–[35], but the application there was dismissed in any event due to the documents sought not falling within the terms of the Act.

(4) Disclosure Orders Against Third Parties on the "Chabra" Basis

29–126 *At the end of footnote 235, add:*

See also *Stokoe Partnership Solicitors v Robinson* [2020] EWHC 3312 (QB), where the principles in both *Solodchenko* and *Kensington International v Congo* were discussed at [29]–[34] by William Davis J, whose decision was upheld on appeal: see *Stokoe Partnership Solicitors v Grayson* [2021] EWCA Civ 626; [2021] 4 W.L.R. 87.

CHAPTER 30

SEARCH ORDERS

A. INTRODUCTION

(1) What is a Search Order?

30–001 *At the end of the paragraph, add:*

An extensive survey of the law on search orders was set out in the Court of Appeal's decision in *TBD (Owen Holland) Ltd v Simons*.[1a] The Court concluded the survey with the following statement of three fundamental principles relating to search orders:

> "First, the purpose of a search order is to preserve evidence, whether documentary or real, and/or property in order to prevent the defendant from altering, destroying or hiding such evidence or property if given notice. The purpose of inspecting documents during the course of the search, to the extent permitted by the order, is to identify documents which should be preserved. Secondly, the facts that justify a search order being made may also in appropriate cases justify the making of without notice orders for the disclosure and inspection of documents and/or the provision of information pursuant to either CPR Part 18 or the court's inherent jurisdiction, but nevertheless the two types of orders are distinct, require separate justification, have different effects and must not be conflated. Thirdly, both search orders and without notice orders for the disclosure and inspection of documents and/or the provision of information must contain proper safeguards for the respondent, and those safeguards must be respected during the execution of the order. It follows from the second point that the safeguards required for without notice orders for the disclosure and inspection of documents and/or the provision of information are different to those required for search orders."[1b]

[1a] [2020] EWCA Civ 1182; [2021] 1 W.L.R. 992.
[1b] At [175].

In footnote 3, replace the final sentence with: **30–003**

The definition of "relevant property" in CPR 25.1(2) is materially the same as that in s.7(1)(b) of the Civil Procedure Act 1997: see para.30–006 below.

Replace footnote 4 with: **30–004**

[4] See the example form of order annexed to CPR PD 25. PD25A para.7.11 states that the example form "may be modified as appropriate in any particular case". However, see the remarks of Arnold LJ at [174] in *TBD (Owen Holland) Ltd v Simons* [2020] EWCA Civ 1182; [2021] 1 W.L.R. 992: "I have to say that I regard the current wording of PD25A para.7.11 as unfortunate. Paragraph 2 of the 1994 Practice Direction was preferable. The standard form of search order, which has been developed over more than 25 years, should be used unless there is good reason to depart from it."

B. PRECONDITIONS FOR THE GRANT OF A SEARCH ORDER

Replace the last sentence of footnote 14 with: **30–011**

The full passage is set out at para.30–022 below.

At the end of the quoted extract, add new footnote 14a:

[14a] Where the high threshold for a search order is not met, practitioners should consider the less draconian option of a 'doorstep delivery up order'. For a discussion of the test to be applied when granting such orders, see *Hyperama Plc v Poulis* [2018] EWHC 3483 (QB), *per* Pepperall J at [12]–[23].

At the end of the paragraph, add: **30–013**

In more recent authorities, the Court has identified five pre-conditions to a without-notice search order, rather than four. However, a close reading of the relevant passages reveals that what is denoted as condition (3) above is simply split into two for the purposes of the explanation in those authorities and the analysis is no different.[17a]

[17a] See, for example: *Bayerische Motoren Werke AG v Premier Alloy Wheels (UK) Ltd* [2018] EWHC 1713 (Ch), per Henry Carr J at [14]; *ArcelorMittal USA LLC v Essar Steel Ltd* [2019] EWHC 724 (Comm); [2019] 2 All E.R. (Comm) 414, per Jacobs J at [98]–[99]; *Calor Gas Ltd v Chorley Bottle Gas Ltd* [2020] EWHC 2426 (QB); [2020] 4 W.L.R. 129, per Fordham J at [8]; and *Koldyreva v Motylev* [2020] EWHC 3084 (Ch), per Meade J at [4].

(1) Extremely Strong Prima Facie Case

At the end of the paragraph, add new footnote 18a: **30–014**

[18a] See *ArcelorMittal USA LLC v Essar Steel Ltd* [2019] EWHC 724 (Comm); [2019] 2 All E.R. (Comm) 414, at [102]: Jacobs J described the first requirement for the grant of a search order as "a strong prima facie case that there is a civil cause of action" but, in that case, the precise formulation did not matter because in fact there was (as Jacobs J put it) "an unanswerable case that there is such a cause of action" because the claimant had already obtained an English judgment.

(3) Clear Evidence that the Defendants have in their Possession Incriminating Documents or Things, and there is a Real Possibility that they may Destroy Such Material Before an On Notice Application Can be Made

30–016 *At the end of footnote 22, add:*

Note that the "major, if not critical, importance" requirement was recently applied in *ArcelorMittal USA LLC v Essar Steel Ltd* [2019] EWHC 724 (Comm); [2019] 2 All E.R. (Comm) 414, per Jacobs J at [98]–[99].

30–018 *At the end of footnote 24, add:*

See also *MX1 Ltd v F* [2018] 3 WLUK 744, at [86], where Vos C refused an application against a "respectable journalist" allegedly involved in an unlawful means conspiracy where there was "nothing by way of significant or strong evidence to the effect that the defendant is an essentially dishonest person who is likely to disobey a court order."

30–019 *At the end of footnote 25, add:*

However, in the recent case of *MX1 Ltd v F* [2018] 3 WLUK 744, at [88], Vos C stated that search orders are appropriate where there is a "clear likelihood that vital evidence will be destroyed" (and in the case before him he held that there was a possibility that evidence would be destroyed, but not a clear likelihood). This is an apparently different formulation of the test, but it is clear from Vos C's reasoning that he did not intend to depart from previous authority.

(4) The Harm Likely to be Caused by the Execution of the Search Order to the Respondent and his Business Affairs Must Not be Excessive or Out of Proportion to the Legitimate Object of the Order

30–022 *At the end of the final sentence of the extract, insert new footnote 29a:*

[29a] Certain precautions will need to be taken when executing search orders whilst COVID-19 restrictions are in place, such as the wearing of masks. These precautions may in turn affect considerations of proportionality. For a recent example of the Court closely scrutinising the practical effect of the execution of a search order during the COVID-19 pandemic, see *Koldyreva v Motylev* [2020] EWHC 3084 (Ch), at [29], where Meade J noted that "the wearing of masks [and] body suits" would increase the "sense of fear and intrusion", particularly upon young children in a residential property. See further *Calor Gas Ltd v Chorley Bottle Gas Ltd* [2020] EWHC 2426 (QB); [2020] 4 W.L.R. 129, at [29]–[30], where Fordham J set out and approved a list of "Covid undertakings" embodied in the draft search order, covering matters such as social distancing, the use of hand sanitiser and the wearing of protective gloves and masks.

Add new paragraph 30–022A after para.30–022:

30–022A This fourth requirement therefore requires various factors to be balanced in the exercise of the Court's discretion as to whether or not to grant a search order. The factors to be weighed in the balance will vary from case to case, but commonly considered factors include the reasons for any delay in applying,[29b] any prejudice suffered by the respondent as a result of such delay,[29c] whether the aims of the order can be obtained through less intrusive means,[29d] and broader considerations of the public interest.[29e]

[29b] *MX1 Ltd v F* [2018] 3 WLUK 744, at [89].
[29c] *Bayerische Motoren Werke AG v Premier Alloy Wheels (UK) Ltd* [2018] EWHC 1713 (Ch), at [16].

[29d] A "doorstep delivery up order" is an example of a less intrusive injunction designed to preserve evidence. For further discussion of such orders, see *Hyperama Plc v Poulis* [2018] EWHC 3483 (QB), per Pepperall J at [12]–[13]. Another order which can be considered in place of or together with a traditional search order is an imaging order (i.e. where a forensic computer expert takes complete copies ("images") of the contents of storage media incorporated in or associated with computers, smart phones and cloud storage): there is not (yet) a standard form for such an order and important points for practitioners to consider with care are discussed in detail in *TBD (Owen Holland) Ltd v Simons* [2020] EWCA Civ 1182; [2021] 1 W.L.R. 992, at [176]–[193]. Mann J discussed the distinction between the taking of an image and the further step of ordering inspection of that image in *A v B* [2019] EWHC 2089 (Ch); [2019] 1 W.L.R. 5832, at [28]–[29]: see further footnote 63a below.

[29e] See *Bayerische Motoren Werke AG v Premier Alloy Wheels (UK) Ltd* [2018] EWHC 1713 (Ch) at [15], where Henry Carr J granted a search order against the manufacturers of counterfeit wheels on the basis of "a clear possibility of danger to public safety", notwithstanding "substantial delay" on the part of the applicants.

D. CURRENT PRACTICE AND PROCEDURE

(2) Procedure

Replace footnote 43 with the following: **30–031**

[43] Practice Direction 2B (Allocation of Cases to Levels of Judiciary), paras 1.1 and 2. See also The Chancery Guide (November 2020) at paras 7.2, 14.2, 14.3, 15.21 and 16.C25 to 16.27 and the County Court Remedies Regulations (2014/982).

(iv) The Form of Order

Delete the second sentence. **30–036**

Delete footnote 50.

In the third sentence, delete the words "or the Commercial Court Guide".

At the end of footnote 51, add:

See also *Frenkel v Lyampert* [2017] EWHC 3121 (Ch), at [90]–[91], where, in the context of a without notice freezing order rather than a search order, Amanda Tipples QC (sitting as a Deputy High Court Judge) recommended providing the judge with a tracked version (or alternatively a schedule) of any departures from the standard form, along with reasons for each modification. The problems which can arise when departures from the standard form of search order are not drawn properly to the Court's attention were set out in *TBD (Owen Holland) Ltd v Simons* [2021] 1 W.L.R. 992, at [18], [25], [26] and [174].

(viii) Computers/servers

Add new paragraph 30–046A at the end of para.30–046:

Applicants should carefully consider whether the availability of an imaging order (see footnote 29d above) renders a 'traditional' search order unnecessary—or alternatively enables its scope to be significantly restricted. Where a claimant has made a without notice application seeking both types of order, the court is likely to follow the recent guidance outlined by Arnold LJ in *TBD (Owen Holland) Ltd v Simons*:[63a] **30–046A**

> "In my view, any court confronted with such an application should first consider whether to grant an imaging order. If the court is prepared to grant an imaging order, then it should be presumed unless the contrary is shown that a traditional search order is unnecessary. Even if the court is prepared to grant a search order at all, careful consideration should be given as to the scope of the order having regard to the imaging order."

[63a] *TBD (Owen Holland) Ltd v Simons* [2020] EWCA Civ 1182; [2021] 1 W.L.R. 992, at [180]. The distinction between imaging as a preservation mechanism and inspection of the preserved material was discussed by Mann J in *A v B* [2019] EWHC 2089 (Ch); [2019] 1 W.L.R. 5832 and by Falk J in *Vneshprombnak LLC v Bedzhamov* [2021] EWHC 1360 (Ch). In *A v B*, search and seizure orders had been made in two cases and included provisions for the taking of images of relevant digital devices during execution. A dispute arose as to whether the claimants should be entitled to inspect the documents (after the filtering out of privileged material) prior to a standard disclosure exercise being carried out by the defendants. Mann J set out at [30] a non-exhaustive list of potentially relevant factors to be taken into account when deciding whether to order inspection by a claimant of an image previously obtained pursuant to an imaging order: the question of whether the defendant can be trusted to carry out the disclosure process himself; which party is better qualified to assess the relevance of particular documents; considerations of urgency; the possibility of applying search terms; any differences in resources between the parties; and the intrusiveness of the exercise and the possibility of irrelevant, privileged and/or confidential material being disclosed to the receiving party. On the facts, a claimant-led inspection process was allowed in both cases.

E. PRIVILEGE AGAINST SELF-INCRIMINATION

30–051 *Replace footnote 67 with the following:*

[67] For example, H. Malek, J. Auburn, R. Bagshaw et al, *Phipson on Evidence*, 19th edn with 2nd supplement (London: Sweet & Maxwell, 2019), Ch.24; C. Hollander, *Documentary Evidence*, 13th edn (London: Sweet & Maxwell, 2018), Ch.21; B. Thanki, *The Law of Privilege*, 3rd edn (Oxford: OUP, 2018), Ch.8; and P. Matthews and H. Malek, *Disclosure*, 5th edn with 2nd supplement (London: Sweet & Maxwell, 2020), Ch.13.

(5) The Privilege Does Not Apply to Material with an Existence Independent of the Will of the Person Relying on the Privilege

30–060 *At the end of the final sentence of the quoted extract, insert new footnote 83a:*

[83a] This analysis was approved and applied by Butcher J at [31]–[32] in *FM Conway Limited v Peter Suggett* [2018] EWHC 3173 (QB).

H. APPLICATIONS TO DISCHARGE A SEARCH ORDER

(1) Immediate Applications to Discharge

30–070 *Replace from "The current example form ..." to the end of the extract with:*

The current standard form of order provides that:

> "The Respondent is entitled to seek legal advice and to ask the court to vary or discharge this order. Whilst doing so, he may ask the Supervising Solicitor to delay starting the search for up to 2 hours or such other longer period as the Supervising Solicitor may permit. However, the Respondent must –
> (a) comply with the terms of paragraph 27 below;[90]
> (b) not disturb or remove any listed items; and
> (c) permit the Supervising Solicitor to enter, but not start to search."

Replace footnote 91 with: **30–071**

[91] *Bhimji v Chatwani (No. 1)* [1991] 1 W.L.R. 989.

SPECIFIC REQUIREMENTS FOR APPLICATIONS FOR AND EXECUTION OF SEARCH ORDERS IN THE PRACTICE DIRECTION 25A (INTERIM INJUNCTIONS) TO CPR 25

Delete footnote 105. **30–079**

CHAPTER 31

OTHER INTERIM REMEDIES

B. "GAGGING" ORDERS

(2) Search Orders

31–010 *Replace footnote 8 with:*

See for example S. Gee, *Commercial Injunctions,* 7th edn (London: Sweet & Maxwell, 2020), para.17–017.

C. PROVISIONAL LIQUIDATORS

31–015 *Replace the words "For that reason" with:*

Even in the case of a non-trading company, an order appointing provisional liquidators will subvert ordinary procedures for the appointment of officeholders, and typically install individuals chosen by one creditor (or a limited section of creditors), conferring upon them extensive powers, obstruction of which would constitute a contempt of court.[20a] For these reasons

[20a] As noted by ICCJ Mullen in *Frasers Group Plc v Debenhams Plc* [2020] EWHC 1755 (Ch), at [12]–[14].

D. APPLICATIONS TO ENFORCE A CROSS-UNDERTAKING IN DAMAGES

(1) The Application to Enforce the Cross-Undertaking

(i) Ordering an inquiry

31–030 *After "insufficient time to hear the inquiry in advance" at the end of sub-paragraph (2), add:*

One situation in which a defendant may be justified in seeking directions for an inquiry to come on before trial of the substantive action arises where there is reason to believe that a claimant may be unable or unwilling to satisfy any award made following the inquiry, and he refuses to provide adequate fortification voluntarily.[48a] In such circumstances, the threat of striking out the claimant's claim if such an award is not satisfied may be the best comfort the defendant (or the court) can have that any inquiry is not in vain.

[48a] There being no mechanism to compel further fortification. The provision of fortification for a cross-undertaking is always voluntary, it is only "required" in the sense that the Court makes the grant of interim orders conditional on its provision. Obviously, once the interim order is discharged and the parties are considering an inquiry under the claimant's cross-undertaking, this method of "requiring" fortification is no longer open to the court (see e.g. *Napp Pharmaceutical Holdings Limited v Dr Reddy's Laboratories (UK) Limited* [2019] EWHC 1009 (Pat), [2019] RPC 22, at [6]–[10]).

Add new paragraph:

In several cases, a respondent to an application for an inquiry under a cross-undertaking in damages, who is claimant in the main action, has sought security for his costs of the inquiry. The position under the RSC was that the court would not award such a respondent security for his costs because he was not a defendant to a claim in the relevant sense.[63a] It now appears settled—at least at the level of the High Court—that that is the position under the CPR as well, even in circumstances in which the application for an inquiry is made by a third party to the proceedings.[63b] **31–036A**

[63a] *C T Bowring & Co (Insurance) Ltd v Corsi & Partners Ltd* [1994] BCC 713.
[63b] *JSC Karat-1 v Tugushev* [2021] EWHC 743 (Comm), at [37]–[81] and *VTB Commodities Trading DAC v JSC Antipinsky Refinery* [2021] EWHC 1758 (Comm), at [138]–[157]. The position might be different in the comparatively rare cases in which it is the claimant who is applying for an inquiry under a cross-undertaking in damages given by a defendant; whether or not the defendant could obtain security for his costs of the inquiry would likely depend—at least in part—on the extent to which the order obtained (albeit wrongly) was a reasonable and foreseeable reaction to the claim brought.

E. ORDERS RESTRICTING MOVEMENT

(2) Bayer v Winter Order

(i) The jurisdiction

Add new paragraph 31–048A after para.31–048:

The Court of Appeal recently summarised the nature and bounds of the *Bayer v Winter* jurisdiction in *Lakatamia Shipping Company v Su* as follows: **31–048A**

> "3. The court has jurisdiction to make a passport order under s.37(1) of the Senior Courts Act 1981 but the grant of such relief is a relatively recent development along with freezing and search orders. The first reported decision concerning a passport order is that of the Court of Appeal in *Bayer A.G. v Winter* [1986] 1 W.L.R. 497 where the defendant was ordered to deliver up his passport and restrained from leaving the jurisdiction until disclosure had been given relating to counterfeit copies of the claimant's products. It was clear that if the defendant was allowed to leave the jurisdiction before disclosure took place there was a serious risk that the order for disclosure would be frustrated.
>
> 4. In his judgment at p.503C Fox LJ stressed that the relief sought was novel and that when exercising the jurisdiction to make an order under s. 37 on the basis that it appeared to be "*just and convenient*" to do so the court needed to keep firmly in mind the consequences for the defendant of having his liberty curtailed in this way:
>
> > "*The time during which the first of those orders should run should—and Mr. Prescott accepts this—be of very limited duration. It is an interference with the liberty of the subject, so that the period should be no longer than is necessary to enable the plaintiffs to serve the Mareva and Anton Piller orders which they have obtained, and endeavour to obtain from the defendant the information which is referred to in those orders.*"
>
> 5. Even with this safeguard in place the jurisdiction is not unlimited. Imprisonment is no longer available as a remedy for the non-payment of debts and it is common ground that the passport order jurisdiction cannot be used as a means of enforcing judgments by requiring the judgment debtor to remain within the jurisdiction and to reside in a particular place until the judgment debt is paid. In *B v B (Injunction: Jurisdiction)* [1998] 1 WLR 329 Wilson J refused to make a passport order restraining a husband who was resident overseas from leaving the jurisdiction until a costs order against him had been satisfied. That, he said, would convert the passport order from an aid to the court's established procedures for enforcing the judgment and make it a freestanding enforcement procedure in its own right.

6. The interference with the liberty of the respondent under a passport order must therefore be for no longer than is necessary to achieve the purpose for which it was granted. How long that actually is will necessarily depend upon the purpose for which it is granted. Most passport orders are granted (as in *Bayer A.G. v Winter*) to enable effective disclosure to be given and in the present case the passport order was limited in duration to the Means Hearing. But in many commercial cases involving foreign defendants the disclosure sought will be voluminous and complex and the time taken to bring on an effective hearing may be lengthy. The judge making the order will need to take into account the effect which being restrained from leaving the jurisdiction will have on a foreign defendant whose home and family life is abroad and to ensure that the terms and conditions of the order are proportionate. How that balance is to be achieved will vary depending on the facts and circumstances of each particular case."[106]

[106a] [2021] EWCA Civ 1187, at [3]–[6].

(ii) Before judgment

31–052 *After "with the order to which it is ancillary.[112]", insert:*

Where compliance with such order is achieved, the court is likely to treat with extreme caution any suggestion that the *Bayer v Winter* restrictions ought to be extended to "hold the ring" pending further interim orders. Generally speaking, *Bayer v Winter* restrictions are to secure compliance with tightly defined obligations. To allow such restrictions to continue simply to maintain the *status quo* or to preserve the court's freedom to act in the future risks losing sight of that function.[112a]

[112a] *Protasov v Derev* [2020] EWHC 2884 (Ch), at [30].

Add new paragraph 31–052A after para.31–052:

31–052A Notwithstanding the stress which the authorities place upon the short-term nature of the restraint, it is fair to say that the court is unlikely to have much sympathy for submissions that a *Bayer v Winter* order has subsisted for too long if the reason for that fact is the respondent's own recalcitrance.[113a]

[113a] This was the case in *Lakatamia Shipping Company Limited v Su* [2021] EWCA Civ 1187, in which a *Bayer v Winter* order was in place for more than three years, but the reason for that fact was Mr Su's "extraordinary resistance" to the court's orders (see [43]).

31–053 *At the end of the paragraph, add:*

The presence of children within the jurisdiction will often be an indication that a respondent is unlikely to quit it.[114a]

[114a] See e.g. *Protasov v Derev* [2020] EWHC 2884 (Ch), at [47].

(iii) After judgment

31–057 *At the end of the paragraph, insert:*

An order compelling a foreign national to remain in the jurisdiction so that effective examinations could take place under CPR 71 was also made in *Lakatamia v Su*.[121a] In that case, the respondent appealed against Waksman J's refusal to discharge a *Bayer v Winter* order, in part because it had the effect of forcing him to remain in the jurisdiction beyond the expiry of his visa, placing him in criminal breach of immigration laws. That appeal was unsuccessful. The Court of Appeal took the view that, in circumstances in which Mr Su had been compelled to remain in the jurisdiction by reason of Court orders (and incarceration for contempt), the secretary of state was likely to grant him leave to remain for such periods and—until an application for such leave was made and refused—Waksman J was entitled to take the view that Mr Su was unlikely to face any criminal consequences flowing from his enforced stay in the jurisdiction.[121b]

[121a] [2021] EWCA Civ 1187.
[121b] *Lakatamia v Su*, above, at [37].

Add new section after paragraph 31–058:

(4) Curfew/Tagging Orders

In *Lakatamia Shipping Co Ltd v Su*, the claimant sought an order requiring the defendant to reside at a specified property for 22 hours a day, and to be fitted with an electronic tag. Foxton J stated that he was not persuaded that he had jurisdiction under section 37(1) of the Senior Courts Act 1981 to make such an order.[124a] While there have been instances in the Family Division in which a party has been tagged pursuant to a Court order, the judge noted that such tagging occurred with the party's consent (as a condition of obtaining an order they sought, or in order to avoid an order sought by another party), and did not suggest a wider jurisdiction to simply impose such severe restrictions on liberty.[124b] **31–058A**

[124a] By which he presumably meant that it would be contrary to settled practice to grant such an order, rather than that that section did not confer power to grant the order in the strict sense. The power of the court to grant injunctions under section 37 against parties over whom it has jurisdiction is, subject to statutory limitations, unlimited, but the extent to which the court will actually use that power is circumscribed by doctrine and practice—see e.g. *Broad Idea International Ltd v Convoy Collateral Ltd* [2021] UKPC 24, at [57]
[124b] *Lakatamia Shipping Co Ltd v Su* [2020] EWHC 865 (Comm), [2020] 1 WLR 2852, at [62]–[80].

F. APPLICATIONS TO CROSS-EXAMINE ON AFFIDAVIT OF ASSETS

(2) Principles upon which the Court Acts

At end of paragraph, insert new footnote 134a: **31–061**

[134a] This paragraph was cited with approval by the court in *Atkinson v Varma* [2019] EWHC 2054 (Ch) per Mr Adam Johnson QC (sitting as a Deputy High Court Judge) at [18].

Add new paragraph 31–063A after paragraph 31–063:

Mr Christopher Hancock QC, sitting as a deputy judge, summarised the principles applicable to applications of this nature as follows: **31–063A**

> "In my judgment, these various authorities, dealing as they do with a variety of different situations, establish the following general propositions:
> 1) The discretion to order cross-examination is broad and unfettered and may be ordered whenever the court considers it just and convenient.
> 2) The purpose of such an order (in any context) is to render the Court process effective.
> 3) The cross-examination must be proportionate and must not be for an ulterior purpose.
> 4) Significant or serious deficiencies in existing disclosure, or in responses to earlier orders, may justify cross-examination.

5) If alternative ways of achieving the same end can be used, these should be used in preference to cross-examination.
6) A change in the Defendant's story may be a good reason to order cross-examination.
7) There may be specific considerations applicable to particular situations in which an order for cross examination is sought.
   a) Cross-examination in relation to an affidavit on disclosure should not be allowed.
   b) Cross examination in relation to asset disclosure should be the exception rather than the rule.
8) There is an important distinction to be drawn between cases relating to the situation before judgment and cases which relate to the situation after judgment. In my judgment, the position is different after judgment has been given, for a number of reasons:
   a) There is no question of the trial process being prejudiced by virtue of a cross-examination procedure having taken place before trial. This possibility clearly troubled Beatson J in the *West London Pipeline* case: see paragraph 84 of that case in particular.
   b) There is a valid analogy between the provisions of CPR Part 71 (relating to attendance of witnesses to give oral evidence in aid of execution) and the current case, even if, as the parties suggest, Part 71 is not itself applicable in terms (a proposition which I would wish to leave open). However, I do not propose in this case to apply a "very low bar".
   c) It is important to bear in mind that this is a case where the very duty sought to be enforced is a duty to give information. This, in my judgment, tends to support the suggestion that the agent or fiduciary should be required to give explanations, and to attend to answer questions in this regard.
   d) It is also important to bear in mind that the order of Knowles J specifically contemplated that there might indeed be a need for cross-examination, following the production of the documents required by virtue of his holdings."[147a]

[147a] *Khouj v Acropolis Capital Partners Limited* [2021] EWHC 1667 (Comm) at [45]. See also a similar summary of the applicable principles in *JSC Commercial Bank Privatbank v Kolomoisky* [2021] EWHC 403 (Ch) at [39]–[44].

31–065 *At the end of the paragraph, insert:*

For another example of the sorts of safeguards which the court might order, see *Kazakhstan Kagazy Plc v Zhunus*, in which Jacobs J ordered that: (a) cross examination be limited to a single day; (b) the examiners provide, in advance, a list of topics to be addressed, a bundle of any documents to which they intend to refer and certain disclosure; and (c) cross examination be limited to the identification of assets against which a WFO could bite.[155a]

[155a] [2019] EWHC 1693 (Comm), at [52].

G. ORDERS (OTHER THAN FOR ASSET DISCLOSURE) ANCILLARY TO FREEZING INJUNCTIONS

(1) Orders Against Solicitors for Disclosure/Information

Add new paragraph 31–074A after para.31–074:

31–074A Applying the above principles, in *Tonstate Group Limited v Wojakovski*, Zacaroli J made an order that a respondent to a freezing order was to identify the source of the funds from which he was paying his legal fees and, if he failed to do so, his solicitors were to provide that information.[170a]

[170a] [2021] EWHC 1122 (Ch), at [102]–[117].

Add new paragraph 31–077A after para.31–077:

As noted above, in *Tonstate Group Limited v Wojakovski*, an order was made requiring the respondent to a freezing order to identify the sources of funds from which he was paying his legal fees. This was justified by the need to ensure that Mr Wojakovski was not using funds subject to a WFO and a proprietary injunction to pay such fees in circumstances in which he had historically failed to cooperate with court orders, had previously made (or allowed his solicitors to make) untrue representations as to the source of his legal funding (and other matters) and had deliberately breached the proprietary injunction to pay fees in other proceedings.[171a] **31–077A**

[171a] [2021] EWHC 1122 (Ch), at [102]–[117].

Chapter 32

THE RETURN DATE

A. INTRODUCTION

(2) The Risks of Consenting to the Continuation of the Injunction Pending the Effective Return Date

32–004 *At the end of footnote 5, add:*

In *Kea Investments Ltd v Watson* [2020] EWHC 472 (Ch), Nugee J referred to this as "the *Chanel* principle" (see [48]–[50]). He noted that the principle was different from the principles applicable to issue estoppel (at [48]) and, by reference to one of his earlier judgments (*Holyoake v Candy* [2016] EWHC 3065 (Ch); [2016] 6 Costs L.R. 1157, at [12]–[17]), concluded that the authorities on the operation of the *Chanel* principle "are not entirely easy to reconcile with each other." The principle was summarised by Garnham J in *Mirchendani v Gheewala* [2020] EWHC 1742 (QB) as follows: "If a party has contested the grant of the interlocutory order, or had the chance to do so and did not take it, the Court will only set aside the order where there has been a material change in circumstances, where the facts on which the original decision had been made had been misstated or where there is a manifest error on the part of the Judge" (see [48]). However, whether the *Chanel* principle is engaged in any given case needs to be carefully considered: see *AA v BB* [2020] EWHC 2490 (Ch) and *Vneshprombank LLC v Bedzhamov* [2021] EWHC 1360 (Ch), at [55]–[71].

In footnote 6, replace the citation for Stephens McBride Piercy Taylor Ltd v McBride with [2014] EWHC 1231 (QB).

At the end of footnote 7, add:

See also *AA v BB* [2020] EWHC 2490 (Ch).

B. BREACH OF DUTY OF FAIR PRESENTATION

(1) A Ground of Discharge

32–020 *At the end of footnote 31, add:*

Carr J referred to the principles to be applied in some detail at [7] of *Tugushev v Orlov* [2019] EWHC 2031 (Comm), quoted with approval by the Court of Appeal in *Valbonne Estates Ltd v Cityvalue Estates Ltd* [2021] EWCA Civ 973, at [47]. In *Valbonne*, the Court of Appeal again emphasised that there "are no hard and fast rules which must be applied" (where there has been material non-disclosure on a without notice application) and that "the court should take into account all relevant circumstances" (at [55]). For further examples where material non-disclosure was so serious, substantial and culpable as to warrant discharge and no re-grant, see *Al-Jaber v Salfiti* [2018] EWHC 3038 (Ch) and *Fundo Soberano de Angola v Dos Santos* [2018] EWHC 2199 (Comm), at [81]–[85].

(3) Discretion to Discharge and Re-grant

32–026 *At the end of footnote 44, add:*

Carr J (as she then was) referred to the principles to be applied in some detail at [7] of *Tugushev v Orlov* [2019] EWHC 2031 (Comm). In *Valbonne Estates Ltd v Cityvalue Estates Ltd* [2021] EWCA Civ 973, the Court of Appeal again emphasised that there "are no hard and fast rules which must be applied" (where there has been material non-disclosure on a without notice application) and that "the court should take into account all relevant circumstances" (at [55]).

C. APPLICATIONS TO VARY FOR (FURTHER) PERMITTED EXPENDITURE: FREEZING ORDERS

(1) Introduction

At the end of the paragraph, add: **32–034**

This approach was adopted by Daniel Toledano QC (sitting as a Deputy High Court Judge) in *National Bank Trust v Yurov*[59a] on an application by a defendant to vary a post-judgment worldwide freezing order in relation to (i) the allowance for legal expenses and (ii) an interest in certain frozen assets; and by Lambert J in *North of England Coachworks Ltd v Khan*[59b] on an application by respondents to a freezing order to permit them to sell frozen assets in order to fund legal expenses for forthcoming committal proceedings and the defence of the underlying litigation.

[59a] [2021] EWHC 164 (Comm), at [14]–[19].
[59b] [2020] EWHC 1972 (QB), at [12].

(2) Living Expenses

At the end of the paragraph, add: **32–037**

In *Vneshprombank LLC v Bedzhamov*[63a] the Court of Appeal discussed the exercise in which the Court engages in setting a figure for living expenses. The question of principle in that case was whether, in setting such a figure, a judge should determine as a question of fact what the defendant's living expenses were before the making of the freezing order; or whether an assessment is required of what the defendant's ordinary living expenses will be after the making of the freezing order, in which the level of expenditure in the past is merely evidence. Males LJ said that: "These are very different exercises. What the defendant was accustomed to spend before the order was made is a question of past fact. . . . What the defendant will spend after the order is made is a different kind of question in which past expenditure is only a starting point. Rather than being a question of past fact, it requires a prediction about the future—a future, moreover, in which the pressure of the litigation and the need to incur (possibly substantial) legal fees to defend the claim may very well lead the defendant to behave differently from how he has behaved in the past." Males LJ concluded that a defendant should be "permitted to spend by way of ordinary living expenses in accordance with his actual past standard of living".[63b] He explained that conclusion by reference to what he perceived to be well-established principles applicable to freezing orders as follows:

> "(1) The purpose of the freezing order jurisdiction is not to provide a claimant with security but to prevent a defendant from taking steps outside the ordinary course which will have the effect of rendering any judgment unenforceable; subject to this, a defendant should be entitled to do as he wishes with his own money. Just as the court will not inquire whether a proposed business expenditure is reasonable or prudent, so long as it is made in good faith, nor is it the business of the court to tell a defendant who has funds available that he cannot spend them on his ordinary living expenses in same way as he has genuinely been accustomed to do before the making of the order. (2) A defendant who has only limited funds available, such that he will or may be unable to sustain his previous level of expenditure on living expenses, will have some hard decisions to make as to how and when to reduce his spending. But these are decisions for the defendant and

not for the court. (3) It is particularly important to ensure that a freezing order does not operate oppressively. The consequences for a defendant against whom an order is made are often severe and can be crippling. That is one reason why the claimant's undertaking in damages is so critical. An order which has the immediate effect of preventing a defendant from spending what he has been accustomed to spend on what are for him his ordinary living expenses creates a particularly acute danger of oppression, not least because of the effect it may have not only on the defendant himself but on members of his family for whom he is responsible. (4) Conversely, the court must be alert to the danger that a defendant will seek to maximise the amount which he is permitted to spend, for example to ensure that as much as possible is kept out of the claimant's hands in the event that a judgment is ultimately obtained, and will therefore exaggerate what he has been spending on living expenses. That would be a form of dissipation of assets which it is appropriate to prevent. (5) That danger can be avoided, however, by the exercise of a healthy scepticism about a defendant's assertions as to the nature and amount of his pre-freezing order expenditure. When appropriate, the court will require convincing support for such assertions. The more extravagant the expenditure, particularly if it appears reckless when seen in the light of the resources available to a defendant, the more sceptical the court is entitled to be. That applies with even greater force if there is reason to doubt the veracity of the defendant's asset disclosure or if his credibility is otherwise open to question, but this should not be viewed as a justification for embarking on extensive investigation of the merits of the underlying dispute or other issues of credibility which can only be resolved at trial. The questions remain questions of fact: what has the defendant been accustomed to spend and what was his actual past standard of living? (6) It may also be appropriate, particularly in a case where there are serious doubts about a defendant's ability to continue to spend money on his living expenses at the same rate as he has been doing in the past, to "ring fence" significant items of expenditure so as to ensure that, while the defendant is permitted to incur them if he wishes, he cannot spend the money on something else, at any rate without further permission from the court."[63c]

Newey LJ and Vos C agreed with Males LJ in relation to the point of principle.[63d]

[63a] [2019] EWCA Civ 1992; [2020] 1 All E.R. (Comm) 911, per Males LJ at [64].
[63b] *Vneshprombank LLC v Bedzhamov*, above, per Males LJ at [65]–[67].
[63c] *Vneshprombank LLC v Bedzhamov*, above, per Males LJ at [68].
[63d] *Vneshprombank LLC v Bedzhamov*, above, per Vos C at [99]–[102].

(3) Legal Advice and Representation

32–042 *At the end of footnote 71, add:*

See also the cases referred to at paras 32–034 and 32–037 above.

32–044 *At the end of footnote 74, add:*

The same approach was followed by Miles J in *AA v BB* [2021] EWHC 1833 (Ch) on an application by a defendant for an order that the claimants would not be entitled to pursue legal action against the defendant's lawyers in respect of funds over which the claimants asserted a proprietary interest paid to the defendant's lawyers as legal fees for the defence of the claim (see [63]–[87]).

(4) Dealings in the "Ordinary and Proper Course of Business"

(i) Generally: the "Angel Bell" proviso

32–050 *At the end of footnote 80, add:*

See also *Vneshprombank LLC v Bedzhamov* [2019] EWCA Civ 1992; [2020] 1 All E.R. (Comm) 911, at [57]–[59].

At the end of the paragraph, add: **32–051**

The Court of Appeal in *Koza Ltd v Ackil*[82a] (in the context of undertakings given by the appellant not to "dispose of, deal with or diminish the value of any funds belonging to [it] or held to [its] order other than in the ordinary and proper course of its business", described by the Court as having the same purpose as a freezing order) summarised the relevant principles as follows:

"i) The question of whether a transaction is in the ordinary and proper course of a company's business is a mixed question of fact and law;
ii) "Ordinary" and "proper" are separate, cumulative requirements;
iii) The test is an objective one, making it necessary to consider the question against accepted commercial standards and practices for the running of a business;
iv) The question is not whether the transaction is ordinary or proper, but whether it is carried out in the ordinary and proper course of the company's business;
v) The questions are to be answered in the specific factual context in which they arise."

[82a] [2019] EWCA Civ 891; [2020] 1 All E.R. (Comm) 301, at [27].

(ii) Applications to permit specific one-off payments/transactions

At the end of footnote 86, add: **32–054**

See also *Vneshprombank LLC v Bedzhamov* [2019] EWCA Civ 1992; [2020] 1 All E.R. (Comm) 911, at [46]–[55] and *Koza Ltd v Ackil* [2019] EWCA Civ 891; [2020] 1 All E.R. (Comm) 301, at [22]–[27].

At the end of the paragraph, add: **32–058**

The case of *Organic Grape Spirit Ltd v Nueva IQT SL*[90a] contains an interesting discussion about when, if ever, a company against which a freezing order has been made can pursue a fledgling business. In that case, the respondent had been made subject to a worldwide freezing order granted under section 25 of the Civil Jurisdiction and Judgments Act 1982 in aid of proceedings which were to be commenced in Spain and applied to vary its terms so that it could pursue a business outlined in the evidence in support of the application but which had not yet been established (for example, the company did not have any employees and its warehouse premises were empty at the time of the application[90b]). The Court drew a distinction between a pattern of past *expenditure* by the company (which the company could show as it had spent substantial sums acquiring equipment for its new business) and a pattern of past *trading* (which it could not show) and said that, in the circumstances, it could not rely on the "ordinary and proper business" exception to the freezing order because "the protection afforded by a freezing order could be significantly eroded if the defendant could claim that transactions fell within the "ordinary and proper business" exception when there was no benchmark against which the activities could be assessed".[90c]

[90a] [2020] EWCA Civ 999.
[90b] *Organic Grape Spirit Ltd v Nueva IQT SL*, above, at [28].
[90c] *Organic Grape Spirit Ltd v Nueva IQT SL*, above, at [29].

D. APPLICATIONS TO VARY FOR (FURTHER) PERMITTED EXPENDITURE: PROPRIETARY ORDERS

32–062 *At the end of footnote 97, add:*

For two recent examples of the application of these principles, see *Fundo Soberano de Angola v Dos Santos* [2018] EWHC 3624 (Comm) and *Skattegorvaltningen (the Danish Customs and Tax Administration) v Solo Capital Partners LLP* [2020] EWHC 2161 (Comm), both of which were applications by defendants to fund their legal expenses out of funds in respect of which the claimants asserted a proprietary interest.

32–068 *At the end of the paragraph, add new footnote 107a:*

[107a] The analysis at paras 32–059 to 32–068 above was cited with approval in *Kea Investments Ltd v Watson* [2020] EWHC 472 (Ch), per Nugee J at [22].

E. PERMISSION TO ENFORCE THE ORDER ABROAD

32–069 *At the end of footnote 108, add:*

In *The Kingdom of Sweden v Serwin* [2020] EWHC 1251 (Comm), the claimant had obtained a worldwide freezing order and proprietary injunction. Butcher J gave permission for the enforcement of the freezing order against the respondents' assets in Sweden because the assets in Sweden had been subject to certain restraints in Swedish proceedings which were due to lapse in the near future, leaving the respondents free to dispose of their Swedish assets.

32–075 *At the end of footnote 113, add:*

Two further recent examples of successful applications to enforce abroad are *The Kingdom of Sweden v Serwin* [2020] EWHC 1251 (Comm) (see n.108 above; enforcement in Sweden was sought) and *Claimants Listed in Schedule 1 v Spence* [2021] EWHC 276 (Comm) (enforcement in Florida was sought). It goes without saying that evidence of the relevant foreign law and procedure will be important. It appears from the judgments in both these cases that foreign law evidence was adduced by the applicants seeking permission to enforce abroad.

CHAPTER 33

RECEIVERSHIP

C. PRINCIPLES GOVERNING THE APPOINTMENT OF A PRE-JUDGMENT RECEIVER

(3) Assets Over which the Receiver can be Appointed

(i) Types of assets

33–007 *At the end of footnote 16, add:*

For such an appointment in a post-judgment case see *Behbehani v Behbehani* [2019] EWCA Civ 2301; [2020] 1 F.C.R. 603.

33–008 *At the end of footnote 18, add:*

See the further judgment in *JSC VTB Bank v Skurikhin* [2019] EWHC 1407 (Comm), mentioned below; and on appeal at [2020] EWCA Civ 1337; [2021] 1 W.L.R. 434, where the Court of Appeal commented with approval on the reasoning of the deputy judge in the original 2015 judgment, at [73] and following.

33–010 *At the end of footnote 24, add:*

For a recent example of such a trial see *JSC BTA Bank v Ablyazov* [2017] EWHC 2906 (Comm).

(4) Principles on which the Court will Act

(i) Introduction

33–021 *At the end of the paragraph, add new footnote 49a:*

[49a] An application to discharge a receivership order is not a "claim" so as to trigger the security for costs jurisdiction: see *JSC VTB Bank v Skurikhin* [2018] EWHC 3072 (Comm).

D. APPOINTMENT OF RECEIVER BY WAY OF EQUITABLE EXECUTION

(1) Jurisdiction and Principles Governing its Exercise

33–023 *After the second sentence, add new footnote 50a:*

[50a] For instance, if the judgment debt is otherwise paid the receivership will fall away. But the order appointing the receiver, once confirmed inter partes (if it was initially made ex parte), will be treated as a final order (and any findings made at that stage will be similarly treated as final and binding between the parties) for the purposes of any subsequent challenge, absent a material change of circumstances: *JSC VTB Bank v Skurikhin* [2019] EWHC 1407 (Comm), at [75]. In that case the court also considered the issues which arose where the material change of circumstance was instigated by the respondent.

33–025 *At the end of the paragraph, add new footnote 55a:*

[55a] And see further the expansive approach adumbrated in *JSC VTB Bank v Skurikhin* [2020] EWCA Civ 1337; [2021] 1 W.L.R. 434, at [76]: "Further, and in any event, the appointment of receivers by way of equitable execution is not limited to circumstances where assets are available for execution. Indeed, the very difficulty in executing a judgment against assets abroad may be the justification for appointing receivers."

At the end of footnote 61, add: **33–027**

So for instance there is no need to attempt to decide hypothetical questions as to whether a foreign court will or will not recognise the order at some future point, so as to obviate pointless and inconclusive debate about difficulties that may or may not, as matters turn out, arise: *JSC VTB Bank v Skurikhin* [2019] EWHC 1407 (Comm), at [74].

At the end of footnote 62, add:

This approach was cited with approval by the Court of Appeal in *Michael Wilson & Partners Ltd v Emmott* [2019] EWCA Civ 219, [2019] 4 W.L.R. 53, at [45]; though it was suggested that suggestions in *Soinco* that the *Angel Bell* exception would never be appropriate in post-judgment freezing orders went too far: see at [55]. The sentence in the main text is too doctrinaire; disruption of the defendant's business *may* be a consideration and the proper approach was set out in the *Michael Wilson* case.

(2) Assets over which a Receiver may be Appointed by Way of Equitable Execution

At the end of the paragraph, add: **33–029**

At this stage, if there is a dispute as to whether the judgment debtor is or is not the owner (in the wide sense discussed in this chapter) of the asset in question, then the court will have to (finally) decide that question on the balance of probabilities.[64a]

[64a] In *JSC VTB Bank v Skurikhin* [2015] EWHC 2131 (Comm) the deputy judge set out the principles as follows: (i) a receiver by way of equitable execution may be appointed over whatever may be considered in equity as the assets of the judgment debtor (at [38] and [45]); (ii) property subject to trust or analogous foreign arrangements would be regarded in equity as assets of a judgment debtor if he has the legal right to call for those assets to be transferred to him or to his order, or if he has de facto control of the trust assets in circumstances where no genuine discretion is exercised by the trustee over those assets ([39] and [45]); (iii) the question was therefore "whether the Court is satisfied that [the judgment debtor] either has a legal right to call for the assets of the Berenger Foundation to be transferred to him or to his order, or has de facto control over the assets of the Berenger Foundation" ([46]); (iv) "at this stage of the proceedings this question has to be answered on the balance of probabilities" ([47]). In later proceedings in the same claim, *JSC VTB Bank v Skurikhin* [2019] EWHC 1407 (Comm), the deputy judge held, at [106] to [114] that de facto control in the sense of a practical likelihood that the recipient of an instruction will follow it, without legal obligation to do so, is not sufficient to found a receivership order; by contrast a right to direct the trustees as to what they were to do with assets was sufficient: this was a right "tantamount to ownership". The judge (at [74]–[76]) rightly distinguished between a pre- and post-judgment receivership; at the earlier stage the threshold that must be crossed will be set at the lower "good arguable case" test because the receivership at that stage is intended to "hold the ring" and prevent dissipation. So the deputy judge held, at [76], that "any such order, made on a purely protective basis, would give the receivers only such powers as were consistent with holding the ring and preventing dissipation of the asset until the question of ownership was finally determined. It would not empower the receivers to sell property that might turn out to belong to a third party. It would contain a cross-undertaking in damages to guard against the possibility that the third party's rights to deal freely with what may turn out to be their own assets had been wrongly subjected to interference."

At the end of the paragraph, add new sub-paragraph (7): **33–030**

(7) In *VB Football Assets (VBFA) v Blackpool Football Club (Properties) Ltd* the court appointed a receiver over the shareholding in the company which operated Blackpool Football Club, to allow a sale of the club as a going concern.[73a]

[73a] [2019] EWHC 530 (Ch).

33–031 *At the end of footnote 74, add:*

It was held in *JSC VTB Bank v Skurikhin* [2019] EWHC 1407 (Comm), at [107], that "a receiver cannot be appointed in terms that compel the trustees to exercise their discretion in favour of a discretionary beneficiary."

E. PROCEDURE

(9) Termination of Receivership

33–044 *At the end of footnote 85, add:*

However, the decision in *McCracken* is bound up in its own particular facts and is of no general application. An application was made to discharge a receivership order in *JSC VTB Bank v Skurikhin* [2019] EWHC 1407 (Comm). The application was dismissed as an abuse of process *inter alia* because the applicant sought to rely upon matters which it could and should have raised at the original *inter partes* application at which the receivers were appointed. An appeal was dismissed: [2020] EWCA Civ 1337; [2021] 1 W.L.R. 434.

Add new paragraph 33–044A after para.33–044:

33–044A A receivership order may be in principle be discharged for a material change in circumstance that has occurred since the order was made. The most obvious example would be if the judgment debt is repaid, thus rendering the receivership entirely nugatory. But a change in circumstances brought about by the respondent itself cannot found such an application.[85a]

[85a] So where the Liechtenstein foundation over which a receivership order was made (on the basis that the judgment creditor exercised *de facto* control over it) purported to exclude the judgment debtor as one of its beneficiaries (at the instigation of the judgment debtor himself) its application to discharge the order was dismissed as an abuse of process: *JSC VTB Bank v Skurikhin* [2020] EWCA Civ 1337; [2020] 1 W.L.R. 434.

CHAPTER 34

PROVING A CLAIM IN FRAUD: EVIDENCE AND OTHER TRIAL ISSUES

A. INTRODUCTION

(2) The Standard of Proof

34–003 *At the end of footnote 4, add:*

For an authoritative restatement by the Court of Appeal, see the decision in *Bank St Petersburg PJSC v Arkhangelsky* [2020] EWCA Civ 408; [2020] 4 W.L.R. 55, per Sir Geoffrey Vos C at [44]–[47].

B. THE LEAD-UP TO TRIAL

(1) Admissibility of Evidence

(i) Evidence improperly obtained

34–007 *At the end of the paragraph, add:*

In *Koldyreva v Motylev*,[11a] it was a relevant consideration that the evidence, while obtained illegally, had not been obtained by the party seeking to adduce it, nor for the purposes of the application in which it was adduced.

[11a] *Koldyreva v Motylev* [2020] EWHC 3083 (Ch), per Meade J at [60].

34–008 *At the end of footnote 13, add:*

See further *Ras Al Khaimah Investment Authority v Azima* [2021] EWCA Civ 349, at [47], where it was considered relevant that the documents illicitly obtained via computer hacking would have been disclosable in due course, and so would have been available to the claimant by the time of the trial in any event, and also revealed "serious fraud" on the part of the defendant.

34–009 *At the end of footnote 16, add:*

Barclay v Barclay [2020] EWHC 1179 (QB), per Warby J at [56].

34–012 *At the end of the paragraph, add:*

The prevailing view now appears to be that the requirements of s.2 are disapplied by the inclusion of documents in an agreed bundle without the additional requirement that a notice be served. Such documents are therefore admissible, and the fact that they are hearsay goes to weight only.[25a]

[25a] See for example *BXB v Watch Tower and Bible Tract Society of Pennsylvania, Trustees of the Barry Congregation of Jehovah's Witnesses* [2020] EWHC 156 (QB), per Chamberlain J at [63]; *Mohmed v Barnes* [2019] EWHC 87 (QB), per Turner J at [41], albeit that the decision of Norris J in *Subsea* was not cited in those decisions.

(2) Authenticity of Documents

34–015 *At the end of the first sentence, add new footnote 27a:*

[27a] Where a further round of evidence is ordered, even if that is because much of the original evidence is struck out, this does not have the effect of resetting the clock for the purposes of serving notice to challenge under CPR 32.19: see *Tuke v JD Classics Ltd* [2018] EWHC 531 (QB), per Julian Knowles J at [108]–[113].

At the end of footnote 28, add:

For the purposes of the *Denton* test, a number of authorities identify such a failure as being 'serious' or 'significant'; see for example *UTB LLC v Sheffield United Ltd* [2019] EWHC 1377 (Ch), per Fancourt J at [27]–[28].

At the end of the paragraph, add:

[28a] Though see the relatively generous approach taken in *Lionwalk Ltd v Singh* [2018] EWHC 1513 (QB) and *McGann v Bisping* [2017] EWHC 2951 (Comm), per Richard Salter QC at [11]–[26]. An application made after the conclusion of a trial, but before judgment was given, was unsuccessful in *Lloyd v Kruger* [2018] EWHC 2011 (Comm) in an addendum to the main judgment.

At the end of footnote 31, add: **34–017**

Conversely, failure to deny the authenticity of a document in a Reply is not tantamount to an admission of its authenticity. See *Berkeley Square Holdings Ltd v Lancer Property Assets Management Ltd* [2021] EWHC 750 (Ch), at [30]–[36].

After "analysis and expert evidence", *add:* **34–018**

[32a] *Takhar v Gracefield Developments* [2020] EWHC 2791 (Ch) is a recent example of such techniques.

(3) Protection/Destruction of Documents

(ii) Illegitimate destruction

At the end of footnote 37, add: **34–025**

For a recent example, see *Bajaj Healthcare Limited v Fine Organics Limited* [2019] EWHC 2316 (Ch), per Michael Green QC at [13]–[25].

At the end of footnote 38, add: **34–026**

See *Ocado Group v McKeeve* [2021] EWCA Civ 145 for a particularly vivid example, where a solicitor acting for a respondent to a search order instructed a manager at the respondent to "burn" an application which had been used as a messenger service, rendering those messages irretrievable and preventing their disclosure in response to the search order and their further use in the proceedings.

At the end of footnote 40, add: **34–027**

Such a remedy is less likely to be proportionate and fair in all the circumstances of the case where the trial has been concluded and the Court is in position to assess the effect of the destruction of documents; *Active Media Services Inc v Burmester Duncker & Joly GmbH & Co KG* [2021] EWHC 232 (Comm), per Calver J at [307].

(iii) Document preservation orders and search orders

At the end of the paragraph, add: **34–029**

[42a] For a discussion of the principles applicable to, and guidance as to, imaging orders by the Court of Appeal see *TBD (Owen Holland) Ltd v Simons* [2020] EWCA Civ 1182; [2021] 1 W.L.R. 992, at [176]–[193].

At the end of footnote 44, add: **34–030**

The distinctions and interaction between search orders and document preservation orders were considered in detail in *Wild Brain Family International Ltd v Robson* [2018] EWHC 3163 (Ch).

(4) Witnesses

(ii) *Witness familiarisation*

34–032 *At the end of footnote 46, add:*

See also *National Bank Trust v Yurov* [2020] EWHC 100 (Comm), per Bryan J at [129].

C. TRIAL

(1) Witnesses

(ii) *Witness reliability and the importance of documentary evidence*

34–042 *At the end of the paragraph, add new footnote 54a:*

[54a] For a review of the approach to assessing conflicting witness recollection, see *Singh v Singh Jhutti* [2021] EWHC 2272 (Ch).

34–045 *At the end of the paragraph, add:*

The difficulties of witness recollection identified in *Gestmin* are now effectively recognised in and codified by the Appendix to CPR PD 57AC.

34–047 *At the end of the paragraph, add:*

The principles in *Gestmin* are now very regularly cited in any case in which the recollection of witnesses plays a significant part in the determination of factual matters.

In footnote 61, after "[2016] EWHC 1793 (Ch)", add:

; [2016] 4 W.L.R. 133.

(iv) *Video link*

Replace paragraph 34–052 with:

34–052 For much of 2020–2021, in person hearings were prohibited or practically impossible, and many cases have been affected by the inability of witnesses or other participants to travel or to attend Court. Accordingly, while it remains the preference of the Court, and of practitioners in general, for witness evidence to be given live and in Court, the Courts have shown a great deal of flexibility in permitting evidence from parties, witnesses and experts to be given remotely. It is likely that this increased flexibility will continue even now that restrictions have been eased, though live evidence will most likely remain the preferred option as Courts and practitioners are broadly agreed that something is lost through evidence being given remotely. CPR 32.3 gives the court the power to allow a witness to give evidence "through a video link or by other means" and extensive guidance is given as to the use of video conferencing in PD 32. Further guidance was given in *Navigator Equities Ltd v Deripaska*,[66a] in particular that details of the arrangements for witnesses giving remote evidence (such as who else may be present with the witness) should be agreed between the parties, and with the Court, in advance.

[66a] [2020] EWHC 1798 (Comm), per Andrew Baker J at [5]–[10].

(v) Ambush cross examination

At the end of footnote 71, add: **34–055**

The principle appears to hold under the disclosure pilot scheme in PD51U: *Byers v Samba Financial Group* [2020] EWHC 2591 (Ch), at [10]–[15].

At the end of footnote 73, add: **34–056**

C.f. *Grove Park Properties Ltd v Royal Bank of Scotland Plc* [2018] EWHC 3521 (Comm), per Males J at [54]. The effect of the decision in *Grove Park* may well be to limit the scope of any perceived requirement to plead matters going to credit arising out of the decision in *Baturina v Chistyakov*, and confirms that such a plea is generally not required.

(vi) Putting the case to witnesses

Replace the words "Lord Phillips MR" with "May LJ". **34–058**

At the end of the footnote 76, add: **34–059**

The question of what amounts to a 'proper opportunity' for a witness to respond was considered at length in *RAS AL Khaimah Investment Authority v Farhad Azima* [2021] EWCA Civ 349, at [83]–[109].

(vii) Can a witness appeal a finding of dishonesty?

At the end of footnote 78, add: **34–061**

[2017] 1 W.L.R. 2415.

(2) Inferences

(ii) Inference from absence or silence of a witness

At the end of footnote 81, add: **34–064**

That the Court is entitled to, rather than obliged to, draw the inference was emphasised outside the civil fraud context in *Manzi v King's College NHS Foundation Trust* [2018] EWCA Civ 1882 at [30]. For an unusual case where adverse inferences were drawn against both parties in a civil fraud case see *Ahuja Investments Ltd v Victorygame Ltd* [2021] EWHC 2382 (Ch), since cited in *Hotel Portfolio II UK Ltd (In Liquidation) v Ruhan* [2022] EWHC 383 (Comm).

In footnote 86, after "[2016]" on the second line, add: **34–068**

EWHC

(iii) Proving fraud by inference

At the end of footnote 92, add: **34–072**

The principles were summarised in *Crypton Digital Assets Limited v Blockchain Luxembourg SA* [2021] EWHC 1172 (Ch), at [16]–[19] and [49].

34–073 *At the end of the paragraph, add:*

In one recent decision,[94a] the inferential weight of the evidence adduced by the claimant was sufficient to reach the standard of summary judgment. Three major issues were raised, each of which gave rise to an inference or strong inference that the defendant had perpetrated a fraud. Taken together, the standard for summary judgment was reached and "despite the very considerable caution requisite in this area", Cockerill J determined that it was appropriate to grant summary judgment.

[94a] *Foglia v Family Officer Ltd* [2021] EWHC 650 (Comm).

(3) Privilege Against Self-Incrimination

(i) What is covered?

Replace paragraph 34–076 with:

34–076 The privilege permits the party to refuse to answer questions which may incriminate him or a spouse. The potential incrimination relates only to any act or omission which is a criminal offence in any part of the UK. Thus, if the answer would expose the witness to proceedings for a criminal offence only in some foreign country, that falls outside the limitations of the privilege. Nonetheless, the Court retains a discretion to excuse a witness from giving evidence where the feared prosecution is under foreign law.[94a] Any person claiming privilege on the grounds of self-incrimination must satisfy the court that there are real, and not fanciful, grounds justifying his fear that the information sought would tend to incriminate him.[95]

[94a] *Compagnie Des Grands Hôtels D'Afrique S.A. v Purdy* [2021] EWHC 1031 (QB), at [54].
[95] *Sociedade Nacional v Lundquist* [1991] 2 Q.B. 310, per Staughton LJ at 324F.

CHAPTER 35

CONTEMPT OF COURT

A. INTRODUCTION

(1) Relevance to Fraud Claims

35–002 *At end of paragraph, add new footnote 2a:*

A wholly new CPR Part 81 came into force with effect from 1 October 2020 by the Civil Procedure (Amendment No 3) Rules 2020, SI 2020/747. The old Part 81 is entirely replaced and the previous Practice Direction to Part 81 has been entirely revoked (without replacement). The new CPR Part 81 was introduced, according to the consultation paper produced by the Civil Procedure Rules Committee, to simplify, shorten and strengthen the procedural rules relating to committal applications in order "to make them operate more fairly and reduce the number of cases where procedural unfairness is found." The new CPR Part 81 was introduced without any form of transitional measures. This created a certain amount of confusion in relation to existing proceedings which had been instituted prior to 1 October 2020. The approach taken in *Secretary of State for Transport v Cuciurean* [2020] EWHC 2723 (Ch), where the committal proceedings commenced well before 1 October 2020, and judgment on liability was handed down on 13 October 2020 after a hearing which took place in July and September 2020, was as follows (see at [4] to [6]):

(1) To apply the old CPR 81 to the interpretation and procedural implementation of the order said to have been breached. The old CPR 81 was in force at that time and to do otherwise would give "an utterly unwarranted retrospective effect to the new rules."
(2) To apply the old CPR 81 to all procedural steps which took place before 1 October 2020.
(3) As to matters post-dating 1 October 2020 to apply the new rules; but if an old rule would be more beneficial to the defendant, to apply that one.

In reality, at least as regards civil contempt, the procedural law of committal has not substantively changed. Two cosmetic changes are that applicants and respondent in committal applications are now to be described as "claimants" and "defendants"; and that committal applications are now described as "contempt applications", defined at r.81.2 as "an application to the court for an order determining contempt proceedings." We have used the new nomenclature in this supplement. Further we have not deleted previous references to the CPR PD81 because, as statements of law, they generally remain valid. In the supplement below we update the references to CPR Part 81. One particular aspect of the new CPR Part 81 is that previous statements of the law contained in the old CPR Part 81 have been excluded; the new Part 81 is purely procedural. But the substantive law has not changed. Our approach has not been to change every reference to the old Part 81 in the main text (which would be very unwieldy), but, where appropriate, to note the change in additional text in footnotes. It seems to be the case that the motive to update Part 81 sprung from comments of courts in criminal contempt cases; the experience of the authors of this work is that the old Part 81 worked perfectly well as regards civil contempt cases and the new Part 81, which is significantly reduced in length, is in fact considerably less helpful in relation to the various issues which commonly arise.

At the end of footnote 3, add: **35–003**

The new Part 81 says nothing about the standard of proof other than that the claimant is now required to state in the contempt application itself that the Court "will only find the defendant in contempt if satisfied beyond reasonable doubt of the facts constituting contempt and that they do constitute contempt" (r.81.4(2)(o)).

Delete paragraph. **35–004**

(4) The Distinction Between Civil and Criminal Contempt

At the end of footnote 8, add: **35–009**

The relevant procedure is now contained in CPR r.81.3, which sets out a compendious set of procedural provisions for the making of any form of contempt application. Importantly there is now no distinction between a false statement in an affidavit or witness statement, and any other document verified by a statement of truth: see r.81.3(5). Permission is required in all such cases. In such a case, an application is made under CPR Part 23: see r.81.3(1) and (6). Permission is sought from a single judge of the Division in which the underling case is proceeding. If permission is granted the contempt application shall also be determined by a single judge of the Division: see r.81.1(7).

At the end of footnote 9, add: **35–010**

See now CPR r.81.3 and r.81.4.

At the end of footnote 10, add:

See also *Cole v Carpenter* [2020] EWHC 3155 (Ch), where it was alleged that the claimant had forged a document referred to in a statement of case and that the statement of case was itself false. The defendant's application for permission to bring a committal application was dismissed on grounds of prematurity and because the issues raised would be in issue at and material to the outcome of the trial. As was recently stated in *TBD (Owen Holland) Ltd v Simons* [2020] EWCA Civ 1182; [2021] 1 W.L.R. 992, at [233]: "In general the proper time for determining the truth or falsity of these statements is at trial, when all the relevant issues of fact are before the court and the statements can be considered against the totality of the evidence." It follows that it will usually be the correct course to dismiss an application brought prematurely rather than simply adjourn it: *ibid*, at [237]–[238]. For an exceptional case where permission was granted in advance of trial see *Advetec Holdings Ltd v Shaw* [2020] EWHC 2660 (QB).

(5) The Decision to make a Committal Application

35–011 *At the end of footnote 20, add:*

Where the defendant's asset disclosure is perceived to be inadequate another common response is to apply to cross-examine the defendant on his affidavit: see paras 31–059 and following above.

B. THE UNDERLYING COURT ORDER OR UNDERTAKING

(1) The Basic Principle

35–012 *At the end of the words "CPR r.81.4", insert new footnote 20a:*

[20a] The general principle is no longer set out in CPR Part 81 at all.

At the end of footnote 21, add:

In relation to the Debtors Act 1869, see recently *Discovery Land Co LLC v Jirehouse* [2019] EWHC 2249 (Ch); [2020] PNLR 1 and *Hussain v Vaswani* [2020] EWCA Civ 1216; [2020] W.L.R.(D) 510. In the latter case a defendant gave a voluntary undertaking to pay a sum of money to the claimant. It was held that breach of that undertaking permitted a finding of contempt of court and the 1869 Act did not prevent the court imposing a sanction of imprisonment.

At the end of the paragraph, add:

However a mandatory order is not enforceable by committal unless it specifies the time for compliance.[21a] An order requiring something to be done on or by a given date can only be breached once: "When a mandatory order is not complied with there is but a single breach." A contempt in failing to do an act by a particular deadline is committed, if at all, when the deadline is not met, and failing to do the act thereafter is not strictly a further or continuing contempt. The defendant is not thereafter in continuing breach.[21b]

[21a] *Temporal v Temporal* [1990] 2 F.L.R. 98. This is because "it is impossible to read implied terms into an order of the court": *Deodat v Deodat* (unreported, 9 June 1978: Court of Appeal Transcript No 78 484), per Megaw LJ.

[21b] *In re Jones* [2013] EWHC 2579 (Ch); [2014] 1 F.L.R. 852, at [20]–[23]. For the implications of this principle in a civil fraud context see *Kea Investments Ltd v Watson* [2020] EWHC 2599 (Ch), at [70]–[82]. These decisions were approved on this point by the Court of Appeal in *Boys & Maugham (a firm) v Moore* [2020] EWCA Civ 1860, at [29]. Of course a claimant can always seek a further order requiring the defendant to take the particular step by a new date.

(2) The Need for Clarity of the Terms of the Order

At the end of footnote 22, add: 35–013

In *Kea Investments Ltd v Watson* [2020] EWHC 2599 (Ch), the court rejected (at [44]–[49]) the proposition that no committal application could be founded on an order where that order cross-referred to another document, while accepting that it would be better practice to ensure that the order contains all the necessary material informing the defendant what he was prohibited from doing (or obliged to do) in one self-contained document.

(3) Service

At the end of footnote 24, add: 35–014

The new Part 81 approaches this matter somewhat obliquely by requiring the claimant to include, at r.81.4(2), statements in the contempt application to the following effect (unless "wholly inapplicable"): "(c) confirmation that any such order [i.e. the order which the defendant is alleged to be in breach of] was personally served, and the date it was served, unless the court or the parties dispensed with personal service; (d) if the court dispensed with personal service, the terms and date of the court's order dispensing with personal service." What is not clear is whether the court can dispense with service of the original order after the making of the contempt application. The old-law, gathered above and restated very recently in *Super Max Offshore Holdings v Malhotra* [2020] EWHC 1023 (Comm) (at [52] and following), makes it clear that that was possible, as did the old CPR r.81.8, the provisions of which are not replicated in the new CPR Part 81. It would be remarkable if that power was no longer available to the court and it is suggested it is, but it is unfortunate that the new Part 81 does not make this clear.

(4) The Requirement for a Penal Notice to be Endorsed on the Order

At the end of footnote 26, add: 35–016

The previous CPR r.81.9 provided that an order could not be enforced by an order for committal unless there was prominently displayed a penal notice on the underlying order. This mandatory provision was mitigated by CPR PD 81, para.16.2, which allowed the court to waive any procedural defect. These provisions are not repeated in the new CPR Part 81 and nor is the form of penal notice that previously was set out at PD 81, para.1 (though it is suggested that that form should continue to be used). Instead the claimant is required by r.81.4(2) to include a statement in the contempt application to the following effect: "(e) confirmation that any order allegedly breached or disobeyed included a penal notice." It is suggested that the old law remains intact (a view supported obiter by the decision of Cockerill J in *Deutsche Bank AG v Sebastian Holdings Inc* [2020] EWHC 3536 (Comm) at [148] and also by Ritchie J in *O'Hara v Whitby-Smith* [2021] EWHC 2806 (QB), at [66]). Again it is unfortunate that the new Part 81 does not make this clear. There is a large body of decisions on the question whether or not to dispense with a penal notice in addition to those noted in the main text. These include: *Masri v Consolidated Contractors International Co SAL* [2010] EWHC 2458 (Comm); *Prosser v Prosser* [2011] EWHC 2172 (Ch); *De Vere v Hither Green Developments Ltd* [2015] EWCA Civ 1365; *JSC Mezhdunarodniy Promyshlenniy Bank v Pugachev* [2016] EWHC 192 (Ch); *Fort Locks Self Storage Ltd v Deakin* [2017] EWCA Civ 404. It is suggested that the ultimate question the court has to ask is whether the claimant properly brought home to the defendant the serious penal consequences of breach of the order such that the defendant suffered no prejudice.

(5) Undertakings

(ii) No requirement for personal service

At the end of the paragraph, add new footnote 30a: 35–018

[30a] None of the provisions referred to in this paragraph are replicated in the new Part 81. It is suggested that the legal position as stated in those provisions remains intact.

(iii) No strict requirement for a penal notice

35–019 *At the end of the paragraph, add new footnote 30b:*

[30b] None of the provisions referred to in this paragraph are replicated in the new Part 81. It is suggested that the legal position as stated in those provisions remains intact. For a recent consideration of the former CPR PD 81, para.2.2 see *Discovery Land Company, LLC v Jirehouse (A Body Corporate)* [2019] EWHC 2249 (Ch); [2020] PNLR 1, at [126]–[127].

(iv) Solicitors' undertakings

35–021 *At the end of footnote 31, add:*

A recent example is *Discovery Land Company, LLC v Jirehouse (A Body Corporate)* [2019] EWHC 2249 (Ch); [2020] PNLR 1, where a solicitor gave an undertaking to the court to procure the payment into court of certain monies which he then breached.

At the end of footnote 33, add:

The provisions of r.81.11 have not been replicated in any way. It is again suggested that the procedural position remains unchanged.

C. THE ELEMENTS OF CONTEMPT

(1) Ingredients

35–022 *At the end of footnote 34, add:*

Masri has been cited consistently up to the present as containing the definitive statement of the elements of civil contempt.

(ii) Intention

35–025 *At the end of footnote 42, add:*

In *Varma v Atkinson* [2020] EWCA Civ 1602; [2021] Ch 180, the Court of Appeal finally and formally disapproved *Irtelli v Squatriti* [1993] QB 83, holding, at [54] (per Rose LJ): "once knowledge of the order is proved, and once it is proved that the contemnor knew that he was doing or omitting to do certain things, then it is not necessary for the contemnor to know that his actions put him in breach of the order; it is enough that as a matter of fact and law, they do so put him in breach."

At the end of footnote 44, add:

See also *Minstrell Recruitment Ltd v Lockett & Anor* [2020] EWHC 3537 (Ch), per Snowden J at [12].

Add new paragraph 35–025A after para.35–025:

35–025A It may well be that the defendant admits the breach and that he committed a contempt, but denies that it was contumacious. The claimant in turn may decline to accept that the contempt was not contumacious. In such a case there will still have to be a trial, albeit turning not on the question of whether a contempt has formally been committed, but in relation to the defendant's *mens rea,* given the vital relevance of that question to sentence. This will be a form of *Newton* hearing. In *Minstrell Recruitment Ltd v Lockett*[44a] the defendant put forward a "basis of plea" document. In *McKendrick v The Financial Conduct Authority*[44b] the defendant gave oral evidence in mitigation and was cross-examined on it.

[44a] [2020] EWHC 3537 (Ch).
[44b] [2019] EWCA Civ 524; [2019] 4 W.L.R. 65.

Add new paragraph 35–029A after para.35–029:

It has been suggested that duress is a defence to an application for committal on the basis that it negatives the required element of intention.[52a] **35–029A**

[52a] See *Truell v Zalinska* [2021] EWHC 1877 (Ch), at [37]. The court left open the question whether the relevant test of duress is the criminal one or that required to avoid a contract. It is suggested that it is the latter.

At the end of footnote 69, add: **35–036**

However, and unsurprisingly, the principle of impossibility does not extend to a case where compliance with the order is not impossible but is difficult or inconvenient: *Westminster City Council v Addbins Ltd* [2012] EWHC 3716 (QB); *Reynolds v Long* [2018] EWHC 3535 (Ch). In *Perkier Foods Ltd v Halo Foods Ltd* [2019] EWHC 3462 (QB) it was held, at [14], that where the defendant raises an impossibility defence he bears an evidential burden (i.e. he must put forward some evidence that compliance with the order or undertaking was impossible) and, once this is satisfied, the burden of proving that compliance was possible passes to the claimant and the standard of proof is the criminal standard. In that case in respect of a number of counts the claimant failed to prove that compliance was not impossible to the criminal standard of proof after the defendant had adduced evidence of impossibility. In *Discovery Land Company, LLC v Jirehouse (A Body Corporate)* [2019] EWHC 2249 (Ch); [2020] P.N.L.R. 1, the court drew a distinction between a case where it subsequently transpires that compliance was impossible and a case where an undertaking was given in circumstances where the contemnor knew compliance was impossible, or was reckless as to whether compliance was possible and nevertheless gave an unqualified undertaking. In the latter case the defendant cannot pray in aid the alleged impossibility of complying with the undertaking (or order as the case may be).

(2) Liability of Company Directors and Other Officers

(i) Introduction

At the end of the paragraph, add new footnote 73a: **35–037**

[73a] The old r.81.4(3) has not been replicated in the new Part 81. Its provisions no doubt continue to reflect the law.

(3) The Position of Third Parties

(iii) Procedural Considerations

At the end of the paragraph, add new footnote 93a: **35–054**

[93a] All of the procedural provisions referred to in paras 35–053 and 35–054 have been rescinded. It appears from the new r.81.3(5) that permission is no longer required for a contempt application against a third party in relation to orders or undertakings made in existing proceedings. Applications are made by application notice under Part 23 in those existing proceedings: see r.81.3(1).

D. THE APPLICATION FOR COMMITTAL

35–055 *Delete footnote 94.*

Delete the last three sentences and replace with:

The previous Part 81 was replaced on 1 October 2020 by a completely new Part 81 which creates a single unified procedural regime for all forms of contempt.

(1) The Application

35–056 *At the end of footnote 96, add:*

See now the new r.81.3.

35–057 *At the end of footnote 97, add:*

The requirements of a contempt application are now stated in the new r.81.4. That relevantly provides as follows (replacing the old CPR r.81.10(3)): "(2) A contempt application must include statements of all the following, unless (in the case of (b) to (g)) wholly inapplicable— (a) the nature of the alleged contempt (for example, breach of an order or undertaking or contempt in the face of the court); (b) the date and terms of any order allegedly breached or disobeyed; (c) confirmation that any such order was personally served, and the date it was served, unless the court or the parties dispensed with personal service; (d) if the court dispensed with personal service, the terms and date of the court's order dispensing with personal service; (e) confirmation that any order allegedly breached or disobeyed included a penal notice; (f) the date and terms of any undertaking allegedly breached; (g) confirmation of the claimant's belief that the person who gave any undertaking understood its terms and the consequences of failure to comply with it; (h) a brief summary of the facts alleged to constitute the contempt, set out numerically in chronological order." For a full analysis of the provisions concerning the statement of the particulars of the alleged contempt, see *Deutsche Bank AG v Sebastian Holdings Inc* [2020] EWHC 3536 (Comm), at [68]–[98]. There the judge, Cockerill J, distilled the test down to the following: "whether the application is clear enough to leave the defendant in no doubt as to the substance of the breaches [alleged again him] at a point when he has still time to meet them." This test allows the court to take into account the background knowledge of the defendant. The judge rejected a submission advanced by the defendant that the application should contain "the precise details of the breach alleged." She took the view that the court was entitled to take account of the welter of previous authority when construing the new rule. It is fair to say that the courts are wise to technical procedural objections made by defendants to committal applications. In *Kea Investments Ltd v Watson* [2020] EWHC 2599 (Ch) the court rejected, at [20]–[28], the submission that, where the claimant wished to assert that the defendant had acted contumaciously, it had to positively allege that fact in the particulars of contempt contained in the application notice (or any schedule to it). Although this ruling was given by reference to the old CPR Part 81 it is likely to be equally applicable to the new version.

After the second sentence in footnote 99, add:

There are signs that courts are taking an increasingly pragmatic approach to these questions, in the face of a growing tendency for defendants to take unmeritorious objections to particulars of contempt. In *Deutsche Bank AG v Sebastian Holdings Inc* [2020] EWHC 3536 (Comm), at [124], the judge doubted whether this strict prohibition on considering the supporting affidavit was justified. Moreover in *Integral Petroleum v Petrogat* [2020] EWHC 558 (Comm) the judge permitted reference to the draft order to explicate the alleged contempt (at [72]).

At the end of footnote 100, add:

These matters are now the subject of provision in r.81.4(2)(o) and (p).

At the end of the paragraph, add:

The new r.81.4(2) now sets out a lengthy list of matters which must be addressed on the face of the contempt application (unless "wholly inapplicable"). These matters range from properly identifying the contempt alleged to other matters designed to ensure fairness to the defendant such as reminding him of his right to be legally represented; his potential entitlement to an interpreter; his right to silence etc. It will be vital for any claimant to a contempt application to ensure that all those matters are properly addressed in the application itself.

At the end of footnote 102, add: **35–058**

The new rules do not refer to amendment of the application but it is suggested that the law has not changed. In *Deutsche Bank AG v Sebastian Holdings Inc* [2020] EWHC 3536 (Comm), the claimant applied to amend its application notice in advance of the substantive hearing. The judge had no difficulty permitting amendments which did not raise new grounds but simply provided further particularisation of existing ones.

(2) Procedural Defects

Delete first three lines (including the first indented quotation) and replace with: **35–060**

Para 16.2 of the former Practice Direction 81 provided that: "The court may waive any procedural defect in the commencement or conduct of a committal application if satisfied that no injustice has been caused to the defendant by the defect." Oddly, no similar provision is to be found in the new Part 81. In *Deutsche Bank AG v Sebastian Holdings Inc*,[103a] Cockerill J, albeit speaking obiter (but surely correctly), held that the court retained the power to cure the types of defect envisaged by para.16.2.

[103a] [2020] EWHC 3536 (Comm).

At the end of footnote 105, add:

A recent example of the exercise of this jurisdiction is *Integral Petroleum v Petrogat* [2020] EWHC 558 (Comm).

(3) Evidence

At the end of footnote 106, add: **35–061**

The new rule is set out at r.81.4(1) as follows: "Unless and to the extent that the court directs otherwise, every contempt application must be supported by written evidence given by affidavit or affirmation." Oddly it does not replicate the old provision that the affidavit/affirmation(s) had to contain all the evidence relied upon. But that surely is implicit.

At the end of footnote 110, add: **35–062**

The rules referred to in this para have now been replaced by new r.81.7, which is much reduced in scope and provides as follows: "(1) The court shall give such directions as it thinks fit for the hearing and determination of contempt proceedings, including directions for the attendance of witnesses and oral evidence, as it considers appropriate. (2) The court may issue a bench warrant to secure the attendance of the defendant at a directions hearing or at the substantive hearing. (3) The court may not give any direction compelling the defendant to give evidence either orally or in writing." It is likely that any direction for evidence to be served by the defendant would be for that to be sworn evidence. The inability of a claimant to seek further information from the defendant is presumably intended to be captured in r.81.7(3).

At the end of the paragraph, add:

But the concern for the defendant's right to silence should not be carried too far. It may be that evidence which has been served but not deployed demonstrates that the charges of contempt, or some of them, are ill-founded. A claimant can of course abandon an application or part of it, by reference to such evidence. Further there is no absolute bar to a claimant seeking to amend its application in the light of evidence which has been served in response, albeit not deployed by the defendant. By contrast it has been recently suggested that any such amendments should not reference the defendant's served but not deployed evidence and nor should they be permitted where they can only be made good by reference to that evidence.[111a]

[111a] *Deutsche Bank AG v Sebastian Holdings Inc* [2020] EWHC 3536 (Comm), at [165]–[174].

35–063 *At the end of footnote 111, add:*

As was noted in *Deutsche Bank AG v Sebastian Holdings Inc* [2020] EWHC 3536 (Comm), at [53(iv)], evidence served by a defendant in advance of the committal hearing, even if it has not been "deployed", may still be used for the purpose of gathering preparatory evidence in reply and drafting responsive evidence (any directions will typically make provision for such evidence). However, pending the actual deployment of the defendant's evidence both that evidence and any evidence in reply remains "in limbo". In *Discovery Land Company LLC v Jirehouse* [2019] EWHC 1633 (Ch) a defendant served an affidavit in response to a committal application. The claimant's application to cross-examine him on the affidavit under CPR r.32.7 was refused. The result is that a defendant may tender (and rely upon) written evidence to the court but decline to be cross-examined on it. Of course the weight to be given to such an affidavit in such circumstances is likely to be (very) limited. It follows that a defendant cannot be compelled to make an election as to (i) deploying at the hearing any affidavit he has served and becoming liable to be cross-examined on it; and (ii) not deploying the affidavit at the hearing. The defendant may deploy the affidavit and yet refuse to be cross-examined on it.

35–065 *At the end of footnote 116, add:*

The principle is now that if a defendant decides to give evidence in chief orally, he may be cross-examined. But he may tender and rely upon written evidence at the hearing without being amenable to cross-examination on it. CPR r.81.4(2)(m) now provides that a defendant "is entitled but not obliged to give written and oral evidence in their defence."

At the end of the first sentence of footnote 117, add:

The court should also specifically inform the defendant at the hearing of his right to remain silent: *ibid.* A failure to do so is likely to render the hearing sufficiently unfair to found a successful appeal by the defendant: see *L (A Child)* [2016] EWCA Civ 173; [2017] 1 F.L.R. 1135; *Douherty v The Chief Constable of Essex Police* [2019] EWCA Civ 55; *Andreewitch v Moutreuil* [2020] EWCA Civ 382; [2020] 4 W.L.R. 54. The appeal court may of course remit the application to be reheard before a different judge, as happened in the latter two cases cited. R.81.4(2)(n) now requires a claimant to state on the face of the contempt application that a defendant has the right to remain silent. It was said in *Pirtek (UK) Limited v Robert Jackson* [2018] EWHC 1004 (QB), at [37], that an inference from silence should not be the sole basis for a finding of contempt; though that will be a rare eventuality in any event. On the facts of any particular case the applicant's case may be bolstered by an inference drawn from the defendant's silence where there is a case to answer and there is no credible explanation for that silence other than guilt of the acts complained of: see *Pirtek*, at [42].

At the end of footnote 120, add: **35–067**

It may also be legitimate to take into account the fact that, when charged with contempt, the defendant gave no evidence or explanation of something of which he would have had knowledge and of which he could be expected to give evidence if it was true. The same principles apply where the defendant, whether or not he has put in written evidence in advance, declines to make himself available to be cross-examined at the hearing of the application: *Integral Petroleum v Petrogat* [2020] EWHC 558 (Comm), at [92], [142].

(4) Service

At the end of footnote 125, add: **35–069**

Service of the contempt application is now provided for by the new r.81.5. Importantly this provides that where a defendant has a legal representative on the record in the underlying proceedings then service on that representative will be good service unless the representative objects. If he does object the matter will go before a judge to determine the issue of service on paper.

(5) The Position of Foreign Respondents

At the end of footnote 133, add: **35–070**

See also *Integral Petroleum SA v Petrogat FZE* [2018] EWHC 2686 (Comm); [2019] 1 W.L.R. 574.

(6) Abuse of Process

Add new paragraphs 35–071A to 35–071D after para.35–071:

In recent years defendants to committal applications have frequently raised abuse arguments as a means of seeking the dismissal of such applications, whether before or at the final hearing of the application. Such arguments have met with varying degrees of success: the courts have shown sensitivity to the question of whether committal applications have been brought for illegitimate or collateral purposes, but on the other hand they have been wary of arguments which are designed simply to avoid a determination of the liability of the defendant. In particular the recent first-instance decision in *Navigator Equities Ltd v Deripaska*[136a] was for a time highly influential in giving claimants real pause for thought in their conduct of committal applications. In that case the judge (Andrew Baker J) was highly critical of the claimant's conduct. In particular he made the following observations:[136b] **35–071A**

(1) Although the hearing of a committal application is not to be equated with a criminal trial, committal proceedings bear several hallmarks of criminal process.
(2) Hence a claimant who brings committal proceedings assumes the role of quasi-prosecutor and therefore must act as a guardian of the public interest alongside any private interest it may have in, say, seeking the enforcement of court orders.
(3) Accordingly, such an application should not be brought with a view to vexing or harassing the defendant, as opposed to the proper purpose of seeking to enforce court orders (or undertakings) or drawing the court's attention to serious misconduct.

(4) It follows that the claimant's subjective state of mind is a relevant consideration.
(5) Further the claimant and his lawyers must act dispassionately and objectively, presenting the facts fairly and with balance and then let those facts speak for themselves before the judge. This is particularly the case where the only proper purpose that might be served by issuing and prosecuting the contempt application is to invite the court in the public interest to identify, pronounce and punish, if appropriate, an historic contempt.[136c]
(6) Accordingly, evidence served in support of such applications should avoid tendentiousness or argumentativeness. Similarly skeleton arguments and legal submissions should avoid adopting an inflammatory or aggressive tone.

The judge struck out the proceedings as an abuse, having held that they were motivated by personal animus and had been prosecuted in a highly-charged, unfair and partisan way.[136d]

[136a] [2020] EWHC 1798 (Comm). Andrew Baker J's judgment was cited many times since and paras [141]–[143] of it were specifically endorsed by the Court of Appeal in *TBD (Owen Holland) Ltd v Simons* [2020] EWCA Civ 1182; [2021] 1 W.L.R. 992, at [246]. However, as pointed out by the Court of Appeal's decision in the appeal against the first instance decision, that was in the context of criminal contempt proceedings.

[136b] See at [137]–[162], passim.

[136c] It is fair to say that this approach was somewhat difficult to apply to the claimant in a fraud claim seeking, say, to enforce compliance with a freezing order (which was not the case before Andrew Baker J in *Navigator*). In such a case the claimant has an immediate, obvious and legitimate interest in seeking to force the defendant to comply with his obligations. The notion that the claimant should proceed as if all that was in play was the public interest is fanciful. Accordingly, whilst of course the claimant should never proceed with undue aggression or unfairness, it is suggested that these dicta should be treated with circumspection in the standard fraud claim.

[136d] The judge ended with these words, at [161]: "In the working generation of 30 years or so during which I have been engaged in commercial dispute resolution in this jurisdiction, principally in this court and in London arbitrations, there has been a significant general increase in hostility and aggressiveness in the conduct of disputes. The taking of any and every point, good or bad, and other failures to display proper independence from the litigating client, is treated too often as if it were a normal or appropriate adjunct of well funded, hard fought, business disputes, particularly if there are issues of dishonesty involved. Where ultimately the court is asked only to decide the outcome of the business dispute, usually to be expressed in terms of a party or parties being told to pay money to another party or other parties, there may be nothing too unfair about that modern style, regrettable though I regard it nonetheless. But when the court is being asked by a private litigant to consider a charge of contempt of court against the other side, especially against an individual whose liberty the claimant therefore seeks to put at risk, a better standard of conduct is not merely desirable, it is essential to the fairness and the appearance of fairness of the process."

35–071B Andrew Baker J's decision in *Navigator Equities* was overturned by the Court of Appeal.[136e] Although much of the decision was specific to the facts of the case, three points of general principle emerge.

(1) The merits of the application are relevant to an assessment of whether it is an abuse of process.
(2) The motive of the claimant (e.g. a personal desire for revenge) in bringing the contempt application cannot be relied upon in founding a strike out application for abuse of process, where: (a) the application is made in accordance with the relevant procedural requirements; (b) it is properly arguable on the merits; (c) it has the effect (and so at least the objective

purpose) of drawing to the attention of the court an allegedly serious contempt.[136f] This second point rested on a reading of Briggs J's decision in *Sectorguard*, which, with respect, appears questionable. In the earlier case Briggs J had referred to the absence of a "legitimate motive" on the part of the claimant in prosecuting the contempt application as a ground for striking it out. The Court of Appeal interpreted this phrase as synonymous with an objectively "legitimate purpose" rather than a reference to subjective motive. This seems a very strained reading of the relevant passage in *Sectorguard*. The Court went on say: "It is correct that Briggs J took into account (at [56]) recent evidence to the effect that two directors of Sectorguard [the claimant] had expressed a wish to have Mr Hare [one of the defendants] put in prison, "whether for contempt or other alleged misconduct, by any means available". But he did so only as a makeweight in circumstances where the application for contempt was hopeless in any event, and it is not apparent from the judgment that there was any suggestion that he should not do so as a matter of principle."[136g] But, with respect, surely this misses the point. What is apparent from the relevant paragraph of Briggs J's judgment (and indeed the preceding two paragraphs, being [54] and [55]) is that when he referred earlier in his judgment to absence of "legitimate motive" he was using the term in its conventional subjective sense. The court sought to distinguish the decision of Foxton J in *Integral Petroleum SA v Petrogat FZWE*[136h] (as to which see below) on the basis that there the court was considering the case of a claimant who was motivated by an improper collateral purpose, e.g. to secure a settlement of the underlying proceedings. It is not clear what coherent distinction can be made between a subjective motive to bring about a settlement and a subjective motive, actuated by revenge (for instance), to obtain the judicial punishment of a defendant.

The Court of Appeal also founded its conclusion that subjective motive should be ignored on the supposed practical difficulties of making assessments of a claimant's mental state. But the courts are well used to engaging in such investigations. The torts of abuse of civil process and lawful means conspiracy, to take just two examples, require an inquiry into the mental state of the claimant.

A further difficulty with the Court's decision was the distinction it drew between civil and criminal contempt. It is clear that in criminal contempt it is a pertinent question for the court to consider whether the claimant is a proper person to bring the application. For instance, in *Newson-Smith v Al Zawawi*[136i] Whipple J refused permission for contempt proceedings to be brought where there was a risk that the application was brought "out of a vindictive desire to harass the Respondent." It is not clear why that should be a relevant question where one party to litigation is seeking permission to bring contempt proceedings against another party for making a false statement in a witness statement, but not where one party is alleging that the other breached a court order. As we have seen (see para.35–007), the taxonomy of civil and criminal contempt has been described as "largely meaningless."

Nonetheless, unless the question is revisited by the Supreme Court, the law is now clear: in civil contempt applications the question of the claimant's motive is irrelevant where the conditions set out above are met.

(3) The judge's conclusion that the contempt application should have been pursued dispassionately by the applicant as the guardian of the public interest with no interest in the outcome was to overstate the position. The claimant did not adopt the role of dispassionate prosecutor: "A private applicant for civil contempt, even where it is no longer necessary to seek enforcement of an order or undertaking, still has a proper private interest in the outcome of the application. Any private litigant will have an interest in the enforcement of a court order or undertaking which has been made to protect its interests. Apart from having this private interest in principle in the upholding of its rights under the order or undertaking, perhaps the most obvious private interest is that of deterrent for the future. That is of particular relevance on the facts here, where the parties continue to be embroiled in other ongoing litigation."[136j]

[136e] [2021] EWCA Civ 1799.
[136f] *Navigator Equities*, above, at [110].
[136g] *Navigator Equities*, above, at [115].
[136h] [2020] EWHC 558 (Comm).
[136i] [2017] EWHC 1876 (QB), at [82]–[85].
[136j] *Navigator Equities*, above, at [135].

35–071C The courts have debated, without finally determining, whether the test of abuse is whether the "predominant purpose" of the claimant is illegitimate or whether the test is the lower one of that being "a real and substantial purpose."[136k] It is suggested that given that the issue of abuse is multi-factorial, involving potentially a range of considerations, it would be wrong to lay down a fixed test. It is adequate to simply pose the question thus: in all the circumstances is this application an abuse of process such that it should be struck out?

[136k] See e.g. *Integral Petroleum v Petrogat* [2020] EWHC 558 (Comm), at [43]–[44].

35–071D A particular risk which the courts are alive to is the extent to which, in circumstances where there is wider ongoing litigation between the parties, a claimant is using the committal jurisdiction to pressurise the defendant into settling that litigation. To threaten or institute committal proceedings to secure such a settlement is itself an abuse of process and indeed a contempt, which is likely to justify the dismissal of the application.[136l] Indeed it may constitute blackmail.[136m] Particular problems can arise in attempts to settle ongoing litigation where there is also an extant committal application. It is not the case that any attempt to globally settle the dispute between the parties necessarily carries with it the implication of impropriety. Otherwise, once a committal application was instituted, it would be effectively impossible to engage in without prejudice negotiations for fear of their being held to be admissible under the "unambiguous impropriety" exception and stigmatised as abusive. Hence the court should not jump too readily to the conclusion that references in the settlement communications to the disposal of the committal proceedings or the timing of the committal proceedings evidence an improper purpose on the claimant's part, or involve the use of the committal proceedings as some form of improper threat.[136n]

[136l] *Integral Petroleum v Petrogat* [2020] EWHC 558 (Comm), at [36] and following. Foxton J said, at [42]: "it can never be proper to seek to use a committal application as a lever to bully a defendant into a settlement."

[136m] See *Ferster v Ferster* [2016] EWCA Civ 77 where the judge at first instance held that a threat of committal proceedings amounting to blackmail was made by one party to another.

[136n] Hence in *Integral Petroleum v Petrogat* [2020] EWHC 558 (Comm), Foxton J declined to strike out committal proceedings where without prejudice correspondence was adduced showing that the claimant had proposed a global settlement. He held, at [66], that the claimant's conduct "did not go beyond that which was permissible in attempting to settle hard-fought commercial litigation." A similar approach was taken in *Cole v Carpenter* [2020] EWHC 3155 (Ch), at [70]–[72]. It seems clear that judges will be sensitive to the realities of modern litigation and will not be over-enthusiastic in finding or holding that claimants who seek to promote global settlements are acting abusively. Necessarily, if there is a contemplated or actual committal application relating to the underlying litigation, then any overall settlement will have to make provision for that. Nonetheless, a claimant should proceed carefully to ensure that there can be no proper suggestion of abusiveness.

At the end of footnote 137, add: **35–072**

In *Navigator Equities Ltd & Anor v Deripaska* [2020] EWHC 1798 (Comm), the judge heard the application to strike out the committal application as an abuse after the claimant's evidence had been given but before the defendant had opened his case.

At the end of the paragraph, add:

Indeed bringing serious breaches of court orders or undertakings to the court's attention is a paradigmatic purpose of the committal jurisdiction.[139a] A committal application can properly be brought in respect of past (and irremediable) breaches.[139b]

[139a] *Sectorguard plc v Dienne plc* [2009] EWHC 2693 (Ch), per Briggs J at [47].
[139b] *Navigator Equities Ltd v Deripaska* [2021] EWCA Civ 1799, at [82(i)].

At the end of footnote 140, add: **35–073**

This power is not the subject of express provision in the new Part 81, but it was confirmed in *Navigator Equities Ltd v Deripaska* [2021] EWCA Civ 1799, at [85], that the court's inherent power to strike out remains; no doubt this power will be exercised after 1 October 2020 just as it was before that date, even absent an equivalent to para.16.1. A similar conclusion was reached by HHJ Eyre QC in *Taylor v Robinson* [2021] EWHC 664 (Ch), drawing on the Court of Appeal's earlier decision in *Taylor v Ribby Hall Leisure Ltd* [1998] 1 W.L.R. 400.

At the end of the paragraph, add: **35–074**

The rule in *Henderson v Henderson* is applicable to contempt applications. So where a claimant issued a second application based on alleged breaches of an order after he had made an earlier application which post-dated the alleged breaches but did not rely upon them, the second application was struck out as an abuse of process in advance of the substantive hearing. The alleged breaches could and should have been relied upon in the earlier application.[142a]

[142a] *Taylor v Robinson* [2021] EWHC 664 (Ch), where HHJ Eyre QC laid out the correct approach, at [87]: "The abuse in such a case consists of bringing the committal application in circumstances when to do so amounts to an unjust harassment of the respondent because the matters relied upon should properly have been advanced in an earlier application. If in such circumstances the court were to decline to consider striking out the application on the grounds of abuse of process until the substantive hearing then to a large extent the abuse against which the principle is directed would already have occurred by the time striking out was considered. In such circumstances the respondent would by having to contest the application to a substantive hearing have suffered the unjust harassment against which he is to be protected."

(8) Timing of Application

35–076 *At the end of footnote 144, add:*

Similarly it was said in *Deutsche Bank AG v Sebastian Holdings Inc* [2020] EWHC 3536 (Comm), at [157], that "It is of course correct that proceedings for contempt of court must be issued without delay." There is a tension between such exhortations and the principle that committal applications should be brought as a "last resort". The reality is that a court will be very wary about striking out a case for alleged delay other than in exceptional circumstances. In *Deutsche Bank AG v Sebastian Holdings Inc* it was contended that the claimant's supposed "inordinate and inexcusable" delay rendered the application abusive. The judge had no difficulty rejecting that contention.

At the end of footnote 146, add:

For an example of a case where the judge decided, on case management grounds, to defer the trial of a committal application arising out of alleged breaches of freezing orders brought while the substantive proceedings were ongoing see *Suppipat v Narongdej* [2021] EWHC 3259 (Comm) where Butcher J said, at [15]: "While I recognise and endorse the general desirability of dealing with allegations of breach of freezing orders or equivalent undertakings promptly and with decision, the question of when there should be a determination of allegations of contempt is an issue to which considerations of proper case management, of proportionality and of the fair allocation of court resources are vital, as they are in other areas. The appropriate course will depend on the facts of the case."

35–078 *At the end of footnote 150, add:*

On this see the cases referred to above under footnote 10.

(10) Entitlement to Legal Aid

35–080 *At the end of footnote 155, add:*

As to the question of whether a court should proceed where the defendant is unrepresented in order to allow legal aid to be obtained see *Brown v London Borough of Haringey* [2015] EWCA Civ 483; [2017] 1 W.L.R. 542; *Re O (Committal: Legal Representation)* [2019] EWCA Civ 1721; [2019] 4 W.L.R. 140; *The All England Lawn Tennis Club (Championships) Ltd & Ors v McKay* [2019] EWHC 2973 (QB); and *Corrigan v Chelsea Football Club Ltd* [2019] EWCA Civ 1964. The new Part 81 now requires the claimant to state on the face of the contempt application that "the defendant is entitled to a reasonable opportunity to obtain legal representation and to apply for legal aid which may be available without any means test." (r.81.4(2)(j)).

After "(10) Entitlement to Legal Aid" insert new section and paragraph:

(11) Court acting on its own initiative

35–080A A novel provision of the new Part 81 is contained in r.81.6(1), which states: "(1) If the court considers that a contempt of court (including a contempt in the face of the court) may have been committed, the court on its own initiative shall consider whether to proceed against the defendant in contempt proceedings." This reflects an inherent power in the court to commit of its own volition and does not involve an alteration of the court's substantive powers. If the court takes this step then it must issue a summons to the defendant which includes the matters set out in r81.4(2), in so far as applicable, and require the defendant to attend court for directions to be given: r.81.6(3). Further "any other party to the proceedings may be required by the court to give such assistance to the court as is proportionate and reasonable, having regard to the resources available to that party": r.81.6(2).

These are problematic provisions and it is suggested that the court will be reticent to rely upon them except in exceptional circumstances, certainly in the context of commercial litigation where the parties are represented. An attempt was made in *Isbilen v Turk*[156a] to persuade a court to utilize the power identified in r.81.6. The court declined to do so, the judge concluding that the court was generally not well placed to commence contempt proceedings. It might be added that in ordinary commercial litigation the party who is the "victim" of the alleged breach can normally be expected to issue a committal application if thought appropriate.

156a [2021] EWHC 854 (Ch), at [32].

E. THE HEARING

(1) The Necessity for a Hearing

At the end of footnote 160, add: **35–082**

The new r.81.8 deals with hearings of contempt applications. The general rule remains that hearings of contempt proceedings shall be in public and r.81.8 makes detailed provision for any derogation from that rule. The new r.81.3 provides for what type of judge can hear a contempt application.

Add new paragraph 35–082A after para.35–082:

Before proceeding the court should ensure that: **35–082A**

(1) (where he is not represented) the person accused of contempt has been given the opportunity to secure legal representation, as he is entitled to;
(2) The person accused of contempt has been advised of the right to remain silent; and
(3) If the person accused of contempt chooses to give evidence, that he has been warned about self-incrimination.[161a]

161a This is drawn from the guidelines stated in *Re L (A Child)* [2016] EWCA Civ 173; [2017] 1 F.L.R. 1135, at [78]. The Court of Appeal emphasised the duty on the claimant's lawyers to assist the court.

At the end of the paragraph, add new footnote 161a: **35–083**

161a This paragraph was cited with approval in *Atkinson v Varma* [2021] EWHC 592 (Ch), per HHJ Johns QC at [5].

(2) Proceeding in the Absence of the Defendant

At the end of footnote 162, add: **35–084**

Cobb J's checklist continues to be cited by first instance judges, and was described as a "helpful summary of the principles" by the Court of Appeal in *Griffith v P (By Her Litigation Friend the Official Solicitor)* [2020] EWCA Civ 1675, at [8]. See also *XL Insurance Company SE v Ipors Underwriting Ltd* [2021] EWHC 1407 (Comm). Under the new r.81.4(2)(o) the claimant must state in the contempt application "that the court may proceed in the defendant's absence if they do not attend...", so alerting the defendant to the potential consequences of non-attendance.

(7) The Standard of Proof and Circumstantial Evidence

35–090 *At the end of footnote 170, add*:

See also *Masri v Consolidated Contractors International Company SAL* [2011] EWHC 1024 (Comm), at [45]–[46].The only reference to the standard of proof in the new Part 81 is to be found in the obligation, imposed by r.81.4(2)(o), on the part of the claimant to state in the contempt application that the court will "only find the defendant in contempt if satisfied beyond reasonable doubt of the facts constituting contempt and that they do constitute contempt." In *Minstrell Recruitment Ltd v Lockett* [2020] EWHC 3537 (Ch), Snowden J held, at [14], that if the claimant contended that the defendant had breached the orders "wilfully or recklessly", then that had to be proved beyond reasonable doubt. On the other hand where the defendant made allegations against the claimant which were said to be relevant to sentence, then the burden lay on the defendant to prove them on the balance of probabilities. The suggestion that the burden lay on the claimant to disprove such allegations to the criminal standard was rejected, and rightly so, it is respectfully suggested.

At end of the first sentence, add:

, i.e. beyond reasonable doubt, or satisfied so that one is sure.[170a]

[170a] In *JSC Mezhdunarodniy Promyshelnniy Bank v Pugachev* [2016] EWHC 192 (Ch), Rose J said, at [41((ii)]: "the criminal standard of proof applies, so that the Bank's case must be proved beyond reasonable doubt—or so that the court is sure. In case the meaning of this formulation were unclear, Phipson on Evidence (17th edn, 2009 at para.6.51) cites the Privy Council in *Walters v. R* [1969] 2 A.C. 26 as indicating that '[a] reasonable doubt is that quality or kind of doubt which when you are dealing with matters of importance in your own affairs you allow to influence you one way or another.'"

At the end of footnote 171, add:

In *Cuciurean v The Secretary of State for Transport* [2021] EWCA Civ 357, Warby LJ held, at [49], that: "A court may be sure of a circumstantial case, built on strands of evidence not all of which are made out to that standard."

At the end of paragraph, add:

On the other hand if a defendant raised a positive defence to the application, it has been said that he carried an evidential burden which he had to discharge before the burden was returned to the claimant.[173a]

[173a] *JSC Mezhdunarodniy Promyshelnniy Bank v Pugachev* [2016] EWHC 192 (Ch), at [41(i)].

F. PENALTIES

(1) Introduction

35–092 *At the end of footnote 176, add:*

However community sentences involving the probation service or unpaid work are only available for those "convicted of any offence": see *R v Palmer* (1992) 95 Cr App R 170 (CA). It follows that they are not available as punishment for contempt: *Minstrell Recruitment Ltd v Lockett* [2020] EWHC 3537 (Ch), at [241].

At the end of footnote 177, add:

The court may also suspend execution of a sentence of imprisonment for a given period of time to give the defendant an opportunity to purge his contempt: see e.g. *Yuzu Hair And Beauty Ltd v Selvathiraviam* [2020] EWHC 1539 (Ch).

Add new paragraph 35–092A after para.35–092:

The new CPR Part 81 provides for the punishment phase of a committal application in the following terms, at r.81.9: **35–092A**

"(1) If the court finds the defendant in contempt of court, the court may impose a period of imprisonment (an order of committal), a fine, confiscation of assets or other punishment permitted under the law.
(2) Execution of an order of committal requires issue of a warrant of committal. An order of committal and a warrant of committal have immediate effect unless and to the extent that the court decides to suspend execution of the order or warrant.
(3) An order or warrant of committal must be personally served on the defendant unless the court directs otherwise.
(4) To the extent that the substantive law permits, a court may attach a power of arrest to a committal order.
(5) An order or warrant of committal may not be enforced more than two years after the date it was made unless the court directs otherwise."

The position has not substantially changed from the previous position.

(2) The Purpose of a Sentence

At the end of footnote 180, add: **35–094**

In *JSC BTA Bank v Solodchenko* [2011] EWCA Civ 1241; [2012] W.L.R. 350, it was said, per Jackson LJ at [45], that the sentence for a civil contempt "performs a number of functions. First, it upholds the authority of the court by punishing the contemnor and deterring others. Such punishment has nothing to do with the dignity of the court and everything to do with the public interest that court orders should be obeyed. Secondly, in some instances, it provides an incentive for belated compliance, because the contemnor may seek a reduction or discharge of sentence if he subsequently purges his contempt by complying with the court order in question."

(i) Punishment

At the end of footnote 183, add: **35–095**

Speaking of some of these decisions, and earlier cases, Jackson LJ said in *JSC BTA Bank v Solodchenko* [2011] EWCA Civ 1241; [2012] 1 W.L.R. 350: "What they show collectively is that any deliberate and substantial breach of the restraint provisions or the disclosure provisions of a freezing order is a serious matter. Such a breach normally attracts an immediate custodial sentence which is measured in months rather than weeks and may well exceed a year." See also *McKendrick v The Financial Conduct Authority* [2019] EWCA Civ 524; [2019] 4 W.L.R. 65 in which the Court of Appeal again reaffirmed, at [40], the strong view the court takes in relation to breaches of freezing orders and indeed court orders generally.

At the end of footnote 184 before full-stop, add:

; *Kazakhstan Kagazy Plc v Zhunus* [2019] EWHC 2319 (Comm) (24 months). In that case the court included a provision in the order that the defendant could apply to vary or discharge that order. The intent of that is, of course, that he can do so if and when he complies in whole or in part with the order or, alternatively, provides an explanation as to why he has been unable to do so

35–097 *At the end of footnote 187, add:*

For an example of where this was done see *Hussain v Vaswani* [2020] EWCA Civ 1216; [2020] W.L.R.(D) 510.

At end of footnote 188, add:

In *Aspinall's Club Ltd v Lim* [2019] EWHC 2379 (QB), the judge fined the defendant but identified an element of the fine which would be remitted if the defendant complied with the order breached by a given date.

35–098 *At the end of footnote 190, add:*

The general rules about costs contained in CPR Part 44 are applicable to committal applications. In *Super-Max Offshore Holdings v Malhotra* [2020] EWHC 1130 (Comm), Sir Michael Burton GBE suggested, at [15], without elaboration, that an order for indemnity costs was the "ordinary course" where a claimant had succeeded.

Add new paragraph 35–098A after para.35–098:

35–098A In recent years the courts have approached sentencing through a structured process which draws upon the approach of the criminal courts:

(1) The court must consider the seriousness of the case, including the culpability of the contemnor and the harm caused, intended or likely to be caused by the breach of the order;
(2) The court should then take account of aggravating and mitigating factors;
(3) The court must then consider whether a fine would be sufficient. If it would, committal to prison cannot be justified, even if the contemnor's means are so limited that the amount of the fine must be modest;
(4) A sentence of imprisonment should only be imposed where the court is satisfied that the contemnor's conduct is so serious that no other penalty is appropriate. It is a measure of last resort;
(5) A sentence of imprisonment must not be imposed because the circumstances of the contemnor mean that he will be unable to pay a fine;
(6) When considering what period of imprisonment to impose, the court should again take into account personal mitigation;
(7) It should then consider what reduction to make, if any, for any admissions made by the defendant;
(8) Having decided on the term of any sentence the court will then finally consider whether that term can properly be suspended. It will take account of the fact that a suspended prison sentence, equally, is still a prison sentence. It is not to be regarded as a lesser form of punishment. Generally matters of personal mitigation will have no role to play in determining the answer to this question. But the court can take account of the impact of a sentence of imprisonment on others when deciding whether or not to suspend the sentence.[190a]

[190a] See generally *Liverpool Victoria Insurance Limited v Zafar* [2019] EWCA 392 (Civ); [2019] 1 W.L.R. 3833; *Sellers v Podstreshnyy* [2019] EWCA Civ 613; *McKendrick v The Financial Conduct Authority* [2019] EWCA Civ 524; [2019] 4 W.L.R. 6; *Kea Investments Ltd v Watson* [2020] 2796 (Ch).

(3) Contumacious Breach

At the end of footnote 191, add: **35–099**

It has been recognised that the maximum term of 2 years is comparatively short and therefore it cannot be reserved for the very worst sort of contempt that can be imagined. In fact there will be a comparatively broad range of conduct which can fairly be regarded as falling within the most serious category and as therefore justifying a sentence at or near the maximum. See generally *McKendrick v The Financial Conduct Authority* [2019] EWCA Civ 524; [2019] 4 W.L.R. 65, at [40].

(4) Sentencing Considerations

At the end of footnote 193, add: **35–101**

The courts treat a breach of a post-judgment freezing order as more serious than breach of a pre-judgment freezing order: see *Kea Investments Ltd v Watson* [2020] 2796 (Ch), at [13]–[14]. In the context of breach of an order made under CPR r.71, Morris J held, in *Hassan Khan & Co v Al-Rawas* [2021] EWHC 3229 (QB), at [24], that "breach of a court order made after judgment made in support of the claimant's rights resulting from that judgment is a more serious contempt of court than breach of a pre-judgment order." A sentence of 24 months was imposed.

After the words "any apology" in sub-paragraph (8), add new footnote 193a:

The weight to be given to an admission will be reduced the later it is made in the proceedings. Sentencing guidelines in criminal cases are of assistance here, so that the maximum reduction will be one-third (from the sentence that would otherwise be imposed), which will be appropriate where the admission is made as soon as proceedings are commenced. Thereafter a sliding scale will generally be appropriate down to about 10% where the admission is made at the trial itself. See *Liverpool Victoria Insurance Limited v Zafar* [2019] EWCA 392 (Civ); [2019] 1 W.L.R. 3833, at [68]. However there is no absolute rule that where an admission is made credit must be given: in *Lakatamia Shipping Company Ltd v Su* [2021] EWCA Civ 1355; [2021] W.L.R.(D) 489, the respondent admitted the contempts alleged very shortly before the hearing. He was sentenced to 24 months imprisonment. His appeal against sentence failed, Carr LJ referring to it as an "exceptional" case. On the other hand the absence of an admission will not aggravate a sentence: *Liverpool Victoria Insurance Limited v Zafar*, at [23]. Courts often set little store by (and are wise to) hollow apologies: see, for example, *Centek Holdings Ltd v Giles* [2020] EWHC 1682 (Ch), at [18].

At the end of footnote 194, add:

Other considerations relevant to sentence, depending on the circumstances, might include one or more of the following: previous good character (though this will rarely carry significant weight in the current context: *Templeton Insurance Limited v Thomas* [2013] EWCA Civ 35, at [45]); the defendant's mental and physical health; where the defendant is a carer, the effect of a prison sentence on any children or vulnerable adults for whom they care (see *Sellers v Podstreshnyy* [2019] EWCA Civ 613, at [36]); the general effect of such a sentence on others; the fact that the claimant has lost on a significant number of counts; the length and stress of the committal trial itself; any delay in the application coming on for hearing. Some of these considerations may be relevant to suspension of a sentence of imprisonment. See generally *Oliver v Shaikh (No.2)* [2020] EWHC 2658 (QB) and *Kea Investments Ltd v Watson* [2020] 2796 (Ch). In *McKendrick v The Financial Conduct Authority* [2019] EWCA Civ 524; [2019] 4 W.L.R. 65, the first instance judge (Marcus Smith J) would have sentenced the defendant to 12 months in prison, but reduced the sentence to 6 months to take into account defendant's admission of and apology for the contempts he had committed and the fact that he had made a bona fide attempt to comply belatedly with the freezing order. The Court of Appeal thought that was a generous reduction: see at [47].

(5) Mitigation

35–102 *At the end of paragraph, add:*

In a substantial case, the sentencing hearing will generally take place after a written judgment on liability alone has been handed down. This will allow the parties to consider carefully the judgment and prepare for the sentencing hearing. It will also allow the defendant to consider whether to take steps to purge any contempts which have been found. At that stage, it is of course possible for the defendant to adduce evidence directly bearing on sentence. If that evidence is challenged, then the claimant may be permitted to cross-examine on it and even to serve evidence in response. But the claimant generally has no right of reply to submissions in mitigation. Where the defendant does not appear at the committal hearing there will often be good reasons to adjourn the sentencing aspect (and, if appropriate, to issue a warrant of arrest so that the defendant may be brought before the court and make representations if he wishes) and to see whether the defendant makes efforts to purge his contempt in the face of an impending sentencing hearing.[195a]

[195a] See *JSC BTA Bank v Solodchenko* [2010] EWHC 2404 (Comm), at [36]–[37] and *Triad Group Plc v Makar* [2020] EWHC 2701 (QB), at [52]–[54]. For cases where a defendant intentionally absented himself from the committal hearing and the court was persuaded to proceed straight to sentencing, see *Russian Commercial Bank (Cyprus) Limited v Khoroshilov* [2013] EWHC 4433 (Comm) and *GML International Ltd & Ors, R (On the Application of GML International Ltd) v Harfield* [2020] EWHC 2667 (QB).

(6) Other Orders

35–105 *At the end of footnote 200, but before the full-stop, add:*

; [2013] Ch 1

(7) Purging Contempt

35–106 *At the end of footnote 201, add:*

For an application of those principles in the civil fraud context, see the two decisions in *Lakatamia Shipping Company v Su* [2019] EWHC 3180 (Comm) and [2020] EWHC 806 (Comm). The new rule is contained in r.81.10.

I. APPEALS

35–115 *At the end of footnote 232, add*:

A more recent example of an appeal against sentence by the claimant is *Liverpool Victoria Insurance Company Ltd v Zafar (Rev 1)* [2019] EWCA Civ 392; [2019] 1 W.L.R. 3833, where a judge had imposed a suspended sentence upon an expert witness who had provided a report to the court which was false.

35–116 *At the end of footnote 233, add*:

And see also section 13(3) of the Administration of Justice Act 1960, which materially provides that "the court to which an appeal is brought under this section may reverse or vary the order or decision of the court below, and make such other order as may be just."

At the end of footnote 234, add:

More recently, in *McKendrick v The Financial Conduct Authority* [2019] EWCA Civ 524; [2019] 4 W.L.R. 65, the Court of Appeal stated that it was reluctant to interfere with sentencing decisions, and will generally only do so if the judge: i) made an error of principle; ii) took into account immaterial factors or failed to take into account material factors; or iii) reached a decision which was plainly wrong in that it was outside the range of decisions reasonably open to the judge. See also *Liverpool Victoria Insurance Limited v Zafar* [2019] EWCA 392 (Civ); [2019] 1 W.L.R. 3833 at [44] and [71], where it was said that "there will be few cases in which a decision as to the appropriate sentence for contempt will be open to challenge in this court, whether on grounds of undue leniency or of undue severity." See also *Lakatamia Shipping Company Ltd v Su* [2021] EWCA Civ 1355; [2021] W.L.R.(D) 489, at [18]. In *Nichols v Chelsea Football Club Ltd* [2020] EWCA Civ 470 the Court of Appeal emphasised that on any appeal against sentence the court will look at the sentence in the round and ask whether it was a proper one, rather than engaging in the fine-tuning of the steps taken by the first instance judge to reach that sentence. Nonetheless it seems that if the Court of Appeal feels that the sentence is too high, then it will allow itself a certain latitude in the application of the principles above: see, for instance, *Lockett v Minstrell Recruitment Ltd* [2021] EWCA Civ 102.

At the end of the paragraph, add

Where the court is satisfied that the sentence was "wrong" then it will reverse the decision below and either remit the case to the judge for further consideration of sanction or substitute its own decision.[236a] In practice, the appeal court will generally wish to adopt the latter course.

[236a] See *Liverpool Victoria Insurance Limited v Zafar* [2019] EWCA 392 (Civ); [2019] 1 W.L.R. 3833, at [46].

Add new paragraph 35–117A after para.35–117:

Where a defendant has been sentenced to an immediate term of imprisonment, the court has jurisdiction to stay that term pending an appeal, whether against the order for committal itself or the sentence. It may be that any appeal is of such complexity that it could not be brought on expeditiously; or that the term of imprisonment is so short that it will have been served or substantially served by the time any appeal comes on, rendering the appeal in large part nugatory.[239a] **35–117A**

[239a] There have been a number of cases where the question of stay has been considered, albeit briefly: see *McKay v All England Lawn Tennis Club* [2020] EWCA Civ 695, *Chelsea Football Club v Nichols* [2020] EWHC 454 (QB); *Super-Max Offshore Holdings v Malhotra* [2020] EWHC 1130 (Comm). In *Kea Investments Ltd v Watson* [2020] EWHC 2796 (Ch), Nugee LJ declined to order a stay where he took the view that the proposed grounds of appeal had limited prospects of success. Of course, in such a circumstance, the defendant may seek a stay directly from the Court of Appeal.

CHAPTER 36

OTHER SANCTIONS FOR PROCEDURAL DEFAULT

B. STRIKING OUT AND DEBARRING ORDERS

(2) The Effect of Debarring and Striking Out

Replace footnote 4 with: **36–007**

See the Glossary to the CPR in Section E of the White Book 2021, Vol.1, para.E1–1.

36–008 *At the end of the paragraph, add new footnote 9a:*

[9a] In *Times Travel (UK) Ltd v Pakistan International Airlines Corp* [2019] EWHC 3732 (Ch), Edwin Johnson QC (sitting as a Deputy High Court Judge) held at [55(5)] that a debarring order does not lead to judgment in default, and that it is still necessary for the claimant to demonstrate to the satisfaction of the court that the claimant is entitled to the relief sought. By contrast, in *Byers v Samba Financial Group* [2020] EWHC 1006 (Ch), Fancourt J distinguished the *Times Travel* case and held that the claimants should not be required to prove their case on the balance of probabilities or adduce evidence in support of that case on issues in respect of which the defendant had been debarred from defending, in circumstances where the basis for the debarring order was a wholesale failure by the defendant to give standard disclosure. To require the claimants to prove their case in such circumstances, without the benefit of the defendant's disclosure, would be to continue the very prejudice which led to the debarring order in the first place. *Times Travel* was distinguished on the basis that counsel for the Claimant had in that case conceded the need to prove its case; and the proceedings only concerned the taking of an account, which "by [its] nature" required the Court to be satisfied as to the amount in which to enter judgment. In *MMD Mining Machinery Developments Limited v Lang* [2021] EWHC 3264 (Comm), a defendant's defence had been struck out for failure to comply with an unless order relating to disclosure. Foxton J, having considered *Times Travel* and *Byers v Samba*, held that the claimants were still required to prove their prove their case on the evidence before the court, but this was in circumstances where the claimants sought a judgment on the merits: see [12].

36–011 *After the second sentence, add new footnote 11a:*

[11a] Though there is probably no absolute rule that a defendant is entitled to test the claimant's case in cross-examination and make further submissions: *Kliers v Schmerler* [2018] EWHC 1350 (Ch), per Murray Rosen QC (sitting as a Deputy High Court Judge), at [16], cited by Foxton J in *MMD Mining Machinery Developments Limited v Lang* (above), at [10]. In the latter case (the facts of which are explained in footnote 9a above), the defendant was permitted to cross-examine the claimants' witnesses, solely for the purpose of testing that evidence rather than advancing a positive case.

36–012 *After the third sentence, add new footnote 13a:*

[13a] *MMD Mining Machinery Developments Limited v Lang*, above, at [10].

36–014 *At the end of the paragraph, add:*

In *Times Travel (UK) Ltd v Pakistan International Airlines Corp*,[20a] Edwin Johnson QC (sitting as a Deputy High Court Judge) held that, where an order debars a defendant from defending, at trial they should not be permitted to participate in the normal way, such as by adducing evidence, cross-examining witnesses or making submissions. It was conceded by the claimants that they were still required to prove their case to the satisfaction of the court.[20b] In the same case the Deputy Judge observed that the court nevertheless retains a residual and narrow discretion or trial management power to permit a debarred defendant to take some part in the trial (which the Deputy Judge exercised in one limited respect). He also considered that a debarred defendant should normally be able to address the court on the form of order to be made following its substantive decision, to point out any errors in its judgment, and to address the court on costs.[20c]

[20a] *Times Travel (UK) Ltd v Pakistan International Airlines Corp* [2019] EWHC 3732 (Ch), at [55(2)].
[20b] *Times Travel*, above, at [23]. Contrast in this respect *Byers v Samba Financial Group* [2020] EWHC 1006 (Ch), noted at n.9a above.
[20c] *Times Travel*, above, at [55(3)]. In *Kim v Lee* [2021] EWHC 231 (QB), Steyn J gave the debarred defendant the opportunity to make submissions on the form of order and costs.

At the end of the paragraph, add new footnote 20d: **36–015**

[20d] See also *Kliers v Schmerler* [2018] EWHC 1350 (Ch), per Murray Rosen QC at [27], holding that the rights of the debarred party to cross-examine and make submissions "are not absolutely lost or retained when a defendant is debarred from defending, unless the court makes this explicit. Absent a previous order to that effect, the trial judge can decide under his or her case management powers (but still of course having regard to the overriding objective) to do what is just and expedient as regard the need and justification for cross-examination and further submissions in the particular case."

(4) Features of the Jurisdiction

At the end of footnote 26, add: **36–020**

In *Byers v Samba Financial Group* [2020] EWHC 1006 (Ch), Fancourt J rejected a submission that a full debarring order was a "normal" or "usual" response of the court to serious non-compliance with its orders, holding instead that "The court must have regard to the circumstances of the individual case, and do what is necessary and proportionate to mark the seriousness of the breach of its order in a way that is consistent with the interests of justice and the overriding objective. The seriousness of the breach, the extent if at all to which it is excusable and the consequences of the breach will be very important factors, but the overriding criterion is the requirement for the sanction to be proportionate and just": see at [122]–[123]. This is consistent with the principles as set out in the remainder of this section: in particular, in identifying the consequences of the breach, the court will ask itself whether that breach gives rise to a continuing risk of injustice in the sense explained below.

At the end of the paragraph, add new footnote 32a: **36–023**

[32a] On the other hand, several recent cases have emphasised the extreme nature of the jurisdiction to strike out following misconduct in the pursuit of litigation on principles set out in *Arrow Nominees*: *Ali v Dinc* [2020] EWHC 3055 (Ch), per Sarah Worthington QC (sitting as a Deputy High Court Judge), at [24]–[26]; *Active Media Services Inc v Burmester* [2021] EWHC 232 (Comm), per Calver J at [302]–[308]; *Palmali Shipping SA v Litasco SA* [2021] EWHC 1161 (Comm), per Foxton J at [16]–[22].

(5) Debarring a party for failure to satisfy previous costs orders

Add new heading as above and new paragraphs 36–030A and 36–030B after para.36–030: **36–030A**

A separate line of authority addresses the situation in which a party seeks to debar their opponent from taking further part in proceedings on the basis of a failure to satisfy a prior interim costs order. The principles were summarised by Sir Richard Field (sitting as a Deputy High Court Judge) in *Michael Wilson & Partners v Sinclair*[50a] as follows:

> "29. In my judgment, the following principles are applicable when dealing with an application that a party to on-going litigation should be debarred from continuing to participate in the litigation by reason of having failed to pay an order for costs made in the course of the proceedings:
>
> (1) The imposition of a sanction for non-payment of a costs order involves the exercise of a discretion pursuant to the Court's inherent jurisdiction.
>
> (2) The Court should keep carefully in mind the policy behind the imposition of costs orders made payable within a specified period of time before the end of the litigation, namely, that they serve to discourage irresponsible interlocutory applications or resistance to successful interlocutory applications.
>
> (3) Consideration must be given to all the relevant circumstances including: (a) the potential applicability of Article 6 ECHR; (b) the availability of alternative means of enforcing the costs order through the different mechanisms of execution; (c) whether the court making the costs order did so notwithstanding a submission that it was inappropriate to make a

costs order payable before the conclusion of the proceedings in question; and where no such submission was made whether it ought to have been made or there is no good reason for it not having been made.

(4) A submission by the party in default that he lacks the means to pay and that therefore a debarring order would be a denial of justice and/or in breach of Article 6 of ECHR should be supported by detailed, cogent and proper evidence which gives full and frank disclosure of the witness's financial position including his or her prospects of raising the necessary funds where his or her cash resources are insufficient to meet the liability.

(5) Where the defaulting party appears to have no or markedly insufficient assets in the jurisdiction and has not adduced proper and sufficient evidence of impecuniosity, the court ought generally to require payment of the costs order as the price for being allowed to continue to contest the proceedings unless there are strong reasons for not so ordering.

(6) If the court decides that a debarring order should be made, the order ought to be an unless order except where there are strong reasons for imposing an immediate order."

[50a] *Michael Wilson & Partners v Sinclair* [2017] EWHC 2424 (Comm), at [29]. In *Siddiqi v Aidinantz* [2020] EWHC 699 (QB), Saini J set out, at [30], a summary of the principles applicable to an application to stay a claim until an existing costs order is paid. That summary did not refer to the decision in *Michael Wilson & Partners v Sinclair*, but is thought to be consistent with it. Notably Saini J held that the working or default rule is that a litigant should not be able to continue with his or her claim without satisfying an existing and non-appealed final costs order.

36–030B The interaction between these principles and those set out in the previous section has received little attention in the case law. In *Orenga de Gafforj v Orenga de Gafforj*,[50b] the Court of Appeal determined an application for a debarring order against a husband in matrimonial proceedings, following his failure to comply with previous orders, including orders for costs. Applying principles derived from *Hadkinson v Hadkinson*, the Court made a debarring order in "unless" form in respect of certain orders, but declined to do so in respect of a prior order for costs, on the basis that non-compliance with the latter order was not an insuperable impediment to the course of justice (in contrast to the husband's breach of a litigation services payment order, which was). No reference was made to the *Michael Wilson & Partners* line of authority.

[50b] *Orenga de Gafforj v Orenga de Gafforj* [2018] EWCA Civ 2070; [2019] 1 F.C.R. 73, at [11].

D. CONTROLLING DISCLOSURE AND USE OF DOCUMENTS

(1) Introduction

36–032 *Replace footnote 54 with:*

See CPR r.31.23, Practice Direction 51U para.23.1 as applicable in the Business and Property Courts (false disclosure certificates), and CPR r.81.3.

(2) Taking Control of the Disclosure Process

Add new paragraph 36–036A after para.36–036:

36–036A The decision of Teare J in the *Nolan Family* case was followed by Foxton J in *Lakatamia Shipping Co Ltd v Su.*[61a] A judgment debtor had failed to comply with orders requiring him to disclose his assets and produce various documents. To assist the claimant in identifying assets against which to enforce, the judge made an order (pursuant to s.37 of the Senior Courts Act 1981 and the court's inherent jurisdiction) requiring the judgment debtor to sign mandates to his email and social media providers, authorising them to disclose to the claimants and an independent lawyer the details of the accounts. Foxton J held that an application for such an order should be approached on the basis of the test for a pre-judgment search order (see para.30–012 above). Having concluded that the test was satisfied, the judge granted the order subject to certain safeguards to protect the privacy of the judgment debtor, namely that the independent lawyer, having accessed and gathered documents from the relevant accounts, should not hand over obviously irrelevant documents to the judgment creditor, and any documents obtained could be used only for the purpose of enforcing the judgments of the court.[61b]

[61a] *Lakatamia Shipping Co Ltd v Su* [2020] EWHC 865 (Comm); [2020] 1 W.L.R. 2852.
[61b] *Lakatamia v Su*, above, at [28] and [43].

Replace paragraph 36–039 with:

This statement of principle was referred to by Mann J in *A v B*,[66] a decision in two similar cases in which imaging orders had been made and a dispute arose as to whether the claimants should be entitled to inspect the documents prior to a standard disclosure exercise being carried out by the defendants. Mann J endorsed the approach of Tugendhat J in *CBS Butler Ltd v Brown*,[66a] save that Mann J did not consider that the existence of substantial reasons for believing that a defendant was intending to conceal or destroy documents in breach of his disclosure obligations was a prerequisite to the making of this type of order in every case. Other circumstances might also justify that approach. Mann J set out[66b] a non-exhaustive list of potentially relevant factors, directed towards the situation in which a prior search order has been obtained: the question of whether the defendant can be trusted to carry out the disclosure process himself; which party is better qualified to assess the relevance of particular documents; considerations of urgency; the possibility of applying search terms; any differences in resources between the parties; and the intrusiveness of the exercise and the possibility of irrelevant, privileged and/or confidential material being disclosed to the receiving party. On the facts, a claimant-led inspection process was allowed in both cases. **36–039**

[66] *A v B* [2019] EWHC 2089 (Ch); [2019] 1 W.L.R. 5832 at [28]–[29]. The same statement of principle was also referred to with apparent approval by Arnold LJ in *TBD (Owen Holland) Ltd v Simons* [2020] EWCA Civ 1182; [2021] 1 W.L.R. 992, at [184].
[66a] [2013] EWHC 3944 (QB).
[66b] *A v B*, above, at [30].

Add new paragraph 39–039A after para.39–039:

CBS Butler v Brown and *A v B* are extreme cases in that the claimants sought to deprive the defendants of control over the disclosure process before it was even due to take place. The factors enumerated by Mann J in *A v B* illustrate that cases involving search orders are likely to be in their own category. Outside the context in which a search order has already been shown to be justified, a particularly strong case is likely to be required before the process can be taken out of the defendants' hands without the usual disclosure process being allowed first to run its course. Even after that has happened, it is unlikely that the necessary threshold will be met simply by showing that a party has breached his disclosure obligations. The court's focus is likely to be on questions such as whether, despite the breach, such an intrusive order is necessary to preserve the fairness of the trial process, and whether it would be a proportionate response to the breach. Each case **36–039A** will turn on its facts. In *Vilca v Xstrata Ltd*,[66c] Foskett J did not doubt that jurisdiction existed to order a "re-review" of the defendants' disclosure to be carried out by an independent lawyer. But he held that this would be "most unusual" and would require strong grounds. A lawyer's mistaken judgment in withholding a particular document from disclosure was held not to warrant the making of such an order on the facts of *Vilca* itself.

[66c] *Vilca v Xstrata Ltd* [2016] EWHC 1824 (QB), at [33].

(4) Preventing Reliance on Documents Disclosed Late

36–043 *At the end of footnote 71, add:*

In the Business and Property Courts, disclosure is presently governed largely by CPR Practice Direction 51U, but the general principles set out in the text are equally applicable in this context: see, for example, paras. 3.3, 8.3 (Models C, D and E in particular) and 12.5 of the Practice Direction.

E. PAYMENT INTO COURT

36–044 *At the end of footnote 74, add:*

Under CPR Practice Direction 51U which presently applies in the Business and Property Courts, see for example para.8.3 which sets out the requirements for each of the so-called Disclosure Models.

Replace the second sentence of footnote 75 with:

For some rare examples of cases in which the power has been exercised, see *Shaw v Palmer* [2004] EWHC 388 (QB), per Newman J; *Lazari v London and Newcastle (Camden) Ltd* [2013] EWHC 97 (TCC); [2013] CP Rep. 26, per Akenhead J; and *Coral Reef v Silverbond Enterprises Limited* [2019] EWHC 887 (Ch), per Deputy Master Linwood.

CHAPTER 37

ENFORCEMENT OF JUDGMENTS

(1) Post-Judgment Freezing Injunction

(i) Introduction

At the end of the paragraph, add: **37–006**

A post judgment freezing order may be made against the judgment debtor and third parties. Such third parties may be joined to the proceedings for the purposes of being subject to the freezing order on the basis that they are involved in the threatened or actual dissipation, with the jurisdiction to grant such orders effectively mirroring the *Chabra* jurisdiction.[4a]

[4a] See for instance *New York Laser Clinic Ltd v Naturastudios Ltd* [2019] EWHC 3944 (Comm).

(ii) Principles on which the Court will act

37–010 *At the end of footnote 11, add:*

However, for a recent example, where the factors relied upon did not suffice to establish a risk of dissipation, and the refusal to grant a freezing injunction was upheld on appeal, see *Les Ambassadeurs Club Ltd v Songbo Yu* [2021] EWCA Civ 1310.

At the end of footnote 12, add:

See, for a recent example, *Scott v Giles* [2018] EWHC 3705 (QB).

At the end of footnote 14, add:

See also *FM Capital Partners Ltd v Marino* [2018] EWHC 2612 (Comm), at [38]–[41], for a recent example where the specific factors relied upon as evidence of dissipation were, broadly, rejected but the finding of dishonest conduct in the proceedings was central to the grant of a post-judgment freezing injunction. See also *Iranian Offshore Engineering & Construction Co v Dean Investment Holdings SA* [2019] EWHC 107 (Comm).

At the end of footnote 15, add:

In *Michael Wilson and Partners Ltd v Emmott* [2019] EWCA Civ 219; [2019] 4 W.L.R. 53, at [56]–[57], it was held first that the fact that a post-judgment freezing injunction would increase pressure on defendants to honour judgment debts did not make it illegitimate and secondly, quoting *Nomihold,* that "it will sometimes and perhaps usually be inappropriate to include the [Angel Bell] exception in a post-judgment Mareva injunction"; but that there was no presumption to that effect. The Court should not even start from the position that the exception is or is not appropriate, but should determine the matter on the facts of the case. See also *Kazakhstan Kagazy Plc v Zhunus* [2018] EWHC 369 (Comm) per Picken J at [167].

At the end of the paragraph, add:

It is worth noting that the procedural safeguards which come into play in applications for freezing injunctions made prior to judgment apply with equal force in a post-judgment situation, such as the duty of fair presentation. Thus in *Rugby BC v Tayton*,[16a] the applicant council, having obtained a post-judgment freezing injunction without notice, was liable for costs when it was found to have breached the fair presentation requirement and failed to provide a note of the hearing to the respondent.

[16a] [2020] EWHC 898 (QB).

(iii) The duration of a post-judgment freezing order

37–012 *At the end of footnote 20, add:*

In *Scott v Giles* [2018] EWHC 3705 (QB), the duration of the post-judgment freezing injunction was limited to 18 months. Contrast with *Markham v O'Hara* [2019] EWCA Civ 397, where a post-judgment freezing order was only partially discharged 10 years after judgment, where a risk of dissipation and the possibility of enforcement remained.

(iv) *The terms of a post-judgment freezing order*

Replace paragraph 37–013 with:

The position on the inclusion of the ordinary course of business exception, which is included in pre-judgment freezing orders as a matter of course[21], was considered in depth in *Emmott v Michael Wilson & Partners Ltd.*[21a] It is now clear that: (i) the exception is not necessarily inappropriate in a post-judgment freezing order; (ii) there is no presumption or starting point in terms of the inclusion or exclusion of the exception in a post-judgment freezing order; (iii) the correct test is as set out in *Nomihold,* that "'it will sometimes and perhaps usually be inappropriate' to include the exception in a post judgment Mareva injunction", and the issue is a matter for the discretion of the Judge. The impact of a pending or extant appeal on the inclusion of the exception was not considered in *Emmott* but has been considered previously; the existence of an appeal is one of the factors which a judge will take into account in determining whether to include the exception.[22] Similarly it may be inappropriate for the legal costs and living expenses exceptions to continue.[23] But if the defendant is seeking to appeal the decision then it would very rarely be appropriate (certainly if permission to appeal has been given) to grant a freezing order which prevents it using its assets to pay its legal costs of mounting that appeal. 37–013

[21] See para.32–047 and following.
[21a] [2019] EWCA Civ 219; [2019] 4 W.L.R. 53.
[22] *Soinco v Novokuznetsk Aluminium Plant*, above, at 421, per Colman J; *Masri v Consolidated Contractors International SAL* [2008] EWHC 2492 (Comm), at [35], per Tomlinson J; *Mobile Telesystems Finance SA v Nomihold Securities Inc* [2011] EWCA Civ 1040; [2012] Bus L.R. 1166, per Tomlinson LJ at [34].
[23] In *One Life Ltd v Roy* Court of Appeal (Civ Div) Transcript No 128 of 1997 (30 January 1997) the Court of Appeal accepted that where a tracing claim had been upheld by the judge it would no longer be appropriate for there to be a living expenses exception: the money no longer belonged to the defendant.

(2) Appointment of Receiver to Preserve Assets

At the end of the paragraph, add: 37–020

Though a respondent to a receivership order may subsequently apply to set aside the appointment, it is to be noted that he cannot rely on evidence or argument which could have been, but was not, deployed at the time of the appointment.[32a]

[32a] See *JSC VTB Bank v Skurikhin* [2019] EWHC 1407 (Comm).

(3) Writ Ne Exeat Regno/Passport Order

At the end of footnote 36, add: 37–022

See *Lakatamia v Su* [2021] EWHC 935 (Comm) for a recent example where a passport order was extended in circumstances where an examination on the respondent's means had been adjourned. The purpose of and justification for the order, to support the order for examination, remained the same. Mr Su's appeal was dismissed by the Court of Appeal: [2021] EWCA Civ 1187. Giving the lead judgment, Sir Nicholas Patten acknowledged the importance of such orders being in place for no longer than necessary but found that on the facts of the case, which were described as "extraordinary", the extension of the order was justified. The Court declined to set down any kind of maximum time period for such orders, which had to be judged on a case by case basis according to their particular facts,

C. OBTAINING INFORMATION TO ASSIST IN ENFORCEMENT

(1) CPR Part 71

(i) Summary of provisions

37–032 *At the end of the paragraph, add:*

However, the material and information sought must be relevant to the question of enforcement. Accordingly, a request for disclosure and inspection of the respondents' passports in *Hassan Khan & Co v Al-Rawas*,[47a] intended to demonstrate that the respondents had lied about their whereabouts and damage their credibility, was refused.

[47a] [2018] EWHC 3730 (QB), at [48], [57].

37–034 *At the end of the paragraph, add:*

The 'judgment' need not even be for an assessed sum. In *Pluczenik Diamond Co NV v W Nagel (A Firm)*,[51a] an order was made under Part 71 for examination of a judgment debtor even though the only parts of the judgment that remained outstanding were costs liabilities which had not been agreed or subject to assessment.

[51a] [2019] EWHC 3126 (QB).

At the end of footnote 49, add:

Teare J described it as "anterior to" enforcement in *Sucden Financial Limited v Fluxo-Cane Overseas Limited* [2009] EWHC 3555 (Comm).

(ii) Procedure on application

37–035 *At the end of the paragraph, add:*

In *Vale SA v BSG Resources Ltd (In Administration)*[53a] it was held that the judgment creditor does not require any good reason to apply without notice; it is simply permitted to do so under the rules. Nonetheless the usual requirements for without notice applications, such as the duty of fair presentation, will apply. Those requirements can be avoided by making the application on notice.

[53a] [2020] EWHC 2021 (Comm), at [35]–[36].

37–038 *At the end of the paragraph, add:*

See to the contrary, in the case of an EU judgment enforceable under the Judgments Regulation, *Alfreds Chefenacker v Darko Horvat*.[59a] In that case, Deputy Insolvency and Companies Court Judge Baister decided that the applicant, with the benefit of an EU judgment, was a judgment creditor as defined by CPR 70.1(2)(a) and (b) (based on the interaction between the Judgments Regulation and the CPR) and so could invoke Part 71 in aid of enforcement. However, following Brexit, the case is likely now of diminishing relevance.

[59a] [2020] EWHC 506 (Ch), at [17].

After the second sentence, add: **37–042**

Similarly, the Court's control over the questioning can ensure that the examination is not oppressive, because it trespasses onto matters which are the subject of separate, ongoing proceedings,[64a] or because of the risk that the examinee is forced to give self-incriminating evidence.[64b]

[64a] *Vale SA v BSG Resources Ltd (In Administration)* [2020] EWHC 2021 (Comm), at [42]–[55].
[64b] *Lakatamia v Su* [2020] EWHC 426 (Comm).

At the end of the paragraph, add: **37–047**

A respondent who has failed to cooperate, for example by failing to provide documents in advance of the examination as ordered or failing to answer questions truthfully, may in exceptional circumstances be subject to an order for a second cross examination.[72a]

[72a] *Lakatamia Shipping Co Ltd v Su* [2020] EWHC 426 (Comm), at [31]–[39], [43].

At the end of footnote 76, add: **37–051**

See also *Motorola Solutions Inc v Hytera Communications Corp Ltd* [2020] EWHC 980 (Comm) (overturned on appeal on other grounds).

D. EXECUTION

(1) Assets Directly Held by Third Parties

At the end of footnote 84, add: **37–057**

See also *Iranian Offshore Engineering and Construction Co v Zavarei* [2020] EWHC 2497 (Comm) in respect of the beneficial ownership of a property said to be owned by the wife of one of the defendants.

(i) Sham trust

At the end of footnote 88, add: **37–064**

For an unsuccessful attempt to demonstrate that discretionary trusts were not genuine, see *Raja v van Hoogstraten* [2018] 2 WLUK 607.

(ii) No discretionary trust

At the end of the paragraph, add new footnote 89a: **37–066**

[89a] No fraud case, or English case, since *Pugachev* appears to have involved consideration or determination of these issues. However in *Webb v Webb* [2020] UKPC 22, the Privy Council considered, and accepted, a similar argument in the context of matrimonial proceedings in the Cook Islands, namely that the powers reserved by the settlor of two purported discretionary trusts were so extensive that the trusts were invalid.

(iii) Section 423 Insolvency Act

37–071 *At the end of sub-paragraph (2), add:*

It is not a requirement of an action under s.423 that, following the transaction which the action seeks to impugn, the respondent has insufficient assets to meet the judgment debt.[92a]

[92a] *Akhmedova v Akhmedov* [2021] EWHC 545 (Fam); [2021] 4 W.L.R. 88, at [103]–[104].

CHAPTER 38

SETTING ASIDE A JUDGMENT FOR FRAUD

A. INTRODUCTION

At the end of footnote 1, add: **38–002**

In *Takhar v Gracefield Developments Ltd* [2020] UKSC 13; [2020] AC 450, Lord Sumption explained the historical origins of the jurisdiction, at [60]: "An action to set aside an earlier judgment for fraud is not a procedural application but a cause of action. As applied to judgments obtained by fraud, the historical background was explained by Sir George Jessel MR in *Flower v Lloyd* (1877) 6 Ch D 297, 299–300. Equity has always exercised a special jurisdiction to reverse transactions procured by fraud.

A party to earlier litigation was entitled to bring an original bill in equity to set aside the judgment given in that litigation on the ground that it was obtained by fraud. Such a bill could be brought without leave, because it was brought in support of a substantive right. If the fact and materiality of the fraud were established, the party bringing the bill was absolutely entitled to have the earlier judgment set aside. In this respect, an original bill differed from a bill of review on the basis of further evidence, which was essentially procedural and did require leave. After the fusion of law and equity in the 1870, the procedure by way of original bill was superseded by a procedure by action on the same juridical basis."

At the end of footnote 3, add:

Cited also in *Takhar v Gracefield Developments Ltd* [2020] UKSC 13; [2020] A.C. 450, at [43].

At the end of footnote 4, add:

There is a substantial jurisprudence concerning fraud in the matrimonial field which this book does not attempt to consider: see for instance *Cathcart v Owens* [2021] EWFC 86.

B. THE PROCEDURAL MECHANISM

(1) Fresh Action

38–004 *At the end of the first sentence, add new footnote 6a:*

See generally *Jaffray v The Society of Lloyds* [2007] EWCA Civ 586; [2008] 1 W.L.R. 75, where the proper procedure where the original judgment/order had already been unsuccessfully appealed was also considered.

At the end of the paragraph, add new footnote 8a:

In *Terry v BCS Corporate Acceptances Limited* [2018] EWCA Civ 2442 the claimant had obtained a default judgment. The defendant tried and failed to set it aside under the normal rules relating to default judgments. Thereafter he issued an application to strike out the claim as an abuse of process on the basis that it was founded on dishonesty and to set aside the judgment. It was held that there was no such jurisdiction and the defendant was confined to the usual remedy of bringing a fresh action to set aside the earlier judgment.

(2) Proceeding by Way of Appeal

38–007 *At the end of the paragraph, add new footnote 15a:*

[15a] The procedural course taken in *Noble v Owens* flowed simply from the fact that the case had been brought before it and, it seems, the court wished to ensure that the appeal was not entirely nugatory. But in the normal way, unless the new evidence is admitted or incontrovertible (which will generally justify an order for a retrial) the disgruntled claimant will simply bring a new action without incurring the cost of a trip to the Court of Appeal. In *Dale v Banga* [2021] EWCA Civ 240, the court considered *Noble v Owens* and considered in which circumstances, short of the new evidence being admitted or incontrovertible, the appeal court should remit the fraud allegation back to the court below. (It needs to be re-emphasised that such a remission does *not* involve the original order being quashed and an order for a retrial; but it does mean that the appellant does not need to issue fresh proceedings to set aside the original judgment). The test for what was described as a "*Noble v Owens* order" was stated as follows:

> "[42]. ...It seems to me that it is necessary to decide whether the new evidence is capable of showing that the judge was deliberately misled by the Respondents and that the judgment may have been obtained by fraud. It must be sufficient to justify pleading a case of fraud. It must be capable of showing that there was conscious and deliberate dishonesty which was causative of the judgment being obtained in the terms it was. The conscious and deliberate dishonesty must be that of a party to the action, or was at least suborned by or knowingly relied upon by a party.

> [43] Secondly, if that threshold test is satisfied, the court must determine whether on the facts and in the circumstances of the particular case, it is appropriate that the fraud issue should be remitted or otherwise dealt with within the same proceedings. There is no question but that the appeal court has power to "refer any claim or issue for determination by the lower court": CPR 52.20(2)(b). The question is whether the discretion to do so should be exercised. It is not possible to list the matters which will be relevant to the exercise of that discretion because they inevitably depend on the circumstances."

The effect of the propounding of this test will inevitably see a revival of such orders even where orthodox jurisprudence propounded over many decades points in favour of the issuing of fresh proceedings without an interim trip to the Court of Appeal. And so it has proved. See for instance *Ras Al Khaimah Investment Authority v Azima* [2021] EWCA Civ 349 where, on the facts of that case, the fraud issue was remitted back to the High Court rather than the appellant being left to start a fresh action to set aside the prior judgment.

After the third sentence of the quotation from Noble v Owens, add new footnote 13b: **38–007**

The rule is now CPR r.52.20(2)(b).

At the end of footnote 15 add:

Now reported at [2018] QB 833. See also *Terry v BCS Corporate Acceptances Limited,* [2018] EWCA Civ 2442 at [34], where the court said, having considered *Noble v Owens*: "In summary, unless the fraud is admitted or the evidence of it is incontrovertible, the issue of fraud must be both properly particularised and proved. This will usually require a fresh action, although in *Noble v Owens* the Court of Appeal adopted what they regarded as being a more proportionate procedure of referring the trial of the fraud issue to a High Court judge pursuant to CPR 52.20(2)(b)." The concept of "more proportionate" here seems to involve nothing more than avoidance of an issue fee: see *Terry* at [89].

C. ELEMENTS TO BE PROVED

At the end of footnote 20 add: **38–013**

Aikens LJ's statement of the law was approved (albeit obiter) by the Supreme Court in *Takhar v Gracefield Developments Ltd* [2020] UKSC 13; [2020] A.C. 450, at [56–57] (per Lord Kerr), at [67] (per Lord Sumption) and at [76] (per Lord Briggs). See footnote 33 below.

At sub-paragraph (3), delete second sentence.

(2) Materiality

At the end of footnote 33 add: **38–016**

However, it seems that the courts have now definitively settled on the test of materiality as set out in *Highland Partners*. See for instance *Takhar v Gracefield Developments Limited* [2020] EWHC (Ch) 2791(the trial of the claim after the Supreme Court decision, where the matter is considered in some detail at [32] to [61]); *Broomhead v National Westminster Bank PLC* [2020] EWHC 1005 (Ch) and [2021] EWHC 105 (Ch); and *Jeffery v Jeffery* [2021] EWHC 582 (Ch). In *Park v CNH Industrial Capital Europe Ltd (t/a CNH Capital)* [2021] EWCA Civ 1766; [2012] W.L.R.(D) 593 it was confirmed, at [50], that the deception need only be "*an* operative cause" for the court acting as it did.

(3) Evidence Not Before the First Court and Not Reasonably Discoverable

Replace paragraph 38–019 with:

38–019 It is self-evident that the fraud relied upon must relate to evidence or material which was not before the first court: the Court must have proceeded on a false understanding.[35a] But what if the material relied upon by the claimant in the second action was, with the exercise of reasonable diligence, available to him before the first judgment was entered? Should that be a bar to the new action, just as applications to adduce fresh evidence on appeal are subject to the well-known (albeit partially modified) *Ladd v Marshall* rules? The position was for some time controversial, with the preponderance of judicial opinion seeming to favour a requirement that the claimant had to show that the new evidence could not with reasonable diligence have been discovered by him before the first judgment. However the law has now been settled by the Supreme Court in *Takhar v Gracefield Developments Ltd.*[36] In that case the claimant had previously sued the defendants alleging that she had transferred property as a result of undue influence. The defendants produced in evidence a document supposedly signed by the claimant which heavily supported their case. The claimant could not recall signing the document and had no explanation for it. She lost her claim. Subsequently she obtained evidence from a handwriting expert which stated that the signature was a forgery. The claimant brought a second claim seeking to set aside the first judgment. A preliminary issue was ordered to be tried as to whether there was a "reasonable diligence" requirement upon a claimant such that she was precluded from maintaining the second claim, given that the handwriting evidence establishing forgery could have been obtained during the first set of proceedings. After a consideration of the significant body of authority bearing on the issue, Lord Kerr, speaking for the majority, concluded that there was no burden upon a claimant to establish that the evidence founding the second claim must not have been obtainable by reasonable diligence for the earlier proceedings. This was because:

> "The idea that a fraudulent individual should profit from passivity or lack of reasonable diligence on the part of his or her opponent seems antithetical to any notion of justice. Quite apart from this, the defrauder, in obtaining a judgment, has perpetrated a deception not only on their opponent and the court but on the rule of law...In my view, it ought now to be recognised that where it can be shown that a judgment has been obtained by fraud, and where no allegation of fraud had been raised at the trial which led to that judgment, a requirement of reasonable diligence should not be imposed on the party seeking to set aside the judgment"[36a]

[35a] See per Lord Sumption in *Takhar v Gracefield Developments Ltd* [2020] UKSC 13; [2020] A.C. 450, at [65].

[36] [2020] UKSC 13; [2020] A.C. 450.

[36a] *Takhar v Gracefield*, above, at [52]–[54]. Apparently conflicting dicta in the decisions of the House of Lords and Privy Council in *Owens Bank Ltd v Bracco* [1992] 2 A.C. 443 and *Owens Bank Ltd v Etoile Commerciale SA* [1995] 1 W.L.R. 44 were not followed. In *Park v CNH Industrial Capital Europe Ltd (t/a CNH Capital)* [2021] EWCA Civ 1766; [2012] W.L.R.(D) 593 it was said, per Andrews LJ, answering a submission that apart from the deception there was another viable basis for obtaining the original judgment, that: "once a judgment is tainted by deceit it is fatally flawed... It is therefore no answer to a claim to set aside a judgment which has been procured by a dishonest representation relating to the claimant's primary case, that he also had an alternative cause of action on which he might have entered judgment without relying on the dishonest representation" (at [51]–[52]).

Add new paragraphs 38–019A to 38–019C after para.38–019:

Lord Sumption, who also commanded a majority, left open the question whether the position would be any different where the fraud was raised in the earlier proceedings, but unsuccessfully, and where "decisive new evidence" then came available. His provisional view, however, was that the same approach as encapsulated in the quotation above should apply.[36b] **38–019A**

[36b] *Takhar v Gracefield*, above, at [66].

One exception to the general rule laid down in *Takhar* was stated as where a party in the first claim had made a deliberate decision not to investigate a suspected fraud (or rely upon a known one). What if X had brought proceedings against Y, and Y had set up a document by way of defence which X suspected was forged but decided not to investigate the matter further? It seems that in such a case X will not be entitled to subsequently challenge the judgment on the basis of the alleged forgery of the document: to do so would be an abuse of process. But there is a further category of case, which the Supreme Court did not in terms address: i.e. where the issue of fraud had been unsuccessfully raised in the earlier proceedings, or could have been raised on the basis of evidence actually known to the losing party at the time but was not through negligence, and the losing party then seeks to set aside the judgment on the basis of the same evidence (or similar evidence) as it had previously done, or sought to do. **38–019B**

This question was considered in some detail by Linden J *in Elu v Floorweald Ltd.*[36c] In that case the claimant tenant brought proceedings against the defendant landlord asserting that it was in breach of its repairing duty. The defendant defended the claim on the basis that it was dishonest; in particular it was alleged that certain invoices for repair works which the claimant had supposedly instructed were forgeries. However the defendant did not plead this case explicitly and the witness evidence it relied upon to demonstrate that the invoices were forgeries was served late and was not admitted in evidence. Nonetheless at the trial it was put to the claimant in cross-examination that her case was fraudulent. The claimant succeeded. The defendant then (in effect) brought an action to set aside the judgment for fraud. The claimant sought to have that claim struck out. She relied on the fact that the evidence of fraud relied upon by the defendant was in fact available to it during the first trial (rather than it could have been available to it with reasonable diligence). Unlike in *Takhar* this was therefore a case where the losing party actually knew of the alleged fraud but failed, through its negligent conduct of the litigation, to properly deploy it. The judge considered the authorities and concluded that the decision in *Takhar* had not altered the rule that any challenge for fraud had to be based on new evidence; nor did it mean that where a party actually knew of the alleged fraud but failed to properly advance its case to that effect (in this case because it did not properly plead it and served its evidence late), the normal rules as to abuse of process did not apply.[36d] However in *Park v CNH Industrial Capital Europe Ltd (t/a CNH Capital)*[36e] the Court of Appeal took a rather more liberal view. Basing itself on Lord Sumption's judgment in *Takhar*, it held that "the fact that the fraud argument could have been raised in the first action is not enough to make the second action an abuse of process." The phrases "new evidence" or "fresh evidence", as deployed in *Takhar,* were held by the Court of Appeal in *Park* to denote "evidence that was not deployed in the action **38–019C** which led to the imputed [sic] judgment, not just evidence that had only come to light since the judgment."

[36c] [2020] EWHC 1222 (QB); [2020] 1 W.L.R. 4369.

[36d] On the applicability of *Takhar* in applications to set aside arbitration awards see *The Federal Republic of Nigeria v Process & Industrial Developments Ltd* [2020] EWHC 2379 (Comm), where Sir Ross Cranston held, at [183]: "If it had been necessary to decide the issue, it seems to me that Mr Howard has the best of the arguments. It is a fundamental principle of our law that, as Lord Bingham said in *HIH Casualty and General Insurance Ltd v Chase Manhattan Bank* [2003] UKHL 6, [2003] 2 Lloyd's Rep 61—referring to what Rix LJ had said in the Court of Appeal—that fraud is a thing apart, it unravels all: [15]. There seems to be no reason why the finality of arbitration awards should be afforded greater importance than the finality of judgments in circumstances of fraud. The statutory bar in section 73 is limited to irregularities discoverable during the arbitration. Otherwise, the effect of section 81(1) of the Act is to preserve the right to challenge the enforcement of an award on public policy grounds under the common law. As Mr Howard contended, there is no reason to interpret the Act so that *Takhar* is confined to common law public policy challenges and not to those under section 68(2)(g)."

[36e] [2021] EWCA Civ 1766; [2012] W.L.R.(D) 593 at [58], [61]. We see in the judgment in this case another example of the court, confronted with what it considered dishonest behaviour on the part of a litigant, seeking to ensure that the law did not stand in the way of what it perceived to be a just result so as to ensure that the dishonest litigant obtained no advantage. *Elu* must now be read in the light of the later decision in *Park* and treated with caution (even though the Court did not doubt the result). In particular, Linden J in *Elu* had cited a dictum of Handley JA in the New South Wales Court of Appeal judgment of *Toubia v Schwenke* (2002) 54 NSW.L.R. 46: "where the action seeks the judicial rescission of a judgment, a plaintiff must prove that he and the court were deceived, and he can only do this by showing that he has discovered the truth since the trial." It was said in *Park* that Linden J had wrongly interpreted this dictum as "a statement of principle that a party cannot set aside the judgment for fraud on the basis of evidence (or facts) which he knew about before trial. Had it been a statement of such a principle, it would be contrary to the decision in *Takhar* and in this jurisdiction the latter must prevail. However, that statement, when read in context, was simply a reflection of the principle referred to earlier in Handley JA's judgment (at [14]–[15]) that a person who has full knowledge of the truth when he acts upon a false representation cannot establish that he was deceived by it": see at [66]. In the light of the decision in *Park* it is clear that [153]–[156] of Linden J's judgment do not represent the law. See further *Read v Eastern Counties Leather Group Ltd* [2022] EWHC 31 (Ch).

38–020 *Delete paragraph.*

(4) Where Perjury is Alleged

38–021 *After sub-paragraph (b) of the passage quoted, add new footnote 37a:*

The reasonable diligence requirement has now been abolished by the Supreme Court in *Takhar v Gracefield Developments Ltd*, above.

D. THE COURT'S APPROACH TO THE JURISDICTION

(2) Prima Facie Case Must be Shown

38–024 *At the end of footnote 45, add:*

See also *Century Financial Holdings Ltd v Jamtoff Trading Ltd* [2018] EWHC 3135 (Comm).

(5) Fraud of Party or Witness?

At the end of footnote 51, add: **38–027**

It was also decided in *Boswell v Coaks* that, where the plaintiff charged fraud against one only of the defendants the claim against the other defendants could not succeed. The fraud of one party on one side of the litigation will not, *ipso facto*, lead to the judgment being set aside against the others. On the other hand, in *Cinpres Gas Injection Ltd v Melea Ltd* [2008] EWCA Civ 9 an individual gave perjured evidence in a legal proceeding in which that individual (H) was being sued alongside another (L). In proceedings to set aside the judgment, it was held that, even though L was not aware of H's perjury, H was "more than a mere witness" for L; H was L's "comrade in arms" and L had "adopted" H's evidence. On that basis the judgment could be set aside as against H and L. Much as the outcome of the appeal seems instinctively right, this reasoning is hard to follow. This outcome is not consonant with the rule as suggested in the main text and suggests a desire on the part of judges, often encountered in the cases, to find the "right answer" on the merits regardless of legal doctrine: understandable perhaps where they are coming face to face with a judgment obtained by false evidence. *Cinpres* has been described as an outlier: see the decision of the Hong Kong Court of Appeal in *Mayer Corporation Development International Limited v Alliance Financial Intelligence Limited* [2019] HKCA 777, at [53]–[59].

At beginning of footnote 56, add:

Re Odyssey is reported at [2000] EWCA Civ 71. The test was there stated whether the connection between the witness and the party "was so close as to make it unjust that it should be entitled to disavow the evidence even though it had no knowledge that the evidence was perjured." See also *Cinpres Gas Injection Ltd v Melea Ltd* [2008] EWCA Civ 9 and *Dale v Banga* [2021] EWCA Civ 240, at [27]. In *Cinpres* it was suggested that, in order for his evidence to be attributed to the party calling him, the witness had to be "a committed member of the team which takes decisions about the litigation" (see at [64]); but that surely puts the issue too narrowly. The facts in *Odyssey* demonstrate the need for a non-doctrinaire approach: what if the witness on whose evidence a litigant's case depends simply leaves the litigant's employment the day before he gives evidence? Does he thereby become a "mere witness" unless he has been a member of the litigation team?

E. RELIEF

At end of paragraph, add new footnote 57a: **38–030**

After the Supreme Court judgment in *Takhar v Gracefield Developments Ltd*, above, there was a trial of the action to set aside the earlier judgment, which was successful. At the consequentials hearing (*Takhar v Gracefield Developments Ltd (Consequential Orders)* [2020] EWHC 3025 (Ch)) the judge ordered the defendants to pay indemnity costs on the basis that they had been found to have forged a document which they had deployed in the first trial in order successfully to deceive the court. But what of the costs of the first action? The costs order in that action had required the claimant to pay the defendants' costs, which she had done, and it followed that, that costs order having been set aside, the defendants were ordered to return the costs to the claimant together with interest. The claimant also sought a costs order (on the indemnity basis) in relation to her costs of the first trial on the ground that that trial had been rendered abortive: there would now have to be a fresh trial of the claimant's original claim. The claimant did not seek her costs of the pleadings, disclosure etc in the first proceedings because those costs had not been wasted. The judge acceded to the claimant's submission, holding at [26]: "The costs thrown away by the first trial having been ineffective in determining the dispute, due to the fraud of the Defendants in presenting forged evidence, have, as a result, been thrown away by reason of their conduct. Even if the Claimant loses at trial, it will not mean she is responsible for the costs incurred in there having been an earlier trial of no effect due to the Defendants' conduct. They are responsible for that, and it is with them that those costs should lie." This analysis is of general application and, with respect, is plainly right. In *Singh v Moorlands Primary School* [2013] EWCA Civ 909; [2013] 1 W.L.R. 3052 Lewison LJ stated, obiter, that he could see no reason why damages should not also be awarded as a remedy on a successful claim to set aside a judgment for fraud.

CHAPTER 39

JURISDICTION ISSUES

A. INTRODUCTION

Replace paragraph 39–003 with:

39–003 The UK government irrevocably triggered its departure from the EU under art. 50 of the EC Treaty on 30 March 2017. There followed a transition period, which ultimately came to an end on 31 December 2021. The final Withdrawal Agreement ("WA") entered into between the EU and the UK explains, inter alia, the position following the conclusion of the transition period in relation to the application in the UK of various bilateral EU treaties, including those relevant to jurisdiction and recognition of judgments. It provides, as relevant to this chapter, that:

(1) The Brussels Regulation Recast (EU) No. 1215/2012 ("the BRR") will continue to apply to all legal proceedings commenced or, where relevant, jurisdiction agreements entered into, before 1 January 2021.[2a]
(2) The BRR provisions relating to enforcement of judgments will apply where judgment was given before the end of the transition period.[2b]

The BRR is likely also to have continued relevance, although not strictly applicable, in relation to claims commenced after 1 January 2021 which relate to earlier proceedings; for example, if there is an application to stay a claim commenced after that date in favour of a set of proceedings commenced before. Otherwise, the BRR will cease to have effect in the UK from that date onwards, by virtue of the UK ceasing to be a member of the EU.

[2a] WA, Art.67(1).
[2b] WA, Art.67(2).

Replace paragraph 39–004 with:

39–004 The UK acceded in its own right, on 1 January 2021, to the 2005 Hague Convention on Choice of Court Agreements ("the Hague Convention"). The EU is already a member, having acceded in 2015. There is therefore, at least to that extent, still legislation regulating the reciprocal arrangements between the UK and the EU as to jurisdiction. However, the circumstances in which that Convention applies are very narrow:

(1) It only applies to exclusive jurisdiction clauses. In other words, it has no relevance other than in relation to choice of law clauses, and it does not

apply to choice of law clauses that are not exclusive, for example non-exclusive or asymmetric clauses.

(2) It also sets out rules as to the recognition of judgments entered pursuant to an applicable choice of law, however those rules apply only to final judgments and say nothing about recognition of interim measures such as freezing orders.

Further, there is an issue that is yet to be resolved as to whether proceedings commenced in the UK between 2015 and 1 January 2021 would be covered by the Hague Convention, given that during that time the UK was a member of the Hague Convention only by virtue of its membership of the EU.

Two new provisions have been inserted into the CPR, at r.6.33(2B)(a) and (b), permitting service out of the jurisdiction without permission in cases (i) within the scope of the Hague Convention; and (ii) outside of the scope of that Convention (for example non-exclusive jurisdiction clauses), where the English court has been nominated (although in the latter circumstance the English court's jurisdiction would be open to challenge on the basis that it was not the *forum conveniens*).

Replace paragraph 39–005 with:

On 8 April 2020, the UK applied to accede to the Lugano Convention. The unanimous consent of the existing members is required in order for such an application to be successful. The other individual state members of the Convention agreed to the UK's accession, however the EU has refused, following the European Commission's Communication to the European Parliament and Council[2c] in which it recommended that the EU should not give its consent. That advice relied on a number of bases, including that the Lugano Convention is designed for countries which have a close regulatory integration with the EU, whereas the UK is now a third party which is not part of the EU's internal market. The Commission did, however, note that the UK had acceded to the Hague Convention, and suggested that the UK should also join the Convention on the Recognition of Foreign Judgments in Civil and Commercial Matters 2019. Given that the latter convention is not yet any part of English law, it is not referred to further herein. **39–005**

[2c] COM (2021) 222 final, 4 May 2021.

Replace paragraph 39–006 with:

The present position in relation to matters that were or would previously have been within the scope of the BRR, therefore, is: **39–006**

(1) In relation to all matters commenced, and judgments entered, before 1 January 2021 that would otherwise have been within its scope, the BRR will continue to apply. The rules in the BRR are set out in Section C below.
(2) The Hague Convention will apply to jurisdiction and recognition of judgments in cases of exclusive jurisdiction clauses. The detail of the rules in that Convention are outside of the scope of this text.
(3) In relation to all matters commenced after 1 January 2021 that are not covered by the Hague Convention, the English common law rules on service out of the jurisdiction will apply. Those are set out in Section F below.

39–007 *Delete entire paragraph.*

39–008 *Delete entire paragraph.*

B. SOURCES OF LAW

39–011 *Replace the first three sentences with:*

Until 1 January 2021, the key piece of EU legislation for these purposes was the BRR. As noted above, that has ceased to have effect in the UK from 1 January 2021; however it still applies to proceedings commenced, and judgments entered, prior to that date. In EU Member States which are signatories to the Regulation, and in the UK to the extent that it is still applicable, it applies in all "civil and commercial matters whatever the nature of the court or tribunal." In relation to the time periods in which it remains applicable, it therefore applies in principle to every civil fraud dispute before the English courts which has an "international element".

Replace paragraph 39–013 with:

39–013 The BRR came into effect on 10 January 2015, meaning that it applies to "legal proceedings instituted" on or after that date. This means that there are now three sets of rules operating in parallel, one for claims "instituted" (meaning, in English terminology, issued) prior to that date; another for those between that date and 31 December 2020 inclusive; and a third for those commenced thereafter. The first category is governed by the BRR's predecessor, Regulation 44/2001, also known as the "Judgments Regulation" or "Brussels I".

39–017 *At the end of paragraph, add:*

As set out above, and with the exceptions there noted, that is also now the case in relation to claims commenced from 1 January 2021 onwards.

C. DEFENDANT DOMICILED IN THE EU

(1) The General Rule

39–021 *At the beginning of paragraph, add:*

As noted above, the remainder of this section applies only in relation to claims commenced prior to 1 January 2021.

(i) Domicile: individuals

39–024 *At the end of paragraph, add:*

In order for someone who resides in England to *cease* to reside there, there must be a "distinct break" in the pattern of the individual's life.[18a]

[18a] See *Shulman v Kolomoisky* [2018] EWHC 160 (Ch), per Barling J at [23], applying the tax case of *R (Davies) v Revenue and Customs* Commissioners [2011] UKSC 47; [2011] 1 W.L.R. 2625.

(ii) Tort

At the end of sub-paragraph (2), add: **39–033**

In *Aspen Underwriting Ltd v Credit Europe Bank NV*,[29a] the Court of Appeal considered that claims for misrepresentation, both under the Misrepresentation Act 1967 and at common law, were not matters relating to a contract for these purposes and, accordingly, fell within Article 7(2). This does not appear to have been addressed when that case was taken to the Supreme Court.

[29a] [2018] EWCA Civ 2590; [2018] 2 CLC 891, per Gross LJ at [135].

At the end of the paragraph, add: **39–042**

For a recent analysis of the significant case law in relation to the question of place of the damage under Article 7(2), see *Griffin Underwriting Ltd v Varouxakis*.[40a]

[40a] [2018] EWHC 3259 (Comm); [2019] 1 W.L.R. 2529, per Males J at [63]–[75].

(4) One of a Number of Defendants

At the end of the paragraph, add: **39–055**

In *Senior Taxi Aereo Executivo v Agusta Westland SpA*,[55a] the court followed the majority *obiter* comments in *Sabbagh*, holding that the claim against the anchor defendant needed to pass a merits test before Article 8(1) was engaged. The Court of Appeal has since confirmed, in *PJSC Commercial Bank Privatbank v Kolomoisky*,[55b] that in a case concerning the equivalent Article of the Lugano Convention (6(1)), which is in materially identical terms to BRR Article 8(1) and which the Court expressly extended thereto, a claimant with a sustainable claim against an anchor defendant which it intends to pursue to judgment is entitled to rely on Article 6(1) even though its sole object in issuing the proceedings against the anchor defendant is to sue the foreign defendant in the same proceedings. The standard required to establish a "sustainable" claim against the anchor defendant was then considered in *Galapagos Bidco SARL v Kebekus*,[55c] where it was said to be the same as the test in the summary judgment or strike out context, i.e. whether there is a serious issue to be tried or whether the claim has a real prospect of success.

[55a] [2020] EWHC 1348 (Comm); [2021] Q.B, 164, per Waksman J at [90].
[55b] [2019] EWCA Civ 1708; [2020] Ch 783, at [102]–[111], per David Richards LJ, Flaux LJ, Newey LJ dissenting.
[55c] [2021] EWHC 68 (Ch), per Zacaroli J at [48].

(5) Exclusive Jurisdiction Based on Subject Matter

Replace paragraph 39–060 with:

In the recent decision of *Koza Ltd v Akcil*,[63] the Supreme Court held, overturning the decision of the Court of Appeal, that where there were two distinct claims which were not inextricably bound up with each other, one of which fell within Article 24(2) and one of which did not, it was not legitimate to maintain that by virtue of an overall evaluative judgment in relation to both claims taken together **39–060** the second should also fall within that Article so that the English court had exclusive jurisdiction in relation to it. Although the claims were related, they were distinct and the English court therefore did not have jurisdiction over the second claim, which did not fall within the wording of Article 24(2).

[63] [2019] UKSC 40; [2019] 1 W.L.R. 4830.

39–061 *At the end of footnote 64, add*:

approved by the Court of Appeal in *JSC Commercial Bank Privatbank v Kolomoisky and Bogolyubov* [2019] EWCA Civ 1708; [2020] Ch 783.

(6) Prorogation

(i) Jurisdiction agreements

39–067 *At the end of footnote 75, add:*

See also the Court of Appeal's recent decision in *Etihad Airways PJSC v Flother* [2020] EWCA Civ 1707; [2021] 2 W.L.R. 939.

(7) Lis Alibi Pendens

(ii) Jurisdiction agreement

39–075 *At the end of the paragraph, add:*

This reversal of priority does *not* apply in cases under the Lugano Convention, which mirrors the language of Brussels I, in which context the rule in *Erich Gasser* still applies: *Mastermelt v Siegrfried Evionnaz SA*.[94a]

[94a] [2020] EWHC (QB), per Waksman J at [26].

(iii) Same parties, same cause of action

39–077 *At the end of footnote 97, add*:

For a recent interpretation of the test see *Nigeria v Royal Dutch Shell Plc* [2020] EWHC 1315.

(v) Claims in "third states"

39–080 *At the end of footnote 102, add:*

; [2018] 1 W.L.R. 3409.

39–082 *At the end of the paragraph, add:*

Perhaps for that reason, there has been a lot of recent case-law in relation to them.[104a]

[104a] See for example *Perform Content Services v Ness Global Services* [2021] EWCA Civ 981; *UCP Plc v Nectrus Ltd* (see fn 102 above); *WWRT Ltd v Tyshchenko* [2021] EWHC 939 (Ch); *Gulf International Bank BSC v Aldwood* [2019] EWHC 1666 (QB).

D. DEFENDANT DOMICILED IN LUGANO STATE

At the end of the paragraph, add: **39–083**

The Lugano Convention applied in the UK by virtue of the UK's membership of the EU. Accordingly, like the BRR, it ceased to have effect in the UK from 1 January 2021, and the position as to its applicability is therefore the same as that in relation to the BRR, as set out in para.39–033 above. The following is subject to that caveat.

F. DEFENDANT DOMICILED OUT OF THE EU / LUGANO STATES

(1) The BRR

Replace the first sentence with: **39–087**

As noted above, the BRR does not apply in relation to proceedings commenced after 31 December 2020. It also does not apply to proceedings commenced prior to that date where the defendant is domiciled outside of the EU. In those cases the English court will apply its own rules to determine its jurisdiction.

(2) Service Without Court's Permission

In footnotes 115 and 117, replace references to "PD 6B para.3.1(6)(d)" with: **39–089**

See the new PD 6B para.3.1(2B), referred to at para.39–004 above, in light of which the pre-existing gateway concerning jurisdiction agreements, PD 6B, para.3.1(6)(d), has been removed.

(3) Order for Service Out of the Jurisdiction

At the end of the paragraph, add: **39–091**

In *Goldman Sachs International v Novo Banco SA*,[127a] the Supreme Court endorsed the three-limb explanation of the "better of the argument" test given by Lord Sumption in *Brownlie* (see above). Further consideration was given to that standard in *Kaefer Aislamientos SA v AMS Mexico SA*,[127b] where the Court said that a relative, rather than an absolute, test applies. For a further consideration of the test, see *Coward v Ambrosiadou*.[127c]

In *Al Jaber v Al Ibrahim*,[127d] a claim was made under a loan agreement for principal and interest, and the first instance judge had granted permission for the claim for the principal sum but not the claim to interest. The Court of Appeal found that that was wrong because the claim for interest was "accessory to" the claim to the principal sum, and that the finding that the principal sum was within the relevant gateway should also have extended to the claim for interest.

[127a] [2018] UKSC 34; [2018] 1 W.L.R. 3863.
[127b] [2019] EWCA Civ 10.
[127c] [2019] EWHC 2105 (Comm), per Andrew Henshaw QC.
[127d] [2018] EWCA Civ 1690; [2019] 1 W.L.R. 885.

39–093 *At the end of footnote 129, add:*

As to questions of law, see *Airbus SAS v Generali Italia SPA* [2019] EWCA Civ 805; [2019] 4 All E.R. 745, at [52]–[53].

(i) *"Necessary and proper party"*

39–096 *At the end of footnote 132, add:*

; [2018] Bus L.R. 1022.

39–098 *At the end of the paragraph, add:*

The decision was overturned by the Supreme Court. Although it was common ground on appeal that the Court of Appeal had applied the correct standard, it was found to have been drawn into conducting a mini trial that led it to making determinations in relation to contested factual evidence. Instead the court should focus on the particulars of claim ("unless, exceptionally, they are demonstrably untrue or unsupportable") and whether, if the facts there alleged were true, the cause of action asserted had a real prospect of success.[134a]

[134a] *Okpabi v Royal Dutch Shell Plc* [2021] UKSC 3; [2021] 1 W.L.R. 1294.

39–099 *At the end of the paragraph, add:*

In *Lungowe v Vedanta Resources* Plc,[137a] the Supreme Court (Lord Briggs JSC) criticised as involving an error of principle the approach taken in previous cases of giving prominence to, or using as a "trump card", the risk of irreconcilable judgments, where it was clear that the claimant would in any event continue proceedings against the anchor defendant in England (in this case, on the basis of domicile in England under Article 4 of the BRR). The judge had given insufficient weight to the fact that the claimant could have sued the defendant in Zambia, with which the case was obviously very closely related, and where the defendant had offered to submit to the jurisdiction, so that all of the related claims could be tried there.

In *ED&F Man Capital Markets Ltd v Straits (Singapore) Pte Ltd*,[137b] the Court of Appeal noted that the multiplicity of proceedings in different jurisdictions, and the accompanying risk of inconsistent judgments, were still important considerations, and said that *Vedanta* could be distinguished in cases where the claimant had no choice but to sue the defendant in England. That basis for distinguishing *Vedanta* was extended slightly further in *PJSC National Bank Trust v Mints*[137c] to the situation where there was no rational choice but to sue the defendants in England, on account of the difficulties, and likely opposition from the defendants, if the claimants sought to enforce a judgment from Russia, which in that case was the other alternative.

It has recently been confirmed that the "necessary and proper party" gateway is not engaged where the anchor defendant has voluntarily submitted to the court's jurisdiction: *ID v LU and BZ*.[137d]

[137a] [2019] UKSC 20, at [66]–[87].
[137b] [2019] EWCA Civ 2073; [2020] 2 All ER (Comm) 551, at [43]–[49] per Flaux LJ.
[137c] [2021] EWHC 692 (Comm), per Sir Nigel Teare (sitting as a High Court Judge) at [66]–[67].
[137d] [2021] EWHC 1851 (Comm).

(ii) *"A further claim is made against the defendant which arises out of the same or closely connected facts"*

In footnote 139, add to citation: **39–100**

; [2018] 1 W.L.R. 6089.

At the end of the paragraph, add:

If a claim for an injunction is permitted to be served out within PD 6B para.3.1(2), permission may be given under para.3.1(4A) to serve further claims seeking injunctions (or other remedies) against the same defendant if those further claims arise out of the same or closely connected facts.[139a]

[139a] *Unlockd Ltd v Google Ireland Ltd* [2018] EWHC 1363 (Ch); [2019] E.C.C. 1, at [48].

(iii) *"Claims in tort"*

At the end of sub-paragraph (2), add: **39–101**

In *FS Cairo (Nile Plaza LLC) v Christine Brownlie*,[142a] the Court of Appeal considered further the issue in *Brownlie v Four Seasons* (given that it had been a split decision and in any event obiter) and decided to follow it. That decision was recently upheld by the Supreme Court, which confirmed that direct damage within the jurisdiction is not necessary for a claim to come within the tort gateway, and thereby confirmed that the test under the common law is different from that under the BRR. It remains to be seen how that decision will be interpreted and applied outside of the personal injury context, particularly in fraud cases, and precisely what level of financial loss will be found sufficient to ground a claim to jurisdiction.

[142a] [2020] EWCA Civ 996, per McCombe LJ at [56].
[142b] [2021] UKSC 45.

At the end of sub-paragraph (3), add:

Of specific relevance in the fraud context, in *Manek v IIFL Wealth (UK) Ltd*,[142b] the Court of Appeal found that misrepresentations made at a meeting in London were "substantial and efficacious acts" committed within the jurisdiction, regardless of whether more important events had occurred elsewhere.

[142c] [2021] EWCA Civ 264, at [51]–[53].

(vi) *"A claim is made against the defendant as constructive trustee, or as trustee of a resulting trust"*

At the end of the paragraph, add: **39–104**

For an interesting recent decision concerning whether cryptocurrency amounted to an 'asset within the jurisdiction' for the purposes of this gateway, see *Ion Science Ltd v Persons Unknown*.[147a] Further, as to the meaning of "constructive trust" and "resulting trust" in this context, see *Ashley v Jimenez*.[147b]

[147a] 21 December 2020, unrep.
[147b] [2019] EWHC 17 (Ch), per Chief Master Marsh at [111]–[112].

(4) Practice and Procedure for Applications

39–109 *At the end of footnote 151, add:*

However, any new evidence must relate to the position as at the permission stage: *Satfinance Investment Ltd v Athena Art Finance Corp* [2020] EWHC 3527, per Morgan J at [41] and [52].

39–115 *At the end of footnote 159, add:*

As noted in footnote 134a above, the Supreme Court considered that even the approach of the Court of Appeal itself in that case amounted to an impermissible mini trial.

CHAPTER 40

CONFLICT OF LAWS

A. INTRODUCTION

At the end of the paragraph, add: **40–001**

Indeed, different governing laws can potentially apply within the same cause of action, if it has caused different damage in different countries.[0]

[0] see *Qatar Airways Group Q.C.S.C. v Middle East News FZ LLC* [2020] EWHC 2975 (QB), at [328(2)].

At the end of footnote 1, add: **40–002**

This principle has been the subject of much recent judicial analysis. It was most authoritatively reiterated in *FS Cairo (Nile Plaza) LLC v Brownlie* in the Court of Appeal at [2020] EWCA Civ 996; [2021] 2 All ER 605, at [177]; followed, in the context of claims in conspiracy, in both *Qatar Airways Group Q.C.S.C. v Middle East News FZ LLC* [2020] EWHC 2975 (QB), at [181]–[188] (in the specific procedural context of a jurisdiction challenge), and *Lakatamia Shipping Co Ltd v Su* [2021] EWHC 1907 (Comm), at [826] and [828]. See also *Iranian Offshore Engineering and Construction Company v*

Dean Investment Holdings [2018] EWHC 2759 (Comm); *Livingston Properties Equities Inc v JSC MCC Eurochem* [2020] UKPC 31. Most recently see the Supreme Court's decision in *Brownlie* (above) [2021] UKSC 45, at [96]–[166], which differentiated between two different aspects of the principle, namely the 'default rule', which treats English law as applicable where no foreign law is pleaded; and the 'presumption of similarity' rule, which says that where foreign law is pleaded, but no detail given as to the content of the law, the Court may apply English law if it is reasonable to presume that the foreign law will be the same as English law on the point.

40–003 *Replace final sentence with:*

Despite that European underpinning, Brexit will have virtually no effect on those rules. That is because, contrary to the position in relation to jurisdiction, rules on conflict of laws are not dependent upon reciprocal enforcement—they simply dictate the law that an English court applies when a dispute with foreign elements comes before it. The UK has therefore simply enacted legislation—in the form of the Law Applicable to Contractual Obligations and Non-Contractual Obligations (Amendment etc.) (EU Exit) Regulations 2019, which provides that although Rome I and Rome II will cease to be part of English law on 31 December 2020, their terms will be incorporated, *mutatis mutandis*, into English law. Therefore, through a different procedural route, the rules set out in the remainder of this chapter will continue to apply in relation to claims commenced from 1 January 2021 onwards. That is for the good, both because it involves minimal disruption, and, more importantly, because those rules are far preferable to the muddled position that existed in English private international law prior to Rome I and Rome II, as briefly summarised below.

B. CONTRACTUAL OBLIGATIONS

40–005 *At end of sub-paragraph (3), add:*

Further, effect may be given to the overriding mandatory provisions of the law of the country where the obligations arising out of the contract have to be or have been performed, in so far as those overriding mandatory provisions render the performance of the contract unlawful: see Article 9(3).[8a]

[8a] In *Banco San Juan Internacional Inc v Petroléos de Venezuela SA* [2021] 2 All ER (Comm) 590, the Court held at [118]–[122] that Article 9(3) had to be applied against the background of the principles which it applies in any event. Although it may be of use where the court in question has no equivalent rule of law, it added nothing to the present case, which concerned illegality—in relation to which England has a significant body of law—and specifically the applicability of the exception in *Ralli Bros* to the general principle that illegality under foreign law does not frustrate or otherwise relieve a party from performance of an English law contract (the exception being that an obligation under an English law contract is invalid and unenforceable insofar as it requires performance in a place where it is unlawful under the law of that required place of performance). Cockerill J concluded (at [122]) that "comity is not intended to provide a trump card" in the event that a rule within the Court's national law, such as *Ralli Bros*, did not apply.

C. Non-Contractual Obligations

(1) Tort/Delict

(ii) Events prior to 11 January 2009

At the end of the paragraph, add: **40–022**

For a recent application of the 1995 Act in the context of misrepresentation, as proof that its provisions are still being litigated, see *Barclay-Watt v Alpha Panareti Public Ltd*,[39a] where the Court found that the general rule had not been displaced and the claim was governed by English law.

[39a] [2021] EWHC 642 (Comm), at [10]–[17].

(iii) Events on or after 11 January 2009

Further, as noted above, where a claim (including claims in unlawful interference, malicious falsehood, and conspiracy) can be broken down into "*sub-causes of action*", each of which has caused damage in different countries, the claimant can choose to divide his claim in that way, each being governed by different laws under Rome II Article 4.[50a] **40–033**

[50a] See *Qatar Airways Group Q.C.S.C. v Middle East News FZ LLC* [2020] EWHC 2975 (QB), at [328(2)].

Remove this paragraph and the heading that precedes it 'E. The Future'. **40–059**

INDEX

ALSO AVAILABLE

Vital supplements to keep your resources current

Bullen & Leake & Jacob's Precedents of Pleadings, 1st Supplement to the 19th Edition, June 2022

Clerk & Lindsell on Torts, 2nd Supplement to the 5th Edition, June 2022

Contractual Duties: Performance, Breach, Termination and Remedies, 1st Supplement to the 3rd Edition, June 2022

Lewin on Trusts, 1st Supplement to the 20th Edition, July 2022

Terrell on the Law of Patents, 2nd Supplement to the 19th Edition, March 2022

Wilkinson's Road Traffic Offences, 1st Supplement to the 30th Edition, June 2022

Zuckerman on Civil Procedure: Principles of Practice, 1st Supplement to the 4th Edition, July 2022